A HISTORY OF RUSSIA

A
HISTORY *of* RUSSIA

BY

V. O. KLUCHEVSKY

LATE PROFESSOR OF RUSSIAN HISTORY IN THE UNIVERSITY OF MOSCOW

TRANSLATED BY

C. J. HOGARTH

VOLUME ONE

New York
RUSSELL & RUSSELL
1960

A HISTORY OF RUSSIA by V. O. Kluchevsky consists of five volumes which were separately published at intervals between 1911 and 1931. They are now, for the first time, issued together as a complete work.

PUBLISHED, 1960, BY

RUSSELL & RUSSELL, INC.

BY ARRANGEMENT WITH E. P. DUTTON & CO., INC.

L. C. CATALOG CARD NUMBER: 60–6033

PRINTED IN THE U. S. A.

NOTE TO THE READER

The four chapters at the end of Volume Five, pages 191–296, were originally the opening sections of Volume One. For reasons unknown to the present publishers, they were omitted when the English translation was begun and were later added as an Appendix to Volume Five.

CONTENTS

CHAPTER I

PAGE

The two points of view in the study of history—The principal factor in the development of Russian social life—The four principal periods of Russian history—The Ancient Chronicle ; its genesis, authorship, and contents . 1

CHAPTER II

Historical value of the Ancient Chronicle—Its importance for later Russian historians—A chronological error—The origin of that error—The work of compiling the Chronicle—Defects in the older versions—The theory of Slavonic unity—Manuscripts of the twelfth century—The divergent points of view of their authors 19

CHAPTER III

Principal factors of the first period of Russian history—The two theories as to its starting-point—The races who inhabited Southern Russia before the coming of the Eastern Slavs—The Ancient Chronicle's tradition concerning the dispersal of the Slavs from the Danube—Jornandes on their distribution during the sixth century—The military union of the Eastern Slavs in the Carpathians—The period and peculiar features of their settlement of the Russian plain— Results of that settlement 28

CHAPTER IV

Juridical and economic results of the settlement of the Eastern Slavs upon the Russian plain—Outline of their mythology and ancestor worship—Coming of the Chozars, and their influence upon Russian trade—Origin of the old trading towns 39

CHAPTER V

The political results of the settling of the Eastern Slavs upon the Russian plain—The Pechenegs in the South Russian Steppes—The fortification of the Russian towns—The Varangians : the question of their origin and the time of their appearance in Rus—The formation of the town provinces : their relation to the tribes—The Varangian principalities—The legend of the invitation sent to the Three Princes : its historical foundation—Activity of the Scandinavian Vikings in Western Europe during the ninth century—Formation of the great Principality of Kiev as the first step towards a Russian State—Importance of Kiev in the creation of a Russian State—Summary 55

CHAPTER VI

PAGE

Policy of the early Kievan Princes—Federation of the Eastern Slavs under the Prince of Kiev—Tax-administration in the Principality of Kiev—Foreign policy and trading relations with Byzantium—Influence of the Greek treaties upon early Russian law—Perils of Russian foreign trade—Defence of the Steppe frontiers—Composition and extent of the Principality of Kiev —Origin, composition, and functions of the princely retinue—Social divisions in the Kievan community—Slave ownership—Successive meanings of the term Rus—Gradual assimilation of Varangians and Slavs .   .   .   77

CHAPTER VII

The order of princely rule in Rus previous to the death of Yaroslav—Partition of the country after that event—The rota system of rule : its origin, theory, and working—Causes of its disruption—*Riadi* (conventions) and feuds—The idea of the *otchina*—*Izgoi* princes—Indirect hindrances to the working of the rota system—The importance of that system .   .   .   94

CHAPTER VIII

Results of the rota system of rule—Gradual political disintegration of Rus during the twelfth century—Reappearance of the great towns as a political influence—*Vietcha* and their conventions with the princes—The effect of princely relations upon the social order of the country during the twelfth century—The political order during the same period—Rise and growth of a sense of popular unity   114

CHAPTER IX

The civil order in Rus during the eleventh and twelfth centuries—The *Russkaia Pravda* as a guide to that order—The two views taken of the Code —Its origin and genesis—Its monetary reckoning—Its sources—Russian law, and enactments of the princes—Judicial decrees of the princes and of the Church —Supplementary sources drawn upon by the codifiers of the *Russkaia Pravda*   128

CHAPTER X

Preliminary questions with regard to the composition of the *Russkaia Pravda* — Process of its collation and elaboration—Its composition and contents—Its relation to previously existing law —The civil order of the period as reflected in its articles—Importance of old legal annals in the study of a given civil order—The distinctions drawn by the *Pravda* between civil and criminal law—Its system of punishments and sums to be paid in compensation—Its original basis and later interpolations—Its relative solicitude for property and the person—Its double demarcation of classes—Its importance as preeminently the code of capital   144

CONTENTS

CHAPTER XI

PAGE

The Church Ordinances of the early Christian princes of Rus—Ecclesiastical jurisdiction as defined in Vladimir's and Yaroslav's Ordinances respectively —Innovations introduced by the Church into the theory of crime and the system of legal penalties—The monetary reckoning observed in Yaroslav's Ordinance as evidence of the period of its composition—The original basis of that Ordinance—The legislative powers of the Church—The process of ecclesiastical codification—Traces of the same in Yaroslav's Ordinance— Relation of Yaroslav's Ordinance to the *Russkaia Pravda*—The influence of the Church upon the political, civil, and social orders of the period . . 165

CHAPTER XII

The principal phenomena distinguishing the second period—The conditions which brought about the disruption of the social order and economic prosperity of Kievan Rus—The life of the upper classes of the community, and the progress of culture and the civic spirit among them—Position of the lower classes—The development of slavery—The attacks of the Polovsti— The depopulation of Kievan Rus—The double stream of emigration thence —The western stream of that movement—A glance at the fortunes of South-Western Rus—The question of the origin of the Little Russian stock— Evidence as to the north-eastward exodus from Kiev—Importance of that movement 182

CHAPTER XIII

Ethnographical results of the Russian colonisation of the Upper Volga—The question of the origin of the Great Russian stock—The Finnish tribes formerly inhabiting the region of the Oka and Upper Volga, and the traces now left of them—Relations of the Russian settlers to the aboriginal Finnish tribes of Suzdal—Traces of Finnish influence upon the Great Russian physical type, form of town-building, popular beliefs, and social composition—Influence of the natural features of the region of the Upper Volga upon the industry of Great Rus and the racial character of the Great Russian stock 203

CHAPTER XIV

Political results of the Russian colonisation of the Upper Volga—Prince Andrew Bogoliubski—His relations with Kievan Rus—His attempts to convert the patriarchal rule of the Suzerain Prince of Rus into absolute rule—His policy in Rostov—His relations with his kindred, with the older towns, and with the senior grade of his retinue—The princely and social feud which arose in Rostov at his death—Opinion of a chronicler of Vladimir upon that feud— Supremacy of Northern Rus under Vsevolod III.—Effect of the political achievements of Andrew and Vsevolod upon the community of Suzdal— Summary of the foregoing 22

CONTENTS

CHAPTER XV

Survey of the position of the Russian land during the thirteenth and fourteenth centuries—The appanage system of princely rule under Vsevolod's successors—The princely appanage—The chief items of evidence with regard to the appanage system—The origin of that system—The idea of separate, devisable rule among the princes of the South—Conversion of Russian princes of provinces into princes subject to the Lithuanian Empire—Strength of the clan tradition among the senior lines of Yaroslav's stock—Relations between the princes of the Upper Volga and the princes of Riazan at the close of the fifteenth century—Fundamental features of the appanage system—Causes of its successful growth among Vsevolod's successors—Absence of impediments to that system in the region of Suzdal 239

CHAPTER XVI

Observations on the importance of the appanage period in Russian history—Results of the appanage system—Questions preliminary to their study—The process of territorial subdivision into appanages—Impoverishment of the appanage princes—Their mutual estrangement—The status of an appanage prince—His juridical relation to private landholders in his appanage—Comparison of appanage with feudal relations—Composition of the community in an appanage—Decline of local patriotism and the territorial sense among the appanage princes—Results of that decline 254

CHAPTER XVII

Moscow begins to combine the appanages into a single great principality—Early references of the Chronicle to Moscow—The original area of the Kremlin—Economic advantages of Moscow's geographical position—The city as the meeting-place of three great roads—Traces of early settlement of the region—Moscow as the ethnographical centre of Great Russia—The river Moskva as a trade route—Political results of the geographical position of Moscow—Moscow as the junior appanage—Influence of that circumstance upon the external relations and internal policy of the Muscovite Princes—Political and national achievements of those Princes up to the middle of the fifteenth century—Summary of the foregoing 272

CHAPTER XVIII

Mutual relations of the Muscovite Princes—System of Muscovite succession—Absence of any juridical distinction between moveable and immoveable property in appanages—Relation of the system of Muscovite princely succession to the juridical custom of ancient Rus—Relations of the Muscovite Princes with regard to kinship and rule—Rise in importance of the senior inheritor—Forms of subordination of appanage princes to their Suzerain—Influence of the Tartar yoke upon the relations of the Princes—Establishment of succession of the Suzerain power in the direct descending line—Coincidence of the family aims of the Muscovite Princes with the popular needs of Great Rus—Importance of the Muscovite feud under Vasilii the Dark—Character of the Muscovite Princes 294

CONTENTS

CHAPTER XIX

PAGE

The Free Town Commonwealths—Novgorod the Great—Its situation and plan—Division of its territory into *piatini* and *volosti*—Conditions and development of Novgorod's freedom—Treaty relations of Novgorod with its Princes—Its administration—The relations of its *vietché* with its Princes—Its *Posadnik* and *Tisiatski*—Its judicial system—Its Council of Magnates—Its provincial administration—Its minor towns, and their relation to the capital—Conclusion 319

CHAPTER XX

Classes of the Novgorodian community—The Novgorodian order of boyars and its origin—*Zhitïe liudi*—Merchants and *tchernïe liudi*—*Kholopi, smerdi*, and *polovniki*—Origin and status of the class of *zemstsi*—Basis of class division in the Novgorodian community—The political order of Novgorod—Origin of the princely and people's parties, and their mutual rivalry—Character and importance of the Novgorodian factions—Peculiarities of the political organisation and life of Pskov—Differences between the political systems of Novgorod and Pskov—Faults of the Novgorodian political system—The general cause of the fall of Novgorodian independence—Prophecies concerning that event 342

HISTORY OF RUSSIA

CHAPTER I

The two points of view in the study of history—The principal factor in the development of Russian social life—The four principal periods of Russian history—The Ancient Chronicle; its genesis, authorship, and contents.

THE degree of scientific interest afforded by the history of a given country depends upon (1) the number of distinctive combinations of conditions therein, and (2) the extent to which the features arising out of those conditions serve to render the circumstances of the social life of that country remarkable. The student may adopt the standpoint either of the sociologist or of the observer of the progress of civilisation. Of these, the general weight of considerations tends, in my opinion, to the adoption of the former, and I propose to make it my own throughout the present work.

The history of Russia affords special facilities for the study of sociology. They originate, firstly, in the comparative simplicity of the processes dominant throughout its course—a simplicity which enables us to examine minutely, not only the working of the historical forces in general, but also the operation and relative potency of those special factors by which the comparatively non-complex composition of Russian social life has been determined; and secondly, in the peculiar circumstances which have influenced Russian development from the very beginning—circumstances which, while imparting to the nation a distinctive character and genius, have communicated also to the national life a special rate of evolutionary progress. Centuries of effort and self-sacrifice have been needed to form the Russian Empire; yet the people by which that State has been formed has not yet taken the place in the front rank of European nations to which it is entitled by its moral and material resources. Adverse historical conditions have combined to cause the internal development of Russia to proceed upon a lower plane than her international status, and to debar her from exercising those national powers of which she is conscious but which she cannot expand to the full.

From the very first moment of their entry into the Russian plain from the slopes of the Carpathians, the Eastern Slavs (the original progenitors of the Russian nation as we now know it) became fixed in a geographical and ethnographical setting widely different from that which fell to the lot of their kinsfolk, the Germanic Slavs. Whereas the latter settled among the survivors and memorials of an old-established civilisation, and thus were enabled to take as guides and instructors the Romans whom they had conquered, the Eastern Slavs found themselves stranded upon a boundless and inhospitable plain, the inhabitants of which had neither civilisation nor memorials to bequeath. Debarred from close settlement by the geographical features of the country, the Eastern Slavs were forced for centuries to maintain a nomad life, as well as to engage in ceaseless warfare with their neighbours. It was this peculiar conjunction of circumstances which caused the history of Russia to become the history of a country for ever undergoing colonisation—a movement continued up to, and given fresh impetus by, the emancipation of the serfs, and remaining in progress to the present day. Issuing in 1861 from the Central Provinces, where it had long been pent up and become artificially congested, the tide of emigration overflowed into Siberia, Turkhestan, the Caucasus, and the Trans-Caspian regions, until it reached the shores of the Pacific itself.

Thus we see that the principal fundamental factor in Russian history has been migration or colonisation, and that all other factors have been more or less inseparably connected therewith. The chief stages of migration group themselves into four periods : which, if named according to the localities in which the Russian population (or such portions of it as helped to make history) was massed during each epoch, may be termed the Dnieperian, Upper-Volgan, Great Russian, and Pan-Russian periods respectively; if according to the political *régimes* in force at the time— the Town Province, Principality, Muscovite Empire, and Russian Empire periods; and if according to their respective economic systems—the Forest Industrial, Free Agricultural Labour, Military Landowning, and Serf Labour epochs of Russian history.

Before entering upon the study of the first of these periods (no matter how we name them), it is essential that we should devote some attention to the genesis and composition of the Ancient Chronicle (the

" Chronicle of Nestor," as it used to be called), which constitutes the prime foundation upon which our history is built. At the same time, although the Ancient Chronicle serves as our chief source of historical information, passing mention ought also to be made of the works of such foreign writers as the Patriarch Photius, the Emperor Constantine Porphyrogenitus, and Leo the Deacon, as well as of certain Scandinavian sagas and a whole series of Arabic scripts. As for the mass of local manuscripts treating only of detached subjects, such as the ecclesiastical establishments, mercantile systems, and so forth, of their day—a mass of documents which swells continually in volume from the eleventh century onwards—they constitute merely the subsidiary details which, fragmentary, diffuse, limited in outlook, and not infrequently obscure as they were, served to form the raw material out of which the compiler of the Ancient Chronicle composed a record, at first disjointed, but afterwards more or less continuous, of the initial two-and-a-half centuries of Russian history. In passing, it may be said, that it is a record cast not merely in the form of bare narrative, but in that of an historical exposition illuminated throughout by the critical outlook of its compiler.

The inscribing of manuscripts was a labour of love to the old Russian bookmen. Following slavishly at first the external models of Byzantine chronography, they soon adopted also its inward spirit and tendency. To these again, in time, became superadded certain specialities of style, a wide and consistent outlook upon events, and a peculiarly just appreciation of historical values. In many cases, also, these bygone writers raised their manuscripts to the highest pitch of artistic development, since they looked upon the labour of inscription and embellishment as not only pleasing to God but beneficial to the intellect. In time it further came about that, in addition to chronicles of the day being compiled either by private individuals for their own edification or by inmates of monasteries for the use of their respective establishments (documents, however, which usually treated of little beyond detached events), there arose also a more or less regular system of official, or governmental, record-keeping. It is clear from a manuscript inscribed to the order of Prince Mstislav of Volhynia in the year 1289 that some such system was not only prescribed at his court, but possessed political significance; since, referring to a castigation inflicted upon the inhabitants of Beresti for some rising or another, the document remarks in the Prince's name: "I have caused this affair to be entered in the customary records." With the rise of the Empire of Moscow this system of official record-keeping attained yet further development. Hitherto the compilers of official manuscripts had been almost exclusively ecclesiastical persons, but at the court of Moscow the work began to be entrusted also to lay clerks. With their accounts of events throughout the country at large these scribes incorporated accounts of purely local happenings, and in time there became accumulated a very large stock of these local memoirs or chronicles. Later on, the compilers of what are commonly known as the Recueils, or Digests, who succeeded the early local chroniclers, collected the multitudinous documents inscribed by the latter, and co-ordinated them into records, more or less continuous, of the country in general, as well as added to them certain independent accounts of events later than those covered by the early documents upon which they were working. In this manner the raw material furnished by those early documents came to serve a national end. In the earlier Recueils we find many alterations made, according as new matter required to be interpolated into the main groundwork of ecclesiastical journals, accounts of detached events, and so on, which formed the constituent portions of each Recueil, until at last the completed manuscript had assumed the guise of a fairly systematic digest of the whole material at disposal. This process of transcription, abridgment, excision, or amplification frequently gave birth to many different versions of the same Recueil—versions differing largely in text, in subject-matter, or in both.

Such, then, in outline, was the early progress of chronography in Russia. To discriminate among this chaotic mass of documents, to classify and group the different versions and copies, to determine their probable sources and authors, to interpret their contents, to reconcile their points of disagreement, and to assign to them their correct scriptory *genera*, constitutes the task—and a very complex one—of experts in chronographical lore. It is a task, moreover, which, though long ago begun upon, and pursued with a considerable measure of success by a long series of investigators, is not yet approaching its conclusion.

Practically the whole of the early documents upon which the Recueils were founded have perished. Like those documents, the Recueils were themselves compiled in different localities and at different periods ; so that, were it possible to combine them into one complete and satisfactory Recueil, they would form—varying as they do both in regard to the area of territory which they cover and the amount of time which they embrace —an almost uninterrupted chronological record of events in Russia at large during a space of eight centuries; albeit a record by no means detailed at every point, nor uniform in style or spirit, nor informed by a consistent outlook upon the world. As a matter of fact, attempts to compile such a general Digest or Recueil have actually been made; in which productions the narrative usually begins with the middle of the ninth century, and proceeds haltingly onwards (its thread interrupted at intervals by many and wide hiatuses) to the close of the thirteenth, or even the beginning of the fourteenth, century as regards the older examples, and to the close of the sixteenth as regards the later. In one or two instances the story even meanders on into the seventeenth or eighteenth century. In this connection it may be mentioned that the Russian Archæographical Society (a body of experts formed in 1834 for the purpose of editing the written memorials of ancient Russia) began in 1841 to publish a "Complete Collection of Russian Manuscripts," and has issued, up to the present time, twelve volumes of that series.

It is through some such process, then, of collection and sifting of raw material that the Ancient Chronicle has come down to us as our oldest source of information concerning events in Russia during the ninth, tenth, and eleventh centuries, as well as during the first ten years of the twelfth. This fundamental record of that period used customarily to be known as "The Chronicle of Nestor," but is now more generally called "The Ancient Chronicle," pure and simple. Any one, however, who were to enter a public library and ask merely for "The Ancient Chronicle" would probably be met with the inquiry: "But which version of it do you require?" The reason is, that no single version has ever yet been discovered in which the Chronicle is set forth in the pure and original form in which it first issued from the pen of its compiler, since in every version we find the text bound up with added narrative matter—matter which, in the later examples, usually extends to the close of the sixteenth century. The two versions to which any one desirous of reading the Ancient Chronicle in its purest form should have recourse are those known as the Laurentian Version and the Ipatievski Version respectively. The former of these is the oldest known script treating of the history of Russia at large, and was inscribed in the year 1377 by "the miserable, greatly-sinning, and unworthy servant of God, the monk Lavrenti,"[1] to the order of Dmitri Constantinovitch, Prince of Suzdal and father-in-law of Dmitri Donskoi; being thereafter preserved at the Rosjdestvenski Monastery in the city of Vladimir on the Kliazma. In this Version we find the Ancient Chronicle proper followed by entries concerning events which took place both in the southern Principality of Kiev and in the more

---

[1] Lawrence.

northern one of Suzdal—entries which continue the story down to the year 1305. The other, the Ipatievski Version, was inscribed towards the close of the fourteenth century or at the beginning of the fifteenth, and first brought to light at the Ipatievski Monastery of Kostroma—whence the name. In this case we find the Ancient Chronicle proper followed by a detailed narrative of events occurring in Russia at large (but more particularly in the Principality of Kiev) during the twelfth century—a narrative excellent alike in its simplicity, its power of graphic description, and its dramatic force. This, again, is succeeded by an equally interesting —it might almost be said, poetical—description of events in the two contiguous Principalities of Galicia and Volhynia during the period 1201–1292. Thus each of these two Versions gives us a fairly complete history of the period comprised between the middle of the ninth century and the year 1110, as well as a less complete record of the two following centuries.

Up to the middle of the nineteenth century, criticism of the Ancient Chronicle was based upon the assumption that it was the work of one writer alone; wherefore critics concentrated their attention upon the personality of the supposed author and upon the task of establishing what might be accepted without cavil as the text of his unaided labours. Later examination of the original script, however, has tended to cast doubt upon the fact of its being in its entirety the original Chronicle of Kiev, and given rise to a theory that the work is only another Recueil (though on a larger scale than the rest) of which the original Chronicle of Kiev forms merely one constituent part. This theory I shall seek to prove.

It is not until the narrative has passed the middle of the eleventh century that the Ancient Chronicle affords us any trace of the personality of its compiler, whoever he may have been, but after that point is reached we do catch certain fleeting glimpses of this bygone bookman of Kiev. For instance, writing under date of 1065 concerning some monstrous fish which had been captured by fishermen in the river Sitomlia near Kiev, the Chronicler remarks: "We gazed at the same until eventide." Whether at that time the writer was already an inmate of the Petcherski Cloister, or whether he merely ran as a boy to look upon the wondrous spectacle, it is difficult to determine. At all events he must have become an inmate of the Cloister before the close of the eleventh century, since, writing of the raid made upon that establishment by the tribe of the Polovtsi in 1096, he says: "They fell upon the Cloister after Matins, when we were resting in our cells." Later on we learn that the Chronicler must still have been alive in the year 1106, since he writes that in that year expired the venerable and saintly Yan, in the ninetieth year of a ripe old age, and "after a life lived in accordance with the laws of God and in an odour of sanctity such as distinguished the Saints of old." "From him," also says the Chronicler, "I heard at times many sayings, which I have duly recorded in my Chronicle." None the less, there are only these few scattered passages to help us to form for ourselves a picture of this old writer. That in his youth he was at least a sojourner in Kiev, and that, later on, he became a monk of the Petcherski Cloister in that city, as well as a "writer of records," is all that we know of him for certain. After the middle of the eleventh century is passed, the narrative of his Chronicle becomes more detailed in its history, and loses much of the legendary stamp which has hitherto clung to its pages.

The question next arises—Who precisely was the compiler of the Ancient Chronicle? It seems that as early as the beginning of the thirteenth century a tradition had arisen and was current within the walls of the Petcherski Cloister that the compiler had been an inmate of that institution, and that his name was Nestor. We find this same Nestor mentioned again, as a "one time writer of records," in a letter sent by Polycarp, Abbot of the Petcherski Cloister in the early thirteenth century, to the Archimandrite Akindin; while the historian Tatischev has it from somewhere or another that Nestor's birthplace was Bieloe Ozero. However that may be, Nestor has a distinct place in ancient Russian literature, not only as the generally reputed compiler of the Ancient Chronicle, but also as the undisputed author of two separate literary works—namely, a life of the Abbot Theodosius of Petcherski, and a narrative of the legendary exploits of the Princes Boris and Gleb.

Now, if the two last-mentioned works be compared with the corresponding passages in the Ancient Chronicle which treat of their respective subjects, we come upon some irreconcilable contradictions. For example, the Chronicle's account of the founding of the Petcherski Cloister declares, in more than one passage, that it was by the Abbot *Theodosius* that the reputed compiler of the Chronicle was admitted an inmate within its walls; whereas, in his "Life of Theodosius," Nestor specifically states that he, "the sinner Nestor," was received into the Cloister by the Abbot *Stephen*, who was Theodosius' successor. This and other contradictions between the Ancient Chronicle and the two separate works above-mentioned are sometimes explained by a supposition that neither the legend of

Boris and Gleb, as detailed in the Chronicle, nor the passages in the Chronicle concerning Theodosius and the Cloister were written by the original compiler of the Chronicle at all, but extracted at some later date from the works of two entirely different writers, and interpolated into the body of the Chronicle. Of these supposed extracts, the legend of Boris and Gleb is usually attributed to Jacob, Abbot of the Petcherski Cloister during the eleventh century, while the other one (the extract containing the passages which conflict with Nestor's own account of his admittance to the Cloister and appearing to have been interpolated into the Chronicle at some period between the years 1051 and 1074) is said (together with a third passage, dated 1091, and relating to the translation of Theodosius' relics) to represent a portion of a similar " Life " of that Abbot, written by some monk who had been a contemporary and pupil of Theodosius, and who, therefore, as an actual eye-witness of the events described, would be more likely to have accurate knowledge of them than could Nestor—who, indeed, could only have written of them according to tales told him by the elder brethren.

Not unnaturally, the above contradictions have caused many scholars to doubt altogether the fact of Nestor being the compiler of the Ancient Chronicle—and the more so since, in the Laurentian Version, we come upon the following unlooked-for Postscript appended to the story of events for the year 1110 : " I, the Abbot Silvester, of the Order of St. Michael, have written these books and documents, in the hope that the favour of God may descend upon Prince Vladimir, upon the Principality of Kiev, and upon myself who am Abbot of this Monastery of St. Michael in the year of grace 6624 " (1116). With some reason, therefore, this Postscript has led many of those who doubt the authenticity of Nestor's authorship to look upon one Silvester, Abbot of the Viebuditski Monastery of Kiev, and a former inmate of the Petcherski Cloister, as the true compiler of the Ancient Chronicle. Yet objections might be raised also to this supposition (though, in my opinion, they would be baseless), since it might be urged that if the Chronicle proper really comes to an end with the year 1110, and the above Postscript was not added by Silvester until 1116, it is not easy to understand why he should have passed over the six intervening years without recording a single event in them, nor why he should have omitted to add the Postscript precisely at the moment when he concluded his narrative. Another objection might be found in the fact that the *litterateurs* of the fourteenth and fifteenth centuries seem invariably to have drawn a clear distinction between the true author of the Chronicle (whoever they imagined him to have been) and Silvester as its mere *continuer*. For instance, in one of the later Recueils (the Nikonian), we come upon the following passage appended to a dramatic account of the terrible raid made by Prince Ediger of Ordin upon Russian territory in 1409: "These things have I set down, not in any man's despite, but as following the example set us in the ancient Chronicle of Kiev. For, indeed, our former rulers were wont to command that every good and every evil thing which might befall in Russia should be recorded without malice and without extenuation, even as the Abbot Silvester did write concerning events which befell under Vladimir Monomakh." This extract alone would seem to show that at least scholars of the early fifteenth century did not regard Silvester as the original author of the Chronicle.

However, it is only by examination of the actual contents of the Chronicle itself that we shall be enabled to form anything like a correct judgment as to Silvester's connection with it. In reality it forms a compound of exceedingly heterogeneous historical material—being, in fact, a Recueil upon a large scale. Jumbled together we find, not only entries for the several years, as well as more detailed accounts of detached events, but also diplomatic documents, such as the Russian treaties with the Greeks of the tenth century, and a letter sent by Vladimir Monomakh to Oleg of Tchernigov in 1098. To these may be added Monomakh's *Pöuchenie*, or "Book of Instruction" (of date 1096), and the works of various ecclesiastical dignitaries, such as the *Pöuchenie* of Theodosius, already mentioned as Abbot of the Petcherski Cloister. In the main, however, the Chronicle is based upon three principal scripts, which divide it practically into as many portions, and may be examined by us in the order in which they occur.

I. The *Poviest Vremennich Liet*, or "Story of the Times." In reading this, the opening portion of the Chronicle, we see that it constitutes a more or less complete and connected narrative; in which respect it differs from the majority of such early manuscripts. Beginning with a description of the partition of the world among the sons of Noah after the Flood, it goes on to treat of the gradual growth and diffusion of the nations; of the first settlement of the Slavones upon the Danube and their subsequent cleavage from that centre; of the Eastern branch of the Slavones which then became formed, and its migrations throughout what now constitutes Russia; of the advent of Saint Andrew to this land; of the founding of Kiev; of the warrings of the Slavones with various races; of their racial characteristics;

of their subjugation by the Chozars; of the tribute which certain of the Slavonic tribes paid to the Varangians, and others to the Chozars; of the ultimate expulsion of those Varangians; of the invitation sent to Rurik and his two brethren; of the exploits of Askold and Dir; and of the manner in which Oleg established himself at Kiev in the year 882. The scriptory form of the narrative is modelled upon that of the ancient Byzantine writers, who usually began their chronicles with an exposition of Old Testament history, and one of whom—Georgius Amartol, who wrote of the ninth century and the first forty-seven years of the tenth— very early became known in Russia through translation into the Slavonic tongues, but more particularly into Bolgarian. Indeed, the *Poviest Vremennich Liet* of which we are now speaking itself names him as one of its prime sources of information—the source whence it derived, amongst other things, the story of the expedition of Askold and Dir against the Greeks in 866. In addition to these extracts from Amartol, the *Poviest* gives numerous legends concerning the Slavones; in which legends, despite their actual prose form, we see preserved the outlines of primitive folk-song, particularly in the case of the one which tells of the raids of the Avars upon the Dulebs (the latter one of the numerous Slavonic tribes). At first the *Poviest* pursues its narrative without giving any dates at all, nor do they begin to appear before the year 852. None the less, their appearance with that year does not seem to be in any way due to the year's importance in the Chronicle, since the manuscript has nothing to show at that point beyond a few jottings, clearly inserted later by another hand than that of the original compiler. Further on in the *Poviest* we come upon dates which are either uncertain or difficult to reconcile with other dates and passages. For instance, under the heading of the year 859, the *Poviest* tells of the levying of tribute by the Varangians upon the Slavonic tribes of the north, as well as by the Chozars upon those of the south : yet when precisely those tributes began to be levied, or when precisely the subjugation of the northern Slavonic tribes by the Varangians took place, the *Poviest* does not say, notwithstanding that no previous mention of those events has been made. The year 862 presents still greater difficulties to the student, since under that date we read of a whole series of non-contemporary events—of the defeat of the Varangians and the subsequent feuds among the Slavonic tribes, of the invitation sent to the Three Princes, of their response thereto, of the death of Rurik's two brethren, Sineus and Truvor, and of the departure from Novgorod for Kiev of Rurik's two boyars, Askold and Dir. In short, we see compressed under a single date the events of several years. The *Poviest* itself declares elsewhere in the course of its narrative that *two* years elapsed between the coming of Rurik and his brethren to Russia and the deaths of Sineus and Truvor! Moreover, this mass of jumbled entries for the year 862 concludes with the following broken passage: "When Rurik was ruler in Novgorod—6371, 6372, 6373, 6374—Askold and Dir went against the Greeks." Thus we see an enumeration of four blank years interpolated into the middle of the sentence and dividing its principal clause from the subordinate. In all probability the chronology met with in the *Poviest*—at all events as regards the ninth century—was not computed by the original author at all, but inserted later, and in mechanical fashion, by some other hand. Certain indications as to the probable date at which the *Poviest* was composed are apparent in the text. Relating, for instance, how Oleg settled at Kiev and began to levy tribute upon the neighbouring tribes, the chronicler observes that Oleg had already commanded the people of Novgorod to pay a similar tribute (of three hundred *grivni* a year) to the Varangians, and adds: "They continued to pay such tribute unto the death of Yaroslav." In one of the later Recueils, however (the Nikonian), the matter is stated differently, as follows: "Oleg commanded the people of Novgorod to pay tribute unto the Varangians, and it is paid by them to this day." Clearly, then, this—an account contemporary with the paying of the tribute—is more likely to be an authentic statement of the facts than the passage given above, which must have been written some time after the event: whence it follows that the *Poviest* must have been composed at least before the death of Yaroslav—that is to say, before the year 1054. That being so, its author could not very well have been Nestor.

It is difficult to define precisely at what point the *Poviest* ends—the precise event at which it breaks off and becomes merged in its continuation. Enumerating the various races with which the Slavones had successively to contend, the narrator says that, after many grievous reverses, the Dulebs suffered a further harrying at the hands of the Pechenegs, and again at those of the Ugri. The onslaught by the last-named tribe is assigned by him, in this passage, to the period of Oleg's rule in Kiev (or, to be precise, to the date 898); by which statement he contradicts another passage in the *Poviest* which says that it was in *915*, when *Igor* was ruler in Kiev, that the Ugri made their incursion into Russian territory. From the conflict between these two passages it seems probable that the narrator of events under Igor had gleaned entirely different historical material to that possessed by the chronicler of events *prior* to that ruler: which is tantamount to saying that during the interval dividing those two periods there had occurred a change of authors. As some indication of the scope originally projected for the *Poviest*, we find prefixed to it the following introduction: "Herein is to follow the Story of the Times, treating both of the origin of the Russian State, of its heretofore rulers in Kiev, and of its progress from this time onward." The first part of this undertaking—to treat of the origin of the Russian State—may be said to have been succinctly fulfilled by the narrator when, speaking of the usurpation by Oleg of the rulership at Kiev, he says: "Oleg took under his rule both Varangians, Slavones, and others—*known together as Rus;*" but inasmuch as the *Poviest* comes to an end with that period, the concluding portion of the narrator's promise—to treat of the further progress of the Russian State—remains unfulfilled.

To sum up, then, we see that the title *Poviest Vremennich Liet* refers properly, not to the Chronicle as a whole, but only to the narrative which constitutes its initial portion and comes to an end at some point during the rule of Oleg; that the *Poviest* cannot well have been written at any date later than the death of Yaroslav; and that the most important subjects of which it treats are the invitation sent to the Three Princes and Oleg's usurpation of the rulership at Kiev.

II. The *Legend of the Conversion of Russia by Vladimir.*—This account in the Chronicle of that mythical event covers a period of three years—namely, 986, 987, and 988. Like the *Poviest*, it is something more than mere narrative, since it contains much that is polemical in tone, particularly as regards its denunciation of all faiths other than the Orthodox. Again, like the *Poviest*, it has manifestly been interpolated into the body of the Chronicle by some later hand than that of the original compiler. Indeed, the date of its composition may be gathered from the text itself. Relating how, at the time of the alleged conversion of the Russian people, the Jews in Russia approached Vladimir to lay before him the tenets of their religion and to beg of him permission to retain them, the narrative states that the Prince asked of them: "Where is your country?" to which they replied, "In Palestine." Then said the Prince, "Is there no room for you there?" to which question his petitioners are represented as having returned the very straightforward, but (to ourselves) perplexing answer: "God was moved to anger at our forefathers, and did cause them to be scattered by the Greeks throughout all lands, and their country to be given over to the Christians." Now, if the writer of the "Legend of the Conversion" had known accurately who were the original conquerors of Palestine, he would have caused the Jews to speak of their forefathers being scattered by the *Romans*, not by the Greeks; and if, likewise, he had known accurately who were masters of Jerusalem in Vladimir's time, he would have spoken of the Holy Land as given over to the *Mahomedans* (*i.e.* to the Turks), not to the Christians. It is this latter error especially which makes it clear beyond all doubt that the author of the "Legend" was writing at a period subsequent to the taking of Jerusalem by the Crusaders—that is to say, at a period subsequent to the year 1099.

The two principal sources for this story of the forcible conversion of Russia by Vladimir appear to be, firstly, popular tradition, and, secondly, a *Life of Vladimir* compiled by some unknown writer shortly after that ruler's death. I say "shortly after that ruler's death" for the reason that in the work itself there occurs the passage, "These events took place a few years before the present time"—that is to say, before the date when the *Life* was written; so that, provided it was composed by some genuinely Russian author, and not by some Byzantine resident in the country, it constitutes one of the oldest memorials in our literature.

III. The *Petcherski Script.*—This, the concluding portion of the Ancient Chronicle, is stated, by a tradition which lack of evidence makes it impossible to disprove, to have been written either at the end of the eleventh century or the beginning of the twelfth by one Nestor, a monk of the Petcherski Cloister of Kiev. Its story breaks off with the year 1110; but where precisely it begins is difficult to determine. We can conjecture that, although Nestor became an inmate of the Cloister only in the year 1074, he nevertheless began his Script with events considerably anterior to that date. In particular, we may assume that the story of the events of 1044 is from his pen, since, writing of the accession of Prince Iziaslav of Polotsk to his father's throne in that year, he not only mentions a bandage with which the Prince had a wound in his head bound up, but adds the comment: "Iziaslav weareth that bandage to this day." Now, Iziaslav died in 1101; so that, upon the whole, we may take it that Nestor began the Petcherski Script with the times of Yaroslav I.

Also, there is ground for believing that Nestor brought his narrative to an end precisely with the close of the story for 1110, and that it was by no mere chance, but for a definite reason, that Silvester came to append his Postscript so long afterwards as the year 1116. I derive my evidence

of this from the actual description of events in 1110, as given in the
Laurentian Version—the one in which the Silvestrian Postscript is to be
found. It would seem that, whether because tidings of current events
did not always reach the Chronicler with due dispatch, or whether for some
other reason, the Chronicler was forced at times to defer the actual task
of writing concerning the happenings of a given year until the year which
followed it, when the consequences or further development of those events
were already known, and so might possibly impart to the comments with
which the Chronicler interspersed his record the appearance almost of
foreknowledge. Nevertheless, he specifically implies, in more than one
passage, that this apparent prescience was due merely to delay in the work
of writing. "Of what is now passing," he says in these passages, "I will
write during the year which followeth." Something of this sort must
have been the case with the concluding year recorded in the Petcherski
Script—namely, 1110. Let me quote an illustration of what I say. Over
the gateway of the Petcherski Cloister there seems to have stood a stone
emblem in the form of a pillar of fire, placed there (so the Chronicler
phrases it) "for all the world to see," and interpreted by him thus : " The
pillar of fire signifieth the Angel of God, sent by Divine command to lead
His people in the ways of Providence, even as in the days of Moses a
pillar of fire led the Children of Israel by night." He then goes on :
" Since, therefore, this emblem surely hath knowledge both of what
is, of what was, and of what is to come, may it not have foreseen,
and acted as our leader in, the late contest, when we repelled the barbarians ? " Now, these concluding words must have been written during
the year *1111*, since it was only *in March of that year* that the Polovtsi
made their great raid upon the Cloister ; yet we find them, not under the
heading of their proper year (for Nestor never came to write a full account
of the raid), but inserted as a comment into his account of events for the
previous year (1110). When, moreover, we take into account the fact that,
although the Ipatievski Version gives practically the same interpretation of
the emblem, in the first instance, as does the Laurentian, the emblem has
nevertheless assumed quite a different significance when we arrive at the
point in the Chronicle where the raid is described *in full* (the pillar of fire
being now identified with the personality of Vladimir Monomakh, who,
with nine other princes, came to the aid of the Cloister)—when, I say, we
take into account all this, it becomes evident that the events of the year
1111 must have been set down in the Chronicle by some other writer than
Nestor, and possibly also as long after that year as 1113, when Monomakh

had succeeded Sviatopolk in the rulership of Kiev. Thus we may take it that, although Nestor's *narrative* comes to an end with the year 1110, he continued his actual *task of writing* into the following year; after which some other writer (Silvester, as I shall seek to show) took up the task of compiling the Chronicle as a whole, and in time appended the Postscript already referred to.

As to the sources from which Nestor derived his information for his particular portion of the Ancient Chronicle—namely, the Petcherski Script of which we are now treating—they were, in all probability, the same as those from which he gleaned the material for his *Life of Theodosius*, since he could have had no personal knowledge of the Abbot during his (the Abbot's) lifetime. Such sources would be tales related to him by eye-witnesses of, or participators in, past or current events, or in any case by persons who might reasonably be supposed by him to have accurate knowledge of them. The Petcherski Cloister would act as a centre to which gravitated all persons of importance and standing in the Russian community of the day—princes, boyars, bishops coming to confer with their Metropolitan of Kiev, and merchants passing up or down the Dnieper on their way to or from the Greek dominions. The Chronicler would also possess a living record of the times in the person of his fellow-inmate, the saintly Yan; who, formerly a boyar and captain of the city guard, and, later, a pupil and close intimate of Theodosius, appears to have given utterance to " many sayings," which Nestor duly recorded in his Script. These various personages would visit the Cloister for a multitude of purposes—to obtain the Abbot's blessing before embarking upon an enterprise, to render thanks to God upon its conclusion, to offer prayer, to beg for the intercession of the monks, to give " of their possessions for the benefit of the brethren and the maintenance of the Cloister," to exchange the news, to meditate, or to confess their sins. Thus it would come about that the Cloister would serve as a focus for all the scattered beams of Russian life, in the concentrated light of which any inmate of the Cloister who might chance to be of an observant turn of mind would be enabled to survey the world of his day from many more points of view than would be accessible to a layman.

Such, then, are the three main portions into which the Ancient Chronicle is divided : namely, the "Story of the Times," the "Legend of the Conversion by Vladimir," and the "Petcherski Script." Examination of the Chronicle makes it evident also that these three several portions are divided by wide chronological hiatuses; for the method of filling up which gaps in the narrative we had better turn (as the best example) to the reign of Igor, which forms part of a period of seventy-three years (913–985), separating Oleg's reign from the point at which the "Legend" takes up the tale. The most important events during this interval fall to the years 941, 944, and 945. In the former of these years took place Igor's first expedition against the Greeks, the story of which is set forth in the Chronicle with the aid of wholesale borrowings from Amartol, as well as from a Greek biography of Vassilii Novi. In the second of these years occurred Igor's second expedition against the Greeks, which is related in the Chronicle solely on the basis of popular tradition. Lastly, under the heading of the third of these years we find set down the text of Igor's treaty with the Greeks, together with accounts of his expedition against the Drevlians, of his death, and of the vengeance wreaked by his widow (Olga) upon his murderers—the whole based, once more, upon popular tradition. Eight more years are filled up with accounts of events having no connection whatever with Russia, but only with the Greeks, the Bolgars, and the Ugri—all of which matter concerning foreign peoples is borrowed, again, from Amartol, and contains interspersed among its text four interludes on the subject of Igor's dealings with the Pechenegs and Drevlians—interludes clearly based upon tradition. The story concerning the period which extends over these eight years and the years 941, 944, and 945 is itself interrupted in places by years left blank and set down merely as figures in chronological order. Apparently the chronicler could find no suitable material for these dates, of which no fewer than twenty-two occur during Igor's thirty-three years of rulership. The remainder of the main interval of seventy-three years of which we are treating is filled up by expedients similar to the foregoing, as also is the gap which occurs between the conclusion of the "Legend of the Conversion" and the supposed commencement of the "Petcherski Script." The sources from which material for the filling up of these gaps was derived appear to have been, firstly, translations from sundry Greek and Southern Slavonic works treating of Russia; secondly, the texts of the various Russian treaties with the Greeks (which treaties constitute the earliest known examples of Russian essays in chronography); and thirdly, popular tradition, developing at times into complete "sagas" or legends, such as the tale of the vengeance wreaked by Olga upon her husband's murderers. This particular species of native Kievan saga continued to serve the Ancient Chronicle as one of its main sources of information throughout the entire ninth and tenth centuries, while distinct traces of it are discoverable also in the early part of the eleventh (as instanced in the legend of Vladimir's heroic battle with the Pechenegs). From these fragments of old Kievan *bilini*, or folk-songs, which we find preserved in the Chronicle it may be conjectured that by the middle of the eleventh century there had become accumulated in Russia an immense stock of legends cast in poetic form, the majority of which bore upon the various Russian expeditions against Byzantium. A second cycle of *bilini* (celebrating, in this case, the many struggles of Vladimir with the nomad tribes of the Steppes) likewise had its origin in Kiev, and is to be found preserved among some of the peasantry of that region to this day. The earlier of the two cycles, however, survives only in the pages of the Ancient Chronicle and—in extremely fragmentary fashion—some of the older Recueils.

The very fact of the occurrence of blank years in the Chronicle reveals to us something of the process by which it was compiled. The compiler seems to have been guided in his arrangement of material by a definite chronological plan, which he placed at the basis of his work and sought to develop by recourse, in turn, to the Byzantine chroniclers, to data afforded him by the Russian treaties with the Greeks, and to traditions preserved among the people of Kiev concerning their former rulers. In the course of the story concerning the origin of the Russian State which follows hard upon the legend of the battle of the Chozars with the Poliani we come upon an interpolation (under date 852) in which, after saying that the Russian State, as such, only came into existence with the accession of Michael III. to the throne of Byzantium after the successful attack upon Constantinople by the Russian forces (as related in the Greek chronicles), the author of the interpolation concludes: " Henceforth, therefore, let us reckon our dates from that event." This interpolation manifestly represents an afterthought on the part of the compiler of the Chronicle, who begins his chronology, in the first instance, with the Flood, and goes on to state how many years elapsed between that event and Abraham, between Abraham and the Exodus, and so forth. Thus computing his various periods, he arrives eventually at the year 882, when Oleg usurped the rulership at Kiev. " Twenty-nine years were there between the first year of Michael and the first year of Oleg, Prince of Kiev, and thirty-one years between the first year of Oleg, Prince of Kiev, and the first year of Igor." Finally, the system comes to an end with the death of Sviatopolk in 1113, the concluding ¡computation being: " Sixty years were there between the death of Yaroslav and the death of Sviatopolk." Now, inasmuch as the latter died, as I have said, in 1113, it follows that this last quotation was written at some date *subsequent* to that year. That is to say, it was written during the rulership of Sviatopolk's successor, Vladimir Monomakh. And since, moreover, the Petcherski Script breaks off (as we have seen) with the year 1110, when Sviatopolk was still living, there can be very little doubt that the whole of the chronological plan found in the Chronicle was the work of another hand than Nestor's, who, if he did not predecease Sviatopolk, had at all events ceased from his labour of writing before that event took place. For these reasons, therefore, it may be taken that the concluding item of chronological reckoning which we find in the Chronicle (the item referring to the interval between the deaths of Yaroslav and Sviatopolk) was set down by the same person who continued the Chronicle during the times of Sviatopolk's successor : which is tantamount to saying that the item was set down at some period between the years 1113 and 1125. *But to that period belongs, beyond doubt, the Silvestrian Postscript.* Therefore I, for one, believe that it was Silvester who compiled the Ancient Chronicle.

To sum up our conclusions with regard to Silvester, the Ancient Chronicle, and Nestor, they may be succinctly stated thus. What is known to us as the Ancient Chronicle is, in reality, a compilation of several different manuscripts, the work of more than one author ; while the task of compiling the whole was carried out, not by Nestor—whose contribution thereto has descended to us only in an abridged and altered form, and constitutes, under the title of the " Petcherski Script," its third and concluding portion —but by Silvester, Abbot of the Viebuditski Monastery of Kiev.

CHAPTER II

Historical value of the Ancient Chronicle — Its importance for later Russian historians—
A chronological error—The origin of that error—The work of compiling the Chronicle
—Defects in the older versions—The theory of Slavonic unity—Manuscripts of the
twelfth century—The divergent points of view of their authors.

OUR next task must be to appraise the true worth of the Ancient Chronicle
as a reliable source of historical information. Valuable though it be as
our oldest compendium of early Russian history, the Chronicle has established a further claim upon our regard by having acted as the model for
later scripts of the same kind, to which productions it was usually prefixed
by their authors.

Analysis of it serves but to heighten our interest in the personality of
its compiler, as also in his methods, for to him is due the credit, not only
of collecting and verifying the necessary historical material, but also of
elaborating a definite system of chronology and maintaining a consistent
outlook upon the events which he records.

The chronological plan upon which the work is based forms a connecting link between its various portions and their contents. Yet, just when
that plan has almost reached its concluding point, we find the compiler
falling into a grave error, through over-reliance upon a Greek source.
It seems that at some period during the eleventh century there had
been translated into the Palaeo-Slavonic language the work known as
the "Chronicle in Brief," or "Abridged Chronicle," of the Patriarch
Nicephorus—a production dating from 828. Now, as we have seen,
the compiler of our own Ancient Chronicle decided to amend his
chronology from the accession of the Byzantine Emperor Michael III.
onwards ; and it was through relying, for this purpose, upon the Greek
script above-mentioned that his error arose. For the precise explanation
of the mistake we are indebted to. the scholar Shakhmatoff, who has set
forth in detail how, at a certain point in the chronological table of the
Nicephorian script (the table which the compiler of the Ancient Chronicle
adopted as the basis of his own, and which extended from the Birth of

Christ to the First Catholic Council), there came to be inserted the figures 318 in place of the figures 325. That is to say, the number of dignitaries attending the Council was inadvertently substituted for the date of the year in which the Council was held. Consequently, the error accumulating, the number of years which elapsed between the holding of that Council and the accession of Michael III. worked out, in time, at 542, instead of 517 ; and, through adding together these two erroneous periods of 318 and 542 respectively, the accession of Michael came to be put at 860 years after the Birth of Christ, or 6360 from the Creation of the World (for Nicephorus' " Abridged Chronicle " reckoned 5500 years as the interval between the Creation and the coming of Christ, not 5508 as we do). Thus there arose an error of eighteen years in computing the date of the accession of Michael III.; the true date being A.D. 842—or, allowing for the Nicephorian system of reckoning from the Creation, A.D. 850. Nevertheless, serious though this initial error undoubtedly was, we find its consequences practically annulled when we arrive at the twelfth century, owing to the corrective agency of the Greek treaties. Still holding to his system of placing the accession of Michael at A.D. 860, but knowing—whether through tradition or conjecture—that the death of Oleg took place in the same year as the Prince made his second treaty with the Greeks, the compiler of the Ancient Chronicle arrived at identically the same number of years for the period elapsing between the accession of Michael and the death of Oleg as that given in the treaty— namely, 60.

It is only due to the compiler of the Ancient Chronicle to say that, considering his difficulties, he emerged from his chronological struggles, if not with complete success, at least with credit. Inasmuch, however, as he assigns the successful attack of the Russian forces upon Constantinople to the year 866 (although it should be assigned, as we now know, to 860), we find it necessary also to antedate certain earlier events which he relates, and place them exactly at the middle of the ninth century. Such, for example, are the feuds which arose among the Slavonic tribes of the North after their expulsion of the Varangians, the invitation sent to the Three Princes, and the settling of Askold and Dir at Kiev. At the same time, inexactitudes with regard to a year or two need not trouble us much, seeing that the compiler himself put only a conditional, conjectural value upon his dates. Confronted, for instance, in the *Poviest* with a series of closely connected events to each of which he could not assign any particular year, he comprised the whole of them within such a period as he thought must surely cover their collective occurrence. His chief service, as regards chronology, lies in the fact that he was able so to arrange the medley of details drawn from Byzantine sources that the original end of the tangled skein of tradition—namely, the first subjugation of the Northern Slavonic tribes by the Varangians—became joined (with an error of not more than a few years in a period of two and a half centuries) on to the real starting-point of Russian chronology—the middle of the ninth century.

Thus, by linking the whole compilation into one definite chronological chain, as well as by sifting historical material from non-historical, Silvester introduced at once more unity and more uniformity into his editorial labours than was usual in those days. Such editorial labours consisted largely in wholesale borrowing from Amartol, who served Silvester not merely as a leading source of information concerning Russia, Byzantium, and the Slavonic tribes of the South, but also as a guide in matters purely academical. Thus, early in the *Poviest* we find Silvester supplementing his account of the partition of the earth among the sons of Noah (borrowed from Amartol) with an independent classification of the Slavonic, Finnish, and Varangian tribes—to each of which he allocates a place in Japhet's portion of the world. Yet it frequently happens that he seeks to explain traditional events of equal importance with the foregoing by resorting to the pages of his favourite authority for *analogous* happenings—a proceeding which causes a certain element of the science of comparative history to enter into his exposition of events. For instance, he supplements the striking passage in the *Poviest* concerning the manners and customs of the early Russian Slavs with extracts from similar descriptions by Amartol of the Syrians, Wallachians, and other races; to which, again, he adds remarks of his own on the subject of the Polovtsi—a tribe concerning which the original author of the *Poviest* could have known practically nothing, seeing that they appeared in Russia only after the times of Yaroslav I. In general, this particular portion of the Chronicle (*i.e.* the *Poviest*) bears traces of such vigorous editing on the part of the compiler of the Chronicle as a whole that the original text is scarcely to be distinguished from the Silvestrian interpolations and amendments. It is clear, also, that the compiler took the utmost care to give his Chronicle the benefit, not only of foreign sources, but also of the ancient Russian memorials. Well acquainted, doubtless, with the Chronicle of Novgorod, he must have borrowed thence the story of the exploits of Yaroslav in that city after the death of his father in 1015, whilst for the relating of what happened in Kiev during that year he seems to have had recourse to the *Legend of Boris and Gleb*, written by the Abbot Jacob early in the twelfth century. We have seen already that it was another than Silvester who drew upon an old biography of Vladimir for the " Legend of the Conversion," yet it was Silvester who added to that from the pages of the *Palaei*—a polemical disquisition on the Old Testament, dedicated to Vladimir by a Greek missionary, and aimed principally at the Mahomedans and certain sections of the Catholics. Likewise Silvester inserted into the record of events for 1097 a circumstantial story concerning the striking with blindness of Vassilika, Prince of Terebovl, written by one Vassilii, an intimate of the Prince ; while (as already mentioned) there are no fewer than three places in the Petcherski Script where we come upon conflicting accounts of Theodosius and the founding of the Petcherski Cloister. It must be confessed that Silvester's adoption of the comparative-historical standpoint led him at times to make sheer confusion of his work, through combining under one date events which, though of similar character, occurred at different periods. For instance, after saying that in or about the year 1071 the city of Kiev was visited by a soothsayer (of whom no mention whatever is made in the actual text of the Petcherski Script), and tacking on to the same a whole disquisition on the subject of " diabolical influence and modes of working," the extent to which devils have power over men, and the means by which they most commonly exercise it (to wit, through sorcerers), Silvester goes on to allot several other non-contemporary events to that date. In fact, he leaves us in no doubt whatever about the matter, since he specifically makes use of the phrases " in the same year," "at the same time," and so on. None the less, two at least of those events must have occurred at a later period.

We see, then, that the compiler of the Ancient Chronicle was no mere recorder of dry events, such as Nestor seems to have been ; and, indeed, the impression that he was an exceptionally cultured bookman, possessed not only of a wide knowledge of both native and foreign sources, but also of ability to use them, is strengthened still further by the occasional flashes of critical acumen which he displays. For instance, he combats the theory that the founder of Kiev was a poor ferryman of the Dnieper, and goes on to insert into the *Poviest* an editorial note, in which he cites a tradition that the founder was a prince by birth, and that, on visiting Constantinople, he was received with great honour by the Emperor in person. Yet as to what that Emperor's name was he has to confess complete ignorance. We see a similar exercise of the critical faculty displayed in connection with the many traditional scenes of Vladimir's baptism. The compiler examines the credentials of each one of them in turn, and finally selects the locality most probable.

Nevertheless, this process of critical selection and rejection does not altogether explain some of the more remarkable omissions in the Chronicle. For instance, in the later versions we come across a series of items to which no place whatever has been assigned in the earlier ones, notwithstanding that those items are not of a nature to excite critical distrust, but consist, for the most part, of entries which it was in no way necessary, nor even possible, to invent. Thus, in the earlier versions we find mentioned neither the building of Ladoga in 862 by the Three Princes, nor Rurik's settling there, nor the slaying of a son of Askold by the Bolgars in 864, nor the return of Askold and Dir to Kiev in 867 after the defeat of their great army before the walls of Constantinople, nor the subsequent mourning in Kiev, nor the great famine there in the same year, nor the victories of Askold and Dir over the Pechenegs. Moreover, in the earlier versions we find the year 979 entirely blank, whereas in the later ones it has two interesting items assigned to it—namely, the rendering of homage to Yaropolk by the Prince of the Pechenegs (in return for which the latter was granted certain "grades and powers"), and a visit paid to Yaropolk, for the same purpose, by certain Greek ambassadors, " who brought with them peace and love, that they might offer unto Yaropolk the same homage as had been rendered by them unto his father and grandfather before him." Finally, in the earlier versions we find omitted from the times of Vladimir a whole series of items connected with the baptism at Kiev of the princes of the Bolgars and Pechenegs, as well as with the various embassies which visited that city from Greece, Poland, Vengria (Hungary), the Papal Court, and the territory of the Czechs. Similar omissions, it may be added, are discoverable throughout the eleventh century, and are due, in all probability, firstly, to faults in the Laurentian Version (which, though the oldest, is by no means the most reliable form of the Chronicle), and, secondly, to reproduction of those faults by careless copyists, despite the fact that the items thus omitted were present in kindred scripts. It may also be that some of those items owed their omission from the earlier versions to the editorial discretion of Silvester, but are found to be present in the later ones through the initiative of copyists, whose frequent practice it was to act as their own editors of what they copied—a fact which may have led them to utilise sources which

Silvester had duly examined and rejected, but which they (the copyists) subsequently adjudged worthy of use for the filling up of spaces which he had left blank.   Yet in some of the ancient Recueils—particularly in those compiled at Novgorod—we find the story of the early centuries of Russian history set down at such striking variance to the manner of its narration in the Ancient Chronicle that it becomes altogether impossible to account for the many divergencies on the theory that omissions were made during the process of collation or inscription.   This led Shakhmatoff to propound a new theory—namely, that there had once been in existence a script yet older than the Ancient Chronicle which, written at the close of the eleventh century, had served as the "foundation-stone" on which the Ancient Chronicle (as exemplified in the Laurentian Version) was built.   However that may be, it would seem, either that the Laurentian Version absorbed only a *portion* of the then current stock of legends concerning the early centuries of Russian history, or that, whereas the earlier versions represent mere *abridgments* of the Chronicle, the later ones represent the Chronicle in its *entirety*.   Of these two suppositions, the latter had the support of (among others) the well-known historian Soloviev.

Perhaps the Chronicle's most noteworthy feature of all is the manner in which it seeks to throw light upon the dawn of Russian history by proving the original unity of the Slavonic stock.   The compiler goes thoroughly into ethnographical details—specifying the various branches of that stock, assigning to them their respective localities, and tracing the several links by which they were connected.   He points out the actual moment in history when the stock first became divided—that is to say, the period when the Ugri settled upon the Middle Danube in the early tenth century and, splitting the Slavonic inhabitants of that region into the Eastern and Western Slavs respectively, at the same time sundered their common nationality and traditions.   He tells us of the influence exercised upon Slavdom by the missionaries Cyril and Methodius, and how the Moravians first adopted the idiom which subsequently developed into the language of Russia and Bulgaria.   One racial origin, he says, was common to the Moravians, to the Slavs of the Danube, to the Czechs, to the Lechs, and to the Poles.   Methodius was Bishop of Pannonia, where he had been preceded in the episcopate by Andronicus, a reputed pupil of St. Paul.   Inasmuch, therefore, as St. Paul undoubtedly preached in Illyria and Pannonia, he must have preached also to the Slavs themselves, since their original home was in those regions. Consequently (concludes the Chronicler) it was through the great Apostle himself that Christianity first reached the early progenitors of Russia. Likewise the Chronicler argues that the Russian and Slavonic stocks were essentially one by origin, since, although it was from the Varangians that our forefathers first acquired the name of "Russians," those "Russians" were none the less a part of the great host of the Slavones. So also (he says) were the Poliani—a branch of Slavdom which derived its distinctive name from the fact that its members selected a *polé*, or plain, as their place of settlement.

In this manner does the twelfth-century Chronicler seek to connect the remote ancestors of modern Russia with the family of Slavonic nations, as also with the tradition that Christianity first reached Russia through Apostolic channels. It is indeed a remarkable phenomenon that a community which, but a century earlier, had been offering human sacrifices to idols should have advanced so rapidly in the scale of civilisation as to have come to recognise the inter-connection between itself and events happening far beyond its territorial limits. Moreover, in the early twelfth century the theory of Slavonic unity demanded all the greater effort to maintain in view of the fact that it was in no way illustrated in practice. At the very period when it was being expounded so eloquently on the banks of the Dnieper, the various branches of Slavdom were either in process of disruption or had already undergone subjection. The beginning of the tenth century had seen the Moravians scattered by the Ugri, and the beginning of the eleventh century the conquest of the first Bolgarian kingdom by Byzantium; while both the Baltic and the Polish Slavs had given way before German pressure, and, with the Czechs, submitted to Catholic influence.

The several divergencies between the two oldest Versions of the Chronicle (the Laurentian and the Ipatievski), as well as between them and certain of the later ones, grow much more marked after we pass the year 1111 than they were before it; which seems to make it clear that from that point onwards the two older scripts cease to be different versions of the same work, and become wholly distinct compilations. Nevertheless, until the close of the twelfth century they continue to give none but identical events, drawn from identical sources—namely, the stock of early local manuscripts which have been referred to in Chapter I. and accounts of detached events written by persons who were either contemporaries of, or had witnessed, or had even participated in, the events related. Yet, although the two Versions avail themselves of common sources of information, they tell their tale in different fashions and in different degrees of detail. Upon the whole it may be said that the Ipatievski Version is more detailed in its narrative than the Laurentian ; yet it should also be noted that, whereas the former draws chiefly upon the literary sources of Southern Russia for its material, and the latter upon those of the Northern regions, the Ipatievski Version not infrequently gives a fuller account of some particular event happening in Northern Russia than does the Laurentian, and *vice versâ*. Lastly, each of these two Versions appears to have possessed its own special sources of information, in addition to those which they shared in common ; wherefore, it may be said that, although they each of them give us a general history of early Russia, they none the less do so in different perspective or settings. In both of them, also, the study of the Post-Silvestrian portion brings us face to face, almost at every step, with borrowings from other writers— now from a chronicler of Kiev, now from one of Tchernigov, of Suzdal, of Volhynia, and so on. From this it would seem that every Russian town of importance in the twelfth century had its own particular chronicler, as also that extracts from the manuscripts of such scribes were granted a place in the Ancient Chronicle according to the more or less important position which their authors' towns filled in the country. For instance, we find the chief place allotted to Kiev, whence both Versions derive the bulk of their material ; while items garnered from chroniclers dwelling in such distant spots as Polotsk or Riazan are only noticed, as it were, in passing. Indeed, the literature of the twelfth century seems to have marched *pari passu* with the life of the people, and, like the people, to have become split up into a number of different local centres of activity. It is difficult to understand how the compilers of the Post-Silvestrian portions of the two Versions were enabled to amass so great a stock of local documents and traditions as they did, and afterwards to co-ordinate them into one connected story. None the less, there can be no doubt that they rendered invaluable service to later historians by preserving for their use numerous historical details which would otherwise have perished.

Again, these two Versions are of inestimable value to us in that the process of compiling them from the primal local records has in no way effaced the distinctive features of the latter as regards style, spirit, local colouring, and political or dynastic bias—nor yet, it may be added, destroyed such internal evidence as those local records afford concerning the relations subsisting between their authors and the communities or governments of their day. It must not be supposed (as is too often done) that those early chroniclers were impartial or apathetic spectators of events. Each of them cherished his own political views, his own local dynastic sympathies or antipathies. Thus we see a writer of Kiev enthusiastically supporting Monomakh and his faction, while another writer of Tchernigov is all for that Prince's opponents, and a third of Suzdal gives vent to his feelings in a string of reproaches against the people of Novgorod for their pride, their " cruel perfidy," their turbulence, their disregard for the sanctity of an oath, and their inveterate habit of deposing their rulers. In his eagerness to defend local dynasties or interests a chronicler of those primitive days never hesitated to colour events, whether by manipulating their details, or by reading into them his own meaning, or by substituting causes for effects. Consequently we see that, whereas it is through the wide variety of local sources upon which they are based that those scripts have acquired their pre-eminent importance in ancient Russian literature, it is through the multiplicity of the local sympathies which swayed their authors that they appear to us so charged with life and movement, that they stand before us as true mirrors of the tendencies, sentiments, and ideals of their day. As we read, for example, in the Ipatievski Version, the account of the fierce combats waged by Iziaslav, son of Mstislav, with the Princes of Tchernigov during the years 1146–1154, we seem to hear, in turns, the voice of a Kievan chronicler whose sympathies lay with Iziaslav, and that of a rival scribe of Tchernigov who was all for Iziaslav's opponents; while, from the moment that the Princes Yuri of Suzdal and Vladimir of Galicia join in the fray, there arises a perfect babel of contending chroniclers from all the remotest corners of Russia. The historian who laboured in the twelfth century made of his characters living, breathing, strenuous human beings. Not only did he record events—he likewise dramatised them, and caused the drama to pass before the eyes of his reader. The Ipatievski Version is peculiarly remarkable for this faculty of dramatisation, and, despite the various conflicting views and interests of the writers drawn upon for its compiling, and the din and bustle of the events described, we find no trace of confusion in the compiler's story, but, on the contrary, every detail, great or small, co-ordinated to the one general outlook with which this bygone chronicler surveyed the world.

CHAPTER III

Principal factors of the first period of Russian history—The two theories as to its starting-point—The races who inhabited Southern Russia before the coming of the Eastern Slavs—The Ancient Chronicle's tradition concerning the dispersal of the Slavs from the Danube—Jornandes on their distribution during the sixth century—The military union of the Eastern Slavs in the Carpathians—The period and peculiar features of their settlement of the Russian plain—Results of that settlement.

PASSING to the study of the first period of Russian history, let me first of all adumbrate its limits, as well as specify the two principal factors which influenced Russian social life during its course.

This period may be taken as extending from prehistoric times to the end of the twelfth century or the beginning of the thirteenth. To define its terminal point more exactly is impossible, since there is no cardinal event dividing it sharply from the succeeding period. We cannot well look upon the coming of the Mongols as such an event, seeing that they found Rus[1] already entered upon a period of migration which they, indeed, helped to accelerate, but did not initiate. At the middle of the eleventh century the territory upon which the great bulk of the Russian population was concentrated stretched in a long, narrow strip coterminous with the basin of the Middle and Upper Dnieper and its tributaries, and extending northwards across the watershed to the mouth of the Volkhov. This territory was politically divided into *volosti*, or provinces, in each of which some large trading town served as the organising and directing centre of local political life. These towns we may call *volost* towns, and the provinces under them town *volosti*. In addition to the political functions which they performed, these *volost* towns served also as the several centres and directors of the economic movement which influenced the Russian industry of that day—namely, foreign trade. All other phenomena of the period—legal enactments, social relations, manners, religion, and achievements of art and learning—were the direct or indirect out-

---

[1] This was the ancient name of the country—the form "Russia" (modelled after the Greek style of nomenclature) not coming into general use until about the close of the seventeenth century.

come of the joint action of the two factors above-named—namely, the *volost* trading town and foreign trade. The first and most difficult historical problem which confronts the student of this period is to determine by what means and under what conditions this particular order of political and economic relations came to be established when the Slavonic population first settled upon the strip of land above-mentioned, and how the two ruling factors of the period—the *volost* town and foreign trade—first came into operation.

In our historical literature we find two views prevailing concerning the dawn of Russian history. The first of these views is expounded in a *critique* of ancient Russian manuscripts, written in the eighteenth century by the renowned German scholar Schlözer, and published at the beginning of the nineteenth. The following are the main outlines of Schlözer's view—a view subsequently shared also by Karamzin, Pogodin, and Soloviev.

Previous to the middle of the ninth century (*i.e.* before the coming of the Varangians from Scandinavia) the great plain lying between Novgorod and Kiev and stretching to right and left of the Dnieper was wholly wild, uncultivated, and unknown. True, it was inhabited, but only by human beings as destitute of government as the birds and beasts of their own forests. Into this desert, tenanted by poor and scattered Finnish and Slavonic savages, the middle of the ninth century saw Varangian immigrants from Scandinavia introduce the elements of social life. The notable picture of the manners of the Eastern Slavs which the author of the *Poviest* has drawn for us when writing of the rise of the Russian State evidently had its influence upon this view. Therein we read that, until their adoption of Christianity, the Eastern Slavs inhabited their forests "even as wild beasts or cattle do live," and, as beasts, again, killed each other, consumed every kind of abomination, and dwelt in clans isolated from, and permanently hostile to, one another. "Each man," says the *Poviest*, "lived alone with his clan, in his own place, and ruled there his clan." If, then, we adopt this view, it follows that we must begin our history with the middle of the ninth century, and begin it, too, with a picture of one of those primal historical processes with which human social life has invariably begun in proportion as humanity has gradually shaken itself free of primitive savagery.

The other view concerning the dawn of Russian history is directly opposed to the first, as well as of later origin in our literature. The works in which it is to be found most fully set forth are those of Bieliaev (a former professor of our University of Moscow) and the well-known *History of Russian Life from the Earliest Times*, by Zabielin.　In brief, it is as follows :—

From prehistoric times the Eastern Slavs dwelt where the Ancient Chronicle knew them, and where, perhaps, they first settled many centuries before Christ—namely, in the great expanse of the Russian plain.　This initial point defined, the exponents of this view go on to postulate a long and complicated historical process by which the primitive union of the isolated clan developed, among these aboriginal Eastern Slavs, into the tribe, towns sprang up as tribal centres, and certain of those towns attained, in time, the status of "elder" or chief towns, and from constituting merely the tribal centres of the Poliani, Drevlians, Sieverians, and so forth, began eventually (about the time of the coming of the Three Princes) to become merged into a general Russian state.

In spite of its simplicity and continuity, this view presents undoubted difficulties to the student, since it gives no precise details as to the time taken by this complicated historical process to develop, nor yet as to the historical conditions under which that development took place.　If we adopt this view we must begin our history long before the birth of Christ— begin it, if not actually with the times of Herodotus, at all events many centuries before the coming of the Three Princes, seeing that, according to this theory, the Eastern Slavs had succeeded in establishing an elaborate and complicated social order, cast in definite political forms, at a period long before the Princes' arrival.　To appraise the two points of view, let us examine our knowledge and traditions of the Slavs.

From ancient Greek and Roman writers we glean many (though not invariably reliable) details concerning the Steppe region of Southern Russia—details which those writers must have acquired through the Greek colonies established there, either from merchants who had connections with those colonies or by personal observation on the spot.　Previous to our era this region was overrun by successive nomad races from Asia— firstly by the Cimmerians, then (in the time of Herodotus) by the Scythians, and lastly (contemporarily with the Roman Empire) by the Sarmatians. With the entry of our own era immigrant hordes of this kind began to succeed each other with even greater rapidity, and the nomenclature of the barbaric inhabitants of ancient Scythia to become more and more complex and diverse—the Sarmatians either giving place to, or becoming divided into, the Gaeti, the Yazigi, the Rhoxalani, the Alani, the Bastarni, and the Dacians.　These races kept pressing forward towards the Lower Danube and the northern confines of the Roman Empire, until, in one or two cases, they succeeded in penetrating into the Imperial provinces themselves, and forming between the Dnieper and the Danube those extensive, but evanescent, kingdoms of the Gaeti, the Rhoxalani, and the Dacians to which even the Romans themselves were forced to pay tribute. Southern Russia served those races only as a temporary halting-place where they could prepare themselves to play a further rôle in Europe by penetrating to the Lower Danube or surmounting the Carpathians. Their passage across the Steppes has left innumerable *kurgans*, or burial mounds, to mark its course—memorials with which the vast expanse between the rivers Dniester and Kuban is thickly strewn. These *kurgans* have been zealously and successfully worked upon by archæologists, and have yielded much valuable historical evidence confirmatory of, or explicative of, the ancient Greek chroniclers who treated of Russia. Certain of those immigrant races, but more particularly the Scythians, who made an extended halt in the Steppe region were brought, through the agency of the Greek colonies established there, into more or less close contact with ancient culture. A mixed Hellenic-Scythian population sprang up around those colonies, the Scythian kings built themselves palaces in the Greek colonial towns, and Scythian scholars journeyed even to Greece itself in the pursuit of learning. In their *kurgans* have been found articles fashioned after the finest Greek models—articles which once adorned the rooms of Scythian dwellings. Nevertheless these data, though of great *general* historical value, refer rather to the history of our *country* than to that of our *people*. Science has not yet succeeded in establishing any direct historical connection between these Asiatic settlers in Southern Russia and the Slavonic population which appeared there at a later date, nor yet in determining the influence of the artistic productions and cultural attainments of these nomads upon the civilisation of the Poliani, Sieverians, and so forth. Indeed, there is no evidence whatever of the presence of Slavs among these ancient races, and the races themselves remain unsolved ethnographical problems. It is true that certain students of historical ethnography have attempted to assign them severally to the Celtic stock or to the Slavonic, but I consider that it is a mistake to do so. The racial stocks into which we now group the populations of Europe do not constitute portions of an aboriginal division of humanity, but were *themselves* historically compounded, as well as became distinct from one another at different periods. Consequently, to seek them amid ancient Scythian genealogy is to attempt to link those bygone races with an ethnographical classification of altogether modern date ; and even if the races in question did possess a common genetical tie with modern Europe, it would still be a difficult matter for each individual European nation of to-day to discover among them its particular and direct forefathers, and to begin from them its history.

To trace the starting-point of the history of a nation, we should look, first of all, to the memory of its people. A nation is an aggregate of individuals not merely *living* together, but *acting* together, and therefore retaining certain traditions of the events in which their community first took part as a whole, and through which it first became conscious of its own unity. Such events generally leave traces upon the national life, as well as upon the national memory, by first of all uniting the nation's forces towards some common end, and then strengthening that initial act of association by some fixed form of social life made obligatory upon all. The earliest traditions current in the national memory, the earliest form of social life adopted to unite the national forces in common action—these, in my opinion, are the two intimately connected factors which define the starting-point of a nation's history. Let us seek them in our own.

The Ancient Chronicle gives us no assistance in this connection, since the point of view of its compiler was altogether different from the one just specified. He was a Panslavist who, starting from the idea of the original unity of Slavdom, endeavoured always to connect the early fortunes of Rus with the general history of the Slavonic race. The Ancient Chronicle makes no mention of the period when the Slavs migrated from Asia to Europe, but finds them already settled upon the Danube. It goes on to say that, after being defeated and subjugated by the "Volkhi," a certain portion of them went and settled upon the Vistula, and became known as Lechs, while others migrated to the Dnieper and acquired the name of Poliani, and others, again, settled in different parts of the forest region and became the Drevlians, and so forth. These "Volkhi " or " Volokhi " are supposed by scholars to have been the Romans ; and inasmuch as we find also in the Chronicle an account of the destruction of the Kingdom of the Dacians by the Emperor Trajan—a state to which his predecessor, Domitian, had been forced to pay tribute—it would seem that Slavs entered into the composition also of that kingdom. I mention this because, with the account of the migration of a portion of the Slavs north-eastwards from the Danube in face of the Roman attack delivered at the beginning of the second century after Christ, this item constitutes one of our earliest pieces of historical information concerning Slavdom, and is given nowhere but in the Ancient

Chronicle. Nevertheless we cannot make it the starting-point of our history, since it does not refer solely to the Eastern Slavs and details a scattering, not a drawing together, of Slavdom.

The Ancient Chronicle does not state in so many words that the Eastern Slavs made any extended halt during their passage from the Danube to the Dnieper, yet, taking its rather obscure reminiscences in conjunction with foreign sources, we recognise that such a halt was made. During the third century after Christ our country suffered a fresh invasion—this time from an unexpected quarter, namely, the shores of the Baltic. The new invaders were hardy sea-rovers from Gothland, who, penetrating up the rivers of the Russian plain, eventually attacked the Eastern Empire. In the following century their then leader, Hermanric, extended his conquests sufficiently to form among the inhabitants of our land a large kingdom, which was the first state known to history as founded by a European people within the confines of what now constitutes Russia. Into its composition entered various races of Eastern Europe, among which may be distinguished the Estians, the Meres, and the Morduines—all of them future neighbours of the Eastern Slavs. Now, Jornandes, the historian of the Gothlanders (from whose writings we glean all that we know of Hermanric's kingdom), also informs us that Hermanric conquered the *Veneti*, or *Venedi*, which was the name given by the Latin writers of the West to the Slavs of the early centuries of our era (their proper name, Σκλαβοι, not appearing, even in Byzantine chronicles, until after the close of the fifth century). Jornandes does not state where the Venedi lived in Hermanric's day, yet he clearly defines their habitat in his own time, the sixth century, since, describing contemporary Scythia, he says that along the northern slopes of the high mountains around the sources of the Visla (Vistula) there was settled the populous race of the Venedi. "Although," he goes on, "the Venedi are now known under many different names, according to their several tribes and places of habitation, their two chief divisions are the Sclaveni and the Anti. The Sclaveni extend northwards along the Visla and eastwards to the Danaster (Dniester), and live not in towns, but in swamps and forests. The Anti—the most powerful of all the Venedi—dwell along the curving shore-line of the Black Sea, from the Danapris (Dnieper) to the Danaster." This shows us that at that time the Slavs held the Carpathian region, and that that region was the centre whence a further diffusion of Slavdom was to take place. During the latter part of the fifth century, as well as throughout the sixth, these Slavs of the Carpathians kept passing the Danube and

attacking the Eastern Empire to such effect that by degrees the whole of
the Balkan Peninsula became permeated with Slavonic population.

Thus we see that the Eastern Slavs halted at least once during their
migration from the Danube to the Dnieper, and that their halting-place
was the region of the Carpathians. This continuous armed pressure of
the Carpathian Slavs upon the Eastern Empire served to weld them into
a military union, which, formed at first of *vatagi* only or companies
selected from each tribal division whenever an expedition was afoot (for
the Slavs of the Carpathians did not attack in whole tribes, as did the
Germanic Slavs when assaulting the Western Empire), developed eventually
into a warlike bond uniting (for the time being) all the tribes in one. Of
this military union and its adoption by the Eastern Slavs we find evidence,
or traces of evidence, in the *Poviest*. There can be no doubt that the
Poviest was written in Kiev—all the signs point to that—and that its author
had a peculiar sympathy for the tribe of the Poliani which inhabited the
Kievan region. More than once we find him drawing a favourable contrast
between their "gentle and peaceable habit" and the brutal disposition of
the other Eastern Slavs, as well as displaying altogether more knowledge
of them than of their fellow tribes. Yet, although he describes a series of
attacks made upon the Slavs successively by the Bolgars, the "Obri,"[1] the
Chozars, the Pechenegs, and the Ugri (omitting, however, all mention
of Hermanric's Gothlanders who preceded them, or of the Huns who
followed the Gothlanders and destroyed Hermanric's kingdom soon after
the death of that leader), it is only with the coming of the Chozars above-
named (with the exception of one short passage relating to the founding
of Kiev) that he makes his first reference to his beloved Poliani. Consequently that tribe would seem to have escaped some of the earlier vicissitudes entailed upon the other Slavonic tribes by the passing of immigrant
Asiatic races through Southern Russia. The only tradition dating from
those early times which seems really to have fixed itself firmly in the
author's memory is a story concerning one of the raids of the Avars upon the
Dulebs—the latter a Slavonic tribe whose ancient habitat was far removed
from Kiev, and whose name had dropped out of history long before the
author's lifetime. Of this raid of the Avars (or Obri) the *Poviest* says :—
"The Obri warred with the Slavones, and overcame the Dulebs, whose
women they captured, for when an Obrin was preparing to set forth he
harnessed neither horse nor ox to his chariot, but, instead, did command

---

[1] The Avars.

some three, four, or five women to be attached thereto ; and thus they drew him. In such manner did this people harass the Dulebs. The Obri were men of great stature and proud of soul : yet God did so wipe them out that every one of them perished, until none of them were left remaining. Wherefore to this day there is a saying in Rus : ' As dead as the Obri.' " To this historical proverb was probably due the fact that the tradition of the battle between the Avars and the Dulebs came to be remembered by the author of the *Poviest*, and to be preserved by him in its pages. On the face of it the tradition bears all the signs of being a *bilina*, or historical folk-song, and may have constituted only one item out of a whole cycle of Slavonic poems bearing upon the Avaric raids and dating from the Carpathian period. But where, we might ask, were the Poliani at the time of these raids, and why are the Dulebs alone represented as suffering so much at the hands of the " Obri " ? We receive an answer from an unexpected quarter.

In the fourth decade of the tenth century—about a hundred years before the composition of the *Poviest*—an Arabic writer named Massudi wrote a work on geography in which he refers to the Eastern Slavs. He states that formerly one of their tribes was paramount over the rest, but that, in time, there arose dissensions among them, so that their union was dissolved and thereafter each tribe elected and obeyed its own prince only. The tribe thus formerly paramount over the rest he calls the " Valinani " (*i.e.* Volhynians), while from the *Poviest* we know that these " Volhynians " were the same as the Dulebs and lived on the Western Bug. Consequently we now see why it was that the Dulebs alone figured in the tradition of the terrible raid of the Avars, since it was they who were the paramount tribe in question, while the other tribes were covered by their name, just as, in later days, all the Eastern Slavs were known as Russians under the covering title (" Rus ") of the bulk of their territory. But at the time of the Avaric incursions neither the Poliani nor Kiev had yet come into existence, and the majority of the Eastern Slavs were still concentrated in the west—upon the slopes and plateaus of the Carpathians and around the great watershed whence flow the Dniester, the Bug, and the tributaries of the Upper Pripet and Upper Vistula.

Thus we find existing among the Eastern Slavs, when halted in the Carpathians during the sixth century, a great military union, with the prince of the Dulebs as its paramount chief. The continuous warring of these Slavs with Byzantium helped still further to cement the bond, and

to weld Eastern Slavdom into a more or less united whole. This initial
achievement of the Eastern Slavs in the direction of consolidating themselves and uniting for a common end was evidently well remembered in
the Rus of Igor's day; with the result that, while our own Chronicler,
writing in the times of Yaroslav I. (a hundred years after Igor's time),
could only preserve a mere fragment of the tradition concerning the
struggles of the Slavonic military union with the Avars, the Arabic contemporary of Igor was able to give almost a complete account of them.

The military union of the Eastern Slavs is a fact which we are entitled
to place at the beginning of our history as a fact well established ; while
as the second fundamental fact of our history we may take the slow
diffusion of those Slavs eastwards from the Carpathians. Previous to
the beginning of that movement the Byzantine writers of the sixth and
early seventh centuries had found the Slavs of the Danube in a state of
great unrest, and all those writers agree in recording continual Slavonic
attacks upon the Eastern Empire throughout the second quarter of the
seventh century. Yet, be it noted, those attacks come to an end with
the close of that quarter, and with them, for the time being, all Byzantine mention of the Slavonic race. The Slavs disappear suddenly, as
it were, from Byzantium's ken—to reappear in its annals only with the
ninth century, when they recommence their attacks upon the Empire
from the *sea* side, by way of the Black Sea, and under the new name of
" Russians " or " Men of Rus." It follows, then, that this cessation of
Slavonic raids upon Byzantium between the seventh and the ninth
centuries was due to the Slavonic exitus from the Carpathians which
began in, or became accelerated during, the second quarter of the seventh
century. But this period of Slavonic unrest and migration coincides with
the period of the Avaric attacks upon the Carpathian Slavs : wherefore we
may take it that the latter was the cause of the former.

Of the halt made in the Carpathians by the Eastern Slavs, and of
their onward movement thence towards the Russian plain, the *Poviest*
makes no mention. On the other hand, it gives certain results, as well as
certain confirmatory evidence, of that movement. In a sketch of the dispersal of the Slavs from the Danube it clearly specifies the two branches
into which Slavdom then became divided—namely, the Western Slavs
(Moravians, Tzechs, Lechs, and Pomerani) and the Eastern Slavs (Serbs,
Croats, and Chrobatians). It is from the latter branch that it derives the
Slavs who subsequently settled upon the Dnieper and other rivers of the
Russian plain, and assigns their habitat, previous to that settlement, to

what now constitutes Galicia and the region of the Upper Vistula. Indeed, the Chronicle seems to have known the Chrobatians as inhabiting that locality up to as late as the tenth century—firstly, through their taking part in Oleg's expedition against the Greeks in the year 907, and subsequently through their fighting against Vladimir in 992. I have already said that the Chronicle makes no mention of the Slavonic migration from the Carpathians to the Dnieper; yet at least it has recorded one of the later *incidents* in that migration. Describing how the Eastern Slavs gradually spread along the Dnieper and its tributaries, it declares that among the *Lechs* were two brothers, Radim and Viatko, who came with their clans and settled, Radim upon the banks of the Sosh, and Viatko upon those of the Oka, and that from those two brothers respectively originated the tribes of the Radimizes and the Vatizes. The settling of those tribes at points so far beyond the Dnieper suggests that their coming represented a belated current of Slavonic colonisation—that the newcomers had been unable to find room for themselves on the right bank of the river, and so were forced to cross and go eastwards. At all events the Vatizes seem to have been the most outlying tribe in that direction. But why did the *Poviest* derive the Radimizes and the Vatizes from the *Lechs*—a *Western* Slavonic tribe? The reason must be that Radim and Viatko hailed from the Carpathian region, and that by the eleventh century (the time when the *Poviest* was written) that part of the world—namely, Red Russia, the former home of the Chrobatians—had already come to be looked upon as the country of the Lechs, and had been the subject of a war between Rus and Poland.

Thus, by comparing the rather obscure statements of the *Poviest* with foreign annals we can determine, to a certain extent, in what manner the two initial facts of our history came about. Let us sum up our conclusions. About the second century after Christ the Slavonic race was swept by the surging currents of racial migration into the region of the Lower and Middle Danube. Previous to that time it had been lost in the heterogeneous kingdom of Dacia, and only now begins to stand out from among the mass of Sarmatian population and to be distinguished as a separate entity both in foreign annals and our own. Although Jornandes states that it was after defeating the *Sarmatians* that the Emperor Trajan founded Nicopolis on the Danube, we know from our own *Poviest* that the race which underwent such a thrashing by the "Volkhi" (*i.e.* by Trajan's Romans) was the Slavonic, and that it was that disaster which first caused it to abandon its settlements on the Danube.

During the next five centuries the Eastern of the two branches into which that race became divided underwent a long, slow process of migration—a process which included an extended sojourn in the Carpathians and eventually landed the Eastern Slavs upon the banks of the Dnieper. Their exitus from the Carpathians was either initiated or accelerated by the attacks of the Avars; which assaults had the effect of dispersing them over territories vacated by other races, even as, in the fifth and sixth centuries, the attacks made by the Huns upon the Germanic Slavs had the effect of dispersing that branch of Slavdom southwards and westwards towards the Roman provinces. Although the story given by Constantine Porphyrogenitus concerning an invitation sent to the Serbs and Chrobatians by the Emperor Herakles in the seventh century, in the hope that they would join him against the Avars, is looked upon with suspicion by historical critics and is full of doubtful details, there is none the less beneath it a certain basis of fact. At all events the seventh century was the period when the rise of certain Slavonic kingdoms (of the Czechs, the Croats, and the Bolgars) coincided with an abatement of Avaric activity, while the same century saw the region where the Gothlanders had formerly ruled undergo colonisation by the Eastern Slavs, and the former territory of the Vandals and Burgundi undergo a similar process by the Lechs.

It is difficult to define the precise moment when the Eastern branch of the Slavs became sundered from the Western, but at all events we have seen that the two branches remained undivided up to at any rate the seventh century. For several centuries longer the Eastern branch remained subject to the influence of peculiar local circumstances and conditions which we shall be better able to note as we proceed to study the Eastern Slavs in their new environment on the Dnieper.

CHAPTER IV

Juridical and economic results of the settlement of the Eastern Slavs upon the Russian plain—Outline of their mythology and ancestor worship—Coming of the Chozars, and their influence upon Russian trade—Origin of the old trading towns.

THE new environment of the Eastern Slavs brought about certain changes in their condition—changes juridical, economic, and political. Collectively these changes helped to determine the order of Slavonic life of which we read in the Ancient Chronicle's record for the ninth, tenth, and eleventh centuries. Let us take the juridical change first.

During their sojourn in the Carpathians the Slavs seem to have preserved the primitive union of the clan as their fundamental unit. At all events evidence of this would seem to lurk in certain obscure and scanty Byzantine passages referring to the Slavs of the sixth and early seventh centuries. According to those passages, the Slavs were governed by a number of *tsarki* and *philarchi* (tribal princes and heads of clans), who were wont to meet together both in councils of *philarchi* and tribal *vietcha* (parliaments) for the discussion of public affairs. At the same time, those Byzantine writers seem to indicate that disagreements and private feuds were not uncommon among the Slavs (as has always been the case in communities based upon the petty union of the clan); so that if those writers are at all to be depended upon it would appear that by the sixth century the Slavonic community was already beginning to emerge from the clan stage into that of the tribe, even though clan exclusiveness still largely predominated. I have referred to the tradition of the Dulebs being paramount tribe in the Slavonic military union; yet it seems difficult to conceive how a warlike bond of this kind could have been organised, still less maintained, among a people so dominated by the petty clan union. At the same time, the objects and constitution of the military bond were so dissimilar to those of the clan union that it may well be that the one was able to exist without in any way affecting the basis of the other. The military union was formed of armed bands of fighting men, chosen from the different clans and tribes at a time when expeditions such as those against the Eastern Empire were in contemplation, and upon the conclusion of these expeditions the comrades in arms would disperse, and return to their kinsfolk and ordinary social relations. In later days it may have been upon a similar basis that the Eastern Slavs combined together to march with the Princes of Kiev against the Greeks. In the interval, however—during the period when the Avars were descending upon Slavdom and when, consequently, the raids of the Slavs upon the Eastern Empire had ceased and the great Slavonic migratory movement eastwards from the Carpathians was in progress—the military union remained in abeyance.

A still more difficult question for us than that of the military union is the question of the form of social life which obtained among the Eastern Slavs during their colonisation of the Russian plain. Writing of their distribution in that region, the *Poviest* gives a list of the different tribes (the Poliani, the Drevlians, the Volhynians, the Sieverians, the Radimizes, the Vatizes, the Krivitches, the Poloczani, the Dregovitches, and the Slavs of Novgorod), and adds that all of these tribes were settled in the river basins of the western half of the plain. Yet this does not help us to determine the *social* composition of those tribes—to decide whether they constituted petty political unions, or merely geographical groups of population in no way politically connected. Massudi tells us that on the break-up of the federation of tribes under the Dulebs the Eastern Slavs became a conglomeration of independent tribes, each of which elected its own prince, and this information is confirmed by a statement in the *Poviest* to the effect that in later days a certain Ki and his two brothers became chieftains of the Poliani, while the Drevlians, Dregovitches, and the rest likewise had their own chieftains. We have seen also that the tradition that Ki was a mere ferryman of the Dnieper is rejected by the scholarly editor of the *Poviest*, who declares him to have been a man of note and princely family. That being so, it may be that Ki's family became the hereditary dynasty of the Poliani, and that something similar obtained among the other tribes also. Even then, however, we do not know the exact governmental importance of those dynasties, not a single name of which has come down to us through tradition. It is true that Mal, the unsuccessful suitor of Igor's widow, appears to have been *one* of the Drevlians' chieftains, as well as the governor of Iskorosten,[1] yet there is nothing to show that he was the *paramount*

---

[1] The town where Igor was treacherously murdered.

prince of the tribe. In the same way, a chieftain among the Vatizes named Chodota, against whom Vladimir Monomakh led two expeditions, is not accorded the distinctive title of *kniaz* (prince) in Vladimir's *Pöuchenie*, but only alluded to in ordinary terms, so that his political status is not apparent. It may be that the various petty chieftains of a tribe looked upon themselves as the descendants of some common ancestor, such as Ki of the Poliani, and therefore maintained clan ties of a sort among themselves, held *vietcha* or councils together (like the *philarchi* during the Carpathian era), and even joined in festivals to commemorate the spirit of a common deified ancestor. The less data to hand in an historical question, the more diverse the possible resolutions of the problem.

So far, then, as can be seen, the union of the clan was still the dominant form of social life among the Eastern Slavs at the time of their settlement of the Russian plain. At all events, this is the only form which the *Poviest* specifies with any clearness. "Each man lived with his own clan, in his own place, and ruled there his clan." This would seem to mean that all the members of a clan lived together in one settlement, and not scattered about among homesteads of other clans. Yet the clan settlements mentioned by the *Poviest* can hardly have been original, undivided unions of one entire stock, since the working of the process of colonisation would inevitably have destroyed any such form of social life. The clan union holds together only so long as its members live in small groups, whereas whole and undivided unions of a single stock always tend to fall apart. Especially would this have been the case in face both of the process of colonisation of which we are now speaking and of the natural features of the country in which it was taking place. As the immigrants spread themselves over the plain they tended chiefly towards its forest strip —the strip to which Jornandes refers when, describing the country lying to the east of the Dniester and along the courses of the rivers Dnieper and Don, he says: "Haec terra vastissima, silvis consita, paludibus dubia." ("This is an immense territory, covered with forests, and almost impenetrable for marshes.") Indeed, it was on the extreme southernmost border of this forest region that Kiev itself arose. In those wilds the Slavonic settlers supported themselves by trapping fur-bearing animals, by forest apiculture, and by primitive husbandry. Yet, inasmuch as spots capable of being utilised for such pursuits were comparatively few and far between, it follows that the immigrants would have to search the thickets and marshes until they found some comparatively dry and open clearing capable of being prepared for agriculture or of being used as a basis for hunting and wild apiculture in the surrounding forest, and these arable spots would be like little islands scattered over a sea of timber and swamp. Upon them the settlers would erect their lonely dwellings, surround those dwellings with earthen fortifications, and clear a space about them for husbandry and for the preparation of appliances for the chase and apiculture. To this day the region around ancient Kiev retains vestiges of such fortified homesteads, the so-called *gorodistcha* [1] (although the term is an absolute misnomer, seeing that each such homestead cannot have occupied much more space than would suffice to accommodate a modern peasant's hut). These *gorodistcha* are usually round (though occasionally square) spaces marked out by the remains of a rampart, and are to be found scattered along the Dnieper at a distance of from four to eight versts from one another. That they date from pagan times is shown by the *kurgans* or old burial mounds which lie near them, excavation of which has made it clear that those interred in them were buried with pagan rites. It was to such isolated homesteads of primitive times that the Byzantine writer Procopius must have been referring when he says that in his day the Slavs of the Danube lived in " small, scattered, remote cots." Similar "remote cots"—perhaps it might be more accurate to say, settlements of one cot each—were built by the Slavonic immigrants when they came to settle upon the Dnieper and its tributaries, as well as when, later, they migrated to the region of the Upper Volga. These homesteads were fortified with earthen ramparts and (probably) a stockade, both as a protection against enemies and to guard the settler's cattle from wild beasts. Indeed, according to the *Poviest*, it was out of three such humble dwellings as these that the great city of Kiev itself arose ; while the fact of its founding being commemorated by him at all may be taken as a sign that the city arose at a date comparatively near to that of the composition of his script. Tradition says that upon three hills near the banks of the Dnieper there settled three brothers, who lived by hunting game in the surrounding forests. Here they built a township, which they called Kiev, after the eldest of the three brothers, Ki. As the head of the clan, Ki would be a *kniaz* only in the original, primitive meaning of that term of ancient clan nomenclature, but, as already seen, the compiler of the Ancient Chronicle saw fit (either on the ground of popular tradition or in

---

[1] Literally, remains of towns, or sites of towns.

accordance with some independent theory of his own) to magnify the title to that of *kniaz* as understood *in the eleventh century*, and thereafter to elevate its bearer to the headship of the hereditary dynasty of the Poliani.

The process of colonisation which I have described could not fail to shake to their foundations the hitherto powerful clan unions of the Eastern Slavs. The clan union rested upon two supports—namely, the authority of the head of the clan and the indivisibility of clan property; both of which supports were reinforced by the religious cult of the clan, or ancestor worship. But the authority of the head of a clan could not well continue to exert undiminished force when the homesteads of his kin had become scattered far and wide among forests and marshes. Consequently, the position of head of the clan in each separate, isolated homestead came to be filled by the head of the individual *family*, or master of the household. At the same time, also, the character of the forest and agricultural industries necessitated by the natural features of the Dnieper region tended to destroy the idea of the indivisibility of clan *property*, seeing that it was the efforts of detached, isolated homesteads only that made the forests exploitable and enabled suitable spots to be cleared for husbandry. Consequently each such arable or forest "lot" was bound sooner or later to acquire the significance of private *family* property, and although the members of a clan might continue to worship the spirit of a common ancestor and preserve common clan customs and traditions, in the domain of property rights and in all the practical relations of life any obligatory juridical bond between the several members of the clan was bound to become more and more a thing of the past. This result is seen the more clearly when, in examining such legal jurisprudence of the period as survives in old Russian annals, we find ourselves unable to trace in it any system of clan *succession*. In the gradual building up of the civil and social life of the individual, it was the primitive Russian *dvor* (that is to say, the complex household, consisting of a man and his wife, their children and near relatives) that served as the next step in the evolution of society—as the intermediate step between the clan and the modern *simple* family—and corresponded to the Roman *familia*. This sundering of the clan union and its dissolution into *dvori*, or complex families, left important traces upon the national customs and beliefs.

In the meagre outlines of Eastern Slavonic mythology which are to be found preserved in our ancient annals, as well as in certain of the more modern ones, we can distinguish two separate systems of religious belief. The first of those two systems is recognisable as the remains of nature worship, for traces are to be found of the sky being worshipped under the name of Svarog, the sun under the names of Dazhbog, Khorse, and Volos, thunder and lightning under that of Perun, and the winds under that of Stribog. Fire and other forces and phenomena of nature are also traceable as deities. Dazhbog and the god of fire were supposed to be the sons of Svarog, and were therefore known as the Svarozhitchi.[1] Like the Greek Olympus, the Russian Mountain of the Gods had its ranks of deities—a sign that the popular memory retained the different stages in the mythological process according as that process developed. Nevertheless we find it difficult to assign those different stages to any definite chronological points. Procopius, for instance, tells us that by the sixth century the Slavs had come to look upon Perun alone as lord of the universe, while, on the other hand, the Ancient Chronicle states that Perun shared that honour with Volos—the latter being characterised also by the appellation of the "Cattle God," or protector of flocks and herds (though possibly also "God of Riches," seeing that in the archaic dialect of the Chronicle the word *skot* or "cattle" still retained its ancient secondary meaning of "money"). The old Russian annals say little of the families of these gods, with the exception of a mention of Svarog's sons, but an Arabic writer of the early tenth century (Ibn Fadlan) tells us that he once saw upon a riverside quay on the Volga (probably at Bolgari, the chief town of the Bolgars) a large image of some pagan god surrounded by smaller images of the wives and children of the deity. "To this image," he says, "Russian merchants were offering prayers and sacrifices." Nevertheless it is not exactly clear what merchants are meant here— whether Varangian merchants or Slavonic. Worship of the true God was not yet generally established,[2] and even in the later days of paganism only its faintest beginnings are to be detected. No churches or priestly class had yet come into existence, but here and there there were to be found soothsayers and magicians, to whom recourse was had for divination and who possessed great influence over the people. In open spots, particularly on the summits of hills, stood images of gods, before which rites were performed and to which sacrifices—sometimes even human ones—were offered. It was before such an idol of Perun, set upon a hill near Kiev, that Igor registered a vow in ratification of

---

[1] -itchi being the plural of the patronymic termination.
[2] i.e. by Vladimir in 988.

the treaty which he concluded with the Greeks in 945, while, thirty-five years later, Vladimir placed upon the same hill a new image of Perun, with a head of silver and a beard of gold, as well as images of Khorse, Dazhbog, Stribog, and other deities, to all of which Vladimir and his people offered sacrifice.

The second of the two systems of religious beliefs current among the Eastern Slavs—namely, ancestor worship—seems to have attained greater development than did the first, and to have preserved its hold more firmly upon the people. So far as we can judge from ancient Russian annals, the central points of this cult were the grandfather and his wives (the latter a testimony to the existence of polygamy among the Slavs), who were looked upon as the protectors of their clan. The deified grandfather was revered under the title of the *tchur*—an appellation which still survives in our compound word *prashtchur*.[1] Moreover, we still see the grandfather's supposed protective power over his descendants preserved in the expression used to exorcise some evil influence or to avert a threatened danger—*Tchur menya !* (*i.e.* " May my grandfather preserve me ! "). While safeguarding his posterity from every sort of evil, the *tchur* also looked after their property, for a tradition which has left its mark upon the language assigns to this ancestral deity a function very similar to that of the Roman *Term*—*i.e.* of being the guardian of the lands and boundaries of his clan. To this day we designate the offence of removing a legal landmark by the word *tchereztchur*[2]—*tchur* having thus come to mean landmark or boundary. The same meaning, too, may help us to explain a certain feature in the ancient Russian-Slavonic burial rite as described by the Ancient Chronicle. After a " wake " had been held over the deceased the body was burnt, and the ashes—duly collected into a small vessel—exposed upon a pillar where the boundary paths of two properties met. Although these pillars were landmarks dividing the field or ancestral homestead of one clan from another, they stood practically in neither of the properties ; whence arose the popular superstition that cross-roads are of ill omen, since no *tchur* can there intervene to protect his kin from harm. All this testifies to the original width and solidity of the clan union. Yet mark that in the popular traditions and beliefs we find the *tchur*—hitherto the guardian only of the *clan*—appearing also under another name— namely, that of the *diediushka domovoi*,[3] or protector, not of the clan

---

[1] =great-great-grandfather.   [2] *Tcherez*=through or across.
[3] =lit., dear grandfather of the home.

as a whole, but of the individual *household*. In other words, we see that, without actually affecting popular traditions and beliefs woven around the clan union, the process of colonisation eventually caused the juridical bond uniting the clan to become dissolved, and clan relations to become exchanged for those obtaining among neighbours and neighbouring households. Nor was this exchange effected without leaving its mark upon the language, for the term *siaber*, or *shaber*, which in its original root-meaning signified "kinsman" (*cp*. the Latin *consobrinus*), acquired, in time, the meaning also of "neighbour" or "comrade."

This juridical sundering of the clan union opened the way for a mutual drawing nearer of clans ; to which end marriage served as one of the principal means. The Ancient Chronicle has noted (though by no means fully or systematically) the various stages of this process as expressed in marriage. The original type of household of which we have spoken— the type composed of an entire family of near relatives—developed, in time, into the clan settlement, of which all the members commemorated a common ancestor, and sought to perpetuate his memory by giving to their settlement some such patronymical title as Zhidchichi, Miriatchichi, Diedichi, Diedogostichi, and so forth. For clan colonies of this kind it was a matter of both urgency and difficulty to provide marriageable girls for their men, since the prevalence of polygamy did not leave sufficient women of the clan to go round, and other clans would not yield their women willingly or for nothing. Hence arose marriage by rape ; to which end kidnapping expeditions were carried out (so the Chronicle tells us) at inter-sports of the clans, at religious festivals held in honour of gods common to all the people (festivals usually held, as the Chronicler phrases it, "near the water"—*i.e.* at sacred springs), or at spots along the shores of lakes or rivers where the inhabitants of the district were wont to assemble. The Ancient Chronicle goes on to outline for us the various subsequent forms of marriage, as indicating the different degrees of culture and enlightenment to which the Russian Slavs had attained in its day. In this respect it places the Poliani upon a higher plane than any of their fellow tribes. Beginning with a description of the heathen manners and customs of the Radimizes, Vatizes, Sieverians, and Krivizes, it remarks that "at their devilish sports he takes a woman to be his wife who first can seize upon her." Rape, in the Chronicler's eyes, was the lowest form of marriage—nay, practically none at all. "In such a deed," he says, "there is nought of marriage." Yet of marriage by rape we see a faint survival to this day—namely, in the game of *gorielki*,[1] so popular with the youth of both sexes. The feuds which would have arisen between the various clans in consequence of their mutual seizure of each other's women were averted by *vieno*—*i.e.* by a sum paid in compensation to the kinsfolk of a captured girl. In time the *vieno* became converted into direct sale of the bride to the bridegroom by her kin, with the consent of the respective clans of the parties, and marriage by force gave place to the more peaceful ceremony of permitted *khozhdenie ziatia po neviestu*—that is to say, of a bridegroom going to fetch his bride and paying for her a sum in compensation for her loss. In the case of the Poliani, however, the Chronicle notes a further stage in inter-clan relations (adding once more the opinion that that tribe had altogether emerged from the savage state in which its barbarous fellows still remained!), since it tells us that among them "the bridegroom goes not to fetch his bride, but she is brought to him at even, and on the morrow there is sent after her what is to be given *with* her." This would seem to point to the institution of the dowry. The passage just given is quoted from the Laurentian Version, whereas the Ipatievski Version gives a slightly different reading: " The bridegroom goes not to fetch his bride, but she is brought to him at even, and on the morrow there is taken what is to be given *for* her,"—which concluding words would appear to refer rather to the old *vieno* than to the dowry. In any case, however, we may take these two readings as indicative of the two stages which followed next upon marriage by rape—namely, the permitting of the bridegroom to fetch his bride on payment of *vieno*, and the bringing of the bride to the bridegroom accompanied by a dowry; from which latter form of marriage originated the term *vodimaia* ("the brought woman") as applied to the legal wife in pagan Rus. From these two forms of marriage, also— the forms which I may call respectively "the going of the bridegroom" and "the bringing of the bride"—arose our modern terms for the marriage rite—namely, *brat za muzh* and *vidavat za muzh*[2] (for our language has preserved many fragments of the past which time would otherwise have winnowed from the popular memory). Marriage by rape; the *vieno* (firstly as compensation for rape, and subsequently as the price paid for the bride); the "going of the bridegroom"; the "bringing of the bride" (firstly in exchange for an agreed sum, and subsequently accompanied by a dowry)—all these successive forms of marriage marched with the various stages in the breaking down of clan exclusiveness, and paved the

---

[1] A kind of blindman's-buff.

[2] =respectively " to take (money) for a husband " and " to give (money) for a husband. '

way for complete clan fusion. Marriage, in fact, melted the clan (if I may use the simile) at both ends, by facilitating both entry to and issue from its ranks. From the fact of the kinsfolk of the bride and bridegroom becoming relations-in-law to one another it resulted that the connection came to be looked upon as an actual form of *kinship*. Consequently, even before the close of pagan times we see marriages beginning to connect whole clans which were formerly distinct. Of course, in its primitive, untouched form, the clan was an exclusive union to which no stranger could gain admittance, and the bride who married into another clan broke all ties of kinship with her own, and the two clans became in no way connected through the marriage; but the clan colonies or settlements of which the Ancient Chronicle speaks were not unions of this primitive kind, but unions formed of *fractions* of clans—*i.e.* of fractions made up of two or more of the many separate households into which the clan had become divided during, and through the action of, the colonising process.

I have entered into these various details concerning the successive forms of pagan marriage obtaining among the Eastern Slavs in order to be able to trace more clearly the weakening of the clan union which began on the Dnieper. My doing so will also help us to explain certain phenomena of family law which we encounter in old Russian annals; in which connection the last-mentioned form of marriage—the marriage accompanied by a dowry—will be found peculiarly important. In fact, the dowry served as the first basis of the separate property of the wife, while its institution also brought about a juridical defining of the position of a daughter in the family, as well as of her legal rights with regard to the family property. Under the *Russkaia Pravda*,[1] a sister could not succeed where there were brothers, but the brothers were none the less bound to provide for her maintenance and to marry her, with an adequate dowry, "to whomsoever they may." This additional obligation of providing the sister with a dowry could not fail to be an unpopular one with the inheritors—as, indeed, is shown by the following piquant proverb expressive of the feelings aroused in the various members of a family by the appearance of a suitor: " The father-in-law loves honour, the suitor loves taking, the mother-in-law loves giving, but the brother-in-law frowns and closes up his pocket." [2] In the absence, however, of brothers, the daughter (if unmarried at the time of the father's death) became legal

---

[1] A legal code compiled by Yaroslav I.—the earliest known in Russian history.

[2] In the Russian original the piquancy of this proverb is partly due to the rhyming of the syllables—an effect lost in translation.

heiress to the whole of the property, in the case of a landowning or free-man's family, and to a portion of it in the case of a serf family. Thus we see that succession was strictly confined within the limits of the family, no provision whatever being made for collateral heirs as participators in the inheritance, and that in building up this type of family and stripping it of all vestiges of the pagan clan union the Christian Church found ready to its hand much existing material prepared during the pagan era—material consisting of, among other things, the marriage with a dowry.

Still more important than these *juridical* changes was the series of *economic* results which followed upon the settling of the Eastern Slavs in the Dnieper region. We see from the *Poviest* that the great mass of the Slavonic population occupied the western half of the Russian plain; and it was by the great river which bisects this plain from north to south that the industry of that population was governed. The vital importance of rivers as affording, in those days, the only means of communication from point to point caused the Dnieper to become the principal industrial artery, the main trade-route, of the western half of the plain. Affording close communication, through its sources, with the Western Dwina and the basin of Lake Ilmen (*i.e.* with the two most important routes to the Baltic), its lower portion united the central plateau and the shores of the Black Sea, while its tributaries, stretching far to right and left, and serving as paths of approach to the main road, made the Dnieper region accessible, on the one side, from the basins of the Dniester and Vistula, and, on the other, from those of the Volga and Don—*i.e.* from the Caspian and the Sea of Azov. All this served, from earliest times, to make the Dnieper a busy trade-route and centre of trade, and it became still more so under the influence of the Greek colonies—colonies with which the northern shores of the Black Sea and the eastern shore of the Sea of Azov were plentifully bestrewn several centuries before our era. Chief among them may be named Olbia, which, colonised by settlers from Miletus six centuries before Christ, stood at the mouth of the Eastern Bug, opposite to the present town of Nicolaiev; Chersonesus in Taurica, on the south-western shore of the Crimea; Theodosia and Panticapaeum (the latter now Kertch), on its south-eastern shore; Phanagoria, in the Taman peninsula, on the Asiatic side of the Straits of Kertch (the old Bosporus Cimmerius); and Tanais, at the mouth of the Don. These Greek settlements had caused the Dnieper to become a trade-route of which Herodotus knew and along which the Greeks brought amber from the Baltic seaboard. Its import-ance from earliest times is referred to also by our own *Poviest*, which adds to its exposition of the geographical distribution of the Slavonic tribes a statement that "there lieth a water-way from the Varaeger (Baltic) to the Greeks by way of the Dnieper, and from the sources of the Dnieper one may pass to the Lovat. The Lovat floweth into the great Lake Ilmen, from which floweth the Volkhov into the great Lake Nevo (Ladoga), whence a gulf leadeth into the Varaeger. From the Varaeger one may sail to Rome, and from Rome to Tsargorod (Constantinople), and from Tsargorod through the Pontus (Black Sea), into which, again, floweth the Dnieper." This circular route girdling the entire continent of Europe must have been used by the Eastern Slavs, while the Dnieper itself became for them the chief artery feeding the popular industry and bringing the tribes into contact with the great trading movement then in progress in the south-eastern corner of Europe. The lower portion of the river's course and the tributaries upon its left bank connected those tribes with the markets of the Black Sea and the Caspian, with the result that these varied facilities for commerce awakened in the settlers a realisation of the natural riches of the country which they occupied. We have seen that it was in the forest region of the plain that the Slavs were chiefly massed—a region which, through its abundance of fur-bearing animals and opportunities for wild apiculture, afforded such ample material for foreign trade that henceforth furs, honey, and wax began to be exported in ever-increasing quantities. This exploitation of forest products, continued for several centuries, left a deep impression upon the social and industrial condition—nay, even upon the national character—of the Russian people, and is the earliest type of industry known in our history.

One circumstance in particular contributed to the success of this commerce. It chanced that, at the period when the Eastern Slavs entered the Russian plain from the West and began to settle its forest strip, there began to spread over the Steppes of South Russia a new Asiatic horde—the Chozars—who had long been roaming the country between the Caspian and the Black Sea. They were a nomad race of Turkish origin, but of different character to any of the hordes which either preceded or followed them. After settling in the South Russian Steppes they began to abandon their wandering mode of life and to engage in peaceful pursuits. They even built cities, whither they repaired in winter time from their summer camps, and to which, during the eighth century, there resorted also a large number of Jewish and Arabic traders. Indeed, the Jewish element became so strong there that eventually the Chozar Khans and their courts (*i.e.* the upper class of the Chozar community) adopted

Judaism. Spreading gradually over the Steppes of the Volga and the Don, this race formed, in time, an Empire centred upon the lower regions of the former of those rivers and having as its capital a city named Itil. This capital city gradually developed into an immense polyglot centre of trade, where there mingled with one another both Christians, Mahomedans, Pagans, and Jews, until, with the Bolgars of the Volga, the Chozars gradually became the intermediaries of an active trade between the Baltic regions of the North and the Arabic peoples of the East. This point was reached approximately at the middle of the eighth century—the period when, under the Abbasides, the centre of the Khaliphate was removed from Damascus to Bagdad. At about the same time the Chozars subjugated the Slavonic tribes which lay nearest to the Steppes—namely, the Poliani, the Sieverians, and the Vatizes. Cconcerning the first-named of these a tradition appears to have been current in Kiev which would go to show that the conquerors produced upon the conquered only the impression of being a very unwarlike, gentle, and easy-going people. The *Poviest* quotes the legend, which is to the effect that when the Chozar warriors came to take tribute of the Poliani they found them massed upon the heights on the right bank of the Dnieper, and said to them : " Pay us tribute." Thereupon the Poliani took counsel together, and eventually surrendered from every hut a sword. This tribute the Chozar warriors bore in triumph to their Khan and his chieftains, saying to them : " Behold, we have taken fresh tribute." " But whence ? " inquired the Khan and his chieftains. " In the forest, on the hills by the river Dnieper," was the reply. " And of what did it consist ? " continued the Khan ; whereupon they showed him the swords. His chieftains, however, at once cried out : " This tribute is not good tribute, O Khan. To us who have gone to seek it of them with one-edged weapons [1] these men have surrendered weapons of *double* edge.[2] Surely it will be that they will one day come to take tribute of us and of others." And so it came to pass, for to this day the Russian population rules the Chozar. From the irony expressed in this legend it will be seen that the Chozar yoke did not press very hardly upon the Slavs of the Dnieper. In fact, although it deprived them nominally of their independence, it brought them great economic advantages, inasmuch as henceforth the Slavs, in their capacity of tributaries to the Chozars, were granted right-of-way over the river trade-routes to the markets of the Caspian and the Black Sea, and thus were enabled, under the protection of their " conquerors," to open up a brisk

[1] Scimitars. [2] Swords.

export trade from the region of the Dnieper. Of the success of this trade we have early evidence. Khordadbih, an Arabic writer of the ninth century and a contemporary of Rurik and Askold, mentions that Russian traders were accustomed to bring merchandise from the remotest quarters of their land to the Greek towns on the Black Sea, where the Byzantine Emperor collected of such merchandise a tenth, by way of toll, after which those merchants made their way along the rivers Volga and Don to the Chozar capital, where the Prince of the Chozars likewise took of their goods a tenth. Thence, says Khordadbih, those traders would proceed to the south-eastern shores of the Caspian, and even convey their wares on camels to Bagdad itself, where the writer had himself beheld them. This information is the more important in that it refers to a period as early as the first half of the ninth century—to a period, in fact, not later than the year 846, or twenty years before the date assigned by the Chronicle to the coming of Rurik and his brethren. How many preceding generations, then, must have been needed to develop these far-reaching and multifarious trade-routes which now spread from the banks of the Dnieper and Volkhov? The Eastern trade from the Dnieper, as described by Khordadbih, must have originated at least a hundred years before he wrote his description of it—*i.e.* at about the middle of the eighth century. Still more direct evidence of the period when that trade began and developed is to be found in the circumstance that in the Dnieper region there have been discovered many hoards of ancient Arabic coins—coins dating, for the most part, from the ninth and tenth centuries, the period of the greatest development of the Eastern trade of the Slavs. In some hoards, however, no coins have been found of later date than the early ninth century, while the earliest of them go back as far as the beginning of the eighth. A few—a very few—coins occur of the seventh century, but only of its closing years. These numismatical data make it clear that the eighth century in particular was the time when the trade of the Slavs of the Dnieper with the Chozars and the Arabic East first arose and flourished. Inasmuch, however, as it was also in the eighth century that the Chozars succeeded in establishing themselves in the South Russian Steppes, it becomes equally evident that it was the Chozars to whom the initiation of Slavonic trade activity was due.

The most important result of this flourishing trade with the East was the rise of the ancient trading towns of Rus. The *Poviest* does not specify the exact periods when these towns—Kiev, Periaslavl, Tchernigov, Smolensk, Lubiech, Novgorod, Rostov, and Polotsk—arose, since, at the

time it began its history, most, if not all, of these cities were already places
of importance; yet a glance at their geographical distribution will suffice
to show that they owed their origin to the growth of Russian foreign trade,
seeing that, for the most part, they stretched in a chain along the principal river route leading "from the Varaeger to the Greeks"—that is to
say, along the Dnieper-Volkhov line. A few only—Periaslavl on the
Trubetza, Tchernigov on the Desna, and Rostov in the Upper Volga
region—were thrown out eastwards from this " base of operations" of
Russian trade, as advanced posts in a flank attack upon the Sea of Azov
and the Caspian. The rise of these great trading towns was the direct
outcome of the complex economic process imposed upon the Slavs by
their new environment. We have seen how, as they settled on the
Dnieper and its tributaries, that people began to live in isolated, fortified
homesteads. Next, with the growth of trade, there grew up among these
isolated settlements a number of trading-centres or places of industrial
exchange, whither fur-hunters and forest apiculturists would assemble
for *gostiba* or barter: whence such spots acquired the name of *pogosti*,
or places where *gostiba* was carried on. Subsequently, upon the adoption
of Christianity, shrines became established at these local rural markets (as
places of the most general resort) and, eventually also, parish churches.
Around the parish church it was customary to inter the dead, and thus
the *pogost* acquired also the importance of being the site of the local
burial-ground. Finally the parish was made to coincide with, or came
to be formed into, a local area of administration, and so developed
into something resembling a *volost*. All these terms, however, are borrowed from a later terminology, since, originally, these developed *pogosti*
were known only as *gostinnia miesta*, or places for *gostiba* (barter). In
time, certain of the smaller *gostinnia miesta* which chanced to lie close to
a busy trade-route developed into markets of considerable size, and from
these larger markets, serving as places of exchange between the native producer and the foreign buyer, there arose those ancient Russian trading
towns which marked the water-route from the Baltic to the Greek colonies
and served as the industrial centres and chief storage depôts of the provinces which subsequently became formed around them.

Such were the two most important economic results with which the
settling of the Slavs upon the Dnieper and its tributaries was accompanied.
To recapitulate them once more, they were (1) the rise and growth of
Slavonic foreign trade with the regions of the Black Sea and the Caspian,
and the forest industries evoked by that trade, and (2) the rise of the

ancient trading towns of Rus, with the industrial provinces attached to them.   Both these new factors in the history of Russia may be assigned to the eighth century.

In concluding this exposition of the economic results of the Slavonic settlement of the Dnieper, it might be well to explain that, in speaking of *Russian* Slavs, *Russian* merchants, and *Rus* generally, I have, so far, been availing myself only of a conventional use of terms.   As a matter of fact, Rus had not yet come into being at all (so far as the Slavs were concerned) during the eighth century, and even during the two centuries following, her Varangian population was still altogether distinct from her Slavonic, and constituted a new and ruling class to which the native population of the country was alien.   In using, therefore, the term *Russian* Slavs, I am referring merely to the Slavs who acquired that name at a *later* date.   It is true that, once established among the Eastern Slavs, the State of Rus began to extend and direct the trading movement which it found already in existence among them ; but to all the industrial prosperity which that State achieved it was the labour of the native Slavonic population—the labour which Rus only stimulated and directed—that contributed the greatest share.

CHAPTER V

The political results of the settling of the Eastern Slavs upon the Russian plain—The Pechenegs in the South Russian Steppes—The fortification of the Russian towns—The Varangians: the question of their origin and the time of their appearance in Rus— The formation of the town provinces: their relation to the tribes—The Varangian principalities—The legend of the invitation sent to the Three Princes: its historical foundation—Activity of the Scandinavian Vikings in Western Europe during the ninth century—Formation of the great Principality of Kiev as the first step towards a Russian State—Importance of Kiev in the creation of a Russian State—Summary.

THOSE *economic* results of the settling of the Eastern Slavs upon the Russian plain which I have described in the last chapter prepared the way for certain *political* results which followed rather later—that is to say, at about the beginning of the ninth century. At that date the Chozar Empire, which had hitherto been so strong, began to totter; the reason of its doing so being that new hordes of Pechenegs, and, after them, of Uzi, began to appear in its rear from the East, and to assault the Chozar stronghold. Indeed, about the year 835 the Chozars found themselves so hard pressed that their Khan engaged Byzantine engineers to build a fortress named Sarkel (known to our Ancient Chronicle as Bielaia Vezha) at a point somewhere on the river Don — probably where the Don approaches nearest to the Volga. Yet even this dam could not hold back the Asiatic flood, and at some period during the first half of the ninth century the invaders seem to have burst westwards across the Don, to have passed right through the Chozar settlements, and to have blocked the hitherto open trade-routes of the Slavs across the Steppes. Of this we have information from two widely-varying sources. In a Latin manuscript of the ninth century—the so-called Bertinski Script — there is a curious story given under date of 839, to the effect that some ambassadors who were sent to Constantinople in that year by "the people of Rus" for the conclusion or renewal of a trading agreement were loath to return home by the way they had come, since they stood in fear of some cruel and barbarous race which inhabited the country through which they would have to pass. These ambassadors are described as men "qui se, id est gentem suam, Rhos vocari dicebant." For the elucidation of the identity

of the barbarous wayside race of whom they stood in awe we must turn to
our own Chronicle, where we find that in some versions of the *Poviest* one
of the first items concerning Kiev is the item that in 867 Askold and
Dir slew a great number of the Pechenegs.   It follows, therefore, that by
the middle of the ninth century that race had penetrated to the neighbourhood of Kiev, and thus had cut off the region of the Middle Dnieper from
the markets of the Black Sea and the Caspian.   Another foe to be
reckoned with by Kiev at that time was the race of the Black Bolgars,
who roamed the Steppes between the Don and the Dnieper and concerning whom our Chronicle records an item that in 864 they slew a son of
Askold in battle.   Clearly the Chozar Empire was no longer in a position
to protect the Russian traders to the East, and the great trading towns of
Rus must undertake their own defence against possible foes from that
quarter.   From this period, therefore, they began to arm their citizens, to
gird themselves about with walls, to introduce military organisation,
and to rely upon trained fighting men.   Thus what were once only
industrial centres and storage depôts for commerce now became converted
into fortified points and armed places of refuge.

One circumstance in particular which contributed to the growth of the
military-industrial population of these towns was the fact that, with the
commencement of the ninth century and the close of the reign of Charles
the Great,[1] the coasts of Western Europe began to be overrun by bands of
armed pirates from Scandinavia, and inasmuch as the greater proportion
of these rovers emanated from Dania, or Denmark, they came to be known
in the West as Danes.   At about the same period, sea rovers from the
Baltic began to make their appearance also upon the river trade-routes
of the Russian plain, where they acquired the local name of Variagi
or Varangians.   Throughout the tenth and eleventh centuries these
Varangians paid constant visits to Rus, either for trading purposes or in
response to invitations from the Russian princes, who raised from among
their number military forces for expeditions of their own.   Nevertheless
the presence of Varangians in Rus is traceable long before that time.   As
early as the middle of the ninth century the Ancient Chronicle knew them
as frequenting the Russian towns, although its eleventh-century recollections
of the past may have been exaggerated a little when they led it to declare
that so many Varangians took up their abode in the Russian trading towns
that they came to form a superstratum of population completely out-
numbering the native inhabitants.   For instance, the *Poviest* tells us that

[1] Of Sweden.

at first the people of Novgorod were Slavones, but that they afterwards became as exclusively Varangian as though the place had been swept by an overwhelming flood from Scandinavia.   In Kiev also and the surrounding region Varangians became especially numerous, and a tradition cited by the Chronicle states that the city not only owed its foundation to them, but was enabled out of the mass of its Varangian population to furnish Askold and Dir with large additional forces with which to proceed from Kiev against Byzantium.   This rather dim tradition would appear to assign the first appearance of the Varangians in Rus to a date during the first half of the ninth century, while foreign sources also show us that that date must have been at least prior to the arrival of Rurik in Novgorod.   The Bertinski Script states that the ambassadors from "the people of Rus" who have been referred to as loath to return home from Constantinople by the way they had come were thereupon dispatched from the Byzantine capital with a Byzantine mission to the German Emperor, Ludovic the Pious, and, being examined at his court as to their nationality, were found to be Svealanders or Swedes—that is to say, Varangians.   To this testimony from a western source, as well as to the tradition cited above from the Ancient Chronicle (the tradition that Askold and Dir recruited their forces from Kievan Varangians) may be added certain passages in Byzantine and Arabic writers, according to which Rus, *i.e.* the Varangians, were already well known in Byzantium and the Arabic East during the first half of the ninth century, both in connection with trading matters and on account of the Russian raids upon the coasts of the Black Sea.   Still further light has been shed upon this important question of the date of the Varangians' first appearance in Rus by the valuable researches of Professor Vassilievski into two ancient manuscript biographies—namely, those of St. George of Amastris and St. Stephen of Surozh.   In the first of these two biographies, written at some date before the year 842, the author relates that on one occasion *Rus*— "*the country of which all men know*"—began a raid upon the southern coasts of the Black Sea, and continued it eastwards from the Propontis until Amastris was reached, while in the other of the two biographies it is stated that within a few years of St. Stephen's death (which took place at the end of the eighth century) a large force *from Rus*, under the powerful Prince Bravlin, seized upon the country lying between Kherson and Kertch, and, after further ten years' fighting, succeeded in occupying Surozh (Sudak in the Crimea).   Other sources, too, seem to identify this "Rus" of the *first* half of the ninth century with the oversea immigrants whom the Chronicle includes among its list of Slavonic inhabitants of the Russian plain during the *second* half of that century. For instance, the name of the king upon whose behalf the ambassadors mentioned in the Bertinski Script visited Constantinople is given as " Chakan "—which probably means that he was the *Khan* of the Chozars, to which people at that time the Slavs of the Dnieper were subject; while the fact that the ambassadors were reluctant to return homeward by the nearest route, through fear of perils to be encountered from barbaric races on the way, points to the presence of Asiatic nomads in the Dnieperian Steppes. Furthermore, the Arabic writer Khordadbih specifically classifies the merchants " from Rus " whom he saw at Bagdad as *Slavs*, come from remote regions of their land. Finally, the Patriarch Photius calls the army which assaulted Constantinople in his day a *Russian* army, although at the same time we know from our Ancient Chronicle that the attack was carried out by the *Varangians* whom Askold and Dir had enlisted at Kiev. Apparently, then, the period alike of the first appearance of the Varangians in the great towns of the Baltic-Black Sea river-route across Eastern Europe, of their rapid increase there, and of their prowess on the Black Sea (where, according to Arabic writers, they ruled supreme during the tenth century), coincides with the beginning and continuance of the sea raids of their kinsmen, the Danes, in the west.

All the signs point to the fact that these Baltic Varangians, these " men of Rus " of the Black Sea, were Scandinavians, and not Slavonic inhabitants either of the South Baltic seaboard or of what now constitutes South Russia, as many scholars suppose. The *Poviest* includes under the term " Varangians " *all* the Germanic races of Northern Europe, but more particularly those inhabiting the territories bordering upon the Varaeger or Baltic Sea—namely, the Swedes, the Norwegians, the Angles, and the Gothlanders. Some scholars regard this generic term of Variagi or Varangians as having been merely a Slavonic form of the old Scandinavian word *vaering* or *varing*, the meaning of which is not altogether clear; while Byzantine writers of the eleventh century knew the Normans (Northmen) who formed a hired bodyguard to the Byzantine Emperor as βαραγγοι. Early in the same century (namely, in 1018) Germans who took part in the expedition of the Polish king Boleslav against Yaroslav of Rus, and who upon that occasion saw much of the population around Kiev, informed Bishop Thietmar of Merseburg (who was then writing his chronicle) that the region of Kiev was inhabited by a vast population consisting chiefly of runaway slaves and "swift Danes" (*ex velocibus Danis*)—and those Germans could hardly have been confusing their own Scandinavian kinsmen with Baltic Slavs. Sweden still contains many ancient burial monuments bearing inscriptions concerning the oversea expeditions of the ancient Scandinavians to Rus, while certain Scandinavian sagas dating back to very early times tell of similar expeditions to the country they call " Gardaric "—*i.e.* Rus, the land of *goroda* or towns. The very inapplicability of such a name to rural Rus shows us that the Varangian immigrants confined themselves chiefly to the great trading towns. Moreover, the names of the early Russo-Varangian princes and their retainers are almost all of them Scandinavian in origin—Rurik appearing as Hrörekr, Truvor as Thorvadr, Oleg as Helgi, Olga as Helga ("Ελγα in the writings of Constantine Porphyrogenitus), Igor as Ingvarr, Askold as Höskuldr, Dir as Dyri, Frelaf as Frilleifr, Svienald as Sveinaldr, and so forth. As for the term " Rus," both Byzantine and Arabic writers of the tenth century distinguish it as a separate name altogether from that of the Slavs over whom " Rus " ruled ; while in his enumeration of the Slavonic races Constantine Porphyrogenitus differentiates clearly between their *Russian* and their *Slavonic* titles, as names belonging to two entirely separate languages.

These Varangians, then, helped to swell the military-industrial class which arose in the great trading towns of Rus under pressure of threatened perils from without. Yet we see them there in quite a different guise, and imbued with quite different aims, to their kinsfolk the Danes. The Dane was a pirate, a sea brigand, whereas the Varangian was a merchant (albeit an armed one) visiting Rus *en route* for wealthy Byzantium—there to take lucrative service under the Emperor, or to engage in profitable barter, or (occasionally) to despoil by force the rich Greek if he could get a chance to do so. That this was the general character of the Varangian is shown by traces left upon our language, as well as by relics of ancient tradition. To this day, for instance, the word *variag* means a pedlar or a retail trader, while the verb *variazhit* signifies to engage in retail trade. It is interesting, too, to find that whenever an armed Varangian was engaged in any other business than trade, and therefore thought it advisable to conceal his identity, he invariably assumed the guise of a merchant proceeding to or from Rus, as the character most likely to win confidence— the most common, the most generally accepted rôle. Take, for instance, the story of the manner in which Oleg induced his rebellious boyars, Askold and Dir, to come forth from Kiev and be slain. " Go tell them," he said to his messenger, " that I am a merchant, and that we are on a mission to Greece from the Princes Oleg and Igor. Invite them, therefore, to come out and greet us, those Princes' boyars." Again, there is a beautiful Scandinavian saga, full of historical details, which relates how when the Scandinavian hero, Saint Olaf, and his retinue were returning home across the Baltic, after long and faithful service of Valdamar (Vladimir), *Könung* (Prince) of Rus, he was driven by a storm on to the coasts of Pomerania, the domain of the widowed Princess Geira Burislavna; whereupon, not wishing to reveal his identity, he gave himself out as a merchant of " Gardaric " (Rus).

According as they settled in the great trading towns of Rus, the Varangians came in contact with, and became gradually absorbed into, a class socially akin to them—namely, the class of merchants who were also men-at-arms; whence they went on to enter into trading relations with the natives, or to hire themselves out to protect the Russian traders and trade-routes—*i.e.* to convoy trading caravans along the great waterways.

In proportion, too, as there arose in the Russian towns an armed class constituted of the native and immigrant elements just mentioned, and the towns became converted into fortified points, the relation of the latter to the surrounding populations also necessarily underwent a change; with the result that, when the Chozar yoke began to relax its grip, those towns which lay among tribes hitherto subject to the Chozars declared themselves independent. As regards the Poliani, in particular, the *Poviest* does not specify the exact circumstances of their emancipation from the Chozar yoke, but states that, after descending the Dnieper to Kiev and learning there that the town was still in fief to the Chozars, Askold and Dir decided to remain where they were, and, having enlisted an additional force of Varangians, proceeded to make themselves rulers over the whole territory of the Poliani. This, however, is sufficiently indicative of the termination of Chozar rule at Kiev. As to the precise manner in which Kiev and the other great towns were governed under the Chozars we have no information, but there can be little doubt that those towns soon followed up their assumption of their own defence by a corresponding political subordination to themselves of their trade-districts or the districts of which each such town was the central storage depôt. This process of placing the trade-districts in political dependence upon the now fortified towns seems to have been begun at least before the coming to Novgorod of the Three Princes—that is to say, before the middle of the ninth century, for it is when relating the story of the invitation sent to Rurik and his two brethren that the *Poviest* reveals to us the interesting fact that those towns had then progressed so far in their political process as each to possess its own tribal *province.* It relates how, when Rurik died and Oleg left Novgorod for the South, the latter began by taking Smolensk and placing in authority there a vice-governor to represent him; on the strength of which, and without further fighting, the Krivizes of that region at once recognised Oleg as their ruler. Next, Oleg took Kiev, and the Poliani hastened to make similar submission. Thus we see entire districts placed in political dependence upon their capital towns—a stage of development which began before, and continued contemporarily with, the Kievan Princes. It is difficult to say by what means this system actually became established. Possibly the trade-districts were driven by the pressure of external danger to make voluntary submission to the towns, but it is more probable that the towns availed themselves of the large military-industrial class which they now contained to subdue the districts by. force of arms. Or sometimes the one may have been the case, and sometimes the other.

Whatever the manner of its attainment, the first local political form known in our history now becomes visible in the shadowy annals of the *Poviest*—namely, the town-provinces; a form which began to be evolved in Rus at about the middle of the ninth century. These provinces were named after their capitals, which served not only as the trade centres of their respective districts, but also as fortified places of refuge. When, later, the Principality of Kiev became formed, and absorbed into itself the whole of Eastern Slavdom, the old town-districts of Kiev, Tchernigov, Smolensk, and the rest, which had formerly been independent, became the administrative areas of the new Principality, and served the early Kievan Princes as ready-made units for division of the land into provinces—a process which continued up to about the middle of the eleventh century.

The question next arises—Were the trading towns responsible for the formation of these provinces, or had the latter a tribal origin? We have seen that the *Poviest* divides the Eastern Slavs into a number of different tribes, and that it specifies, to a certain extent, their distribution. That the new provinces of the Principality of Kiev which became formed during the tenth and eleventh centuries consisted of the Poliani, Sieverians, and so forth, severally united into self-contained political wholes, and not of the old trade-districts of the towns, is disproved by examination of the ethnographical contents of those provinces. If they had had a tribal origin, and had been compounded of whole tribes irrespectively of economic interests, each such tribe would have formed a province by itself—or, in other words, each province would have been composed only of one particular tribe. This, however, was not the case : there was not a single province consisting wholly of one complete tribe. The majority of them included within their boundaries two or three different tribes or parts of tribes, while the remainder were made up of one complete tribe and one or more details of others. Thus the Province of Novgorod included, with the Slavs of Lake Ilmen, a small branch of the Krivizes, whose central (though not capital) town was Izborsk. The Province of Tchernigov comprised the northern half of the Sieverians, a portion of the Radimizes, and the whole of the Vatizes, while the southern half of the Sieverians went to form the Province of Periaslavl. The Province of Kiev consisted of the whole of the Poliani, the greater portion of the Drevlians, and the southern half of the Dregovitches (the latter having the minor town of Turov on the Pripeta as their central point); while the northern half of the Dregovitches (their central town being Minsk) was separated from its complementary half by the western portion of the Krivizes, and entered, with the latter, into the Province of Polotsk. Finally, in the Province of Smolensk were included the eastern portion of the Krivizes and the rest of the Radimizes. Thus we see that the old tribal areas coincided neither with the old town-districts nor with the newly-formed provinces of the Principality of Kiev. Nevertheless, it is possible to tell from the tribal contents of those provinces what was the factor which governed their allotment. If among a tribe there arose *two* great towns, that tribe became split into two portions (as in the case of the Krivizes and the Sieverians); while if, on the other hand, a tribe possessed no great town at all, that tribe became absorbed into a province attached to some other capital town. We have seen that the rise of an important trading town among a tribe depended upon the geographical position occupied by that unit. Consequently such towns as became capitals of provinces arose exclusively among the populations lining the great river trade-routes of the Dnieper, the Volkhov, and the Western Dwina, while tribes remote from those routes possessed no great town of their own, and therefore did not constitute separate provinces, but were absorbed into those belonging to tribes possessing such a centre. No great town, for instance, arose among the Drevlians, the Dregovitches, the Radimizes, or the Vatizes, and consequently those tribes had no separate provinces of their own. From this we see that the factor which governed the formation of the provinces was the great trading towns which arose along the principal river trade-routes and of which none stood among tribes living remote from those routes. In all, there lay between Lake Ladoga in the north and Kiev in the south eight Slavonic tribes. Of these, four (the Dregovitches, the Radimizes, the Vatizes, and the Drevlians) gradually became absorbed—partly before, and partly in the time of, the Kievan Princes—into the provinces of other tribes; while the remaining four (the Slavs of Lake Ilmen, the Krivizes, the Sieverians, and the Poliani) formed, among them, six provinces, none of which (except that of Periaslavl) constituted a self-contained province consisting of one tribe only, but included, with the chief tribe or part-tribe, portions of tribes which possessed no great town. These six provinces were those of Novgorod, Polotsk, Smolensk, Tchernigov, Periaslavl, and Kiev.

To sum up, then, we see that the great fortified towns which became capitals of provinces arose solely among those tribes which were most closely connected with the foreign trading movement, and that, after placing in subordination to themselves the surrounding rural populations of their respective tribes (for whom they served, first of all as trade centres, and subsequently as centres of administration), absorbed into their provinces—both before and in the time of the Kievan Princes—some of the populations of neighbouring tribes which possessed no great town of their own.

The evolution of this earliest Russian political form was accompanied, in certain localities, by the appearance of a secondary local form—namely, the Varangian principality. At industrial centres where Varangian immigrants had congregated in especially large numbers, the conversion of those immigrants from traders or protectors of convoys into rulers was an easy enough transition. Forming themselves into armed industrial companies or trained bands, they selected captains who gradually acquired the status of military governors of the towns protected by their companies. In the Scandinavian sagas these leaders are called *Könings*, or Vikings; which terms have passed into our language in the Slavonic forms of *kniaz* (prince) and *vitiaz* (knight or hero). These words are to be found also among other Slavonic races of the period, who probably borrowed them from the Germanic tribes of Central Europe; but in our own case they reached the language from Scandinavian races considerably nearer to ourselves in antiquity—namely, the Germanic tribes of the North. This conversion of Varangians from immigrant traders to rulers was, as I have said, a simple enough transition where the circumstances were favourable. Take, for instance, the Chronicle's story of how, in 980, with the help of Varangians invited from over the sea, Vladimir defeated his brother Yaropolk of Kiev, and then established himself in that city. No sooner had Kiev fallen than his Varangian allies (who had realised their strength during the siege of the city) said to their employer: " O Prince, this town belongs to us by right, for it is we who have conquered it. We therefore desire to take of every townsman a toll of two *grivni.*[1] And, indeed, it was only by a stratagem that Vladimir succeeded in getting rid of these impertinent mercenaries, and sending them forward to attack Constantinople.

Thus certain of the fortified towns and their provinces became converted into principalities under Varangian *Könings*. Several of these petty states are to be met with during the ninth and tenth centuries, and as examples of them I may cite Rurik's principality at Novgorod, that of Sineus at Bieloe Ozero, that of Truvor at Izborsk, and that of Askold at Kiev. The tenth century also saw established the two notable little principalities of Rogvelod at Polotsk and Tur at Turov on the Pripeta; but inasmuch as the Ancient Chronicle does not specify the exact date of their founding, and only mentions their existence in passing, we may take it that petty Varangian states of this kind came and went very quickly in Rus. .The same phenomenon may be observed at that period among the Slavs of the Southern Baltic seaboard, to which region also Varangians penetrated. To contemporary observers these little principalities must have seemed the result of actual conquest, in spite of the fact that their Varangian founders usually made their first appearance in them with no conquering aim in view, but rather as seeking commercial profit, and not a permanent place of settlement. As an instance of such a view being taken by contemporary observers, we find the Jewish writer Ibrahim—a man well acquainted with the country of the Germanic tribes and thoroughly well-versed in the affairs of Middle and Eastern Europe—writing (at about the middle of the tenth century) in a letter preserved in a work by Al Bekri (an Arabic writer of the eleventh century): " The tribes of the North (among them the people of Rus) have placed certain of the Slavones in subjection, and are dwelling in their midst to this day. Nay, they have become so intermingled with them as even to have adopted their tongue." This can only refer to the Slavonic-Varangian principalities which had arisen at that period along both the South Baltic seaboard and the river traderoutes of Rus.

The rise of these Varangian principalities fully explains the story of the invitation to the Three Princes which we find in the *Poviest*. The story relates that, before Rurik's coming, Varangians had contrived to insinuate themselves among the people of Novgorod and the neigh-

---

[1] The *grivna* was equal to about a pound's weight of silver.

bouring Finnish and Slavonic tribes (Krivizes, Tchudes, Meres, and Wesses), and to take of them tribute. At length, however, the tributaries refused further payment, and drove the Varangians back across the sea; whereupon, left with no rulers to take the place of those whom they had expelled, the natives of the region began to quarrel among themselves, clan to rise against clan, and much bloodshed to ensue. Dismayed at these feuds, the natives took counsel together, and said: "Let us seek some prince to rule over us, and to judge us by the law." So they sent ambassadors across the sea to their late acquaintances the Varangians, and invited whomsoever of them might will to come and rule their (the Novgorodians') fertile and open, but lawless, land. This invitation was responded to by three brothers, who crossed the sea "with their clans"—*i.e.* with their retinues of boyars—and settled in Rus.

Now, if we strip this story of a certain idyllic varnish with which it is overlaid we find revealed a very simple and non-idyllic phenomenon— a phenomenon which has occurred not once only, nor yet twice, in our history of past ages. To set the matter in its true light we must collate all the scattered fragments of the tradition which are to be found strewn through the various versions of the Ancient Chronicle, and we shall then recognise that the strangers were not sent for merely to preserve internal order or to organise a new government, since the tradition says (among other things) that, no sooner had the brothers settled in Rus, than they began "to build them towns[1] and to wage war everywhere." It follows, then, that if the invited began by erecting frontier fortifications and engaging in general warfare, those who extended the invitation must have done so for the purpose of protection from external foes. Further on we read that the princely brothers did not show any great alacrity or willingness in accepting the proposal of the Slavonic-Finnish ambassadors, but did so only after considerable hesitation—"scarce electing to go," as one version puts it, "through fear of the beast-like customs and habits of the Novgorodians." This is borne out by the further information that Rurik did not proceed straight to Novgorod, but decided first to halt at Ladoga, as though he considered that the nearer he remained to his own country, the better chance he would have of taking refuge there if the people of the country did not approve of him. At Ladoga he built a town and erected fortifications—probably to serve the double purpose of protecting the natives from piratical

[1] *i.e.* fortifications.

countrymen of his own and defending himself from the natives if the need should arise. When at length he proceeded onwards and settled in Novgorod, he seems very soon to have aroused dissatisfaction among the inhabitants, for we find it recorded in one version of the Chronicle that two years had not elapsed from his acceptance of the invitation before the people of Novgorod " were offended, saying : 'We are but slaves, and suffer much evil from Rurik and his boyars.'" Indeed, an actual conspiracy arose, but Rurik succeeded in killing the ringleader, " the brave Vadim," and flogged many of his accomplices ; with the result that during the next few years a large number of the male inhabitants of the city deserted from their allegiance, and went and took service under Askold at Kiev.

These scattered fragments of the tradition seem to speak rather of a hiring of Rurik and his brethren for warlike operations against external foes than of a friendly invitation to come and preserve internal order. The truth of the matter is that these Princes and their following were engaged at a fixed rate of pay to defend the country from invasion, but that, subsequently having a mind to increase that rate, they began to do so unbidden and in an arbitrary manner. Hence arose murmuring among the inhabitants, and this murmuring was suppressed by armed force ; until, having thoroughly realised their strength, the hired servants ended by converting themselves into masters, and their fixed pay into a tribute based upon a constantly ascending scale. There we have the simple, prosaic fact which doubt- less underlies this poetical legend of the invitation sent to the Three Princes—the simple, prosaic fact that Novgorod, hitherto free, now became a Varangian principality.

There is nothing in the events related in this story which need be looked upon as unusual or remarkable or peculiar to our own country alone, for they belong to a category of phenomena common enough at that time in the other, the Western, half of Europe. The ninth century was the period when the devastating raids of Scandinavian pirates were at their worst. It is sufficient only to read the chronicles of the ninth-century monasteries of Bertini and Vayast to see that what happened in the West was repeated, with local modifications, in the East. From the year 830 to the close of the century scarcely a year passed without incursions of the Northmen into Western Europe, where they sailed up the great rivers discharging into the German and Atlantic Oceans—the Elbe, the Rhine, the Seine, the Loire, the Garonne, and so forth, and, having penetrated into the interior of the country, proceeded to lay everything waste and to burn even such great cities as Cologne, Treves, Bordeaux, and Paris. Frequently they remained for years in the country which they had invaded; using a fortified camp upon some island situated in the bed of a river as their base of operations, and issuing thence to take tribute of the terrorised inhabitants. Then, having collected as much booty as they required, they would proceed onwards, to repeat the process in another region. Scotland, for instance, was harried by them for years, and at last (in 847) compelled to pay them regular tribute; yet not a year had elapsed before the Scotsmen refused further payment of the levy, and drove the Northmen out of the neighbouring islets where they had established themselves, even as at about the same time the Novgorodians expelled the kinsmen of those raiders. The weaker Carlovingians made treaties with the Danes which, in some of their conditions, remind us strongly of the treaties which the Kievan princes made with the Greeks in the tenth century. The Carlovingians either paid to the invaders a toll of so many thousand pounds' weight of silver, or else made over to them a maritime province on condition that the Danes protected the whole of the country from raids by their fellow-countrymen. In this making over of maritime provinces in the West we see something analogous to the way in which the Varangian principalities arose in the East. Nevertheless it more than once occurred that a band of Danes dominating one French river were paid a fixed sum by the French king to expel or kill some rival band of their countrymen who were raiding another river, and that, no sooner had the first band surprised the second and taken toll of it, than the two would combine, and start raiding the country in quest of fresh booty, even as Askold and Dir, when dispatched by Rurik to assault Constantinople, settled *en route* at Kiev, enlisted Varangian troops, and assumed the rulership of the Poliani, independently of Rurik. Again, in the second half of the ninth century we find great commotion caused along the Elbe and the Rhine by a contemporary and namesake (perhaps also a boyar) of our own Rurik—namely, the Viking Rorich as the Bertinski Manuscript spells his name. This Viking enlisted bands for coast raids, compelled the Emperor Lothaire to place in fief to him several of the maritime provinces of Frisia, and, after more than once taking the oath of allegiance to the Emperor and breaking it again, was expelled from the country. Thereupon he returned to his own land, attained there the sovereign power, and at length ended somewhere an adventurous life. It is also worthy of note that, like the retinues of the early Kievan Princes, these bands of sea raiders consisted both of

Christians and pagans; nor was it an infrequent occurrence, on the conclusion of a treaty, for their Christian members to pass into the service of the French kings whose dominions they had lately been ravishing.

These doings in Western Europe help us to explain events contemporary with them on the Dnieper and Volkhov, and make it possible for us to sum up matters as follows. About the middle of the ninth century a band of Baltic Varangians sailed up the Gulf of Finland and the river Volkhov to Lake Ilmen, and levied tribute upon the Northern Finnish and Slavonic tribes; whereupon those tribes combined their forces, expelled the invaders, and hired a band of other Varangians (warriors whom they called "men of Rus") to protect them from further incursions of this kind. As soon, however, as these hired mercenaries found themselves safely entrenched in fortified camps in the country which they had been engaged to *defend*, they assumed the part of rulers in a *conquered* country. There we have the whole story. The two incidents of prime importance in the affair were, firstly, the agreement between the natives and the foreigners for the protection of the former by the latter from external foes, and, secondly, the forcible seizure of authority by the foreigners. The Ancient Chronicle throws the second of these two incidents into shade, and the first into clear light, as though to make it appear that the cession of authority by the natives to the foreigners was a purely voluntary act. Thus it produces a very fairly plausible version of the origin of the Russian State. For this gloss upon facts there were reasons. We must not forget that, like all our oldest traditions concerning Rus, the story of the invitation to the Three Princes has come down to us exactly as it was known to and understood by the Russian bookmen and scholars of the eleventh and early twelfth centuries—the period of the unknown author of the *Poviest* and of the Abbot Silvester who edited that script and placed it in the forefront of his great historical record. At that period Varangians were still visiting Rus, but no longer as conquerors; and inasmuch as the forcible seizure of authority just referred to had never been repeated, its recurrence seemed at least improbable. On the contrary, the Rus of the eleventh century saw in its princes the establishers of state government and the upholders of that lawful authority under which the Russian community lived and which it conceived to be derived from the invitation sent to the Three Princes from beyond the sea. Therefore both the author and the editor of the *Poviest* must have felt dissatisfied with some of the less edifying details of the legend, and accordingly decided, as thinking historians, to explain facts by results and to improve the occasion with a theory. The *practical* formation of a state may take place in several different ways, but the *theoretical* moment of its inception is the moment when the power which wields the authority of the law therein becomes generally recognised. This, then—the accepted theory of law and order—was the theory which the author and editor of the *Poviest* imported into the legend ; and, indeed, the assembling of a council of the Northern tribes amid the turmoil of clan feuds, the decision to seek a prince who "should rule them and judge them by the law," the sending of a mission to Varangian Rus to invite some one " to come and be prince over and to do his will upon" their great and fertile, but lawless, land,— what is all this but an expression of the stereotyped formula that legal authority is based upon agreement?—an ancient theory, indeed, but one which we find continually recurring as an idea well adapted to an intellect attempting its first assimilation of political ideas. The story of the invitation, as set forth in the *Poviest*, is in no way a *popular* tradition, and bears none of the marks of such. It is simply a parable of the origin of state government—a parable adapted, as it were, to the under-standing of children of school age.

The federation of the Varangian principalities with those of the town-provinces which had hitherto preserved their independence gave rise to the *third* political form adopted in Rus—namely, the great Principality of Kiev. For this form the way had been prepared by the political and economic factors already given. Wherever Varangian princes had made their appearance in the Russian industrial world they had always tended to gravitate towards Kiev, the southernmost town of that world, and the final link in the chain of trading towns which dotted the river route leading from the Baltic to the Greek colonies. It was in Kiev that seekers after trade and profit best throve, for Kiev was the collecting point of Russian commerce, and to it came boat-loads from every quarter—from the Volkhov, from the Western Dwina, and from the Upper Dnieper and its tributaries. Hence, throughout the Chronicle's record of the events of the ninth and tenth centuries there always remain prominent two factors—namely, the ceaseless trend of Varangian immigrants towards Kiev, and the economic dependence of the Russian trading towns upon that city. Whoever was ruler at Kiev held in his hands the keys of the main outlet of Russian commerce : which is why all the Varangian leaders who entered the country from the North tended to gravitate thither. It was Kiev which set them in rivalry and enmity to one another—which led, first of all, Oleg of Novgorod to slay his boyars, Askold and Dir, and afterwards induced Vladimir, of the same northern principality, to slay his brother Yaropolk. Moreover, all the trading towns of Rus stood in economic dependence upon Kiev, for in her met all the threads of their prosperity. She could sap their trade and divide the main artery of the industrial veins of the country by merely allowing no boats to pass her to the markets of the Black Sea and the Sea of Azov. Therefore it was beyond all things to the interest of the towns to live upon good terms with her, if they wished to have free exit to the trade routes traversing the Steppes. This common interest on their part is shown very clearly in the Ancient Chronicle's story of the first princes who established themselves at Kiev. After deserting Rurik's service, his boyars Askold and Dir descended the Dnieper without hindrance, occupied Kiev almost without fighting, and assumed the lordship over the territory of the Poliani. The cause of their success is largely explained by their subsequent policy, as I will show. The Ancient Chronicle tells us that after the death of Ki (the founder of Kiev) the Poliani suffered great loss at the hands of the Drevlians and other neighbouring tribes, but that, after Askold and Dir had established themselves in Kiev, those two boyars first of all subjugated the Drevlians, Pechenegs, and Bolgars, and then set out for Constantinople with their army reinforced by a band of newly-enlisted Varangians. Photius, Patriarch of Constantinople, who was a contemporary and eye-witness of the assault upon that city, says, in a rescript upon the subject, that the men of Rus contrived the attack very skilfully by creeping up to the walls at a time when the Emperor Michael III. had just departed with an army and a fleet against the Saracens, and so had left his capital defenceless from the sea side. Of course the Russians of Kiev were well acquainted with the sea route to Constantinople, as well as perfectly well able to procure intelligence of how matters stood in the city; so that even the Greeks themselves were surprised at the suddenness and unusual swiftness of the attack. Photius also tells us that the expedition was mooted, in the first instance, after the Greeks had broken a trading agreement, and finally undertaken for the purpose of avenging an insult done to some Russian merchants (probably for non-payment of a debt). Consequently we may take it that its chief object was to re-establish forcibly trade relations which the Greeks had abruptly sundered. Hence it follows that trade relations must have been in existence before, at all events, 860, the year of the attack, and that Kiev stood in the position of arbiter of those relations. We recognise further that those relations must have been of long standing—that they must have originated in the first half of the century, seeing that it was to conclude some commercial agreement that the ambassadors from " the people of Rus " whom we find mentioned in the Bertinski Script had paid their visit to Constantinople in 839. We see a precisely similar series of phenomena repeated under Oleg, who followed in Askold's footsteps. Descending the Dnieper unhindered, just as Askold had done, he took Smolensk and Lubiech on the way without any trouble, and then occupied Kiev without a blow struck after he had once got rid of his former boyars Askold and Dir. Thus established in the city, he began to build a ring of defences around it, as a protection against attacks from the Steppes; which done, he led the united forces of a majority of the tribes to make a fresh assault upon the walls of Constantinople—an assault which, like the former one, ended in the conclusion of a treaty of commerce. It follows, therefore, that (like the former attack, again) this assault was made for the purpose of re-establishing trade relations which had become broken off in some manner; while, inasmuch as upon each occasion the Russian leader was supported by the majority of the tribes, it seems clear that the latter must have had foreign trade as their common ruling interest, especially in the case of such of them as dwelt near the Volkhov-Dnieper route. At all events we read in the Ancient Chronicle's account of Oleg's expedition hat, in addition to the tribes immediately subject to him, there took part i 1 the affair two non-subject tribes—namely, the Dulebs and the Chrobatians, both of which lived in the region where the Upper Dniester and the two Bugs issue from the slopes and foot-hills of the Carpathians. Thus we see that, while the expeditions against Constantinople and the task of defending Rus against the nomads of the Steppes served to unite in friendly co-operation the whole of the industrial community dwelling upon the trade routes of the Dnieper, the Volkhov, and other rivers of the plain, the same interests served also to unite the riverside trading towns of Rus in fealty to the Kievan Prince of the day, to whom the twofold importance of his city naturally assigned the lead at such junctures.

Kiev stood in the position, not only of principal advanced post in the defence of the country against the Steppes, but also of central export depôt for Russian trade. These two facts alone were bound to prevent the city from remaining a mere Varangian principality after falling into Varangian hands, as did the principalities of the same kind which arose about at the same period at Novgorod, Izborsk, and Bieloe Ozero, as well as, later, at Polotsk and Turov. Trading connections with Byzantium and the Arabic East, as well as with the markets of the Black Sea, the Sea of Azov, and the Caspian, not only turned the popular industry towards exploitation of the forest wealth of the country, but also concentrated upon Kiev the country's most important commercial traffic. To make, however, that traffic secure it was indispensable to have inviolable frontiers and free passage along the rivers of the Steppes, as well as, at times, to bring armed pressure to bear upon foreign markets for the securing of advantageous terms in them. All this could be attained only by the united forces of the *whole* of the Eastern Slavonic tribes, and this circumstance entailed forcible impressment into the service of those tribes which lived at a distance from the principal trade-routes and so had no inducement to support the Kievan Princes of their own free will. For that reason both foreign sources and our own have a good deal to say about the warlike operations of the first rulers of the Principality. The researches of the great authority Vassilievski into the biographies of Saints George of Amastris and Stephen of Surozh have proved, beyond all practical doubt, that the first half of the ninth century saw Rus already raiding the coasts—even the southern coasts —of the Black Sea. Nevertheless, it was not until the time of the Patriarch Photius that Rus ventured to attack Constantinople itself. Previous to that event Photius had heard reports of an important change having begun in Rus—a change which had its origin in Kiev. In a rescript concerning the Russian attack upon Constantinople, as well as in an encyclical letter, he says that the Russians, who had hitherto been wholly unknown and " of no account," had suddenly become "most renowned and glorious" after that deed of daring. Such valour, he explains, must have been inspired in that people through the fact that it had recently subjugated the tribes which lived around its territory, so that the success had made it "boundlessly proud and bold." This means that, as soon as ever the great Varangian Principality of Kiev was formed, it organised a concentration of the forces of the whole country, and so brought about the first Russian enterprise undertaken for a common end—that end being the securing of trade relations.

Such were the conditions the combined action of which brought the great Principality of Kiev into being. At first this State formed merely one of the many *local* Varangian principalities, since Askold and his brother Dir originally settled there simply as Varangian *Könings* whose activities were limited to protecting the province attached to the city from foreign foes and to supporting its trade interests; while Oleg, who followed in their footsteps, only continued their work. To that work, however, the military-industrial position of Kiev soon communicated a wider importance. The province attached to the city shut off from the south the whole of the country bordering upon the Baltic-Greek trade route — an area having trade interests identical with those of Kiev itself. Consequently it was not long before the other Varangian principalities and town-provinces of Rus were driven, willy-nilly, to unite themselves under the authority of the Kievan Prince, until the federation thus formed acquired the importance of a Russian State. This process of federation was necessitated by the political and economic dependence upon Kiev in which the various petty Varangian principalities and town-provinces had been placed by the downfall of the Chozar power in the Steppes.

In view of these facts I do not think that the arrival of Rurik in Novgorod can properly be regarded as the beginning of the Russian Empire, seeing that there arose there, when he came, but a local, as well as only a very short-lived, Varangian principality. No ; the Russian Empire was founded through the deeds of Askold and, after him, Oleg at Kiev. From Kiev it was, and not from Novgorod, that the political federation of Russian Slavdom originated, and it was the petty Varangian state which those two Vikings there founded that constituted the first germ of that union of all the Slavonic and Finnish tribes which may be looked upon as having been the primal form of the modern Russian Empire.

A state becomes possible when there appears among a population hitherto divided into disconnected sections, all of them animated by differing, or even mutually hostile, aspirations, either an *armed force* capable of knitting those several disconnected sections into one or a *common interest* sufficiently strong to subordinate to itself their various mutually hostile aspirations. Both these factors — the armed force and the common interest—played a part in the forming of the Russian State. The common interest was evoked by the fact that, as soon as the Pecheneg invasion began to flood the Steppes, the trading towns of Rus became conscious of the need of an armed force capable of protecting both the frontiers of the country and the river trade-routes running through the Steppe region. The chief point of departure whence the Russian caravans set out for the markets of the Black Sea and the Caspian was Kiev. As soon, therefore, as an armed force made its appearance in the city and proved itself capable of satisfying the defensive requirements of the country, the trading towns and their attached provinces made voluntary

submission to it. That force was the Varangian prince and his Varangian following. Once become the supporter and protector of the
common interest which had brought the great trading towns of the
country under his authority, the prince, with his following, no longer
remained an armed force merely, but became also a political power. Next,
availing himself of the resources which that fact afforded him, the prince
proceeded to subjugate to himself such other tribes as did not share
in the common interest and took but little part in the commercial
traffic of the land; until, with the subjugation of those tribes, there
at length became established the political federation of the whole of
the Eastern Slavs.

I repeat, then, that the creation of the Russian State was effected both
by the common interest and by the armed force, for the former agency
allied itself with the latter. The needs and perils of Russian trade first
called into action (for the protection of that trade) an armed body of men,
with a prince at its head; after which, that body of men, supported by the
majority of the tribes, subdued the rest of the population. If we read carefully the Ancient Chronicle's account of the Kievan Princes of the ninth
and tenth centuries we shall see clearly revealed this two-fold, military-
industrial origin of the Principality of Kiev—the earliest form of the
Russian State. The first tribes to join the Principality and to support its
princes in their expeditions abroad were those which were attached to the
great trading towns situated upon the principal river trade-route. Those
tribes submitted themselves to the authority of Kiev of their own free will.
Even the Slavs of Novgorod who had invited the three brothers to come
from over the sea, who had attempted to rebel against Rurik, and who had
been deserted by Oleg and Igor in favour of Kiev, now entered loyally
into fealty to the latter. To effect the subjugation of some of the other
tribes only one expedition was necessary, and that too without any
fighting (as in the cases of the Krivizes of Smolensk and the Sieverians).
On the other hand, there were tribes far removed from the trade-routes
and possessing no great trading towns (*i.e.* no important fortified trade
centres) which long held out against the authority of their new rulers, and
were subdued only after stubborn and repeated resistance. Thus several
arduous expeditions were needed to subjugate the Drevlians and the
Radimizes, while similar efforts against the Vatizes did not prove successful until the very end of the tenth century—fully a hundred years after the
first founding of the Principality.

Such was the final result of the series of complicated juridical, economic, and political processes which began with the settling of the Eastern Slavs upon the Russian plain. Let me recapitulate those processes.

We found the Eastern Slavs of the seventh and eighth centuries in a state of transition—in a state of increasing social disintegration. The military union which they had formed among themselves in the Carpathians was in process of being dissolved into its constituent tribes, while the tribes themselves were being broken up into clans, and even the clans were becoming weakened through diffusion among the isolated *dvori* or family homesteads which the Eastern Slavs adopted as their unit of habitation after their settlement upon the Dnieper. In time, however, the influence of new conditions in this region brought about a kind of reflex movement of association—the connecting element in the new system of social relations being, not blood kinship, but the economic interest evoked jointly by the peculiar features of the country and by external circumstances. In other words, the facilities offered by the southward-flowing rivers of the plain and the imposition of a foreign (*i.e.* the Chozar) yoke served jointly to attract the energies of the Eastern Slavs to the building up of an active foreign trade. That trade, in its turn, caused the inmates of the various scattered *dvori* to assemble together at certain rural trading-spots, or *pogosti ;* which, later, developed into great trading towns, with trade-districts attached. Early in the ninth century there arose new external dangers, necessitating a fresh series of changes. The great trading towns first armed and fortified themselves, and then became converted from mere trade-depôts into political centres, while their former trade-districts developed into areas of administration or provinces, a certain number of which became Varangian principalities. Finally, through the federation of these Varangian principalities and of such of the town-provinces as had hitherto preserved their independence there came into existence the great Principality of Kiev—the earliest form of the Russian State.

I may conclude this chapter by recalling the fact that, when beginning the study of the first period of our history, I expounded the two theories which are most generally adopted with regard to the starting-point of that history; stating that some authorities date the point only from about the middle of the ninth century (when—so they state—the Varangian invaders found the Eastern Slavs living in a state of rude, anarchic barbarism), while other authorities derive our history from a period long before the Birth of Christ. Since, therefore, we have finished studying our historical factors and their consequences with regard to this period, we are in a better position than before to appraise those two theories; and in my opinion our history is neither so old nor so modern as many people think.   On the one hand, I consider that it began long after the opening of the Christian era; while, on the other hand, I believe that by the middle of the ninth century it already had behind it a past of rather over two centuries.

CHAPTER VI

Policy of the early Kievan Princes—Federation of the Eastern Slavs under the Prince of Kiev—Tax-administration in the Principality of Kiev—Foreign policy and trading relations with Byzantium—Influence of the Greek treaties upon early Russian law—Perils of Russian foreign trade—Defence of the Steppe frontiers—Composition and extent of the Principality of Kiev—Origin, composition, and functions of the princely retinue—Social divisions in the Kievan community—Slave ownership—Successive meanings of the term Rus—Gradual assimilation of Varangians and Slavs.

THE common interest which created the Principality of Kiev (namely, the defence of the country and of its foreign trade) governed also its further growth, and guided both the foreign and the domestic policy of the early Kievan Princes. Of the fundamental springs of that policy we can gain a sufficiently clear idea—and that without any great critical effort—from the half-historical, half-legendary traditions of the Ancient Chronicle concerning Oleg, Igor, Sviatoslav, Yaropolk, and Vladimir.

It was impossible that Kiev could remain merely the capital of a local Varangian principality, for she had a pan-Russian importance as being the central point of the commercial and industrial traffic of the country. Consequently it was not long before she developed into the head of a great political federation. The policy of her first prince, Askold, seems to have been limited to preserving the external safety of what then constituted her province, nor, despite Photius's remark about the inordinate pride of Rus after her subjection of neighbouring tribes,[1] does the Chronicle at any point show that Askold ever assumed the offensive against the population which encompassed his Poliani. Oleg, however, who succeeded him, lost no time in enlarging his dominions and endeavouring to bring under his sway the whole of Eastern Slavdom. This process, however, is described in the Chronicle with a rather suspicious continuity—with a rather suspicious adding to Kiev of exactly a tribe a year. In 882, says the Chronicle, Oleg took Kiev, while in 883 he subdued the Drevlians, in 884 the Sieverians, and in 885 the Radimizes; after which there occurs a long series of vacant years. Upon the whole, therefore, we may take it that the foregoing items represent rather a series

---

[1] See page 72.

of beliefs or imaginings on the part of the Chronicler than a series of actual facts. However that may be, the end of the tenth century saw the whole of the Eastern Slavonic tribes placed in subjection to the Prince of Kiev, and their names disappearing in favour of those of the new town-provinces. As the Kievan Princes proceeded with the enlarging of their dominions, they established in the conquered territories a system of tax-administration, for which the town-provinces served as a ready-made administrative basis. Likewise the Princes appointed governors, or *posadniki*, to all the great towns—officials who were sometimes sons or near relatives, sometimes paid retainers, of the Prince, and each of whom had his own retinue and local forces. Indeed, these *posadniki* acted so independently of, and maintained so slender a connection with, the central government at Kiev that to all intents and purposes they were as much *könings* as the Prince of Kiev himself, who stood to them merely in the relation of a senior among equals, and was distinguished from them only by the title of "Great Prince," as against the more simple one of "Prince" borne by the *posadniki*. Nevertheless, for the further aggrandisement of their superior, the *posadniki* also received the title of "Great Prince" when it came to a question of diplomatic documents. Thus in Oleg's first treaty with the Greeks (907) we find him demanding *ukladi* (*i.e.* maintenance allowances) for Russian merchants visiting Constantinople from the towns of Kiev, Tchernigov, Periaslavl, Polotsk, Rostov, and Lubiech, "where dwell the Great Princes who are under Oleg." In fact, these town-provinces were so many petty Varangian principalities affiliated to a larger one at Kiev, the status of whose Prince at that time was merely that of chief of a military union and had, as yet, acquired no dynastic significance.

It sometimes happened that when the *posadnik* of a town-province had subjugated a given tribe for his Suzerain he received that tribe in fief, with the right of collecting tribute from it for his own benefit, just as, in the West, the Danish Vikings received maritime provinces in fief from the Frankish kings, with the right of exploiting them. In this manner we find a certain *voievoda*[1] of Igor's named Svienald conquering the Slavonic tribe of the Uluzes (who dwelt upon the Lower Dnieper) and then being granted the right of levying tribute both upon them and upon the Drevlians; with the result (says the Chronicle) that his *otroki* or pages lived even more sumptuously than did Igor's own retinue.

The chief administrative aim of the Kievan government was the collection of tribute and taxes, and no sooner had Oleg established himself at

[1] A commander of military forces.

Kiev than he proceeded to put their collection upon a systematic footing. Olga also made periodical tours of the subject tribes for the purpose of fixing and collecting "dues and taxes, tribute and tolls." *Dan* (the comprehensive term embracing these various imposts) was usually paid in kind, more particularly in furs, but in the case of the agricultural, nontrading Radimizes and Vatizes we learn that during the ninth and tenth centuries they paid their *dan* (first to the Chozars, and, later, to the Princes of Kiev) in the form of a "*skilling*" for every plough. By "*skilling*" we must understand some species of foreign coin then in circulation in Rus—probably the Arabic silver *dirgem*, of which the current of foreign trade swept vast quantities into the country. *Dan* was collected in two ways—either through the tribes bringing it to Kiev themselves (the method known as the "*povoz*" or "bringing"), or through the Prince of Kiev and his retinue making a tour of the provinces to collect it (the method known as the "*poludie*" or "visiting"). In his work *De Nationibus* (written in the middle of the tenth century) Constantine Porphyrogenitus draws a graphic picture of a *poludie* made by the Russian Prince of his day. As soon as the month of November had arrived the Prince, "with all Rus" ("μετὰ πάντων τῶν Ρῶς"—*i.e.* with the whole of his retinue), set out from Kiev "ἐις τὰ πολίδια" (literally, "for the towns," though "πολίδια" probably represents rather Constantine's rendering of the Russian term *poludie* as it sounded to his ears on the lips of his Slavonic informants). The Prince, he goes on, visited all the territories of the tribes paying *dan* to Rus, and was entertained by them through the winter; after which—in April, when the ice was gone from the Dnieper— he returned home to Kiev. In the meanwhile the tribesmen had spent the winter in felling trees and hollowing them out into boats. Then, when spring came and the rivers were open, they floated these boats down the Dnieper to Kiev, hauled them out upon the bank, and sold them to the Prince and his retinue as soon as the latter returned from the *poludie*. After this the Prince's retinue rigged and loaded their purchases, and, when June came, proceeded down the river to Vitichev, where they waited a few days for the convoy to be reinforced from other points on the Dnieper—from Novgorod, Smolensk, Lubiech, Tchernigov, Vishgorod, and so forth. Finally the combined fleet descended the Lower Dnieper, and set sail across the Black Sea to Constantinople.

In reading this account of Constantine's it is easy enough to conjecture what were the goods with which Rus loaded her summer convoys of boats before dispatching them to Byzantium. Undoubtedly those goods consisted of the *dan* paid in kind—paid in such products of the forest as furs, honey, and wax—to the Prince and his retinue during their winter tour of the tribes. To these commodities would be added slaves, for not only was the gradual subjugation of the Slavonic and allied Finnish tribes accompanied by the enslavement of a large proportion of the conquered population, but we are told by the Arabic writer Ibn Dasta that the warriors of Varangian Rus made stealthy raids by boat for the sole purpose of slave-catching. Another rare item, only to be found in the pages of Leo the Deacon, is to the effect that the Emperor Zemisches concluded an agreement with Sviatoslav by which *corn* also might be imported into Constantinople by the Russians.

The chief actors in this great commercial movement were the Prince of Kiev and his retinue. To their official convoys were added also the vessels of private merchants, in order that the latter might make the voyage to Constantinople under the protection of the Prince's representatives, and in Igor's treaty with the Greeks we read that " each year the Great Prince of Rus and his boyars may send to the Great Greek Emperor as many ships as the Prince may desire, together with his commissioners and guests "—that is to say, together with the official traders of the Kievan government and private merchants. The account of a *poludie* which I have cited above from the pages of Constantine Porphyrogenitus makes it clear that a vital connection existed between the annual political tour of the Kievan government and the economic life of Rus. The *dan* collected by the Prince as ruler formed also the material of his expeditions as trader ; and although, as *köning*, he governed, he none the less, as a Varangian, remained an armed merchant. This *dan* he shared with his retinue, who, constituting both his instrument of rule and the chief mercantile class in Rus, acted as the prime lever in both the political and the economic routine of the state. In winter the retinue administered the country, visited the tribes, and gathered in the *dan*, while in summer it sold in foreign markets what it had collected during the winter. In what I have cited from Constantine Porphyrogenitus we have a clear and concise indication of the importance of Kiev as the political and industrial focus of early Russian life. The foreign trading expeditions of the Kievan government not only created and supported an extensive boat-building industry among the Slavs of the Dnieper basin —an industry finding a ready market each spring at Kiev—but was also the means of causing large numbers of traders and vessels to join the official convoys from every corner of the region bordering upon the Baltic-Greek trade-route, and so still further to swell the volume of foreign commerce.

The same complex economic process caused also the silver *dirgems* of Arabic currency and the golden *zastezhki* of Byzantine workmanship to be wafted from Bagdad and Constantinople to the banks of those Russian rivers where archæologists since have found them.

Such, then, was the *domestic* policy of the Princes of Kiev during the ninth and tenth centuries. It is not difficult to see what was the fundamental economic interest which directed that policy and united the various heterogeneous, isolated portions of the country into a political whole. That fundamental interest was the *dan*, which, passing through the hands of the Prince and his retinue, went to feed the foreign trade of Rus. The same economic interest, again, ruled the *foreign* policy of the early Kievan Princes. That policy was directed to two principal ends—namely, the acquiring of oversea markets and the keeping open and secure of the trade-routes leading to those markets. According to the Ancient Chronicle, the most notable feature in the foreign history of Rus up to the middle of the eleventh century was the series of military expeditions undertaken by the Kievan Princes against Constantinople. Reckoned up to the death of Yaroslav, they numbered, in all, six, without counting Vladimir's expedition of 988 against the Byzantine colony of Chersonesus in Taurica. These expeditions against Constantinople included the one made by Askold in 860 (formerly assigned to 865), the one made by Oleg in 907, the two made by Igor in 941 and 944 respectively, Sviatoslav's second expedition against the Bolgars in 971 (which subsequently became converted into a war with the Greeks), and Yaroslav's (son of Vladimir) expedition in 1043. It is sufficient to know the causes of the first and last of these enterprises to understand the prime motive which inspired them all. As regards Askold's expedition, Photius tells us that Rus was first angered by the murder of some of her merchants in Constantinople, and finally moved to action by the refusal of the Byzantine government to make reparation for the insult or to renew the trading relations thus broken off. Again, the reason why Yaroslav sent his son with a fleet against the Greeks in 1043 was that some Russian merchants had been assaulted in Constantinople, and one of them killed. Thus we see that the chief cause of these expeditions against Byzantium was the determination of Rus to support or to re-establish trade relations which had become interrupted; while the same reason accounts for the fact that these expeditions usually ended in the conclusion of a treaty of commerce. Of such treaties, only four have come down to us—namely, two made by Oleg, one made by Igor, and a short one (or the preamble of one) made by Sviatoslav. All these documents were drawn up, in the first instance, in the Greek tongue, and then translated (with certain necessary changes of form) into the language best understood in Rus. As we read them we quickly realise what was the common interest which connected Rus and Byzantium in the tenth century, for we find fully defined in these documents both the system of annual trade regulations which were to obtain between the two countries and the private relations which were to be observed between Russian merchants visiting Constantinople and the mercantile community resident there.

Every summer, Russian traders made their way to Constantinople for the trading season. This season lasted six months only, since Igor's treaty shows us that no Russian merchant was allowed to remain in the city through the winter. Throughout their stay in Byzantium Russian traders were lodged in the suburb of San Mamo, where formerly there stood a monastery dedicated to St. Mamant ; while, from the period of the conclusion of Igor's treaty onwards, Imperial officials used to require of the visiting merchants a document signed by their Prince and specifying both the number of vessels dispatched from Kiev and the names and descriptions of all who had sailed in them, whether official representatives of the Kievan government or private merchants. This was done "in order" (so the Greeks caused it to be inserted into the treaty) "that we may know that all do come in peace," and constituted a precautionary measure against the intrusion of pirates into Constantinople under cover of the Russian convoy. Throughout their stay in the Greek dominions both the Prince's official traders and the private merchants included in the expedition were accorded free board and "baths" by the Byzantine government —a sign that these annual trading expeditions were regarded by the Greeks not merely as private affairs, but as official missions from the friendly court at Kiev. Indeed, according to Leo the Deacon, this significance of the Russian trading expeditions was specifically defined in a treaty made by Sviatoslav with the Emperor Zemisches, in which the Emperor bound himself to receive "as allies and as hath alway been done" all Russians visiting Constantinople for trading purposes. In return Rus was to perform certain reciprocal services for the Greeks within the confines of the Byzantine Empire. An instance of these services is given in Igor's treaty, which bound the Prince of Rus not to permit the Black Bolgars of the Crimea to ravage the district of Kherson. In addition to free maintenance while in Constantinople, the official trading commissioners of the Prince of Kiev received an allowance in accordance with their rank, while private merchants received a sum paid monthly and varying according to the relative seniority of the towns from which they came—Kiev ranking first in this regard, then Tchernigov, then Periaslavl, and so on. Yet the Greeks must have had no little distrust of the "men of Rus," however apparently peaceful their mission, seeing that the regulations required the Russian merchants to go unarmed when bringing their wares into Constantinople, to enter the city by one gate only and in parties of not more than fifty at a time, and to be accompanied by an Imperial official to see to the proper treatment of the buyers by the sellers—"lest " (in the words of Igor's treaty) "the Russians entering the city should create a mischief." This treaty also stipulated that the Russian visitors should be exempt from tolls. Trade was done almost wholly by barter ; which accounts for the comparatively small number of Byzantine coins found in the old Russian hoards and *kirgans*. Russian furs, honey, wax, and slaves were exchanged for Greek silk-stuffs, gold,[1] wine, and fruit. Finally, when the trading season came to an end every Russian ship received *gratis* from the Imperial Government provisions for the journey home, as well as such shipping tackle—anchors, cables, ropes, sails, and so forth—as required to be made good.

Such was the system of trading relations between Rus and Byzantium which became established by the treaties of Oleg and Igor. The system's cultural importance for the former country is self-evident, and I need say no more than that it was the chief means of preparing the way for the introduction of Christianity to Rus. Yet there was a side of the system other than the cultural which began to exercise a strong influence upon Russian life long before the coming of Christianity. I refer to the *juridical* side, to which was due the treaties' legal definition of the relations to be observed between the Greeks and Russian traders visiting Constantinople, as well as a like definition of civil or criminal offences which might arise out of such relations. These offences were to be set down " both according to Greek law and statute and according to Russian law " : whence arose the code compounded of two different systems of jurisprudence which we find in the treaties, and in which it is sometimes difficult to distinguish from one another their two constituent elements, namely, Byzantine law and Russian law (the latter, again, a compound of Varangian and Slavonic usage). Yet, although these treaties have great scientific interest for ourselves as constituting the oldest memorials in which at least an *outline* of early Russian law is to be distinguished

[1] See reference to *zastezkhi* on p. 81.

(even though, in places, the closest study of them cannot determine with certainty whether we have before us the pure Russian code or some Russo-Byzantine alloy), they probably exercised less influence upon the making of that law than did the actual trading relations which obtained between Rus and Constantinople, seeing that those relations were so dissimilar to anything obtaining in the Russian home trade that any new Greco-Roman juridical theory introduced through their means could not fail to make an impression upon the minds of Russian jurisprudents. At all events this was the case with the *terminology* of Greco-Roman law, for we find it insinuating itself (for example) into more than one of the clauses of Oleg's treaties. Those clauses stipulate, among other things, that if any Russian member of the Imperial service (and there were many such) should die intestate and "possessed of none proper to him," his property should pass to "his lesser kinsfolk in Rus." Of course this "proper to him" represents the Latin "*sui*" of Greco-Roman legal terminology, while "his lesser kinsfolk" (or simply "his kinsfolk," as some of the older manuscripts have it) represents the Latin "*proximi*" or the Greek "οἱ πλησίοι"—*i.e.* collateral relatives. With regard to the social incidence of early Russian law, it should be said that, inasmuch as the Russian traders who took part in this commerce with Byzantium belonged preponderantly to the governing class—the class always differentiated from native Slavdom, at first through its racial origin, and later through its vested privileges—it follows that the early law of the land was the work of this privileged class rather than of the indigenous element. Indeed, it can be seen that the latter had no share whatever in the making of it, except in such cases where popular usage proved incapable of assimilation with the newer jurisprudence. But to all this we will return when we come to study the *Russkaia Pravda*.

The second principal task of the Kievan Princes as regards foreign policy (the first being, as described, the establishment of trade relations) was to maintain and protect the trade-routes leading to the oversea markets—a task which became a matter of much greater difficulty when once the Pechenegs had made their appearance in the Steppes lying to the southward of Rus. Constantine Porphyrogenitus (whose account of the annual Russian trading expeditions to Byzantium I have already quoted) gives us also an excellent picture of the difficulties and dangers which needed to be overcome by Russian merchants before they could reach their destination. The joint convoy of vessels belonging to the Prince, the boyars, and private merchants which had assembled at Vitichev, below Kiev, would leave that point in June, and encounter, as the first obstacle to be surmounted, the cataracts of the Dnieper. As we all know, the course of the river cuts, for a distance of some seventy versts between Ekaterinoslav and Alexandrovsk, through ramifications of the Avratinski heights, which cause it to take a wide sweep to the east. Throughout the whole of that distance the banks of the river rise in precipitous cliffs to a height of some thirty-five *sazhens* [1] above the level of the water, and in places converge considerably inwards. At such points the bed of the river is thickly strewn with rocky boulders, as well as bordered by broad ledges projecting round or sharpened edges far into the current; so that, although the ordinary pace of the water outside the cataracts does not exceed some twenty-five *sazhens* a minute,[2] it passes through the rapids—with a rush and a roar and a dashing of spray from the boulders—at a speed almost six times that pace. At the present day the cataracts are ten in number, but in the time of Constantine Porphyrogenitus they numbered only seven. Although (says Constantine) the small dimensions of the Russian vessels were all in their favour in passing through the rapids, at certain points the slaves had to be landed upon the bank, and told off in batches of six to tow the convoy under the lee of the shore, where rocks were fewest; while, at the more dangerous cataracts, the whole ships' companies had to disembark, and, after throwing out armed detachments into the surrounding Steppe for protection from the Pechenegs who infested it, to draw the vessels out of the water, and then either drag them on rollers past the cataract or carry them that distance on their shoulders. The cataracts safely negotiated, the traders offered sacrifices of thanksgiving to their gods, and re-embarked for the Dnieper estuary. There they halted for a few days on the Island of St. Eleutheria (now Berezan), for the purpose of rigging up sea-going tackle in preparation for the voyage across the Black Sea, and then finally set sail for the mouths of the Danube, hugging the coast throughout, and continually pursued (though not farther than the mouths of the Danube) by the Pechenegs, in the hope that the Russian convoy would be driven ashore by a storm. The whole of this account by Constantine makes it clear how absolutely indispensable to Russian trade an armed escort was which was capable of protecting the Russian traders during their progress to Byzantine markets. It also makes it clear that Constantine had some reason for appending to his story the remark: "This is a troublous voyage, full of perils and mischances."

[1] About 250 English feet.   [2] About two miles an hour.

In addition to besetting the Russian trade-routes through the Steppes, the nomads were forever raiding the Steppe frontiers of Rus. Hence arose the third principal task of the Kievan Princes—namely, to fortify and hold the confines of their territory against the barbarians of the Steppes. According to the *Poviest*, Oleg had no sooner settled at Kiev than he began to build a chain of fortifications around the city; while Vladimir, after remarking, "It is not good that there should be so few defences around Kiev," erected additional earthworks upon the Desna, the Trubetz, the Stuga, the Sula, and other rivers of the region. These fortified posts were manned by warriors ("best men," as the *Poviest* calls them) impressed from among the various Finnish and Slavonic tribes which were settled upon the Russian plain; and, as time went on, ramparts and stockades were constructed to connect the whole chain of forts together. The result was that in the ninth and tenth centuries the entire southern and south-eastern frontiers of what then constituted Rus were protected against nomad incursions by a long line of entrenchments and stockades. Practically the whole of Vladimir's tenure of rule was spent in stubborn warfare with the Pechenegs, who ranged in eight hordes along both banks of the Lower Dnieper, each horde being subdivided into five sections. Constantine Porphyrogenitus tells us that, in his day, these hordes habitually wandered within as short a distance of Kiev as a day's march; wherefore, since, as we have seen, Vladimir built defences upon the Stuga, a tributary on the right bank of the Dnieper, it follows that the southern frontier of Rus must then have run with that river, and have been distant only a day's march from Kiev. By the beginning of the eleventh century, however, we see that the struggles of Rus with the nomads had met with considerable success, for in 1006 (or 1007?) there passed through Kiev a German missionary named Bruno, who was on his way to preach the gospel to the Pechenegs. Vladimir (whom Bruno subsequently described in a letter to his Emperor, Heinrich II., as "Senior Ruzorum") entertained the missionary, and tried hard to dissuade him from visiting the Pechenegs, saying that he would not find a soul among them to save, but would only meet with a miserable death in the attempt. His representations proving unavailing, he then offered to escort Bruno to the frontier, "which he had fenced for a great distance with a strong barrier, by reason of the foemen who roamed outside it." Finally, arrived at a certain spot, Vladimir dismissed his guest through a gate in the line of fortifications, with the remark: "Behold, I have brought you to the place where my territory ends and that of the foemen begins." Now, we are told that this journey to the frontier took *two* days to accomplish ; and inasmuch as we have already noted that, in the time of Constantine Porphyrogenitus (*i.e.* at about the middle of the tenth century), the line of fortifications along this frontier lay at a distance of only *one* day's march from Kiev, it follows that half a century of stubborn fighting under Vladimir had enabled Rus to push her boundary forward a whole day's march into the Steppe—*i.e.* to advance it as far as the line of the river Rhos, where Vladimir's successor, Yaroslav, subsequently built additional forts and manned them with captured Lechs.

Thus we see that the early Kievan Princes continued the policy originated before their time by the fortified trading towns of Rus—namely, the policy of maintaining trade relations with oversea markets and protecting the frontiers and trade-routes of the country from the nomads of the Steppes.

Having now described the policy of the early Kievan Princes, let us sum up its results, as well as touch upon the composition of Rus in the middle of the eleventh century. By that time the Kievan rulers had carved out for themselves a wide expanse of territory, of which Kiev was the political centre. The population of their dominions was of mixed composition, since there had gradually become absorbed into the Principality not only the whole of the Eastern Slavonic tribes, but also a certain number of the Finnish—the latter comprising the Tchudes of Bielozersk and the Baltic, and the Meres of Rostov and Murom. Among these Finnish tribes Russian towns had arisen at an early date, such as Yuriev (now Dorpat) among the Tchudes of the Baltic, and Murom, Rostov, and Bielozersk among the more easterly tribes of that race. The three towns last mentioned were founded earlier than Yuriev, which was called after Yaroslav's Christian name of Yuri (George)— the town of Yaroslav on the Volga (also built in Yaroslav's time) representing his titular appellation. In this manner the Principality of Kiev had come to stretch from Lake Ladoga in the north to the river Rhos in the south, and from the Kliazma in the east to the head of the Western Bug in the west. Galicia—the ancient home of the Chrobatians—can scarcely be counted, since in the tenth and eleventh centuries it was disputed territory between Rus and Poland. Both the lower course of the Oka (the upper course of which formed part of the eastern frontier of Rus) and the lower portions of the Dnieper, the Eastern Bug, and the Dniester seem to have lain outside the then territory of the Prince of Kiev, but on his eastern flank he still retained the ancient colony of

Tmutorokan, connection with which was kept up by way of the left tributaries of the Dnieper and of the rivers discharging into the Sea of Azov.

This huge territory, then, with its vast heterogeneous population, formed the Principality of Kiev, or State of Rus. Yet the State of Rus did not yet constitute the State of the Russian *nation*, for the reason that the Russian nation had not yet come into existence. All that had been accomplished in that direction was that the ethnographical elements had been prepared out of which, by a long and difficult process, the Russian nation was eventually to be compounded. Meanwhile those various heterogeneous elements were mixed together in mechanical fashion only, since the moral tie of Christianity was slow in its working, and had not yet succeeded in embracing even the whole of the Slavonic tribes of the country (the Vatizes, for instance, not becoming Christianised until the beginning of the twelfth century). Of the mechanical ties connecting the various sections of the population the chief was the State system of administration, with its *posadniki, dan,* and taxes. With the nature and origin of the authority wielded by the Prince who stood at the head of that administration we are already acquainted, and know that he derived his authoritative status from those Varangian captains of city companies who first began to appear in Rus during the ninth century, and whose original functions were to protect the trade, the Steppe trade-routes, and the oversea markets of Rus, in return for certain payment from the native Slavonic population. In time, however, the lust of conquest, as well as contact with foreign political forms, caused certain borrowed features to creep into the character of the authority of these mercenary Princes, with the result that their authority ended by becoming the supreme governmental power. During the tenth century, for instance, we frequently find the Prince styled " Kagan " or " Khan "—a title borrowed from his Chozar suzerain ; while Ilarion [1] does the same by Vladimir, in a laudatory work on that Prince which he composed at about the middle of the eleventh century. With the coming of Christianity, however, there set in a new trend of political ideas and relations in Rus, and it was not long before the recently created priesthood imported from Byzantium the notion that a sovereign ruler is appointed of God to establish and maintain the internal order of his state equally with its external security. Consequently we find Ilarion writing that " Prince Vladimir did often and amicably commune with his holy fathers the bishops, to the end that he might learn of them how to establish law among a people

---

[1] Metropolitan of Kiev in the eleventh century.

which had not long known God." The Ancient Chronicle also describes Vladimir as conferring with the bishops, and being told by them that he ought to punish robbers, "seeing that he had been appointed of God to deal retribution unto the wicked and favour unto the good."

Next let us glance at the *composition* of the community governed by the Prince of Kiev. The upper class therein—the class which the Prince employed as his instrument both of rule and defence—was formed of his retinue, and divided into an upper and a lower grade. The former grade consisted of "prince's men," or *boyars*, while the latter grade was made up of *dietski* or *otroki* (pages)—the original collective term for this lower grade being *grid* or *gridiba* (Scandinavian words meaning "servants of the household"), and subsequently the Russian terms *dvor* and *slugi* (meaning respectively "household" and "serving-men"). As already seen, the retinue derived its origin from the armed merchant class of the great trading towns, and had not, as yet, become wholly distinct from that class, either politically or economically. True, the retinue was first and foremost a military class, but then the great towns were themselves organised upon a military basis, and maintained each of them a local force called a *tisiatch*[1]—the *tisiatch*, again, being subdivided into a number of *sotni*[2] and *desiatki*.[3] Each *tisiatch* was commanded by a *tisiatski*, who was elected by his fellow-townsmen and confirmed in his appointment by the Prince of Kiev, while the *sotni* and *desiatki* were commanded by *sotskie* and *desiatskie* respectively. These elected officers constituted the military governing board of the town and its attached province, and appear sometimes in the Ancient Chronicle under the name of the *startsi gradskie* or town wardens. Whenever an expedition was afoot, they and their men marched with the Prince on the same conditions as his retinue; and although the latter constituted his immediate instrument of government, the town wardens had at least a *consultative* voice in the Prince's *duma* or state council. "Vladimir," says the Chronicle in writing of the times of that ruler, "loved well his retinue, and delighted to consult with it concerning the administration of the land, and concerning the military forces, and concerning the statutes." Indeed, we find even the momentous question of the adoption of Christianity being debated by Vladimir in council of boyars and wardens of towns. In addition to being associated with the Prince and his retinue in matters of government, these wardens seem to have been invited to all court ceremonies; whence it would appear that, with the boyars, they

---

[1] Literally, a thousand.   [2] Hundreds.   [3] Tens.

constituted the aristocracy of the country. For instance, we find a feast given by the Prince on the occasion of the dedication of a new church being attended, not only by the boyars and *posadniki*, but also by "the wardens of all grades." In the same manner, Vladimir commanded that "*boyare, otriki, sotskie, desiatskie*, and men of eminence" should all of them receive invitations to his baptismal feast at Kiev. Yet, while constituting the ruling and military class, the retinue still remained an integral part of that mercantile section of the community from which it first originated, and continued to take an active share in foreign trading operations. In the middle of the tenth century the mercantile section of Rus was still almost wholly Varangian in composition, not Slavonic. Of this we see an instance in the fact that, out of the twenty-five trading commissioners who represented Igor in the drawing up of his treaty with the Greeks in 945, we find not a single one bearing a Slavonic name, while out of the twenty-five or twenty-six private merchants who were associated with them in that duty, not more than two or three of them appended signatures recognisable as Slavonic. In addition to the evidence which this association in diplomacy affords of the close connection existing between the mercantile class of Rus and the Kievan government, the treaty also confirms our view of the part played by Varangians in the Russian oversea trade of that period. Yet to foreign observers of the day the two classes represented respectively by the Prince's retinue and by the town merchants evidently appeared to constitute a single social stratum, under the collective name of Rus, for we find Eastern writers of the tenth century speaking of Rus as a people engaged exclusively in war and trade, as well as living solely in towns and possessed of no rural landed property. Certainly, no traces of landownership on the part of the upper classes can be detected in our annals before the eleventh century; while the period when landownership came to constitute a sharply-cut economic and juridical dividing-line between the retinue and the town mercantile community was later still. The *Russkaia Pravda* founded its social divisions solely upon the relation of individuals to the Prince as sovereign ruler, so that a boyar, in acquiring land, became a privileged landowner for the reason that he was a privileged servant of the Prince. The original foundation, however, upon which social divisions in the Russian community were based was undoubtedly slave-ownership. In certain clauses of the *Russkaia Pravda* we find mentioned a privileged class which bore the now obsolete title of *ognistchané* —a term interchangeable in other clauses of the Code with the more familiar one of " prince's men." That the *ognistchané* were a class of especial social importance is shown by the fact that the assassination of one of their number was made punishable by the payment of a double amount of wer-gild. If, then, we take into consideration the additional fact that passages in certain of our other more ancient annals undoubtedly give the word *ognistché* the meaning of slaves, we are justified in supposing that, before the era of the Princes, *ognistchané* was a term applied to a mercantile class which traded solely in slaves, and therefore ranked as the aristocracy of the land. Yet, although it was not until the eleventh century that the retinue became sharply divided from the mercantile class, either politically or economically, we can none the less discern a certain *racial* distinction between them. True, the retinue gradually absorbed into itself the native military forces of the Slavs; yet the signatures of the Prince's commissioners appended to the tenth century treaties with the Greeks show us that the *nachodniki*,[1] as the Chronicle calls the alien Varangian element, constituted the preponderant majority in the then composition of the retinue. The same element must have continued to maintain its predominance into the eleventh century, for we find that the Russian community of that period still looked upon a boyar as necessarily a Varangian. In a curious old work dating back to the early days of Christianity in Rus—namely, a volume of sermons suitable for Lent—we come across a homily upon the subject of the Pharisee and the publican, in which the author says, *apropos* of the virtue of humility : " Boast not of thy birth that thou art noble. Say not that thy father is a boyar, and that the twain martyrs of Christ were thy brethren." The concluding sentence of this passage refers to two Varangian Christians, father and son, who suffered martyrdom at the hands of Kievan pagans in the year 983 : which makes it clear that, in the eleventh century, a boyar was looked upon as necessarily a kinsman and compatriot of the martyrs referred to, notwithstanding that (as we know from the Chronicle) not a few native Slavs had been created boyars during the preceding century. The homily, then, must have been written at a date when the racial reconstitution of the retinue was in process of accomplishment, but no corresponding change of social ideas had yet had time to take place.

It was to the retinue in its double capacity of the Prince's arm of government and of the chief trader in the State that the term " Rus " was first applied—a term of which neither the historical origin nor the etymology have ever yet been satisfactorily explained. The author of

---

[1] Literally, " finders " or " explorers."

the *Poviest* supposed the term to be a *racial* appellation, as denoting the Varangian stock in general from which our early rulers sprang; while at a later period (*i.e.* in the tenth century) the word acquired a *social* meaning, and was taken by Constantine Porphyrogenitus and Arabic writers to apply solely to the upper classes of the Russian community, more especially to the Prince's retinue. Next, the term "Rus" became a *geographical* expression, as denoting the *Russian land* (the term "*Russkaia zemlia*" appears for the first time in Igor's treaty of 945)— *i.e.* the province of Kiev, whither the bulk of the early Varangian immigrants had gravitated. Finally, in the eleventh and twelfth centuries, when the fusion of Rus (in its racial application) with the native Slavonic element had become complete, the terms "Rus" and "*Russkaia zemlia*" acquired a *political* significance (though still retaining their geographical one), and began to be applied to the whole of the territory subject to the Princes of Kiev, as well as to the whole of the Christian Russo-Slavonic population included therein. As yet, however, (*i.e.* in the tenth century,) the military-industrial upper class was preponderantly Varangian in composition, and altogether distinct from the native lower classes—*i.e.* from the bulk of that indigenous Slavonic population which still paid *dan* to alien Rus, or the Varangian element; and it is only later that we find this native Slavonic stratum beginning to figure in our annals, not merely as a native population paying tribute to alien rulers, but as the inferior orders of a pan-Russian community—*i.e.* as an aggregate of inhabitants homogeneous with the upper stratum of Russian society, but possessed of inferior rights, as well as liable to different obligations, to those of their superiors. Thus at this period of our history we can observe in operation a process of two distinct races, fortuitously thrown together in common social life under a common governing authority, undergoing gradual assimilation in the face of race-dominance by the one over the other. Likewise we can now discern the peculiar factor which caused this process to differ from similar ones known to us in the history of Western Europe. That factor was the circumstance that, previous to the process of assimilation, the alien metal had become charged with a certain measure of native alloy; which circumstance served both to deprive the new social order of any very sharp-cut lines of demarcation and to soften the asperities of social antagonism.

Such, then, was the composition of Rus at the middle of the eleventh century. From that point onwards until the close of the century—*i.e.*

until the end of the first principal period of our history—the political and social order of Rus (of which the foundations were laid by the old trading towns, and added to by the early Kievan Princes) underwent considerable development. Of that development we will speak in the next chapter, beginning with the new factors which arose upon the death of Yaroslav.

CHAPTER VII

The order of princely rule in Rus previous to the death of Yaroslav—Partition of the country after that event—The rota system of rule: its origin, theory, and working—Causes of its disruption—*Riadi* (conventions) and feuds—The idea of the *otchina*—*Izgoi* princes —Indirect hindrances to the working of the rota system— The importance of that system.

THE social forces and historical conditions which helped to create the political order established in Rus after the death of Yaroslav (*i.e.* after the middle of the eleventh century) were many and various, but the real basis of that order was the system of princely rule which then became operative.

It is difficult to say precisely what system of rule obtained under Yaroslav's predecessors, nor, indeed, whether any system obtained at all. Sometimes the princely power seems to have passed from one ruler to another according to seniority of birth—as in the case of Oleg, who though, by tradition, Rurik's nephew only, succeeded his uncle in place of Rurik's son Igor. Again, the rulership seems to have been centred in the hands of one prince alone only when no other grown-up princes were available, so that, up to the middle of the eleventh century, sole rule appears to have been rather a political accident than the established political system. Usually, when the sons of the reigning prince arrived at years of discretion, he awarded them each a province during his lifetime, irrespective of their precise age when receiving it. Thus Sviatoslav, though still a minor at the time of his father's death, had been prince of Novgorod for some years when that event took place; while at a later period, when Sviatoslav was setting forth upon his second expedition against the Bolgars of the Danube, he himself apportioned a province of Rus to each of his sons. Vladimir did the same on a similar occasion. All these sons governed their provinces as their father's *posadniki*, and, as such, paid into the paternal exchequer a given amount of *dan*, collected from their several territories. Thus the Chronicle tells us that, as governor of Novgorod under his father, Yaroslav paid Vladimir an assessed annual *dan* of two thousand *grivni*: "which," adds the

Chronicle, " is what *posadniki* of Novgorod were ever wont to pay." When, however, the father died, all political ties between his sons seem to have become automatically sundered, nor are any traces to be found of younger princes remaining filially subject to the elder brother who succeeded to the father's throne at Kiev. Family law, apparently, held good between father and sons, but not between brothers: which explains the many feuds which arose among the sons of Sviatoslav and Vladimir. At the same time, faint traces are to be found of the idea of seniority by birth—an idea voiced by one of Vladimir's sons, Prince Boris, when, upon the death of his father, his retinue urged him to seize the throne of Kiev and thus supplant his elder brother Sviatopolk. "Bid me not raise hands against my elder brother," said Boris; "for, inasmuch as our father is dead, it is for my brother to take the father's place."

On the death of Yaroslav the rulership of Rus seems finally to have ceased to be centred in the hands of one prince alone, for, according to the Chronicle, none of Yaroslav's successors assumed "the whole Russian rule" or became "the autocrat of the Russian land." This was probably due to the fact that Yaroslav's family ramified rapidly with each successive generation, and that the country became correspondingly divided up among the various princes as they attained maturity. These continual subdivisions of Rus must be closely followed if we wish to gauge the system of princely rule to which they gave rise and understand clearly its bases. Likewise it is necessary to distinguish the plan or norm of that system from its practical development. The former must be sought in the practice of the system during the first few generations after Yaroslav, since after that period the force of circumstances caused it to fall into abeyance in all but the conceptions of the princes themselves. It frequently happens in life that, though men may be compelled by circumstances to resign the practice of some old-established rule to which they have long been accustomed, they still retain the *idea* of it in their inner consciousness, since memory, being a thing personal and individual, is, in general, more conservative, more inert, than life, which varies for ever with the collective efforts, the collective errors, of humanity at large.

At his death Yaroslav divided his dominions among his five sons and one grandson (the latter Rostislav, son of Yaroslav's son Vladimir, who predeceased his father). Of the Princes of Polotsk who constituted a collateral branch of Yaroslav's house (being sons of Yaroslav's elder brother Iziaslav, son of Vladimir by Rognieda), but had been disinherited at an earlier date and awarded no share in the general government of the country, we need take no account. According to the Chronicle, Yaroslav made his testamentary disposition verbally—assigning to the eldest son (Iziaslav) both Kiev and Novgorod (thus investing him with command of both ends of the Baltic-Greek trade-route); to his second son (Sviatoslav) the province of Tchernigov, the region around Murom and Riazan, and the distant colony of Tmutokoran (founded upon the site of the old Greek Tamatarch—now Taman); to his third son (Vsevolod) the comparatively small and isolated province of Periaslavl (the old capital of which is now the capital of the government of Poltava) and the region around Suzdal and Bielozersk; to his fourth son (Viatcheslav) Smolensk; and to his fifth son (Igor) the province of Volhynia (of which the town of Vladimir—built in the time of St. Vladimir and situated upon the Luga, a tributary of the Western Bug—was the capital). As for the grandson (Rostislav), he received only the district of Rostov, situated in the middle of his uncle's '(Vsevolod's) province of Periaslavl. It is easy to see the main idea which inspired Yaroslav in this partition of Rus, since the productive values of the various provinces corresponded precisely to the relative degrees of seniority of their inheritors. That is to say, the older the prince, the better and richer was his allotted province. It is interesting also to note that the three senior towns—Kiev, Tchernigov, and Periaslavl—followed one another, in Yaroslav's disposition, in exactly the same order as we find them placed in the Greek treaties (in which documents they are expressly enumerated according to political and economic importance). We have seen that eleventh-century Kiev owed its position as the wealthiest town in Rus to the fact that it was the focus of Russian trade; and although foreigners of the day may have been somewhat inclined to exaggerate its opulence and population (Thietmar of Meresburg, for instance, describing Kiev as an extremely great and powerful city, possessed of *four hundred churches* and eight markets, and Adam of Bremen declaring Kiev to have been the Orthodox rival even of " that shining glory of the East," Constantinople herself), our own annals furnish us with the even more startling information that in the great fire of 1071 the city lost *seven hundred churches !* Next to Kiev in wealth and importance ranked the portion of the second brother—Tchernigov; then Periaslavl, and so on.

The question now confronts us — How did Yaroslav's immediate successors contrive to adopt their method of ruling the land to the periodical changes taking place in the *personnel* of the princely family? Did they remain permanent rulers of the provinces originally allotted to them, or, if not, under what system did those provinces devolve? Yaroslav's dying speech to his sons (which is given at length in the Chronicle) does not help us much, for, although charged with fond paternal feeling and studded with exhortations to his heirs to live at peace with one another, it contains only two references to the *political* relations which the testator desired his successors to observe. The first of those references occurs when, after naming the territories allotted to each inheritor, he inculcates in the younger members of his family obedience to the eldest brother as to a father—"since, for you, he shall be as in my place"; while the second reference is contained in the words subsequently addressed to the eldest son where the testator says : " If brother shall commit wrong against brother, then shalt thou befriend the one wronged." That is all there is to be gleaned from the speech itself. Nevertheless, other sources provide us with two complementary items of evidence. In the story of Boris and Gleb written by the Abbot Jacob of Petcherski [1] we read that Yaroslav bequeathed his throne, in the first instance, to his three eldest sons only—not to the whole five of them.[2] This constitutes our first item. Our other one is to be found in the Chronicle itself, which states in a later passage that Yaroslav, loving Vsevolod above all his other sons, said to him before his (Yaroslav's) death : " If God should ever grant unto thee to attain the power of my throne (*albeit by right of succession only*, and not by force), then, when death come to thee, command that thou be laid where I shall lie—close beside my tomb." These sources are sufficient to show us that Yaroslav had a clear idea of the system of succession which he desired his sons to adopt with regard to the throne of Kiev. That system was the system of succession in order of seniority. Let us observe how far it was actually carried out and the manner in which its theory worked in practice.

In 1057 Yaroslav's fourth son, Viatcheslav of Smolensk, died, leaving a son behind him ; whereupon his elder brothers transferred Igor (Yaroslav's fifth son) from Volhynia to the vacancy at Smolensk, and replaced him, in Volhynia, by their nephew, Rostislav of Rostov. Next, in 1060,

[1] See p. 22.
[2] This constitutes a well-known norm of family relations, and, in later days, formed one of the bases of the *miestnichestvo* system. According to this norm, only the three eldest brothers in a family of brothers and sons (*i.e.* of uncles and nephews) constituted the first, the ruling, generation in the family—the remaining brothers, with the nephews, being relegated to the second, the subordinate, generation, and all of them placed upon a level with one another. The *miestnichestvo* system, however, placed the eldest nephew upon a level with the fourth uncle, while making the remaining nephews rank strictly according to the seniority of their fathers.

Igor himself died, leaving sons behind him. None the less, neither they nor their cousin Rostislav were awarded Smolensk (in succession to Igor) by the elder brothers of the family, and Rostislav in particular, conceiving himself wronged, declared a feud against his uncles, and went off to Tmuto-koran to raise forces for that purpose. Next, in 1073, Yaroslav's second and third sons (Sviatoslav and Vsevolod) took it into their heads that their eldest brother, Iziaslav, was intriguing against them, and therefore expelled him from Kiev, where he was succeeded by Sviatoslav; Sviatoslav himself being succeeded at Tchernigov by Vsevolod of Periaslavl. Again, in 1076, Sviatoslav himself died, leaving sons behind him, and was succeeded at Kiev by Vsevolod of Tchernigov. Soon afterwards, Iziaslav returned to Rus with Polish reinforcements, whereupon Vsevolod voluntarily surrendered Kiev to him, and himself returned to Tchernigov. Next, in 1078 some of the dispossessed nephews tried by force to seize the supreme power, and in the struggle to restrain them Iziaslav fell; whereupon Vsevolod—now the last surviving son of Yaroslav—transferred himself once more to the suzerain throne at Kiev. Finally, in 1093, Vsevolod himself died; whereupon there entered upon the scene the *second* generation of Yaroslav's issue—*i.e.* the grandsons, of whom Sviatapolk, son of Yaroslav's eldest son Iziaslav, succeeded to the throne of Kiev.

These instances will suffice to show us the system of princely rule which became established after the death of Yaroslav. In short, we see that the princes did not remain permanent, irremovable rulers of the provinces origin-ally allotted to them, but that, according as changes occurred in the family through death, one or more of the members junior to the deceased were promoted to provinces superior to those which they had previously held. This process of promotion was based upon a definite rota, and carried out in exactly the same order of seniority of the princes as the order in which the original allotment had been made. The system expressed, before all things, the idea of the indivisibility of the princely power, for, although the princes divided that power among themselves, they never parted with a share of it to an outsider, but succeeded each other strictly according to seniority : nor until the end of the twelfth century was this idea ever lost sight of by the descendants of Yaroslav who ruled the country during that period. Striking examples of its working are to be found in the Ancient Chronicle. For instance, on the death of his father in 1093, we find Vladimir Monomakh considering certain suggestions which had been made to him to assume the throne of Kiev and supplant his cousin and senior, Sviatopolk, son of Iziaslav. Finally, saying to himself, "If I should seat myself upon the throne, then will there arise a feud between myself and Sviatopolk, seeing that his father sat thereon before my father," he bade Sviatopolk assume the suzerain power. Again, in 1195 Monomakh's great-grandson, Rurik of Smolensk, took it into his head that he and his brothers came next in rightful order of seniority to Monomakh's grandson, Vsevolod III. of Suzdal; wherefore he sent messengers to Yaroslav of Tchernigov (Vsevolod's fourth brother) with the demand: "Do thou and all thy brethren swear to us upon the cross that ye will seek nor Kiev nor Smolensk to our despite, nor to that of our sons, nor to that of all our house of Vladimir. For, inasmuch as our grandfather Yaroslav did apportion unto us the Dnieper, ye have nought to do with Kiev." [1] Understanding that the demand, though voiced by Rurik, emanated from the head of Rurik's line (Vsevolod of Suzdal), Yaroslav addressed his answer direct to the latter, saying: "Behold, we have agreed not to seek Kiev to thy despite, nor to that of thy nephew Rurik, and by that agreement will we abide. Yet, shouldst thou bid us renounce Kiev *for ever*, then are we neither Ugri nor Lechs, but grandsons of one grandfather with thyself. Wherefore, so long as thou livest, we will not seek Kiev; but when thou art gone—then let Kiev fall unto him unto whom God may grant it." Although the principals in this dispute were of the fourth and fifth generations of Yaroslav's house, their words show clearly that the theory of succession by rota, founded upon the unity of the princely family and the indivisibility of its ancestral heritage, was still being strictly adhered to.

Such was the peculiar system of princely rule which became established as the political order immediately after the death of Yaroslav. Let us state it once more in the simplest terms. The Suzerain Prince of Rus now possessed dynastic importance, and none but descendants of St. Vladimir were entitled to style themselves "Great Prince." Sole rule was ended, as also was bequeathal of rule. Instead of dividing up their ancestral heritage into perpetual portions and bequeathing them to their posterity at death, Yaroslav's successors constituted themselves transferable rulers, and moved from province to province according to a definite rota. This rota was fixed by the relative seniority of the individual, and served, in its turn, to fix the adjustable relation between the number of

---

[1] As a matter of fact, this statement of Rurik's was inaccurate, since it was not the immediate region of the Dnieper that Yaroslav allotted to Sviatoslav and Vsevolod, but provinces eastward of that river—namely, Tchernigov and Periaslavl.

eligible princes and the number of provinces (*i.e.* of areas of territory subject to princely rule).   Even as the provinces constituted a territorial scale, graded in order of wealth and importance, so the princes constituted a genealogical scale, graded in order of seniority; and it was upon the exact relation between these two scales—the genealogical scale and the territorial, the scale of princely *personnel* and the scale of provinces—that the system of princely rule was based.   At the head of the scale of princely *personnel* stood the eldest of the family, the Prince of Kiev, who not only had for his share the richest province, but was entitled, by right of seniority, to certain other privileges and prerogatives superior to those of his younger kin.   For the reason, too, that, as head of the dynasty, he stood in the relation of "father" to the younger members of the family (who were bound to "walk in obedience unto him") he was accorded the distinguishing title of "Suzerain Prince"; while the theory that he was "in the father's place" was a juridical fiction designed to preserve that political unity of the princely family which might otherwise have given way under the stress of conflicting governmental interests.   The Suzerain Prince assigned to juniors their provinces, installed them therein, inquired into and adjudicated upon their disputes, made due provision for their orphaned families, and acted as general guardian of, and "thought and made divination concerning," the whole territory of Rus.   But, though paramount ruler both of the country and of his kindred, it was usual for him, on all important occasions, to summon his fellow-princes to a family council, to see to the execution of their resolutions in council, and, in general, to act as both director and executor of the family's will. In all history, probably, there is no such curious system of rule to be seen in operation as the one described.   Taking its chief principle—succession by rota in order of seniority—as our guide, we may call it the *rota system*, as distinguished from the *appanage system* which followed it and which first came into force during the thirteenth and fourteenth centuries.

Next let us examine the question of the *origin* of the rota system.   Its principal bases were, firstly, the possession of the supreme power as a whole by the princely family *collectively*, and secondly, temporary tenure of power over an allotted area by each separate prince *individually*.   In the system, therefore, we must distinguish carefully between the collective right of rule enjoyed by the princely family as a whole and the rota whereby that right was sought to be maintained.   The origin of this curious family system of state rule is sometimes ascribed to the influence exerted by the native domestic order of the land upon its political order, as leading the immigrant Varangian princes to adopt the clan ideas and relations which they found prevalent among the Eastern Slavs at their coming, and to build upon them their method of governing the country. This explanation cannot be accepted without great reserve, seeing that clan relations were already in process of disruption at the time when this theory declares the early princes to have adopted them. But we need not dwell upon that. The presence of family relations in an order of state government is no uncommon phenomenon. Such relations are present, for instance, in monarchies, since in them the sovereign power and its attached prerogatives descend in order of seniority of the reigning family. In fact, it is a phenomenon due rather to legislative enactments than to any domestic order of the people, while it should be remembered that the very position of dynasties tends to confine their state relations within a family ring. At all events there was nothing of the monarchical idea among the Russian princes of the eleventh century. In those days, joint rule, with the eldest of the family as "father," was looked upon as simpler and more intelligible. Nor do clan relations explain the *working* of the system, since we see no similar system in operation in the domestic life of the early Russian Slavs. Indeed, had clan law been taken as its basis, the system might have assumed more than one different form to what it did. The eldest prince, for instance, might have constituted himself sole ruler, retaining the junior princes merely as his coadjutors or executors of his commands, instead of as actual territorial rulers. That was what Vladimir did with his sons—appointing them to provinces as his *posadniki* only, and frequently transferring them from one province to another. Again, the joint family heritage might have been divided up into permanent heritable lots, as was done by the successors of Clovis of the Merovingians, or, in our own case, by the successors of Vsevolod III.

Thus we still have to explain whence and how there arose the idea of the system of transferable rule in order of seniority, as well as the idea of the importance not only of maintaining an exact relation between the seniority of the princes and the politico-economic importance of the several provinces, but of readjusting that relation at each successive change in the *personnel* of the dynasty. To understand this phenomenon properly, we must try and enter into the political views of the Russian prince of the period. The princes collectively formed a dynasty, the authority of which was generally recognised. As yet, however, the idea of a prince as a territorial ruler bound by permanent ties to the territory which he governed had not arisen. So far from that, Yaroslav's early successors were still much what their forefathers of the ninth century had been—that is to say, river Vikings whom even the threat of perils from the Steppes could scarcely induce to quit the boat for the saddle, and to whom the old Varangian notion that they were not so much armed rulers or administrators as armed protectors engaged "to watch over the Russian land and to contend with unclean barbarians" was still an article of faith. Remuneration for this service, then, they looked upon as their political right, and the defence of the country as their political obligation—the one serving as the source of the other. These two ideas exhausted the whole political views of the prince of that period—exhausted what I might call his working, everyday political views, as distinguished from such Sunday, fête-day views as he might possibly borrow from books or imbibe from the clergy. At the same time, he had before him, as constant reminders of the insecurity of the whole political ground beneath his feet, both the feuds constantly occurring among his family and the frequent intervention of the citizens of the great towns in the family's affairs. For instance, Yaroslav's eldest son Iziaslav was twice expelled from Kiev—the first time by the Kievans themselves, and the second time by his brothers Sviatoslav and Vsevolod. On each occasion he regained his position with Polish help, but his attitude is clearly expressed in the speech which he subsequently addressed to his brother Vsevolod when the latter, in his turn, had been expelled from Tchernigov and had betaken himself disconsolately to his now reinstated brother at Kiev. Iziaslav, a kind and simple-hearted man, who knew, perhaps, better than did his brothers how affairs really stood, said to the downcast Vsevolod: "Grieve not, my brother. Remember how it hath also been with me. First did the people of Kiev drive me forth and despoil my goods, and then didst thou and thy brother do likewise. Have I not wandered, stripped of all my possessions, in foreign lands—I who had done no wrong? Nay, fret not thyself, my brother, but let us share the Russian land together, that, if we hold it, we hold it together, and if we lose it, we lose it together, and I lay my head with thine." This was not the speech of an independent ruler of Rus, but of a hired public servant prepared at any moment to surrender his post. Like their forerunners, the captains of the Varangian trained bands, Yaroslav's successors still remained competitors for the richest towns and provinces ; only, since they now constituted a close family ring, instead of a miscellaneous crowd of seekers after trade bargains and high rates of pay, they sought to replace the haphazard and irregular working of individual enterprise or individual prowess with a collective, permanent, and obligatory rule of seniority, and

came to look upon themselves less as guardians of the state in return
for payment or under contract than as its protectors in fulfilment of an
inherited duty imposed upon each of them in proportion to his aptitude
for the task of defending his territory. Of this aptitude for protective
duties the arbiter was, as regards sons, the father, and as regards brothers,
their degree of seniority. According to his degree of seniority, a prince
received not only a more or less rich province, but also a province more or
less liable to attack, since, at that time, both the right of a prince to govern
a province and his fitness to defend it were determined by that self-same
seniority. The richness of a province and its need of protection were
directly proportionate to one another, since they both of them depended
upon the proximity of that province to the Steppes, whence came the
foes of Rus and beyond which lay the oversea markets of Russian trade.
Similarly, the richness of a province was in inverse proportion to the
security of its position, since, the nearer it lay to the Steppes (*i.e.* to the
lucrative oversea trade markets), the more exposed was it to attack. Consequently, whenever a prince advanced a step upward in seniority, his
sovereign powers had to be increased to balance his increased obligations
in the matter of rule and defence. Hence it is probable that it was this
peculiar relation between the strategic position and the economic importance of the several provinces (together with, of course, other incidental
conditions) that first suggested to the princes the idea of the rota system
of rule.

Having thus pointed out the principle, the theory, of the rota system
of government, as illustrated in the practice of Yaroslav's immediate
successors, let us examine its historical development in the hands of
subsequent generations. What precisely was that system? That is to
say, was it a mere theoretical formula shaping the political ideas of the
princes, or was it an historical actuality, a political rule, by which their
actual conduct and relations were determined? To obtain an answer to
that question we must draw a strict distinction between the bases of that
system and its casual development—*i.e.* between its root-principles and
their adaptation to chance circumstances in the course of princely relations.

We have seen that the juridical bases of the system were, firstly, the
right of the princely family collectively to rule the whole of the country in
perpetuity; and secondly, the right of each prince to hold temporary rule
over a portion of the country, according to his degree of seniority—the
second of these bases serving as a means of maintaining the first. This
seems to have been the only system which Yaroslav's successors deemed to

be either right or possible—namely, to rule the land as their family heritage ; while the reason why they regarded the root-principles upon which the system was based as clear and indisputable was that those principles limited the system to the simplest possible of relations—to such relations as would naturally obtain in an exclusive circle of near kinsfolk.   In proportion, however, as that circle began to widen, and the inter-relations of the family to become more complex and intricate, there began also to arise questions not easily admitting of resolution on the strict basis of the system's principles.   Hence was initiated a gradual working out of those principles in detail—a process which entailed their application to occasions when the difficult question of relative seniority was in doubt. This, in its turn, gave rise to quarrels among the princes, for Yaroslav's heirs had never established any exact method of determining seniority. Hitherto, indeed, they had had no need to do so, seeing that (as mentioned above) relations with them were of the very simplest—merely relations proper to a family of fathers and sons, in which union the parent would naturally take precedence of the children, and the eldest brother of his juniors.   Later generations of Yaroslav's house, however, began to find these simple family relations difficult to maintain after the stock had multiplied and become split up into several parallel branches, each of which furnished princes so nearly equal to one another in age that to distinguish between their rival claims to priority of birth was a matter almost of impossibility.   Indeed, even to *count* the princes who make their appearance in the Chronicle during the latter half of the eleventh century is a task of the most arduous kind, seeing to what an extent the various branches of the stock had now multiplied and produced degrees of kindred at once numerous and complicated.   Hence, every change in the *personnel* of the princely house gave rise to disputes either about the order of seniority or the order of rule.   One occasion of quarrel there was which occurred with especial frequency.   Seniority was determined by two conditions—by the order of generations or distance from the founder of the dynasty (genealogical seniority), and by the order of birth or comparative ages of the different individuals constituting a generation (physical seniority).   In the simple family we generally find these two seniorities coincident, so that the member of the family senior according to the one is senior also according to the other ; but with the enlargement of the family—*i.e.* with the appearance of a third generation within the lifetime of the father and sons—this coincidence frequently becomes broken, for at that point the physical seniority may begin to diverge from the genealogical, and the comparative ages of the members of the family to cease to correspond to the genealogical distance at which they stand from the original founder—*i.e.* from the grandfather. Owing to this, the custom of the early princes to marry early and die late often caused a nephew to be older than an uncle. Monomakh, for instance, had eight sons, of whom the fifth, Viatcheslav, once said to the sixth, Yuri Dolgoruki : "When thou wert born I was already bearded." That being so, Viatcheslav's eldest son—and, *a fortiori*, the eldest son of Viatcheslav's elder brother, Mstislav—must also have been born before Yuri Dolgoruki. Thus the question frequently arose as to which was the senior of the two—an uncle younger than a nephew in years, but older by generation, or a nephew older than an uncle in years, but younger by generation ; nor is it too much to say that by far the greater proportion of the princely feuds of the eleventh and twelfth centuries were caused by this conflict of seniority between older nephews and younger uncles—*i.e.* by the conflict between physical and genealogical seniorities originally coincident. Apparently the princes had not the wit to devise any exact system of seniority which should decide every disputed point in their genealogical relations, with the result that there arose two distinct sets of conditions inimical to the smooth working of the rota system of rule. The one set of conditions owed its rise to the results of the system itself, and the other to difficulties purely incidental—difficulties which might have been rendered inoperative if the princes had had the sense to decide their differences in a peaceable manner. Let us examine the principal conditions in each of these two sets.

I. *Riadi (Princely Conventions) and Feuds.*—Disputes arising among the princes as to seniority or the order of rule were decided by one of two methods—namely, either by a *riada* or convention concluded between the disputants in the presence of all the princes assembled in council, or (if no such agreement was arrived at) by a feud or trial of arms. These feuds of the princes belong to the same order of phenomena as *riadi*, and had a juridical origin, seeing that they served the princes as a means of settling their political quarrels in very much the same manner that the *polé*, or legal duel, served private individuals as a means of deciding their civil law-suits. Like the *polé*, also, the feud was known as "the trial of God," and was usually opened with the formula of "God be between us" or "Let us be judged of God." Yet, though its aim (as also that of the *riada*) was rather to re-establish the working of the rota system of rule than to establish a new system in its place, both the *riada* and the feud introduced into the composition of the system certain elements foreign to its nature, since the one method set aside the natural ties of blood kinship in favour of hard and fast bargaining, and the other the moral authority of seniority in favour of armed force. A prince could now acquire seniority, not by right of age or succession, but by inducing or compelling his rival to yield him recognition of his claim. All this resulted in there being added to physical and genealogical seniority a third species—namely, *juridical* seniority ; which, being based either upon concession or upon compulsion, had no real existence in fact, and there-fore was purely arbitrary.

II. *The Theory of the Otchina or Grade of the Father.*—The supreme power was vested in the princely family as a whole, and not in individual members of that family, while the order of seniority in the latter with regard to ascent of sons in the family scale and the rotation of their juris-diction over provinces was based upon repetition by successive generations of the exact relations in which the fathers had stood to one another. Since, then, a son was required (genealogically speaking) to assume the exact place in the chain of relationship which had been filled by his father before him, that place became known as his (the son's) *otchina*.[1] Yet the *otchina*, in this original sense, was a purely mathematical idea, while many causes—divergencies between the order of births and the order of deaths, personal characteristics, and so forth—combined to prevent sons from invariably repeating the exact genealogical order of their fathers : with the result that, according as the original genealogical relations between the sons of the different fathers became more and more complex with each succeeding generation, the sons were forced more and more to change places with one another, and so to follow in quite a different order to that of their fathers. This difficulty caused the *otchina* gradu-ally to acquire another, a territorial, significance. That is to say, a not unnatural transition from the meaning of the father's "place" in the *family* scale to the meaning of the father's "place" in the *scale of provinces*[2] caused the *otchina* to connote *the actual territory* which a given father had ruled. This not only facilitated the distribution of the provinces among the sons, but also served as a reference to which recourse could be had when difficulties arose concerning the genealogical relations of the various sons to one another. In 1097 formal recognition was accorded to this new territorial significance of the *otchina* at a princely council held at Lubiech for the purpose of attempting to put a peaceful end to an old-

[1] From *otets*, father.   [2] *i.e.* the scale of provincial rule.

standing feud between Yaroslav's grandsons and the dispossessed nephews of his two sons, Iziaslav and Vsevolod. In this attempt the council was successful, and it was formally resolved that in future " each do retain his own *otchina*," *i.e.* that each of Yaroslav's grandsons should be left in unmolested possession of the province which had been awarded to the grandson's father by Yaroslav. Thus Kiev became the *otchina* of Sviatopolk, son of Iziaslav ; Tchernigov that of Oleg, son of Sviatoslav; Periaslavl that of Monomakh, son of Vsevolod ; and so on. Yet subsequent events show that the rule thus promulgated by the council had no permanent force, and so did not finally replace the rota system with a system of succession to separate and permanent territorial *otchini*. In short, the rule was limited in its application to the then reigning princes. However, since they were all of them sons of Yaroslav's immediate legatees (*i.e.* Yaroslav's own sons), the repartition of the land among the generation of princes who followed them (its repartition, that is to say, in such a manner that the territorial *otchini* of the inheritors should coincide with their genealogical *otchini*) was. a matter of no difficulty. It was only later that difficulties arose—that genealogical relations began to grow more complex and the princes took to disregarding such relations when it was a question whether a son, or whether some other near relative, should succeed to a given province. The result of it all was that each branch became more and more identified with, and confined to, a particular province, and that each particular province began more and more to be looked upon as the special *otchina* of its own branch. In 1139, for instance, Vsevolod, son of Oleg of Tchernigov, attempted, as Suzerain Prince of Kiev, to induce one of Monomakh's sons to leave his late father's province of Periaslavl for Koursk, but was met with the reply : " I wish rather to die in the *otchina* descended to me from my father and grandfather before me. My father sat not in Koursk, but in Periaslavl, and there I would end my days." It is clear also that more than one attempt was made by Monomakh's line to extend the territorial significance of an *otchina* to Kiev, the senior province. Between the years 1113 and 1139 there succeeded each other upon the Kievan throne Monomakh and his two sons, Mstislav and Yaropolk—thus dispossessing the original lines of Iziaslav and Sviatoslav. As soon, however, as Yaropolk was dead, Vsevolod of Tchernigov, the head of the long dispossessed line of Sviatoslav, sent to the newly-elected Prince, Viatcheslav, third son of Monomakh, who had been invited to assume the throne by the Kievans themselves, a demand that he should withdraw ; whereupon Viatcheslav answered : " I have come hither by the will of the elders of the city and to fill the place of my brethren before me. Nevertheless, if thou dost desire this throne, I will forsake this my *otchina*, and give place unto thee, and yield unto thee Kiev." Again, in 1154, another descendant of Sviatoslav's—Iziaslav, son of Davidoff, whose father had never sat at Kiev—assumed the throne; whereupon the former instance was reversed through Monomakh's son, Yuri Dolgoruki, sending him word to withdraw, saying: "Kiev is *my otchina*, not thine." These instances show us that Monomakh's sons at least *attempted* to convert Kiev into the *otchina* of their line, just as Tchernigov had been converted into that of the line of Sviatoslav. It is clear also that the territorial significance of the term facilitated the question of the distribution of the provinces among the princes on occasions when calculations of relative seniority had become entangled, and that thus a possible political danger was averted, since otherwise the various feuds and jealousies which arose among the princes according as the lines of the princely house diverged might easily have assumed the character of a war of possible dynasties for the possession of the entire country. Given favourable circumstances, any enterprising head of a line might have taken it into his head to "hold of himself the whole Russian land" (as, indeed, it did occur to the Vsevolod above-mentioned), and, having seized Kiev, to reshuffle the provinces among his own immediate kin—provided, that is to say, that the latter did not answer in the words of Monomakh's son : " Our father sat not in Koursk."

In general, then, we see that the main effects of the territorialising of the term *otchina* were to shatter one of the principal bases of the rota system—namely, the *indivisibility* of family rule, and to cause the land to become broken up into a number of genealogical areas governed as inherited patrimonies instead of as provinces succeeded to in order of seniority.

III. *The Displacement of izgoi Princes from the Rota.*—The two generations continuously operative in ordinary human society are fathers and sons, so that the sons of Yaroslav's descendants entered the chain of succession according as their fathers dropped out of it, and occupied places in that chain in the same order as their fathers had done; while grandsons, on the other hand, stepped into their fathers' places only according as those fathers ceased to be sons—*i.e.* according as the *grandfathers* dropped out of the chain. Hence it followed that the political career of a prince was determined by his father's movement in the chain of generations. Now, it did not always happen that the order of births in a family coincided with the order of deaths; with the result that occasionally a prince's father died before the grandfather, and thus left the grandson with no father's place to step into, seeing that the grandfather had never, by dropping out of the chain, enabled the father to enter it.   In such cases the grandson became an *izgoi*, or " orphaned " prince—a perpetually portionless grandson, a genealogical minor.   Possessed of no genealogical *otchina*, he lost also his territorial—*i.e.* he forfeited his right to a place in the rota through having, as it were, missed his turn.   Princes thus prematurely " orphaned," *i.e.* deprived of their father during the lifetime of their grandfather, were provided for by their senior kinsmen, who apportioned them districts in perpetuity without, however, allowing them to participate in the *general family* distribution of rule.   Thus these *izgoi* princes became disjointed fragments of the princely house—such fragments as, in the eleventh century, were represented by Volodar and Vassilko, sons of Yaroslav's grandson Rostislav, to whom were allotted certain townships in Red Russia, and who eventually formed of those townships a separate principality.   Through similar circumstances there arose during the following century the outlying principalities, firstly, of Murom and Riazan—formed of districts originally awarded to the *izgoi* Prince Yaroslav, son of Sviatoslav, and youngest of the princes of Tchernigov; secondly, of Turov and Pinsk on the river Pripet—formed of districts allotted to the *izgoi* line of Sviatopolk, son of Iziaslav and grandson of Yaroslav; and thirdly, of Goroden (Grodno)—formed of territory assigned as a perpetual heritage to the *izgoi* line of Igor, son of Yaroslav, whom we originally saw ruling in Volhynia, and subsequently in Smolensk. All these *izgoi* princes were preceded, in the predicament of dispossessed heirs, by the princes of Polotsk, descendants of St. Vladimir's eldest son by Rognieda—although in this case the princes owed their position, not to the death of their father, but to other and special circumstances. Such displacement of *izgoi* princes from the rota was the natural outcome of the system based upon that rota, and was necessary for its due maintenance ; yet it none the less tended to limit the circle of princes and provinces embraced by the system, and so to introduce into the latter relations foreign and hostile to its nature.   If we glance at the geographical position of the territories which were allotted to *izgoi* princes and so helped to restrict the area of country governed under the rota system, we shall see that all those territories were far removed from the centre of Russian life.   The rota system, while dependent upon the warmth of family feeling for its support, was based also upon the exact correlation of two scales

—the genealogical scale and the territorial; and this correlation was maintained even during the process of its disruption. Consequently, once become (if I may use the term) genealogical terminations, *izgoi* princes were kept at the very foot of the family ladder, at the very furthest point from the titular "father," the Suzerain Prince of Kiev, and allowed to rule only such territorial fragments, such outlying portions of Rus, as lay remote from "the Mother of Russian towns." In short, it was as though the life-blood of clan feeling beat warmly and strongly around the heart of the country, Kiev, but grew weakened and chilled in proportion as it approached the extremities of the land.

These conditions, then, constituted the first of the two sets which, arising out of the bases of the rota system of rule, and serving the princes as their means of supporting that system, tended also to its overthrow. Indeed, in this lay the innate contradiction of the system—that the results of its fundamental principles served both to support it and to dissolve its fundamental principles. In other words, the rota system brought about its own disruption by entailing upon itself consequences of which it could not support the working. But in addition to this set of conditions emanating from the system itself and tending to its disruption there operated a second set of forces—two in number—towards the same end. Let us consider each of them in turn.

I. *Personal Prowess of the Princes.*—It not infrequently happened that notable exploits performed by one prince or another earned for the doer great popularity in Rus, and so facilitated his gathering into his hands more territory than he was entitled to under the rota. For instance, at one period during the twelfth century, well-nigh the whole of Rus was under the sway of Monomakh's line alone, for the reason, in general, that that line was the most wealthy in talents, and, in particular, that one of its members—Monomakh's daring grandson Iziaslav, son of Mstislav, and Prince of Volhynia—had been bold enough to declare a feud against his uncles, to seize their thrones by force and "add them unto his head," in defiance of all seniority, and to continue to hold them as rightful booty of war. It was he, again, who first gave utterance to a view of the rota system which cut right across all established tradition when he said: "A place should not go to a head, but a head to a place"—meaning thereby that an office of state need not necessarily go to a suitable aspirant, but that an aspirant was wise to aim at an office which suited him. By this dictum he placed the personal equation above rights of seniority.

II. *The Chief Towns of Provinces.*—Another influence which inter-
fered with calculations of princely seniority, and so helped still further to
hinder the working of the rota system of rule, was the intervention in
state affairs of chief towns of provinces, upon whose interests the innumerable feuds among the princes to which such calculations gave
rise had a most deleterious effect.   Nevertheless, those towns cherished
their own dynastic sympathies in the feuds, and did not always
accord their sympathies to the rightful prince.   For instance, Monomakh's sons were popular even in towns belonging to their rivals,
the line of Sviatoslav of Tchernigov.   Sometimes the townsmen would
be so carried away by their feelings as to fly straight in the face of
princely calculations and summon to their throne some popular favourite
instead of the prince standing next upon the rota.   This intervention of
the towns in questions of succession—a phenomenon which helped so
much to add to the complexities of seniority—began within a comparatively
short time of Yaroslav's death.   In 1068 we find the Kievans expelling the
then Suzerain Prince, Iziaslav, and replacing him with Vsoslav, one of
the *izgoi* princes of Polotsk, who had previously been thrown into prison
by the direct line.   Again, in 1154 the Kievans invited Rostislav of Smolensk to come and be co-ruler with his uncle, the nominal Suzerain Prince
Viatcheslav—saying to him: "For thy lifetime Kiev is thine"—*i.e.* that
they would recognise him as their prince for life, irrespective of any princes
senior upon the rota.   Novgorod in particular felt the consequences of the
princely feuds, inasmuch as that province was usually ruled by the eldest
son (or, failing him, by the next nearest relative) of the Suzerain Prince,
and so had to suffer a corresponding change of ruler whenever a change
took place at Kiev.   Indeed, the frequency of those changes was so adverse to Novgorod's prosperity that, by the time a sixth change of prince
had occurred there within a period of less than fifty years from the death
of Yaroslav, the citizens began to feel that it would be well for them to
have a permanent prince of their own choosing.   Accordingly in 1102 the
reigning prince there was Monomakh's son Mstislav, who had been selected
for the position when quite a child, and brought up for the purpose.
Monomakh, however, and the then Suzerain Prince of Kiev (Sviatopolk)
took it into their heads to remove Mstislav from Novgorod, and to follow
established tradition with regard to his successor—*i.e.* to replace him with
a son of Sviatopolk himself; but no sooner did they hear of this being
done than the Novgorodians dispatched commissioners to Sviatopolk,
with the message: "Novgorod hath sent us to say this unto thee.   We

desire neither thee nor thy son. Send thy son unto us only if he hath two heads. Already have we Mstislav, given unto us by Vsevolod his grandfather, and reared by us to rule Novgorod." The Suzerain Prince disputed long and earnestly with the commissioners, but they held their ground, and eventually retired in triumph with Mstislav. Thus we see that, although the princes did not always yield implicit deference to the intervention of the great towns, they at least had to reckon with such intervention and its possible consequences.

Now that we have examined the two sets of conditions which militated against the stability of the rota system of rule we are in a better position to answer the question recently propounded in these pages concerning the probable significance of that system—namely, whether it ought to be looked upon as a mere political theory, a mere political ideal, of the princes, or whether it was an actual political order—and, if the latter, to determine what were the extent of its duration and operative force. We now know that the system was both the one and the other— that it was both a political theory and a political actuality, and that for more than a century and a half after the death of Yaroslav it operated always and never—that is to say, always partly, but never in whole, since, although it retained its force (as regards the application of its fundamental principles to the entangled relations of the princes) up to the very end of the twelfth century, it never attained such development, such practical elaboration, as enabled it wholly to disentangle those relations, and thus to obviate all princely disputes. Indeed, it was that very inability of the system to resolve all princely differences that brought about its downfall and mutilation—or at all events its weakening ; with the result that in the working of the rota system we see a continuous process of self-disruption, a continuous struggle against the destructive effect of the system's own results.

Nevertheless, such a phenomenon is not an uncommon one in the history of communities—the phenomenon, that is to say, of a community holding conscientiously to an order of life which it believes to be the right one, yet which serves its interests badly at every step. Yet (the question might be asked) what other system could have been set up in its place in Rus at that period, and could *any* system have been permanently maintained there ? In answering that question we must draw a clear distinction between the order of princely relations and the territorial system of Rus. The territorial system was not dependent upon the princes alone, nor even chiefly upon them, but had its own foundation and supports. In the same way, the order of government maintained by the princes was not wholly the outcome of their own creation, nor could it ever have been so. It was not for that purpose that the Three Princes were summoned, nor for that purpose that they came. What the natives required of them was the help of their swords against external foes, not their capacity for ruling, seeing that there was already established in the country a regular—albeit a multiform—system of local government. It is true that the Princes usurped the *headship* of that system, but the system itself was not of their making, nor, as yet, had their questions of family seniority become so much state relations as a means of attaining equal division of the territorial spoil. It may have been that the long protractedness of their protective functions at length inspired them with the idea that they were natural rulers and lords of the earth, and, as such, entitled to seize the supreme power; but if so, this view of themselves was pure assumption on their part, and neither founded upon right nor consonant with the facts.

CHAPTER VIII

Results of the rota system of rule—Gradual political disintegration of Rus during the twelfth century—Reappearance of the great towns as a political influence—*Vietcha* and their conventions with the princes—The effect of princely relations upon the social order of the country during the twelfth century—The political order during the same period—Rise and growth of a sense of popular unity.

In the last chapter we examined both the social needs and aspirations which evoked and maintained the rota system of rule and the conditions which militated against its working. Let us now study the two series of results which, arising out of the combined action of those adverse conditions, helped to complete the political order established in Rus by the end of the first principal period of our history.

The first of those two series of results was the double political disintegration of Rus—disintegration dynastic and territorial. In proportion as the princes multiplied, so did the various lines of the princely house drift further and further apart and become estranged. First of all, the house of Yaroslav split into two hostile branches—namely, the line of Monomakh and the line of Sviatoslav. Next, the former of those two branches became subdivided into the lines of Iziaslav of Volhynia, of Rostislav of Smolensk, and of Yuri of Suzdal, while the latter line, again, split into those of David of Tchernigov and Oleg of Novgorod-Sieversk.[1] Each of these several lines, become mutually hostile through the working of the rota system of rule, began more and more to assume permanent rule over its particular sphere of influence, until, *pari passu* with the cleavage of the princely house into local branches, the land became divided up into a number of provinces wholly distinct from one another. We have seen that the early princes established the policy of making all the provinces dependent upon Kiev, but with the death of Yaroslav that system began to come to an end. The *posadniki* nominated to the great towns by the Prince of Kiev gave place to an ever-increasing swarm of local or provincial princes, who ceased to pay regular *dan* to the Suzerain, but offered in its place only occasional and voluntary tribute; while, still

---

[1] In the province of Tchernigov—not to be confounded with Novgorod the Great.

114

further to hasten the political disintegration of the Russian land, the division of rule among the several lines of the princely house was accompanied by a sundering of the *territorial* tie which hitherto had bound the various provinces together.

Nevertheless, in proportion as the provincial princes increased their independence from above, they became restricted from below. The continual shifting of rulers from throne to throne and the many quarrels which accompanied that movement all combined to weaken the territorial authority of a prince. Bound to his sphere of rule by no dynastic or personal ties, he came and went so quickly that he represented for his province as much a political accident as a wandering comet represents, for astronomers, a celestial one. Naturally, in time the population began to long for some sedentary authority—some authority around which it could group itself, and which it could look upon as a permanent, not a transitory, force. Such a political force had arisen in Russian history before, and then sunk into abeyance again. That force was the influence of the great towns. It will be remembered that, before the coming of the early princes, the great towns had been rulers of their own provinces, but that with the arrival of the Varangian Vikings the old military administrative boards of those towns—consisting of the wardens, the *tisiatskie*, and the rest—had either become absorbed into the princely retinues or had been left with no practical functions to fulfil. In other words, the military administrative boards had ceased to be elected by the popular voice or to be drawn entirely from the native element, but had become paid official bodies nominated by the Prince and confined exclusively to the class of "prince's men." Now, however, that the authority of the princes was beginning to wane, in consequence of their innumerable feuds and the frequent changes of local ruler, the importance of the great towns began to wax in corresponding proportion, until at length the increased political influence of the towns caused the extinct order of wardens to become replaced by *vietcha* (town councils) representative of the citizens as a whole. These *vietcha*—which the Chronicle describes as appearing for the first time at Kiev and Novgorod in the early eleventh century (or, to be precise, in the year 1015, when Yaroslav was entering upon his struggle with Sviatopolk)—made their voices heard in public affairs with ever-increasing insistence as the century advanced, until, by the opening of the century following, they had come to be a local phenomenon with which the princes had to reckon in all their calculations and to conciliate with *riadi* or conventions. Frequently these conventions defined some point of governmental policy so strictly as to subordinate the prince completely, as regards that particular point, to the *vietché* of his capital town. Such was the convention which the Kievans exacted from Igor of Tchernigov when, in 1146, he was about to assume the throne of Kiev in succession to his brother Vsevolod. The Kievans, it seems, had suffered much at the hands of Vsevolod's local judges or *tiuni;* wherefore, before they would allow Igor to succeed his brother, the townsmen (*i.e.* the local *vietché*) demanded of him an undertaking that he would preside in person over his tribunals, and not delegate the duty to *prikazchiki* or clerks. This undertaking Igor gave, and was then permitted to ascend the throne.

The new order of phenomena represented by these conventions between princes and *vietcha* continued in force throughout the eleventh and twelfth centuries, and introduced into Russian political life an important change—or rather, embodied an important change resulting from the onward march of events. Although the princely house still retained in its hands the monopoly of supreme power and the individual princes continued to hold temporary sway over their provinces in order of seniority, each branch of the princely stock had begun to confine its sphere of rule solely to that part of the country where its influence most lay. The majority of these spheres of influence (or *zemli*[1] as the Chronicle calls them) were identical with the old town-provinces of Kiev, Tchernigov, Periaslavl, Smolensk, Polotsk, Novgorod, and Rostov; while the few that were not so identical, but had been formed at a later period, were the provinces of Volhynia, Galicia, and Murom-Riazan. Of these *zemli*, three—namely, those of Kiev, Periaslavl, and Novgorod— still remained subject to the princely house as a whole, while the remaining seven had become the special spheres of influence of one or another of the separate lines of that house. For instance, Polotsk was the peculiar domain of the line of Vladimir's son Iziaslav; Tchernigov was that of the descendants of Yaroslav's son Sviatoslav; Volhynia, Smolensk, and Rostov were those of Monomakh's posterity; and so with the rest. But princely relations had now ceased to be a matter personal only to the princes themselves, since they had become dependent also upon the goodwill of the capital towns. Even the Suzerain Prince of Kiev retained his throne under him only by keeping on good terms with the local *vietché*, lest his boyars and townsmen should address to him the reminder: "Thou remainest here only so long as thou dost hold with the people of Kiev."

[1] Literally, "lands."

Thus, without entirely overriding the sovereign rights of the princely house, the *vietcha* of the great towns had come to rank at least *equal* in importance with the local princes.

This safeguarding of their political interests by conventions with the princes caused the great towns gradually to become a rival political force to their nominal rulers, and even, towards the end of the twelfth century, to acquire an ascendancy over them. During that period the various provincial communities came more and more to look to the permanent *vietcha* of their capital towns for guidance, and less and less to the temporary local princes who might be in their midst one moment and gone the next. The *vietché* had the advantage of being a single unit, whereas the princes were usually many in number, seeing that an entire *zemlia* was seldom the sphere of one ruler alone, but more often divided up into several minor principalities, according to the number of adult princes included in its particular line. For instance, in the *zemlia* of Tchernigov were included the minor principalities (known locally as *kniazhia volosti* or *kniazhia nadielki*[1]) of Tchernigov itself, Novgorod-Sieversk, Koursk, and Trubtchevsk. Consequently, in proportion as the local *vietcha* and the local princes came into rivalry with one another (to the constant disadvantage of the latter), the great towns and their provinces became more and more politically independent, until, by the end of the twelfth century, the entire Russian land had become split up into a number of local, slenderly-connected district principalities.

Such was the political order described by the Chronicle as becoming established during the latter half of the twelfth century and ousting the rota system of rule. At the same time, that very system, combined with the conditions militating against it, helped to create—or at all events to call into operation—a series of ties which tended to bind the various portions of Rus, if not into a political, at least into a permanent territorial whole. Those ties constitute the second [2] of our two series of results of the rota system of rule, and may be enumerated as follows.

I. First of all we must reckon the influence of the agents who were primarily responsible for the political disintegration of Rus—namely, the princes themselves. Although the populations of the various local principalities might look with indifference upon questions of princely seniority, and feel only weariness at the constant feuds to which those questions gave rise, they at least could not afford to disregard the *consequences* of those feuds, seeing that such consequences were frequently fraught with

---

[1] " Princely districts " or " princely lots." [2] See p. 114.

the gravest of results for the people. Moreover, in spite of the decline of the princes' authority, those nominal rulers still remained identified with many local interests and aspirations which could not but be affected by the feuds, as well as by the political changes which resulted from those contests. Thus the ceaseless migration of princes from province to province brought about a certain interchange of local sympathies and ideas, so that a change of rulers in one part of the country was bound to produce an effect in parts lying altogether remote from the centre of disturbance. For instance, let us suppose that a prince of, say, the line of Monomakh ascended the throne of Kiev. The first thing he would do would be to send his eldest son to rule Novgorod. Arrived there with his boyars and retinue, that son would proceed to allot to his followers all the more important government posts in the province and (as the old annals have it) "*sudi sudit, riadi riadit, vsiakia gramoti zapisivat*—*i.e.* "to hold courts, to conclude conventions, and to sign charters." Next, perhaps, some prince of the line of Tchernigov or Volhynia would oust the Suzerain from Kiev; whereupon the Prince of Novgorod would likewise have to vacate his throne in favour of some newcomer—probably a newcomer hostile to his predecessor. Upon that there would arise for the people of Novgorod the important question as to whether or no the new prince was acquainted with the old customs, the old etiquette and procedure, of the province, or, if he were not, whether he would ever go to the trouble of making himself acquainted with them. As a matter of fact, it frequently happened in such cases that mere hostility to his predecessor led the newcomer to refuse to conform to ancient usage in his manner of "holding courts" and "concluding conventions," and to disregard all "charters" (*i.e.* legal or governmental instruments) which had been signed by the last prince. Thus, by drawing the local life, the local interests, of the various portions of Rus into its revolutions, the maelström of princely succession prevented the provinces from becoming wholly isolated and self-centred. True, they were still far from the point of being animated by a single national spirit, a consciousness of common interests, a realisation of territorial unity; yet they were learning to heed one another's fortunes and to follow with interest events occurring near or at a distance. Thus we see that the rota system of rule was the means of originating a tendency destined, in time, to develop into a consciousness of common material ties binding the whole country into one.

II. A similar part to that of the princes was played, in this connec-

tion, by their boyars and retainers. The more the princely stock multiplied and the fiercer waxed the struggle with the Steppes, the more did
the class of "prince's men" increase in numbers. Although no precise
data are available as to the usual size of a prince's retinue, we know that
the older princes maintained very large courts, and that they were emu-
lated in this respect by the wealthier of their juniors. For instance, we
find Sviatopolk boasting that he possessed five hundred *otroki* (pages)
alone, while in 1208 a single "trial of arms" in Galicia (at that time a
very rich province) accounted for the deaths of as many boyars, not to
speak of those who escaped. Indeed, it was a common thing for the
senior princes or the more wealthy of their juniors to lead into the field
a force of from two to three thousand men-at-arms. Further evidence of
the magnitude of the military-governmental class is to be found in the
fact that every adult prince (and in the latter half of the twelfth century
such princes could be numbered by scores) had his own retinue, whether
a large or a small one. We have seen that in the tenth and eleventh
centuries the military-governmental class was almost wholly Varangian in
composition. With the twelfth century, however, there began to figure in
it many elements other than the native Slavonic or the Russified Varangian—elements drawn from the Polovtsi, Chozars, Ugri, Lechs, Lithuanians, Tchudes, and other races encompassing Rus. The fact of the
princes being transitory, moveable rulers communicated to their boyars a
similar mobility. If the rota of seniority brought about the promotion of
a prince from a poorly endowed throne to a better one, his boyars found
it to their advantage to move with their master; while if, on the other
hand, the issue of a feud compelled that master to vacate a better throne
for a worser one, it was equally to the advantage of his boyars to remain
where they were. Such transference of service from prince to prince was
made easy for the boyar by the unity of the princely stock, while the
unity of the land made it equally possible for him to change his province
as occasion might serve—in both cases without incurring the stigma of
treachery. This power of mobility conferred upon the boyar by the rota
system of rule likewise had the effect of making it difficult for the senior
boyars who held the chief posts of government to continue to occupy
those posts for any great length of time in the same province—still less
to make those posts hereditary, as was done in the feudal West and in
neighbouring Poland. Although the list of boyars mentioned by name in
the Chronicle between the death of Yaroslav and the year 1228 reaches
a total of some hundred-and-fifty, not more than half-a-dozen instances

occur in which the death of a prince left a boyar in the service of his late master's son, or in which a change of princes found a boyar electing to remain in his old province ; while not more than two instances occur in which the important office of *tisiatski*, or military prefect of a provincial capital, was filled by two successive members of one and the same boyar family. It was due also to this power of mobility that the strongest of all ties binding a class to a given locality—namely, the tie of landowner-ship—made such little headway among the official section of the com-munity. Although isolated instances occur of boyars owning estates during the eleventh and twelfth centuries, it is none the less clear that the system developed but slowly among them, and did not constitute their main economic interest. To tell the truth, they preferred other sources of income—the taking of an active share in trading operations, and the receipt of pay at a fixed rate from the princes. We even know exactly what that rate was, since, speaking of times previous to his own day, the compiler of the Chronicle's record for the thirteenth century remarks that a boyar never had to say to his master : " O Prince, I lack two hundred *grivni*." These two-hundred *grivni*, then, must have been the customary amount of a twelfth-century boyar's salary.

III. A third unificatory influence established by the rota system of rule was the prestige which that system conferred upon the city of Kiev. Kiev was the central knot of the tangled skein of princely relations—the point to which the maelström of princely succession tended, and at which it attained its zenith. The amenities of life there, family traditions, the honour inherent in the status of titular "father," the ecclesiastical import-ance of the city—all these things combined to make Kiev the goal of every prince's desire. Never for a moment, as he revolved in the whirl-pool of the provinces, would a young prince take his eyes off the metro-polis, or cease to see it even in his dreams. This yearning of the princes for Kiev finds poignant expression in the prose-poem " *Slovo o polku Igorevè* " ("The story of the expedition of Prince Igor "). In 1068 the Kievans rose against the then Suzerain Prince, Iziaslav, and, expelling him from the city, elected to the throne Vsoslav of Polotsk, who had been cast into prison by his elders. Vsoslav held the throne for seven months only—had hardly touched it, as it were, with the point of his spear before he was forced to return Polotsk : yet all his life long he could never forget Kiev. Whenever (says the *Slovo*) the bells of St. Sophia at Polotsk were ringing to early Mass, the poor dethroned prince would seem to hear in them the bells of St. Sophia at Kiev. This feeling of devotion to the metropolitan city which inspired the princes so passionately was shared also by the populations of even the remotest of their provinces, since the people had now learnt to look upon Kiev as at once the seat of government of the Suzerain Prince, the point of departure for the many doughty expeditions which he sent against the pagans of the Steppes, the *cathedra* of the highest dignitary of the Russian Church, and the depository of that Church's most venerated relics. We find this feeling finely summarised by the author of an ancient Russian hymn where, forgetful for the moment of Jerusalem, he sings : " Kiev, holy Kiev, is the mother of all towns."

IV. While increasing the territorial importance of the chief city of Rus, the rota system of rule contributed also to the advancement of social life and citizenship in even the remotest corners of the land. The more princes entered the field, the more complete did the disintegration of Rus into small principalities become. Every prince, on reaching maturity, was accorded his own particular portion of territory ; with the result that the outlying regions of the country became more and more divided and subdivided up. In each new principality a town would be selected for the local capital, to which would come the newly-created prince and his retinue, and proceed to add to it churches, monasteries, mansions, and a palace—all of them modelled upon Kievan patterns. In this manner there became introduced into the remotest corners of the land certain stereotyped forms, fashions, and settings of life, for which Kiev served as the model, and through which Kiev communicated to the outlying provinces such culture, such social tastes and ideas, learning and art, as were hers. In this manner the rota system of rule caused the princes to contribute largely to the social and intellectual fertilisation of Rus, even as birds of passage contribute, through the medium of chance-dropped seeds, to the physical fertilisation of the soil.

Having now obtained our two mutually antagonistic series of consequences arising out of the conflict between the rota system of rule and the conditions militating against its working, we are in a position to determine the exact nature of the political order of that period, and to assign to it its correct political form in the terminology to which we are accustomed. To the question, then, as to whether Rus of the twelfth century was a single homogeneous state, controlled by a single supreme authority, we can reply that, although such an authority certainly existed in the land, it was neither a monarchical nor an autocratic power, but, on the contrary, one of only very conditional, limited importance. The princes were not plenipotentiary lords of the country, but its military protectors and administrators ; being recognised as the wielders of the supreme power only so long as they proved themselves capable of repelling external foes and maintaining internal order. Only within those limits could they legislate. Likewise, it was not for them to found a new territorial system, seeing that the necessary plenipotentiary powers for doing so were not theirs through existing laws, nor were likely to be conferred upon them in the future. Certainly, the princes introduced not a little that was new into the inter-territorial relations of Rus, but this they effected rather through standing by and allowing events to take their course than through any actual exercise of authority ; while, although the new element which they caused to be introduced into inter-territorial relations caused them, in their turn, to become the prime instrument in the unification of the country, that element owed its introduction less to their actual authority than to the reaction against it—*i.e.* to the intervention of the great towns. In short, the prime agency responsible for the conversion of Vladimir's posterity into a dynasty and for investing the paid guardians of Rus with a monopoly of hereditary administrative power was the mere natural sequence of princely generations—that, and no more ; and although this simple fact never received formal recognition from the country, the reason was that the country had no machinery at its disposal for doing so. When changes of provincial rulers occurred it was with the princes separately, and not with the princely house as a whole, that the great towns opened negotiations.

Thus we see in opposition to one another two antagonistic forces—the unity of the princely house and the disintegration of the country into politically distinct provinces. At the first glance, Rus of those days would appear to have been a territorial federation—a union of self-governing provinces or *zemli ;* yet the only real political bond uniting the various portions of the land was the princely house. Even the very unity of that house did not constitute a state institution, but only a natural fact—a fact to which the country was, if anything, indifferent, or even actively opposed. Indeed, the essential difference between Rus of the twelfth century and a federation lay in the fact that, whereas the latter order of union is based upon a definite political agreement, the system of collective princely rule which obtained in Rus had for its base only the factor of its origin—a genealogical, not a political factor, and that, while entailing upon the princes general solidarity of action, this factor provided them with no fixed rules of procedure nor any definite system of inter-princely relations. Moreover, a federation needs to contain federal sources of power capable of making their influence felt in every quarter of the federated territory; whereas, although Rus of the twelfth century possessed two such potential sources —namely, the Suzerain Prince and the princely council, the authority of the former was based only upon a genealogical fact, not upon a constitutional agreement, and so, being neither exactly defined nor securely confirmed, had no sufficient means of working, was in process of becoming converted into a purely honorary distinction, and never at any time possessed aught but a very conditional importance, seeing that the junior princes considered themselves entirely at liberty to oppose their Suzerain whenever they held his action to be irregular or non-paternal. The same with the authority of the princely council. Though convened at intervals by the Suzerain Prince for the purpose of debating questions of legislation, seniority, or defence, the princely council never succeeded either in uniting all the princes or in having the binding force of its decisions defined. For instance, at a council held at Vitichev in the year 1100, the cousins Sviato-polk, Monomakh, David, and Oleg (all of them of the line of Sviatoslav) decided to punish David of Volhynia for blinding Vassilko of Terebovl, and to relieve the latter of his province, on the ground that he was no longer fitted to govern it. Not only, however, did Rostislav's two sons, Volodar and Vassilko, refuse to recognise this decision, but, upon some of the senior princes proposing to compel them to do so by force of arms, Monomakh—the most prominent of those who had been present at the council—declined to join in the expedition, saying that he recognised the right of Rostislav's sons to disregard the council's authority, seeing that, by a former council held at Lubiech in 1097, Terebovl had been confirmed to Vassilko in perpetuity.

Thus we see that neither the authority of the Suzerain Prince nor the authority of the princely council communicated to the Russian land the character of a homogeneous state, of a political federation in the strict sense of the term, but that the country represented an aggregation of provinces united only through their princes. In other words, it was a genealogical, not a political, federation—a union based upon the mere fact of the kinship of its rulers and neither voluntary in its origin nor binding in its action. In fact, it represented one of those social constitutions peculiar to the middle ages in which political relations arose out of private rights. Yet the land was not divided into portions wholly and absolutely distinct from one another, for there were not a few ties tending to bind it into a homogeneous whole: *only*, those ties were not political bonds, but ties racial, social, religious, and economic. That is to say, there was no unity of *state*—only a unity of territory and population, the threads of which were woven, not of laws nor statutes, but of such interests, customs, and social relations as, later, became crystallised into laws and statutes. These connecting ties—these interests, customs, and social relations—were constituted (to recapitulate them once more), firstly, of the consciousness of common needs and aspirations which the working of the rota system of rule engendered in the provinces; secondly, of the pan-territorial character conferred upon the two upper classes of the community (the clergy and the boyars) through the same agency; thirdly, of the pan-territorial importance of Kiev as the common focus of the industrial and the religious life of the country; and fourthly, of the homogeneity of the forms and settings of life which the working of the rota system of rule caused to be introduced into every quarter of the Russian land.

Thus we see that the second of our two sets of results of the rota system constituted, in its entirety, the awakening in the Russian community of a feeling of popular, as well as of territorial, unity: and it is in that fact, perhaps, that we must seek an explanation of the peculiar footing upon which both our people and our historical literature have always stood towards the Rus of Kievan days. Russian historians and the Russian population generally have never failed to treat the memory of bygone Kiev with a sympathy hard to understand when we consider the chaotic impression produced upon the mind by a study of its greatest period. Not only are there few traces of Kievan Rus and its conditions of life to be found now surviving in our land, but one would naturally suppose that the traditions of Kiev itself, with its incessant turmoil, its never-ending princely feuds, and its struggle with the pagans of the Steppes, would have left anything but a grateful impression upon the popular mind. Yet many a poetical and religious legend has been preserved concerning the ancient seat of St. Vladimir, including the proverb that, as to Rome, all roads lead to Kiev. The Russian nation still knows and remembers the city of princes and heroes, of the Cathedral of St. Sophia and the Cloister of Petcherski, and loves and reverences its memory above that of any of the subsequent capitals of the land. Vladimir on the Kliazma has long ago been forgotten of the people, to whom it was never really known. Moscow only oppressed the people, and so was feared and respected, but not loved. As for St. Petersburg, it is neither feared nor respected nor loved. On the other hand, Kiev, with all its faults and failings, has never lost its hold upon the popular affections, and historians, whatever their school, have always agreed in painting the bygone life of the city in the brightest of colours. Why is this? I will proceed to show the reason.

Ancient Kievan life connoted much that was stupid, unnecessary, and violent—much of what Karamzin calls "the senseless brawlings of the princes." To the common people those feuds meant loss only, so that, although we, as observers of a later day, derive a certain æsthetic pleasure from contemplating the din and bustle arising out of the play of clan—or rather, of genealogical—feeling among the princes, as well as out of their passionate longing "to acquire for themselves glory or to yield their lives for the Russian land," the general mass of the population cherished altogether different feelings towards what we look upon as the fascinating life and movement of the tempestuous eleventh and twelfth centuries. Nor can the principal actors in the drama[1] have taken the same view of it as we do. Hemmed in by an ever-increasing host of difficulties and dangers, internal and external, they began to become more and more sensible that those difficulties and dangers were not to be combated by isolated local efforts alone, but that the whole community must be brought to co-operate in the task. Under Yaroslav and Monomakh that task was fairly easy to accomplish, since those two Princes were rulers sufficiently strong to enlist the resources of the entire country ; but with Monomakh's departure from the scene there came a time when his less virile descendants were so hopelessly involved in a maze of conflicting interests and relations that the community awoke to the fact that it must solve its own difficulties and undertake its own defence. In devising means to this end the inhabitant of Kiev was brought to think more and more of the dweller in Tchernigov, the dweller in Tchernigov of the citizen of Novgorod, and all three of them of the Russian land—of a common territorial cause. This awakening in the community at large of a solicitude for the Russian land as a whole, this birth of a common territorial cause which it was incumbent upon each man to support, constituted the fundamental factor of this particular period—the factor to which were directed all the otherwise heterogeneous, divergent, and often mutually antagonistic aspirations of boyars, clergy, capital towns, and other social forces of the day. Now, an historical epoch in which a people at large takes an active and extensive share in public affairs, so that it realises itself to be a complete entity, as well as an entity that is working for a common cause, invariably leaves a deep-cut and lasting impression upon the tablets of the popular memory ; while the ruling ideas and sentiments which that people cherishes during

[1] *i.e.* the princes.

the given epoch usually find expression in phrases recurring with sufficient frequency to become stereotyped.   Such a phrase was the term " *Russkaia zemlia* "—" the Russian land "—which we find forever in the mouths of princes and chroniclers during the eleventh and twelfth centuries, and which may be taking as summarising the chief historical factor emerging from that period of our history—the factor that, although the Russian land, of which the various ethnographical elements were first of all mechanically mixed and then politically compounded by the early Kievan princes, was now in process of losing its political unity again, it was also awakening to a consciousness of itself as a complete popular entity.   This, then, is the reason why subsequent generations have always revered the memory of Kiev : for Kievan Rus was the cradle of Russian nationality.

Of course, no direct evidence of this factor can be adduced from any particular passage in any one of our ancient annals ; yet it creeps in everywhere—appears in every manifestation of the spirit and tendency of the age.   Take, for example, the early twelfth-century story of Daniel Polomnik's [1] presentation of a Russian lamp to Our Lord's Tomb in Jerusalem.   Approaching King Baldwin with a request for the necessary permission, he was kindly received by that monarch, who had known Daniel of old, and was, moreover, a good-hearted and peace-loving man. " What needest thou of me, O monk of Rus ? " asked the King.   " O Prince and Master," answered Daniel, " I do but seek to set a lamp upon the Tomb of Our Lord, in the name of all Rus, and of all her princes, and of all Christian people in her land."   This is the more striking an instance in view of the fact that the course of public affairs had caused Daniel's province of Tchernigov to be one of the first to become politically distinct from the other provinces, while the character and external policy of its princes had afforded even less encouragement to sentiments of Russian territorial unity than had been the case under other provincial rulers. Nor does any hint of those obstacles to pan-territorial sentiment appear in the *Slovo o polku Igorevê*, although the author of it, like Daniel, hailed from the province of Tchernigov—being a member of the princely retinue there.   Indeed, the whole poem is inspired by a sense of the territorial unity of Rus, and takes but little account of local sympathies and aspirations.   For instance, as the contingents from Novgorod-Sieversk and Koursk are setting forth to do battle with the hosts of the Steppes,[2] the *Slovo* exclaims : " O *Russian land*" (not " O province of Tchernigov "), " already art thou sinking behind thy hills ! "   Again, it calls the local forces

---

[1] =Daniel the Pilgrim.   [2] In this case the Polovtsi.

Russian regiments, speaks of their subsequent defeat as a sacrifice for *the Russian land*, and applies the same pan-territorial term to the region where widespread grief followed upon the news of the disaster. Nor is it only upon his own princes—upon the rulers of Tchernigov, the line of Sviatoslav— that this poet of Novgorod-Sieversk calls to take vengeance for "this dis- grace to our times and to *the Russian land*." No ; he extends his appeal also to the widely-distributed line of Monomakh—to Vsevolod of Suzdal, and to Rurik and David of Smolensk, and to Roman of Volhynia. Yet, although the term "the Russian land" has now become so prevalent, of the term "the Russian *people*" there occurs, as yet, not a single instance. Of all the elements entering into the composition of a state, the one most readily intelligible to the popular mind, the one which has always most served to determine nationality, is *territory*. For the time being, there- fore, the feeling of popular unity expressed itself only in the idea of a common *fatherland*, not in a consciousness of national character or of an historical destiny, nor yet in a conception of duty to the public weal. Yet that a dim idea of responsibility towards fatherland had already arisen in Rus seems evident from the fact that at the council held at Lubiech in 1097 we find the princes clinching an oath which they had sworn with the following curse upon whomsoever should break it : "Upon him be the Holy Cross and the whole Russian land !"

CHAPTER IX

The civil order in Rus during the eleventh and twelfth centuries—The *Russkaia Pravda* as a guide to that order—The two views taken of the Code—Its origin and genesis—Its monetary reckoning—Its sources—Russian law, and enactments of the princes—Judicial decrees of the princes and of the Church—Supplementary sources drawn upon by the codifiers of the *Russkaia Pravda*.

WE have now studied the political order obtaining in Rus during the eleventh and twelfth centuries, and must next turn our attention to a more intimate sphere of life—to the *civil* order of the period, the daily private relations between individuals, the interests and ideas by which those relations were governed and confirmed.

First of all, let me outline the personal-juridical side of the civil order of the time. Hitherto an idea has always been prevalent in our historical literature that the private juridical life of ancient Rus is to be found most fully and faithfully expressed in the *Russkaia Pravda*—our oldest legal code. Yet, before making use of that code as a mirror of observation, we should do well to examine how far it is altogether reliable in this respect: for which purpose let us take, first of all, its origin and genesis, and thereafter its composition.

Two views obtain as to the origin of the *Russkaia Pravda*. Some observers see in the Code, not an official document come straight from the hand of the legislator, but a private summary of jurisprudence compiled by some old-time Russian lawyer or lawyers for his or their own particular use. Others, on the contrary, believe it to be, not only an official document, but the actual text of its original author—though corrupted in places through that repeated process of copying which (as in the case of the Ancient Chronicle) has given rise to different versions of the same work.

In the older of these versions we see, from a heading prefixed to the first article, that the Code purports to be the "judgment" or "ordinance" of Yaroslav, while in more than one subsequent article we come across a statement that Yaroslav "did thus judge" or "did thus ordain." The first conclusion which might be drawn from this is that the *Russkaia*

Pravda represents a code compiled solely and personally by Yaroslav for the guidance of his tribunals, more especially since certain of our other ancient annals append to his name the title of "Pravosud," or "the Judge," and state that he was a framer of laws. Yet, if we look more closely into it, we shall see that it contains evidence altogether rebutting this conclusion, as follows :—

I. In the Code we come across ordinances made by Yaroslav's *successors, i.e.* by his sons and his grandson Monomakh, to the latter of whom, in particular, must be assigned a law against usury. This alone shows that the Code was not the sole work of Yaroslav.

II. The text of some of the articles clearly does not give the original wording of the lawgiver, but, in its place, some explanation or paraphrase of an annalist who is describing how the given law came to be framed. This is the case with the second article of the Code, which is really an addendum—or, more correctly speaking, an amendment—to the first article treating of "vengeance for murder."[1] This second article says: "When Yaroslav was dead, his sons Iziaslav, Sviatoslav, and Vsevolod did assemble in council with their retinues, and did abolish vengeance for murder; but all else that Yaroslav had ordained did his sons confirm." Of course, this is not the text of a law at all, whether by Yaroslav or any one else, but either an annotation on the part of some one or a part of the minutes of the princely council.

III. No reference whatever is made in the Code to a well-known form of old Russian legal procedure, namely, the *polé* or legal duel. Yet we know from other sources that the *polé* was in force both before the period of the Code and for a long while after it. For instance, Leo the Deacon (a Byzantine writer of the tenth century) says, in his account of Sviatoslav's expedition against the Bolgars, that the Russians of his (Sviatoslav's) day were wont to settle their private differences "by blood and slaying." Of course, this rather ambiguous term might be taken as referring to the vendetta, were it not that we have confirmatory evidence of the *polé* from a contemporary of Leo's, namely, the Arabic writer Ibn Dasta, who gives an account of the legal duel as practised in the early tenth century. According to him, any one in dispute with another man might summon his opponent before the Prince's court, where the arguments on both sides would be expounded and the matter adjudicated upon by the Prince in person. Should, however, both sides be found unwilling

---

[1] This law allowed the near relatives of a murdered person to seek out and kill the murderer.

to accept the Prince's decision, then the final issue was left to the arbitrament of arms, and he who wielded the more cunning blade won the suit. Thus there can be no doubt that the *polé* had a place in Russian legal procedure long before the days of the *Russkaia Pravda*, while there is evidence also to show that it was practised as long *after* that period as the beginning of the thirteenth century. How is it, then, that the *Russkaia Pravda* came to take no cognisance of this most important and very largely utilised resource? The answer to that question is that, although the *Pravda* knew of the *polé*, it purposely ignored its existence, for the reason that the clergy (who formed a considerable proportion of the ruling class) stoutly opposed the legal duel as a relic of paganism, and even ordained ecclesiastical penalties against any one who should practise it. Nevertheless, although their efforts in this direction did not meet with entire success until fully the end of the sixteenth century, the solidarity between their ideas and those of the *Russkaia Pravda* should be carefully noted.

IV. Although several versions of the Code are extant, the principal ones number only two, and are known as the full version and the short version respectively. Of these, the former made its appearance earliest in our literature, for we meet with it in a Novgorodian *Kormtchaia*[1] of the end of the thirteenth century, whereas of the short version no earlier example is known than that contained in a fifteenth-century copy of the Chronicle of Novgorod. Moreover, the full version of the *Pravda* is always to be found in what might be termed the same circle, the same company, while the short version usually makes its appearance in works of a purely literary character and possessed of no practical legal value, more especially in copies of the oldest version of the Chronicle of Novgorod. The company most affected by the full version is that of the ancient *Kormtchi*, but it also consorts, on occasions, with the series of canonical manuals known under the collective name of the "*Mierilo Pravednoye*," or "Standard of Righteousness." Of the chief members of this ecclesiastical circle in which the full version of the *Pravda* lived and moved and had its being I will give a brief summary.

The old Novgorodian *Kormtchaia* above referred to as the first work to introduce the full version of the *Pravda* to our literature is a Slavonic translation of the Byzantine "Nomocanon" or "Digest of Canon Laws (κανόνες) and Imperial Laws (νόμοι) affecting the Church"—an authority by which the Church in Rus was wholly guided in those days (as, to a

---

[1] An ancient compendium of Russian ecclesiastical law.

certain extent, the Russian Church is to-day) as regards its internal administration in general and its spiritual jurisdiction in particular. This *Kormtchaia* is always to be found bound up with a series of treatises supplementary to its second portion—the portion which treats of the Imperial laws. Chief among those treatises are, firstly, an abstract of the Law of Moses; secondly, an Eclogue ("'Εκλογὴ τῶν νόμων" or "Selection of Laws")—a digest compiled in the early eighth century under the direction of the Iconoclastic co-Emperors Leo the Isaurian and his son Constantine Copronymus, and containing a number of ordinances relating to family and civil law, as well as an addendum concerning penalties for criminal offences; thirdly, a treatise known alternatively as "*Zakon Sudni Liudem*" ("A Law for the Judging of the People") and "Constantine's *Sudebnik*"[1]—a Slavonic rendering of the penalties enacted in the above Eclogue, but of earlier appearance in our literature than the original, and purporting to have been drawn up for the use of the Bolgars shortly after their conversion to Christianity in the ninth century; fourthly, the *Procheiron* ("'O πρόχειρος νόμος" according to its Greek title, "*Zakon Gradski*" according to its Russian, and "*Jus Civile*" according to its Latin)—a legal digest compiled by the Byzantine Emperor Basil the Macedonian in the same century; and fifthly, a summary or extract of the Church ordinances made by our first two Christian princes, Vladimir and Yaroslav. It is with one or other of these works that the full version of the *Russkaia Pravda* always appears; so that it cannot be looked upon as an independent memorial of bygone Rus, but merely as a supplement to this, that, or the other work on ecclesiastical law.

V. Examination of these supplementary treatises of Byzantine-ecclesiastical origin reveals to us a certain connection between them and the *Russkaia Pravda*, seeing that some of the latter's articles seem undoubtedly to have been framed with the help of the former. For instance, in the abstract of the Law of Moses we find a clause relating to robbery by night which reads thus in the Book of Exodus: "If a thief be found breaking up, and be smitten that he die, there shall no blood be shed for him. If the sun be risen upon him, there shall be blood shed for him." Of course, the meaning of this is, that if a thief should be caught between sunset and sunrise it would be no murder to kill him; but if, on the other hand, he should be caught between sunrise and sunset the act of killing him would become murder, and the doer of that act would himself have to suffer the penalty of death. Now, in the *Pravda* we find a clause on

---

[1] Code of law.

the same subject, but reading thus: " Whoso shall be found by night in a storehouse or doing a deed of pillage, the same shall be slain as a dog; but if he be taken and held until sunrise, then shall he be brought before the Prince's court for judgment. Howbeit, if he hath been slain after that witnesses have beheld him bound, then for his slaying shall there be paid a mulct of twelve *grivni.*" The connection between these two ordinances will be apparent, save that that of Moses has become Russified in the *Pravda* to the extent of being adapted to local conditions and recast in native forms of expression. Take another example. In both the Eclogue and the *Procheiron* we find a short clause that " a slave shall not bear witness." Now, in addition to absolute slaves, there existed in ancient Rus a class of semi-slaves, known as *zakupi,* concerning whose qualification to testify before a legal tribunal we find, in the *Pravda,* the following clause: " No slave shall bear witness, and if there be not freedmen to hand, then shall there be summoned to testify a boyar or a *tiun,*[1] but in no case a simple slave. Howbeit, in a suit of lesser sort, and if the need be instant, there shall be summoned to bear witness a *zakup.*" In this we see another instance of the adaptation of ancient law to later Russian conditions, as well as of the Russification of its phraseology. Again, we find among the articles of the *Zakon Sudni Liudem* an ordinance dealing with the offence of mounting another man's horse without permission from the owner. " Whoso shall, unbidden, seat himself upon the horse of another, he shall receive three strokes." This ordinance is reproduced *verbatim* in the *Pravda,* except that for " strokes" is substituted " *grivni.*" Evidently Rus in the days of the *Pravda* was averse to corporal punishment. Finally, the *Zakon Sudni Liudem* contains an ordinance (borrowed, in its turn, either from the Eclogue or from the *Procheiron*) relating to a slave who should commit a robbery " abroad"—*i.e.* not upon the premises of his master. If, in such a case, the master still wished to retain the dishonest slave in his service, he was bound to compensate the complainant; but if he no longer wished to retain the culprit, the latter became the absolute property of the person whom he had robbed. Now, although we find a very similar enactment in the *Pravda,* it binds the master to compensate the complainant in *any* case; in addition to which, certain regulations are added for dealing with the culprit's family or with any freeman or freemen inculpated in the same offence. Thus we see that, although they did not always borrow *verbatim* from the compendia of ecclesiastical law above-mentioned, the compilers of the *Russkaia Pravda*

[1] Local magistrate.

took them as a guide both in selecting such *casus* as seemed to them to call for legal specification and in determining questions of law to which an answer was lacking in our native jurisprudence.

This process of examination of the *Russkaia Pravda* throws a certain light upon its origin. We have seen that the Code was not the work of Yaroslav alone, but that its composition was continued into the twelfth century—long after his death ; that it does not always present us with the original or exact text of a given law, but, in its place, with a mere explanation or paraphrase of that law ; that it ignores the legal duel which undoubtedly was practised in Rus throughout the eleventh and twelfth centuries, despite the Church's ban ; that it is not an independent code, but a complementary portion of a *Kormtchaia* or compendium of Canon law ; and that its composition was largely influenced by those digests of Byzantine ecclesiastical jurisprudence amid which it usually makes its appearance. To what conclusion, then, does this lead? To, in my opinion, the conclusion that the text of the *Pravda*, as we now read it, was inspired, not in princely circles, but in ecclesiastical—in those circles, in fact, with whose aims and requirements the compilers of the Code were best acquainted and the most sympathetic. That would account for the ignoring of the legal duel, as also for the fact that no reference is made in the Code to political offences, to offences against women and children, or to offences of the tongue. Of these transgressions, political offences would not be subject to ecclesiastical jurisdiction at all, while the other two classes of misdemeanour would be subject only to *special* ecclesiastical courts, not to Church discipline in general. On the other hand, the princely courts existing before the middle of the eleventh century had no need of a written code to guide them, seeing that, in the first place, the old system, based upon legal custom, by which the Prince and his judges had always hitherto been influenced in their dispensation of justice still held good ; that, in the second place, the process of law most generally in force at that time was the argumentative process or *priá*,[1] so that, if the court had forgotten, or chose not to remember, a given legal custom, it was sure to be reminded of it by one or both of the contending parties, who conducted their case in person, and between whom the court adjudicated rather as an impartial president or passive spectator of the proceedings than as a tribunal having any authority in the matter ; and that, in the third place, the Prince, as supreme legislator, could always, at

[1] = contention or argument.

a pinch, make good his legal memory, or decide some doubtful point, by the simple expedient of making a new law out of hand.

Yet, although the princely courts might contrive to do without a written code up to the middle or end of the eleventh century, such a source of reference was absolutely indispensable to the ecclesiastical tribunals. With the adoption of Christianity by Rus, the Russian Church became invested with a dual jurisdiction, for not only did it acquire authority in *some* spiritual matters over *all* Christians in Rus, but likewise authority in *all* matters over *some* Christians in the land—the latter section of inhabitants constituting a distinct ecclesiastical community of which we shall presently see the composition. The ecclesiastical court for spiritual matters extended its jurisdiction to all Christians, and based its procedure upon the Byzantine *Nomocanon* and the Church ordinances enacted by the first two Christian princes of Rus, while the ecclesiastical court for civil and criminal matters extended its jurisdiction only to the particular section of inhabitants named above,[1] and perforce based its procedure upon the native local laws of the country. It was this latter necessity, indeed, which first gave rise to that demand for a written code of law which resulted in the appearance of the *Russkaia Pravda*. Two causes contributed to that demand—namely (1) the fact that the first ecclesiastical courts of Rus had no previous knowledge of old Russian legal customs, and (2) the circumstance that those courts soon began to feel the lack of a digest of native law which should supersede, or at all events mitigate, certain indigenous legal customs which offended the moral and legal sensibilities of the new Christian judges—all of whom had been brought up on the civil and ecclesiastical jurisprudence of Byzantium. That the *Russkaia Pravda* emanated from circles familiar with Byzantine and Southern Slavonic law is shown by its very terminology, since we meet in it with words altogether foreign to the Russian tongue, but derived rather from the Greek and Southern Slavonic languages. Of the former an instance is to be found in the term *bratutchado*—a clumsy Russism representing the Greek ἀδελφόπαις or cousin, and, of the latter, in the word *vrazhda*, which signified, in the old Southern Slavonic dialect, either penalty for murder or any legal process in general. Finally, the *Pravda* shows its connection with Byzantine jurisprudence by its *form*, since it is a small code of the synoptical species which, at the period in question, was understood by Byzantine ecclesiastical jurisprudents alone.

The basic forms of jurisprudence are two—namely, legal custom and

---

[1] Namely, the ecclesiastical community.

law. Of these, legal custom is the natural, original form in which all jurisprudence is cast during the early stages of social life. It is a form gradually evolved through continuous adaptation to individual circumstances and relations of life of rules elaborated by the popular juridical instinct working under the influence of historical conditions. In time, consonance with the moral and juridical conceptions of a given people combines with continuity of action to communicate to those rules that physiologico-obligatory force of custom which we call tradition. On the other hand, law connotes rules established by some supreme governing authority for the satisfaction of the current needs of a given state—rules which the pressure of those needs endows with an obligatory force, to which the governing authority contributes with all the means at its disposal. Law, therefore, comes later than legal custom, and, while primarily only complementary to, or directory of, the latter, begins gradually to supersede it, and to replace it with fresh jurisprudential rules. *Codification* of law comes later still, and usually combines within itself, as well as with one another, the two foregoing forms of juridical obligation. Nevertheless it is a process which, in its usual acceptation, establishes no new juridical norms, but merely reduces to a system such rules as have become established already through legal custom or through law, and adapts them to the changing manners and juridical conceptions of the people or to the needs of the state. Yet that very process of regulation and adaptation of existing norms insensibly leads the way to a change in them, and so to the introduction of new jurisprudence. For example, it was Roman tradition which first gave rise, in Byzantium, to a new system of codification—the system already referred to as the synoptical form : yet that form, the original model of which was taken from the Institutes of Justinian, became improved upon at a later date in two of the manuals which usually accompany the *Russkaia Pravda* in the pages of the *Kormtchaia*—namely, the Eclogue and the *Procheiron*. The synoptical form of codification consists of short, systematic expositions of law which are the productions rather of legal erudition than of legal elaboration—explanations of jurisprudence rather than aids to its mental assimilation. The headings or titles of the articles into which such codes are divided read like the theses of a course of readings in civil law, while, in addition to the textual portions (emanating from the original legislative authority), we find included in the type further explanatory or complementary summaries of the contents of the various portions. Such complementary summaries were the rule among the Greeks during the eleventh and twelfth centuries—the period when the codification of the *Pravda* was in process in Rus on Byzantine lines: which furnishes us with additional evidence that, although it was the needs of the local ecclesiastical courts which first caused the work to be undertaken, it was the Byzantine method of codification which gradually imparted to that work its scriptory form and character. The result was the *Russkaia Pravda*—an attempt on the part of the Church to compile a general standard code of jurisprudence which should reconcile local legal customs and laws with ecclesiastical ideas and relations. I repeat, therefore, that, in my opinion, our primal digest of Russian law originated, not in the civil sphere of ancient Russian life, but in the ecclesiastical.

We are now in a position to answer the question first propounded when we began our study of this Code—namely, whether the Code was an official production, the work of the princely legislative power, or whether it was a private digest devoid either of official origin or obligatory force. It was neither the one nor the other. Although it did not emanate from the princely legislative power, it likewise did not remain a private digest of law, but acquired an obligatory force over at least one section of the Russian community—namely, the section subject to ecclesiastical authority in non-ecclesiastical matters—and was to that extent recognised by the princes themselves. Moreover, we may reasonably suppose that, in time, the operation of the *Pravda* passed beyond the limits of ecclesiastical jurisdiction. Up to the middle of the eleventh century, old-established legal custom made it possible for the princely courts to dispense with any written code of law; but after that point, advancement in civil conditions, together with the introduction both of Christianity and a Byzantine ecclesiastical jurisprudence strange to Rus and to all her hitherto accepted ideas and relations gradually brought about a weakening of native legal custom and a throwing into confusion of the juridical memory of the courts. At every step a judge found himself confronted with questions to which he could discover no answer in ancient native custom, nor yet a means of extracting one, even by the utmost stretch of reasoning. This was bound, sooner or later, to call forth in judicial circles a demand for a written exposition of the then existing judicial system, but one, of course, adapted to the changed position of affairs. The *Russkaia Pravda* solved the difficulty to a large extent, for it furnished answers to many of the new questions of law and, moreover, endeavoured to adapt itself to the new ideas and relations now obtaining. In fact, in my opinion, although the Code was binding only in the realm of ecclesiastical jurisdiction, it gradually came to serve also as a guide for the princely courts—not as carrying any authority, but as an aid to the elucidation of the existing civil law.   Thus we are entitled to look upon the *Pravda* as an example of old Russian *codification*, but not of old Russian *legislation;* and it is in this fact, perhaps, that an explanation must be sought of the surprising circumstance that, while its norms were taken from many different works bearing on civil and ecclesiastical law, we find those works nowhere cited in the Code itself as the sources upon which it drew.

At what period, then, was the task of codification performed?   An answer to that question is imperative if we are to complete what has been said concerning the origin of the *Pravda*.   In the old Chronicle of Novgorod we read that in 1016, when Yaroslav was dismissing to their homes those Novgorodians who had helped him in his struggle with Sviatopolk, he "gave unto them a law" and "signed unto them an ordinance," with the words: "Walk ye by this, and maintain that which I now sign unto you"—a charge which we find immediately followed in the Chronicle by a copy of the short version of the *Russkaia Pravda*, together with the ordinances added to it by Yaroslav's sons.   In all probability, however, this introductory episode or tradition was invented merely as an excuse for inserting the version in question under that particular year (1016).   We may therefore ignore it.   Apart from that, we know that Vladimir Monomakh introduced into the Code an ordinance against usury, and that, consequently, the *Pravda* was still in process of composition in the early twelfth century ; but inasmuch as this particular ordinance does not appear in the short version, it follows that the latter must have been composed *before* Monomakh's time—*i.e.* at a date not later than the *beginning* of that century.   As for the date when the full version—the complete form of the *Pravda*—assumed final shape, I propose to show, from the monetary reckoning observed in the Code, that that date should be assigned to some period during the latter half of the same century, or else to the beginning of the thirteenth.

As we have seen, the penalties enacted by the *Pravda* for civil and criminal offences were chiefly *pecuniary* penalties, and were reckoned in *grivni kūn* and fractions of the same.   Until the German term *phūnt* made its appearance in our language (itself derived from the Latin *pondus* or "weight") the *grivna* represented in Rus a pound's-weight, while *kuni* (*kūn* as printed above is the genitive plural) represented money in general, since our present word *dengi* is of Tartar origin, and dates only from the thirteenth century. A *grivna kūn*, then, was a pound's-weight of money, and took the form of an ingot of varying shape, but usually oblong. Up to the introduction of the rouble—*i.e.* up to the fourteenth century, or rather earlier—such ingots or *grivni* served as the highest medium of exchange in the Russian market, and were divided into twenty *nogati*, twenty-five *kuni*, or fifty *riezani*—the *riezana*, again, being subdivided into *vekshi*, though how many is not certain. Neither have we any exact knowledge as to what furs were represented by these several units—all that we know being that they did represent monetary values in furs, and that *kuni* in particular also stood for *all* furs passing from hand to hand in the market as currency. At the same time, metallic currency made its appearance in Russian trade at an early date, for, as already described,[1] a large number of "hoards" of Arabic *dirgems* of the eighth, ninth, and tenth centuries have been discovered, and are still being so, in various regions of European Russia. The "hoards" thus found are, for the most part, small ones, containing only about a pound's-weight of silver—such "hoards" as that found at Murom (which amounted to more than two pound's-weight of metal, or over eleven thousand coins) being a great rarity. It is likewise a curious fact that the majority of such "hoards" comprise, besides whole *dirgems*, a number of broken pieces— halves, quarters, and even smaller fractions of those coins. For instance, in a "hoard" of tenth-century *dirgems* discovered at Riazan there were unearthed only fifteen whole coins, but nearly nine hundred pieces, the smallest of which were equal to about a fortieth part of a *dirgem*. This can only mean that the people of Rus clipped and cut up the coins to serve as small change, for the native coin, the Russian *srebrennik* (about equal to the *dirgem* in weight), did not begin to be minted until Vladimir's day, and then, apparently, only in small quantities. In time a definite market ratio came to be established between the *dirgem*, with its fractions, and the fur values from which those fractions acquired their names ; with the result that there arose reckonings in two currencies— currencies often quoted indifferently by our ancient annalists, as shown by the typical passage "For a foxskin five *nogati*, and for three foxskins forty *kuni* less a *nogata*" which occurs in a twelfth-century manuscript. The *Russkaia Pravda* tells us the actual measure of the ratio, for, in reckoning certain judicial fines in units of five *kuni* apiece, it adds to each unit the words "two *nogati* of furs"—*i.e.* or two *nogati* of furs. Hence we may take it that one *nogata* of those commodities was equivalent to

1 See p. 52.

two and a half metal *kuni*; and inasmuch as the Arabic chronicler, Ibn Dasta, says, when writing of the Bolgars in the early tenth century, that they had abandoned reckoning in *kuni* of furs in favour of reckoning in metal coin, and that the price of each fur at that time was two and a half *dirgems*—the same number of *dirgems* as the *Pravda* has shown us to have been paid also of *kuni*—we may take this (in conjunction with the fact that the markets of that day were remarkable for their fixity of prices, and that prices ruling in the Bolgarian market cannot but have been influenced by those ruling in the Russian) to mean that the metal *kuna* formerly used in Rus was identical with the Arabic *dirgem*.

The *grivna* varied in weight at different periods according to the changing value of silver. For instance, we see from the Greek treaties of Oleg and Igor that its weight in the tenth century averaged only about a third of a pound, while actual examples which have come down to us weigh about a sixth more. From our knowledge of the history of Russian currency we are led to ascribe these examples to the eleventh century or the early part of the twelfth—*i.e.* to the times of Yaroslav, Monomakh, and Mstislav I. After that period, however, the course of events brought about a great restriction of Russian foreign trade, so that the flow of valuable metals from abroad was reduced, silver rose in price, and the weight of the *grivna* is stated by annalists of the late twelfth and early thirteenth centuries to have fallen by one-half—*i.e.* to only a quarter of a pound. Of course, this reduction in the bulk of the *grivna* affected also the monetary reckoning. Though now lighter in weight in consequence of the increased dearness of silver, the *grivna* still retained its old purchasing power, since commodities had cheapened in proportion ; but inasmuch as the foreign silver coins which served as change continued to be valued according to the *grivna's former* weight, while furs, used as money, continued, like the *grivna*, to retain their old purchasing power, a change necessarily took place in the market ratio both of furs [1] and of other commodities to the *dirgem* and other units of metallic currency. The *nogata* of furs,[2] formerly worth two and a half *dirgems* or *kuni*, was now worth only the same number of half-*dirgems* or *riezani*, while the half-*dirgem* or *riezana* bought in the market what could formerly only have been purchased for a whole *dirgem* or *kuna*. In time the prevailing custom of calling foreign coins by the names of the fur units to which they were equivalent caused the *riezana* to be renamed the *kuna*, and fifty of them to go to the *grivna* instead of twenty-five of the old *kuni*. This explains

---

[1] As goods. [2] As currency.

why monetary penalties expressed in *riezani* in the short version of the *Pravda* become everywhere *kuni* in the full version, and that without the change of a single figure in the amounts.   Since, then, as we have seen, it was with the close of the times of Mstislav I. that the *grivna* began to fall rapidly in weight and the *riezana* to be called the *kuna*, we may reasonably suppose that it was during the latter half of the twelfth century or at about the beginning of the thirteenth that the *Russkaia Pravda* assumed its final shape in the full version.   And if its initiation may be ascribed to the times of Yaroslav, it follows that the process of its elaboration was spread over a period of not less than a century and a half.

Now that we have examined the origin of the *Russkaia Pravda* and determined the approximate period of its composition, we are in possession of *one* of the necessary bases for answering the second question propounded when we first began our study of the *Pravda*—namely, the question as to how far that Code can be looked upon as a full and reliable guide to the ancient legal system of Rus.   The other basis required for that purpose is a knowledge of the sources utilised by the compounders of the Code, as well as of the degree to which they availed themselves of those sources.   These latter were to a large extent determined by the purpose and origin of the *Pravda*, which was designed to be a code drawn up for the use of a court exercising jurisdiction over church people in non-ecclesiastical matters.   For that reason, therefore, it was bound to draw its norms from both ecclesiastical and non-ecclesiastical sources.   Let us consider the latter first.

Under the Russo-Greek treaties of the tenth century, a Russian who should draw his sword upon a Greek, or a Greek who should draw his sword upon a Russian, was to be punished with such monetary fine as "is usual under Russian law."   The "Russian law" here referred to was, of course, old pagan legal usage based upon custom, and served the codifiers of the *Pravda* as their first and principal source.   Yet to call it simply "old pagan legal usage based upon custom" might lead to some misunderstanding, or even to some inexactitude, seeing that the subject is a much more complicated one than such a definition might lead one to suppose.   Was, then, the "Russian law" of the treaties the same as the law obtaining at the period when the codifiers of the *Russkaia Pravda* were utilising the former as a source?   We read that, when making peace with the Greeks under the walls of Constantinople, Oleg—still a true Varangian, as also were the majority, if not the whole, of his retinue—swore "by Russian law" to keep the peace thenceforth, and invoked in witness of his oath "*his* gods" Perun and Volos.   This shows us that in those days "Russian law" was simply the old legal custom of Rus, *i.e.* of that mixed Varangian-Slavonic class which ruled the Eastern Slavs and took the lead in commerce with Byzantium.   Although this "Russian law" or unwritten legal custom was of the same mixed origin and composition as was the class whose life it regulated, it would be a matter of some difficulty to distinguish in it its constituent elements, the Varangian and the Slavonic, more especially through the medium of the *Russkaia Pravda*. Two centuries of life in association are quite sufficient to fuse into an organically indissoluble whole the customs of two originally separate races.   The conditions and relations of life into which both the immigrant Varangian element and the native Slavonic entered in the great trading towns which sprang up along the Dnieper and other rivers of the plain were primal, aboriginal conditions and relations of life, and thus had no ready-made norms, whether of Varangian or Slavonic legal custom, to go upon.   Next, in the ninth century, the Varangians of those towns converted themselves into a ruling class—or at least into the dominant element of one, while in the century following we find that class, as represented by Oleg and his men, not only swearing by Slavonic gods as their own, but becoming, through services of war and trade with Byzantium, the means of introducing Byzantine legal customs and ideas into Rus. From that the Varangian element went on also to introduce into Russian jurisprudence and administration certain legal and administrative ideas of its own, and thus, in Igor's time, to pave the way for the coming of Christianity and a further development of Russian law.   Next we see that Varangian element furnishing Rus with her first Christian martyrs [1] while Vladimir was, as yet, but a pagan; until finally, by the time that the codification of the *Russkaia Pravda* had been entered upon, the descendants of those early Varangian immigrants had become so completely Slavonicised as to look upon lately arrived immigrants of their own race who professed the Catholic faith as foreigners and "Varangians without baptism."

Thus, in the form in which Russian law reached the codifiers of the *Russkaia Pravda* there were expressed all the various conditions of life which succeeded one another in the great towns during the ninth, tenth, and eleventh centuries; and, although its roots were laid in separate Varangian and Slavonic pagan customs, they were roots to which many and varied influences caused such growth, such accretions of new social relations arising out of two centuries of mechanical and racial fusion, to

[1] See p. 91.

accrue, that there resulted from them a formation entirely distinct from, and additional to, the old system of legal custom which had hitherto obtained among the non-urban Slavonic population. We see, then, that Russian law, the main source of the *Pravda*, was compounded both of primitive Slavonic usage and of the law of Varangian Rus—*i.e.* the Rus of the towns, and that the period of its composition extended over the ninth, tenth, and eleventh centuries.

In addition to Russian law, there were sources whence the codifiers of the *Pravda* derived norms for amending and developing that law. Of these, the most important were the legislative enactments of the Russian princes. Thus, in the second article of the full edition of the *Pravda* we find set forth, first of all, the law made by Yaroslav's sons for the abolition of vengeance for murder in favour of a monetary penalty, and then further articles specifying the costs and other points of procedure to be observed in murder trials. As for the idea itself of the power, the right, and the imperative obligation of a supreme ruler to regulate the life of the community by the exercise of his will, we know that it reached Rus with Christianity, and was steadily inculcated by the Church.

Another of the secondary sources made use of by the codifiers of the *Pravda* was the series of judicial pronouncements of the princes which subsequently became converted into precedents—the most usual method of law-making in primitive days. Such, for instance, was the decree of Iziaslav, son of Yaroslav, which condemned the inhabitants of Dorogobūtz to pay a double amount of wer-gild for the murder of a *stari konukh* or head stableman of the Prince's suite, and which was afterwards inserted into the *Pravda* as a general law placing all such functionaries upon a level with the senior grade of the retinue as regards the penalty for their assassination.

To these two secondary sources must be added also those ordinances which, suggested by the Church, were enacted by the princes. Traces of such ordinances being made are to be found in an old manuscript relating to Vladimir, which says that when robbery was on the increase in Rus the bishops suggested to that ruler that a sterner penalty should be substituted for the existing monetary fine ; with the result (so we may take it to be) that there was inserted into the *Pravda* the article which enacts that a robber should suffer, not a pecuniary penalty, but wholesale confiscation of his property and the sale of himself and his family into foreign slavery. This secondary source of the *Pravda* served as the principal means of bringing the influence of Byzantine ecclesiasticism (and, through it, of Roman law) to bear upon Russian life. That influence was of great importance, not only because of the new juridical norms which it caused to be introduced into Russian law, but also because of the diffusion which it brought about of those general juridical definitions and ideas which constitute the basis of all jurisprudence. It was through that influence that the Church was enabled to extend her jurisdiction to cover family relations, as well as to use her newly-acquired judicial and legislative powers to readjust those relations to her canonical ordinances, and her canonical ordinances to local conditions : for which reason we may take it that from the above secondary source were derived, directly or indirectly, all those portions of the *Pravda* which deal with the system of succession, the guardianship of minors, the legal position of widows, and the relation of the latter to their children.

Among other supplementary authorities to which the Church and her legal codifiers had resort in selecting and formulating *casus* for legal enactment may be mentioned those added portions of the *Kormtchi* among which the full version of the *Pravda* is usually to be found, and whose very presence among the contents of such a work as a *Kormtchaia* was a sufficient guarantee of their authority as a legal source. At the same time, however, the old ecclesiastical jurisprudents of Rus did not neglect less authoritative sources when suitable material was discoverable in them for the purpose ; and although to trace them in the *Pravda* is no easy task, some evidence of their co-operation shows forth in places. For instance, we meet, in the *Pravda*, with a series of articles relating to assaults committed with the hand, foot, and other members of the human body—a series almost identical with one to be found in the so-called " Eclogue according to the *Procheiron* " (a private digest ascribed to the great canonist of the early tenth century, Zachariah). The *Pravda* awards compensation for damage to an eye or nose at the rate of thirty *grivni*, while the Eclogue assesses the injury at thirty *sikli* (Eastern money). The same with regard to the knocking out of a tooth. This particular Eclogue was a private Greek compilation only, and so cannot have been extensively known among the old Russian jurisprudents. At all events it has left few traces upon our ancient legal literature. That being so, we are justified in drawing the conclusion that, if this parity of penalties between the Eclogue and the *Pravda* is not mere coincidence, the sources drawn upon by the compilers of the Russian code were both various and surprising.

CHAPTER X

Preliminary questions with regard to the composition of the *Russkaia Pravda*—Process of its collation and elaboration—Its composition and contents—Its relation to previously existing law—The civil order of the period as reflected in its articles—Importance of old legal annals in the study of a given civil order—The distinctions drawn by the *Pravda* between civil and criminal law—Its system of punishments and sums to be paid in compensation—Its original basis and later interpolations—Its relative solicitude for property and the person—Its double demarcation of classes—Its importance as pre-eminently the code of capital.

BEFORE proceeding to examine the contents of the *Russkaia Pravda* we must decide the very difficult question of the manner of its composition—of the methods by which the codifiers availed themselves of their various sources.

Two methods of utilising those sources are noticeable in the *Pravda* —namely, the method of borrowing *form*, and the method of borrowing *material*. The first of these two methods was the one most generally employed with regard to foreign (*i.e.* Byzantine) sources, and the second with regard to native. In the last chapter we examined evidence bearing upon the origin of the code, and cited instances of the former method as applied to the supplementary treatises in the *Kormtchi*. It is a method which cannot but have had a marked educational value in the development of Russian law, since it taught the old codifiers to recognise and define human relations, to penetrate to the meaning and spirit of jurisprudence in its relation to life. In short, it gave practical finish and expression to juridical theory. Likewise it communicated to the *Pravda* a feature which Byzantine synoptical codification derived from two influences —namely, the influence of Roman law and the influence of Christian teaching. Of these, the first-named tended to communicate to a given code a purely jurisprudential character, while the second tended to convert it also into a work of edification: both of which tendencies are to be found in our *Pravda*. Yet the principles of the latter vary greatly in places, owing to the reason that its moral and psychological views, as well as its practical aims, were closely bound up with practical calculations of existence. Instances of this combination of moral and practical tendencies are to be found in those of its articles which enact (1) that a slave shall not be punishable for theft by the Prince's court, "seeing that a slave hath not his freedom," and (2) that the lender of a sum of more than three *grivni* without witnesses shall be disqualified from recovering the sum by legal process.

However important the method of borrowing form may have been as regards the *Pravda* in particular, the other method—the method of borrowing material—has been of still greater importance in the history of positive law in general. It is never difficult to discover in a given source the particular article from which the *Pravda* derived its norm for the corresponding point of law. The real difficulty is to discover whence that norm originated in the *first* instance. Let us stop here for a moment to consider a certain bibliographical point. In old Russian legal literature, more especially in that section of it which emanated from the Church, we meet with articles of Russian origin which are at once identical with one another and devoid of all apparent connection with the works in which they occur. For instance, in the "*Zakon o Kazniech*" or "Law of Penalties" (a Slavonic translation of an old Byzantine treatise [1]) we find an article enacting that a childless widow who married a slave should be scourged and have her head shorn; while a widow with children who should be guilty of the same offence should not only undergo the above penalties, but forfeit to her children the whole of her property, save only such a bare moiety of it as should be necessary for her personal maintenance.[2] To this Byzantine article, however, we find the Slavonic translator (or some other person) adding an extraneous addendum wholly opposed to Byzantine law—an addendum enacting that not only should a widow marry a slave if she wished, but she should thereupon become entitled to all the usual legal benefits attaching to a second union. However, we do not find this unauthorised clause reproduced in the section of the *Pravda* which treats of family law. Again, among some articles borrowed by an old copy of the *Mierilo Pravednoye* from the Eclogue there occurs a clause specifying the procedure to be observed in cases of theft when both the stolen goods and the thief have been apprehended in a district other than the one in which the crime was committed. This

---

[1] This Byzantine treatise formed one among a volume of such works which the late Professor A. S. Pavlov compiled and edited under the title of "*Knig Zakonnich*" or "The Book of Laws."

[2] This was in accordance with Roman law, which prescribed, as a general principle, that a master or mistress should not marry their slave.

clause also has no visible connection whatever with its context. Similar stray articles are to be found in the *Pravda*, but only in later copies of the full version. Thus, in a fifteenth-century copy we come across an article dealing with the case of a bailee who absconds with his trust, and ranking the offence as presumable theft instead of as mere failure to restore—a delinquency hitherto punished on a lower scale than theft. This article does not stand among the other clauses treating of theft, but at the very tail-end of the Code, together with another extraneous article referring to the amount of compensation to be paid in cases of wrongful arrest or flogging. Again, in some copies of the *Pravda* we meet with added or interpolated articles which find no place at all in other copies of the Code. One such article—an article relating to theft—is particularly out of place in the *Pravda*, seeing that it is a mere amendment to a clause in Yaroslav's Church Ordinance, and therefore wholly unintelligible without its parent item. Yet, curiously enough, it does not appear in any single copy of the Ordinance, but only as an extraneous addendum to the *Pravda*. Finally, there are articles—whole groups of articles, in fact —which have no connection whatever with anything in our old legal literature, yet appear (with certain textual differences between them, but identical substance of contents) in every copy of the *Pravda*. Of these the article defining the sources of slavery is a typical example.

Of course these do not constitute all the articles of this miscellaneous kind; yet the instances which I have given will serve to illustrate their general nature. They throw a certain amount of light upon the manner in which the *Pravda* was composed, for they show us that the task of systematic codification of compilations of this kind was preceded by a detailed elaboration of individual norms, and that these norms were subsequently collated into more or less complete digests, or used to amend digests already in existence. The work of codification was carried out by that section of the clergy, both immigrant (*i.e.* Byzantine) and native, which formed the *entourage* of the early episcopal thrones in Rus, and served as the bishop's immediate instrument of Church rule and judicial administration. No other class in the Russian community of that day possessed the requisite resources for such a task—whether resources of general culture or resources of specialised legal erudition. Records which have come down to us from the eleventh and twelfth centuries show us that the transition from paganism to Christianity was accompanied by many grave difficulties for the new converts. The clergy and the ecclesiastical judges had constantly to consult the bishops on questions which they themselves were incompetent to decide, but to which it was advisable that answers should be returned *ex cathedrâ*. Such questions related mostly to church practice and discipline, but also to purely legal matters—to usury, to ecclesiastical penalties for murder and other criminal offences, to marriage, to divorce, to unlawful cohabitation, to testimony on oath before a court of law, to slavery, and to the relation of ecclesiastical jurisprudence to slavery. We read that an inquiry as to what a devout Christian ought to wear elicited the pronouncement that anything was proper—even bearskin! Another episcopal dictum was to the effect that a slave should not be punished for theft in the Prince's court, "seeing that a slave hath not his freedom." Gradually these pastoral directions became adjusted to judicial practice, converted into juridical norms, and crystallised into articles of law as occasion arose. Next, the various scattered articles were collated into groups or sectional digests, and these, again, with emendations, into successive editions of a complete code.

The *Pravda* contains certain internal evidence which enables us not only to estimate the part played in its composition by this process of gradual elaboration and grouping of articles, but also to explain why the different versions of the code differ so much in extent, in order of articles, and in wording. Of the two principal versions of the *Pravda*—the full and the short—the short is divided into two parts, of which the first contains seventeen articles defining murder, assaults of various kinds, offences against property, and sums to be paid in compensation for damage, while the second part specifies the penalties to be awarded in each case, as well as certain details relating to judicial costs and expenses. In the full version we find these articles of the short version's developed and set forth in greater detail; to which may be added that this version also incorporates into the general scheme of the Code those ordinances enacted at the council of Yaroslav's sons which the short version gives only separately and in bare outline. In fact, the short version might almost be taken for an abstract of the full were it not for two reasons. In the first place, an article in the short version which enacts that the master of a slave who has committed an assault upon a freeman must compensate the complainant or else hand over the slave to him to be killed has added to it, in the full version, a clause that, although Yaroslav "did thus judge," his sons established as an alternative that the complainant might either kill the peccant slave or else sue the slave's master for damages. From this it follows that the article in the short version, not the amended article in the full, must be looked upon as Yaroslav's original enactment. The other objection to the possibility of the short version being a mere abstract of the full is the fact that, of the two, the former holds (as we have seen) to an older system of monetary reckoning than does the latter. In short, we may take it that the short version represents an early attempt to codify the legislation established by Yaroslav and his sons (though, of course, the version does not itself constitute Yaroslav's own original *Pravda*), and that the full version represents a later and more finished attempt in the same direction, together with additional norms established by legislation of Monomakh's and by later practice. Yet it is a difficult matter, in the full version, to distinguish clearly between the various portions which gradually became added to it. In the older copies this process of addition seems to have been carried out in purely mechanical fashion. At about the middle of such copies we come across an article defining "monthly interest," while immediately following it is the ordinance above referred to as having been enacted by Monomakh for the limiting of such interest. At this point the dividing line between the two portions of the Code is drawn—the first portion being headed "*Sud Yaroslav Volodimerich*" or "*Ustav Yaroslavl Volodimericha*," and the second portion "*Ustav Volodimer Vsevolodicha*." [1] Yet these headings refer only to *the first article* in each part, not to each part as a whole. For instance, article one of the first part is an ordinance made by Yaroslav (or in his time) for dealing with cases of murder, and enacts that, where the deceased has blood relatives, they may avenge the crime by slaying the murderer, but that if no such relatives be extant, the murderer shall be mulcted in a fine. Article two, however, cannot have been made either by Yaroslav or in his time, since it amounts to a mere statement that Yaroslav's sons abolished family vengeance for murder, and substituted for it, as the invariable penalty, a fine. The truth is that the *Pravda* does not consist of *two* non-contemporaneous portions only, but of several. Indeed, some of the articles contain evidence in themselves of the period at which they were composed. For instance, one article names twelve *grivni* as the penalty for a blow with a naked sword, while another one names three for a blow with a sword when sheathed, notwithstanding that the latter class of assault would be as capable as the former of inflicting a wound, or even death. Again, one article names twelve *grivni* for a blow with a cudgel, while another one names

[1] These three titles=respectively, "The Judgment of Yaroslav, Son of Vladimir," "The Ordinance of Yaroslav, Son of Vladimir," and "The Ordinance of Vladimir, Son of Vsevolod."

only three for a blow with a pole, although, as before, the two classes of assault would be equally serious in their effect. These apparent discrepancies are explainable, however, if we consider the process by which the *Pravda* was composed. Inserted into the older examples of the *Kormtchi* and the *Mierilo Pravednoye* we find an Abstract of certain ordinances "concerning hearings"—the majority of these ordinances being derived from Byzantine sources, and the rest from Russian. Now, although this Abstract must have been the source whence the *Pravda*, in its turn, derived its articles enacting the above three-*grivni* penalties, the *amounts* of the penalties named in the original source read differently in different copies. For instance, although the Abstract names no precise monetary penalty for a blow with a cudgel, but leaves it to the discretion of the judge to inflict what amount he thinks fit, for a blow with a naked sword some copies name a fine of *nine grivni*, and others a fine only of three. Yet no real discrepancy is here. The article in the *Pravda* which awards twelve *grivni* for a blow with a naked sword was framed during the second half of the twelfth century, when the *grivna* weighed a quarter of a pound: consequently we may suppose that during the earlier part of the century, when the weight of the *grivna* was *half* a pound, the penalty amounted to *six grivni*. Indeed, a treaty concluded between the people of Novgorod and the Germans in the year 1195 gives that identical amount as the fine to be paid for a blow with a "weapon." "Six olden *grivni*" is the term used in the document: by which are meant six *grivni* of the half-pound weight which had been the standard during the earlier part of the century. But between those two periods of *grivni* of half-pound weight and quarter-pound weight respectively there occurred an interval when the *grivna* weighed a *third* of a pound. During this interval, then, the penalty of six *grivni* according to the half-pound standard must have stood at nine *grivni*, seeing that the *grivna* had then decreased in weight from half a pound to a third of a pound; and inasmuch as those nine *grivni* would be equal, as ingots, to three pounds' weight of silver, they came to be set down in the articles of the Abstract as "three *grivni*" in the sense of *weight*, and not in the sense of *ingots* at all. When, therefore, these articles were transferred from the Abstract to the *Pravda* they were made to replace articles identical with them in substance, but having their monetary penalties calculated according to another standard of *grivna*-weight—namely, the quarter-pound standard. If to that we add that Monomakh's ordinance above referred to was undoubtedly based upon the half-pound *grivna*, it will be seen that the *Pravda's* scales of monetary penalties expressed in turn every fluctuation of currency which occurred in the Russian market during the twelfth century. Additional evidence that the compiling of the Code must be assigned to more than a single period of Russian history is afforded by other passages in the text. I have already mentioned an article enacting that a slave should not be fined for theft by the Prince's court, "seeing that a slave hath not his freedom " : yet in another part of the Code we find it enacted that the master of a slave who has stolen a horse is bound to repay to the owner of the animal an amount identical with the sum which the court would have exacted from the slave had he been a freeman, while a third article, coming at the very end of the Code, ordains that the master of a slave who has been guilty of any act of robbery whatsoever shall either "ransom" the culprit or hand him over as a gift to the person whom he has robbed—the latter alternative a course of which no mention is made in the earlier two articles. From this it might be supposed that each of these three successive clauses was enacted to supersede the others ; yet, on the whole, I think that the character of the Code justifies us in assuming that the differences between the three articles arose out of the fact that each section of the *Pravda* in which the articles severally occur was compiled at a different period to the others, and that the articles themselves refer to occasions which, though similar to one another, differ in some slight degree which has not been made sufficiently clear by the codifiers. We must remember that in the *Pravda* we have to do with an attempt to combine into one general code norms from any and every source, and not with legislation which replaced one norm with another.

This tendency on the part of the *Pravda* to embrace all possible material is overdone in places. For instance, we find the section on family law interspersed in promiscuous fashion with scales of salaries to be awarded to city prefects in charge of fortifications and to bridge-builders responsible for the construction and up-keep of bridges (to which some versions add, at the end of the Code, a further ordinance allotting various bridge-dues among the wards of Novgorod)—all thrown in amid those supplementary articles to which I have referred. Again, to another article limiting the rate of interest on invested capital to fifty per cent. per annum we find added, in some versions, a fanciful estimate of profit and loss drawn up by some country landowner or another of (apparently) the province of Rostov. Taking the above rate of interest as his basis, the unknown agriculturist has set down a complete calculation of the profit which he might look to receive during twelve years from his cattle, bees, and crops, as well as the amount of remuneration which would be due to his wife and daughter for the same period for their work on the estate! Although this curious old estimate is rich in interesting details of Russian estate-management during the twelfth and thirteenth centuries, such interpolations make it much more difficult for us to distinguish between the various component parts of the Code and to apprehend the proper order of its articles. In general, the order of subjects in the Code shows a tendency to pass from graver offences to lighter, thence to ordinances approximating to the realm of civil law, and thence to civil law proper.

We see, then, that the *Russkaia Pravda* is a collection of articles and groups of articles of different periods, and that it has undergone various processes of revision: also, that the only portion of it which can rightly be looked upon as the original *Pravda* of Yaroslav is that portion of the older articles in which the juridical system of his day is reproduced. This much decided, we are in a position to approach the question of the extent to which the Code is a full and faithful exponent of the Russian jurisprudence of its time. The question is one entirely of the manner in which the *Pravda* made use of its sources, especially of old Russian unwritten law.

The *Pravda* was prevented by the very circumstances of its origin and purpose from covering every department of Russian life, since, in non-ecclesiastical matters, it was obliged to limit itself only to such as came within Church jurisdiction—which, as we know, extended, in that regard, only to the clergy and lay supernumeraries of the Church. On the one hand, therefore, the Code could not touch upon political questions, while, on the other hand, it had to omit matters of a spiritual character which were subject only to special ecclesiastical laws, and, in all else, to reproduce merely the practice of the princely courts (except in cases where slight digressions from that practice were permitted to the ecclesiastical tribunals by virtue of special powers given them for the purpose). The whole relation of the *Pravda* to the Russian jurisprudence of its day is a subject deserving of a course of investigation to itself, but I will nevertheless confine my remarks strictly to such points as seem to me the most notable.

We have seen that the *Pravda* did not recognise the *polé* or legal duel —unless a certain recognition of that practice is to be discerned in a rather obscurely worded article which occurs in one of the older examples of the short version.   This article says that, should a man assaulted appear in court with the wounds or bruises still upon him, his evidence shall be accepted without corroboration, but that, if no such marks be visible upon his person, the testimony of a second witness shall be necessary for the plea to be received.   Should, in the former case, (adds the article,) the man assaulted be unable to take " personal vengeance " upon his assailant, the latter shall be fined three *grivni* for the assault and a further sum in "recompense to the physician."   What, then, was the "personal vengeance" referred to?   If it meant personal administration of corporal chastisement combined with legal inability of the chastised to defend himself, the proceeding would amount practically to a sentence of corporal punishment, with the complainant as executor of the judicial decree. If, on the other hand, the defendant was permitted to defend himself from the chastisement, we have something very like the legal duel. However, in the full version of the *Pravda* we find this article denuded of all vestiges of personal vengeance by order of the court, and enacting, instead, that, on proof of his case—whether by evidence of bodily injury or by the testimony of a second witness—the complainant shall be awarded compensation by the judge.   " But if " (continues the article, in effect) " the complainant shall seem to the court to have been the aggressor in the affair, he shall receive no compensation, no matter what injuries he may have sustained, nor shall the defendant be held responsible for such injuries, seeing that they were incurred in the struggle which inevitably ensued from the complainant's aggressive action."   The same tendency of the full version to set aside the system of personal vengeance by judicial decree is found in another instance.   The short version permitted the sons of a family to avenge an injury done to their father—this being conceded " that the sons may be appeased."   For this enactment, however, the full version substitutes a fine equal to half the monetary penalty for murder, as well as a sum to be paid in compensation to the complainant equal to a quarter of that penalty.   Thus we see that, though making concessions at first to local juridical custom, the ecclesiastical courts gradually consolidated themselves sufficiently to be able to insist upon the principles which they had made their own.

Furthermore, the *Pravda* does not recognise the death penalty, in spite of the fact that an early thirteenth-century treatise included among the contents of the Petcherski *Paterik*[1] shows that the graver offences were frequently visited with sentences of hanging when the accused was unable

---

[1] A work descriptive of the lives of the Saints.

to pay the fine customarily levied for his misdemeanour. The *Pravda's* silence on this point can be explained in two ways—namely, either by the fact that the more serious crimes (such as homicide and theft) could be dealt with only by the ecclesiastical courts in conjunction with the princely tribunals (the death sentence, probably, being awarded always at the instance of the latter), or by the fact that the death penalty is totally opposed to the Christian view of mankind. That it is so opposed was recognised even by Monomakh, for, in the course of his *Pöuchenie*, he lays a strict injunction upon his sons never to kill either a bad man or a good, however great the provocation. A like ethical view would explain the silence of the *Pravda* both upon the question of torture as a legal process and upon the non-responsibility of a master for the death of his slave if the latter should succumb to the effects of his beatings. Nevertheless, however much the Church might discountenance this immunity of slave-owners, she was powerless to deprive them of it, and could visit the offence only with spiritual discipline and penance. Thus we find an old code of ecclesiastical penalties—a code commonly ascribed to Georgius, Metropolitan of Rus during the eleventh century—roundly prescribing that " whoso killeth a slave, the same shall be guilty of murder, and shall do penance for the act." With regard to torture, the *Paterik* above-mentioned gives us a description of the " tormenting" of two monks of Petcherski by command of one of Sviatopolk's sons, in order to compel them to reveal where a Varangian hoard lay buried in their monastery. Of course this "tormenting" may have been merely an isolated act of caprice on the Prince's part, and in no way an authorised legal process : yet, if such a method of examination was at all a regular feature in the procedure of the princely courts, it is easy to understand that the *Pravda* would in any case have passed it by in silence.

In short, the omission of the Code to mention the points enumerated may be taken to represent the profound protest of the Christian jurists of the period against the customs of ancient paganism, as well as against the cruelties of the later *régime*. Yet the work also contains omissions and discrepancies which can only be explained on the ground of incompleteness of codification, and it is not until we remember the process by which it was compiled that we shall cease to look for system or symmetry in its pages, seeing that it was not the outcome of any single, complete conception, but a mosaic of heterogeneous items pieced together according as the requirements of ecclesiastical legal practice demanded. For instance, the articles on slavery which are to be found appended at the tail-end of the

Code mention only three of the sources of that bondage—namely, public sale, marriage of a person to a slave without a previous guarantee of freedom from the slave's master, and entry into domestic service without a similar agreement ; yet other articles in the *Pravda* show us that slavery was imposed also for such offences as theft and horse-stealing, and (occasionally) for insolvency, while certain of our other ancient annals add to that the circumstance that slavery was frequently made a corollary to imprisonment or disfavour in the Prince's eyes. These articles of the *Pravda's* on slavery constitute a special section to themselves, as well as one of the latest sections to be introduced into the Code—a sort of chapter explanatory of slavery alone, and composed altogether independently of the main section in which the articles occur. The reason of this is that the requirements of legal practice obliged the framer of the articles to formulate only such sources of slavery as arose out of private transactions, and to omit those which were due to criminal or political causes.

In studying the relation of the *Pravda* to the Russian law of its day we must not forget the position of the Russian codifier of that period, who had to deal with a haphazard system of judicial practice in which ancient custom conflicted with new juridical theories and requirements, and human relations rose up and confronted the courts in guises wholly unforeseen by the law or judicial by practice ; with the result that those courts were constantly being thrown into confusion and perplexity, and the task of the codifier in selecting and formulating the norms which he required became a most arduous one. Although the *Pravda* devoted its chief attention to those fundamental, elementary enactments of material law which life and the ruling interests of life demand for the punishing of offences and the righting of wrongs, and although the procedure to be observed in cases of loss or theft of property (especially where the thief or the property was a slave) is defined with particular care in the Code, its numerous articles do not furnish us with a single word in answer to a question of great interest for the recorder of a social order and its juridical ideas—namely, the question whether the prosecution of crime in Rus was undertaken by private persons or by the State. We can only suppose the latter, seeing that every judicial decree was accompanied by a fine to the Prince's government. With regard to this point, however, let us turn to annals contemporary (or nearly so) with the *Pravda*. In an old work concerning the Petcherski Cloister there is a story that some thieves once planned to waylay and rob an inmate named Gregory, a pupil of Theodosius', but were unsuccessful in the attempt, since Gregory overcame them, and calmly dismissed them with his blessing. As soon, however, as the city prefect of Kiev heard of this he caused the would-be robbers to be arrested and thrown into prison; whereupon Gregory, distressed that they should suffer on his account, paid their fine and once more "dismissed" them. The story is clear in its wording as to this second "dismissal" being the act of Gregory himself, and not of the Prince's court; whence it would appear that the city prefect no longer had power to keep the culprits in prison after their fine had been paid to the state, even though it was paid by another hand than their own. Likewise, a curious old twelfth-century manuscript tells us that once upon a time some of the clergy repaired to Bishop Niphont of Novgorod with, among other questions, the problem, "Is it, or is it not, lawful to ordain a man to the diaconate who has committed a theft?"; to which (so we are told) the Bishop replied: "If the theft was a great one and not to be amended in private, but resulted in that the thief was arraigned before the Prince and his boyars, it would not be seemly to admit such a man a deacon; but if the theft was amended in private and in secret, then the sinner may be ordained." From this it is clear that the Bishop did not regard it as contrary to public policy to hush up even the gravest of crimes if a mundane and hole-and-corner agreement with the prosecution were feasible: and if to that we add that the *Pravda* expressly ordained that the winning or acquitted party in a suit or a criminal case should pay to the judge a *pomochnoe* or "contribution" for the assistance which that functionary had rendered him during the hearing, it would seem that the so-called justice of that period worked out in there being three parties to every suit— namely, judge, prosecutor, and defendant, and that, while each of them began by being hostile to the other two, an alliance between any two of them settled the suit to the detriment of the third.

We have now completed our examination of the *Pravda* sufficiently to be able to answer the question of the extent to which it is a reliable guide to the legal system of its day. Although we can trace in it a lack of sympathy with those legal customs of ancient Rus which smacked of paganism, it reproduces the procedure of the princely courts without either insisting upon such amendments to that procedure as, in ordinary practice, were adopted by ecclesiastical courts having jurisdiction in non-ecclesiastical matters or seeking to abolish local legal custom by substituting new norms for old ones. No; its methods of attaining its ends were different. It merely ignored such details as it thought should be eliminated from legal practice (*e.g.* the legal duel and private vengeance by judicial decree), while at the same time it supplemented the existing law by formulating such legal *casus* and relations as that law had not hitherto touched upon—*casus* and relations arising out of such matters as (for example) hereditary succession and slavery.   Yet there was much of the existing law which it did not reproduce at all, for the reason either that there was no practical need for its formulation, or that, in the then confused state of the princely courts, such formulation was impossible.   For these reasons, then, we may look upon the *Russkaia Pravda* as a *reliable*, but not as a *complete*, guide to the legal system of its day ; since, although it supplemented and developed the existing law with details which it elaborated and set forth with a skill to which the princely jurists probably could never have attained, it replaced none of that law with fresh jurisprudence, as well as omitted some of its more pagan features.   In short, the *Russkaia Pravda* might be described as constituting an excellent, but slightly cracked, mirror of the Russian legal system of the eleventh and twelfth centuries.

Now let us study the civil order of the period in so far as it is possible to do so from the contents of the *Pravda*.   We have seen that one of the results of the rota system of rule of the eleventh and twelfth centuries was to draw the different portions of Rus together in the various relations of life : from which it follows that in studying the civil order of the period we shall be observing the working of one of the elements of the territorial or popular unity communicated to Rus by the system of rule in question.

The civil order of a state is compounded of exceedingly complex relations—relations juridical, moral, family, and economic.   Those relations are created and evoked by personal interests, feelings, and ideas, and constitute the sphere of *personality*.   Yet so diverse are the motive springs of those relations that they would effectually be prevented from preserving any measure of system or harmony among themselves unless the personal interests, feelings, and ideas referred to had some common connecting force which was recognised as binding upon the whole community.   Such a force is needed to limit the play and mutual antagonism of those personal interests, feelings, and ideas, and to regulate them by private rules and restrictions : which rules and restrictions constitute *jurisprudence*, while the force thus safeguarding the interests of society and giving expression to social relations constitutes *custom* or *law*. Personal interests are usually voluntary in origin, and personal feelings and ideas invariably involuntary, while all of them are so intangible in

their nature as to be useless as a standard for gauging the trend of a
nation's life or measuring the extent of a nation's development. The
only possible standard for that purpose is the sum of those normal, obligatory, and universally recognised relations which, formulated in the shape
of jurisprudence, thereby become accessible to the student. Such relations
are founded and maintained by the ruling views and interests of their
period, and thus enable us to estimate its material conditions and moral
structure. In short, the study of ancient legal memorials permits us to
probe to the very roots of social life.

In touching upon the contents of the *Russkaia Pravda* we need only do
so sufficiently to give us an idea of the chief interests and motives which
inspired the Russian community of its day. Like all legal codes, it constitutes, in the main, an attempt to limit, by juridical means, all such acts
as connote injury, physical or economical, to one person at the hands of
another. For some such acts the Code awards monetary compensation to the injured party, while for others it metes out official penalties at
the hands of the government—thus differentiating clearly between civil
and criminal law. This is an important fact for the historian of that
period. Yet the dividing line between those two kinds of acts and of law
is not always drawn very distinctly in the *Pravda* : so that to separate the
criminal element from the civil, and to lay hold of what German jurists
call the *Schuldmoment*, is sometimes a matter of difficulty, and a
task rather for the moral instinct than for juridical analysis. Moreover,
legal methods of punishing a criminal act or determining a given stage
or degree of criminality varied greatly in olden times. For instance, Oleg's
treaty with the Greeks stipulated that a thief caught in the act should
make *treble* restitution, *i.e.* restore the stolen property and *twice* its value ;
while by Igor's treaty such a thief had to make only *double* restitution,
whether he were caught in the act or apprehended later. The *Pravda*, on
the other hand, enacts that the *master* of a slave who commits a theft, not
the slave himself, shall make the necessary restitution (a double one in
this case, as in the last), as a penalty for his criminal neglect in exercising supervision over his servant. In civil suits also a sum was always
exacted from the losing party ; so that, in reality, the point where the
Pravda draws the dividing line between a criminal offence and a civil
infringement of the law is the point where the resultant case or suit
ceases to involve a contribution to the government's coffers, but puts
one, instead, into the pocket of an individual. As for moral responsibility
for a crime—responsibility either towards the individual or towards the

community—the *Pravda's* conceptions do not seem to have risen beyond a purely material view of the matter. Yet the Code was not wholly lacking in moral instinct. For instance, it distinguishes clearly between unpremeditated murder (such as might be committed "in a dispute" or "through an affront") and murder done with preconceived intention; between an inadvertent infringement of the law and a wilful crime; between an act involving injury to health or limb (*e.g.* the cutting off of a man's finger with a sword-blow) and an act less dangerous in its nature but involving an affront to honour (*e.g.* a blow with a cudgel, pike, or the open hand, the tearing out of a man's hair or beard, and so forth). Of these two classes of acts, the *Pravda* visits the latter with penalties four times heavier than it does the former, while it also takes no account of serious assaults committed in response to an insult: thus showing that the Code was primarily the code of a class of men who always had a sword ready to their hand—namely, the class of military-governmental retainers of the Prince. That these distinctions between different classes of assaults and other acts according to their *moral* bearing represent a later stratum introduced into the Code is shown by the fact that, early in its pages (namely, in its second article), it prescribes only the normal, not the four-fold, penalty for a blow with a cudgel or pike. The source of this stratum of four-fold penalties and increased visitations for the crimes of theft, arson, and horse-stealing (to the simple fine for which there afterwards became added sequestration of property and sale of the offender into slavery) may be easily guessed, seeing that (as already noted) it was at the instigation of the *bishops* that Vladimir first raised the punishment for the first of those three special offences.

For all crimes other than those three offences the *Pravda* ordained a fine to the Prince and a sum to be paid in compensation to the person or persons injured by the offence. Both fine and compensation were reckoned in *grivni;* so that, in reality, the *grivna* served as the standard by which criminality, honour, even life itself (seeing that for the more grave offences a sentence of hanging was sometimes substituted by the Prince's courts) were measured. It is not possible for us to determine the exact market value of silver at that period, but we can at least estimate what its present-day value by *weight* would have been. In the twelfth century that metal was far more costly than it has ever been since the discovery of America—some economists say as much as four times more so. However, if we take twenty silver rouble-pieces as constituting a pound's weight of the metal, we find that the *grivna* of the eleventh century and early part of the twelfth would be equal now to about ten roubles, and the *grivna* of the later part of the twelfth century to about five. The monetary penalty for murder was known as *vira* or wer-gild, while the compensation to be paid to the relatives of the deceased was called *golovnitchestvo* or "head money." *Vira* was apportioned in three degrees, according to the social status of the deceased—eighty *grivni*, or double *vira*, being paid for the murder of a boyar or any member of the senior grade of the princely retinue, forty for that of a simple freeman, and twenty, or half *vira*, for that of a woman, or for such grave acts of mutilation as the cutting off of a nose, hand, or foot, as well as for blinding. *Golovnitchestvo* varied as much as did *vira* (or even more so) with the social position of the deceased. For instance, in the case of the murder of a boyar, the compensation to be paid was exactly equal to the amount of the penalty itself (*i.e.* eighty *grivni*), while in the case of a simple freeman it amounted only to five *grivni*. This almost invariable exaction of a fine to the Prince's government and a sum to be paid in compensation to the injured party or parties constituted the *Pravda's* whole system of punishments. The basis of that system is clear enough. The *Pravda* distinguished strictly between an injury or an affront done to an individual and injury done to property. At the same time it regarded even the former class of injury mainly from the standpoint of the industrial loss which such injury might cause to the community, and if it meted out a heavier penalty for the cutting off of a hand than for the cutting off of a finger, the sole reason was that the former mutilation rendered the sufferer a less efficient worker than the latter. Since, then, the *Pravda* regarded crime chiefly in the light of action inimical to industry, it appointed for every case a sum in restitution—a sum which should be approximately equal to the industrial loss caused by the given offence. So long as personal vengeance by judicial decree obtained, this restitution was based simply upon the rule, "A life for a life, a tooth for a tooth," but when restitution passed to another, a monetary, basis, the rule came rather to read, "A *grivna* for a *grivna*, a rouble for a rouble." This was the basis adopted by the *Pravda*. For the prevention of crime, for the repression of the criminal instinct, the *Pravda* made no provision. All that it had in view was the *material results* of crime, and for that reason punished the criminal only with *material loss* to correspond—saying to him, in effect: "Kill or steal as much as you like; *only*, for all that you do in that way you must pay according to the scale which I hereby appoint." Further, or higher, than that the *Pravda's* moral instincts did not go, for they were based only upon those of primitive law.

In this connection it is interesting to compare some of the *Pravda's* articles with one another. We find an identical penalty of twelve *grivni* awarded for stealing a beaver out of another man's trap, for disregarding a landmark, for knocking out a tooth, and for killing another man's slave. Again, identical penalties (this time of three *grivni* apiece, with compensation of one *grivna*) are allotted for cutting off a person's finger, for striking a man in the face, for dealing him a sword-cut resulting in a wound but not in death, for destroying another man's fowling-net, for removing his hunting implements, and for converting a freeman into a slave without judicial authorisation. Arson and horse-theft are the crimes most heavily punished of all—being visited more severely even than murder or grave acts of mutilation. From this we see that the law valued property more than its owner—that, in the law's eyes, the product of labour was of more importance than the living instrument by which that product was obtained. The same view of the individual and of property is repeated in the series of articles treating of slavery; in which we read (for instance) that an insolvent merchant might be sold into slavery by his creditors, and that a semi-slave who obtained an advance of wages from his or her master or mistress, and then ran away without repaying the same, might, upon recapture, be bound into full slavery. Thus the law valued and safeguarded the integrity and security of capital more than it did the freedom of the individual—a man's personality constituting an asset only in so far as it was allied with property. By the same standard also was his social importance measured. This will best be seen by examining the composition of the community (the lay portion of it, that is to say) as reflected in the *Pravda*.

The Code divided the community into two portions by a double system of dividing lines—political and economic. Politically it divided the people into an official class and a non-official class: a class which had direct relations with the Prince and a class which had not—a class of "prince's men" and a class of "simple men." The former of these classes was confined to that military-governmental section of the community which constituted the Prince's retinue, served as his instrument of rule and defence, enjoyed greater rights and privileges than the inferior class, and had the lives of its members protected by a double payment of *vira*. The other class—the class of "simple men"—embraced the whole of that general mass of freemen which constituted the tax-paying portion, urban and rural, of the community. Whether or not there ought to be added to these two classes a third and lower one—the class of *kholopi* or slaves—is doubtful. Certainly the *Pravda* itself did not regard *kholopi* as constituting a class at all, nor even human beings, but rather as chattels or beasts of burden. For that reason it punished the murderer of a slave other than his own, not with *vira* and *golovnitchestvo*, but with an ordinary fine to the government and the payment of such a sum to the owner of the slave as would have been awarded him for the loss of any other article of property. With regard to a master who murdered *his own* slave, the *Pravda* began by not punishing him at all, but eventually the Church introduced a new view of the relation of the law to the slave, and, declaring him to be a human being, meted out ecclesiastical penalties for his murder. Consequently, in the end, the princely courts had to follow suit. There are items in the *Pravda* which show that, previous to Yaroslav's death, a slave who struck a freeman might be killed by the latter, but that, after Yaroslav's death, his sons replaced this ordinance with an enactment permitting the person assaulted either to kill the slave or to sue the master for damages. Judging, then, by social practice, if not by actual law, we may take it, upon the whole, that slaves constituted a definite class in the composition of the then Russian community—a class distinguished from the two superior to it by the fact that on the one hand, it served, not the Prince himself, but private persons, and that, on the other hand, it paid no taxes. Thus we see that political relations to the Prince caused the three chief sections of the community to consist of (1) freemen serving the Prince personally, (2) freemen not serving him personally, but liable for taxes to him, and (3) non-freemen serving private persons and exempt from taxes.

As to the three *economic* classes into which the *Pravda* divided the community, the first of these consisted of what the Code calls boyars—not the boyars whom we know as princes' retainers and warriors, but a class of privileged landowners. This class sprang from the ranks of the "prince's men," while those of the "simple men" produced a class of *smerdi* or state copyholders, as well as one of *naimiti* or *zakupi*—i.e. semi-slave allotment-holders under a master. Of these, the *smerdi* were freemen who farmed State lands with their own stock and implements, while the *naimiti* or *zakupi* were serfs who farmed portions of a master's estates for themselves with that master's stock and implements. In each case, then, the distinction between the several classes was mainly one of property, though also, to a minor extent, of juridical rights. For instance, a boyar-landowner who had no sons might leave the whole of his property, moveable and immoveable, to his daughters, whereas the *smerd* in like case could do so only as regards his *moveable* property—the rest reverting to the Prince and his government. Again, both the boyar-landowner and the *smerd* were freemen, while the *naimit* or *zakup* was only half-free—a serf, though not an absolute slave. That this was the position of the *zakup* is shown, in the *Pravda*, by the facts (1) that his master might administer to him corporal chastisement, (2) that he was subject to certain civil disabilities, such as disqualification from bearing witness in any but minor legal suits—and then only when no freeman was available for the purpose,[1] and (3) that he was absolved from responsibility for certain offences such as theft; his fine being paid for him in such cases by his master, who thereafter could bind him into full slavery. Thus we see that, although the three economic classes in no way coincided with the three political, they, like the latter, were distinguished from one another by special rights—those of the political classes being based upon their relation to the princely power, and those of the economic upon their relation to property. In short, the *Pravda* rated capital as a social force equal in importance to the princely power itself, since not only did capital effect its own demarcation of classes in the Russian community, but it could compel the princely power to recognise it.

The importance of capital in the *Pravda's* eyes appears again in such of its articles as touch upon contracts and obligations with regard to property. The *Pravda*—or rather, the jurisprudence which produced it—had only a dim idea of crime as an offence against the moral order, and therefore devoted its chief attention to the exact definition and circumscription of proprietorial relations. We find it drawing a strict distinction between the entrustment of property to a bailee (its term for that transaction—*poklazha*—appearing to be a Slavonic translation of the Greek term καταθήκη) and a loan; between a simple loan—*i.e.* a loan without interest, as between friends—and one made at an agreed, fixed rate of interest; between a short-date and a long-date loan; and between fixed interest on a trade venture or company speculation and chance interest accruing in the form of *extra* profit or dividend. Likewise we find set forth in detail the procedure to be observed by creditors in the liquidation of a debtor's affairs—the procedure varying according as the bankruptcy of the debtor was due to his own fault or to misfortune. In general we

[1] See p. 132.

notice, as we proceed, a continuous increase in the forms of credit trading operations to which the *Pravda* refers in its pages, while the wealth of norms, definitions, and cases which it lavishes upon its jurisprudence with regard to capital is in marked contrast to the poverty of the articles included among its jurisprudence with regard to the person.

Such are the main features of the *Russkaia Pravda* as illustrative of the basic, ruling interests and motives in life of the Russian community of Kievan days. The Code is first and foremost an exposition of the rights of capital. Upon labour, upon the manifestation of human energy, it looks as upon the mere instrument by which capital is created. All the most important legal processes which it formulates have to do with capital ; all its most stringent injunctions are directed rather against acts detrimental to capital than against those inimical to the security of the person. In it capital furnishes not only the means of restitution in civil and criminal offences, but likewise the basis of its whole system of penalties and indictments. The individual is looked upon not so much as a member of the community as a possessor or a non-possessor, a producer or a non-producer, of capital. If he were neither a possessor nor a producer of that commodity he lost his right to freedom and to the civil qualifications of a citizen. For the same reason a woman's life was valued at twenty *grivni* only, or "half *vira*." Yet capital, in those days, was extremely costly. For short-date loans no exact rate of monthly interest is to be found prescribed in the *Pravda*, but for loans of one year or upwards an article fixes the annual rate at fifty per cent. Vladimir Monomakh alone attempted to modify this usurious system, by ordaining that interest should in no case be suffered to accumulate to the amount of more than one-half of the original principal, and that such interest should be recoverable only during the first two years of the loan—after which period nothing but the principal could be sued for, and even that under pain of forfeiture if the lender should be proved to be demanding more than his two years' interest. At the same time, for loans which it was expressly agreed to spread over three or more years he allowed interest, throughout, of forty per cent. Little attention, however, seems to have been paid to these restrictive enactments, for, although we read that Bishop Niphont of Novgorod[1] charged his questioners to denounce usury among the laity, and to instruct them to exact only "merciful" interest of from three to five *kuni* in the *grivna*, we find that Monomakh had not long been dead before "merciful" interest was once again being

[1] See p. 155.

assessed at the rate of from sixty to eighty per cent.—half as much, or nearly twice as much, as the legal rate! In fact, it was not until the thirteenth century, when the great trading towns were beginning to lose their importance as a factor in the industrial life of the people, that the clergy at last found it possible to insist upon "light" interest being charged—*i.e.* interest of three *kuni* or seven *riezani* in the *grivna*, or at the rate of from twelve to fourteen per cent. This fact, combined with the hard, *bourgeois* character of the *Pravda*, points clearly to the social centre whence the jurisdiction originated which served as the basis of the Code. That centre was the great trading town. Consequently, study of the civil order of the period, as revealed in the pages of the *Pravda*, brings us face to face again with the force which did so much to establish the political order of the period—namely, the force represented by the great trading town and its *vietché*. This force, then, it was which, combined with capital, determined both the civil and the political order of the eleventh and twelfth centuries.

CHAPTER XI

The Church Ordinances of the early Christian princes of Rus—Ecclesiastical jurisdiction as defined in Vladimir's and Yaroslav's Ordinances respectively—Innovations introduced by the Church into the theory of crime and the system of legal penalties—The monetary reckoning observed in Yaroslav's Ordinance as evidence of the period of its composition —The original basis of that Ordinance—The legislative powers of the Church—The process of ecclesiastical codification—Traces of the same in Yaroslav's Ordinance—Relation of Yaroslav's Ordinance to the *Russkaia Pravda*—The influence of the Church upon the political, civil, and social orders of the period.

In the course of our examination of the *Pravda* I called the Code a reliable, yet an incomplete, exponent of the legislation of its period. My reason for doing so was that the close of the tenth century witnessed the permeation of the old materialistic jurisprudence with a new tendency which, emanating from the Church, was based rather upon moral feeling than upon economic interest. Annals such as the Church Ordinances of Vladimir and Yaroslav illustrate that tendency, and therefore help to throw light upon a side of ancient Russian life which is scarcely touched upon in the *Pravda*.

Relating how, in 996, Vladimir devoted a tenth part of his revenues to the support of the cathedral church which he had built in Kiev, the Ancient Chronicle adds the remark : " This he did confirm with a vow." This vow is repeated in the work known as his Church Ordinance, wherein he binds his successors to preserve inviolate the enactments which it contains, and which he had framed according to the decrees of the Catholic Councils and the laws of the Greek emperors—*i.e.* according to the Nomocanon. We find the oldest of the many copies of this Ordinance bound up with the same Novgorodian *Kormtchaia* of the late thirteenth century which contains our oldest copy of the *Russkaia Pravda*. Although time has greatly corrupted the text of the Ordinance and thickly overlaid it with a mass of emendations, alterations, interpolations, and additions (a sign, nevertheless, that the Ordinance long held its place as an authority on legal practice), it is no very difficult matter to reconstruct, if not the original text, at all events the juridical framework of the Code with sufficient clearness to give us at least an idea of the theoretical basis upon which it was built.

In the main the Ordinance constitutes an exposition of the powers possessed by the Church in what was, for her, a new sphere of activity, since it was a sphere in which she was less concerned with the saving of souls than with the supervision of temporal matters approximating closely to tasks of state. On the one hand she had to aid the temporal power in building up the social organisation of the community and maintaining the political order of the land, while, on the other hand, she had to exercise jurisdiction over the whole body of Christians in Rus—a jurisdiction covering family relations, sacrilege, the care of Christian shrines and monuments, heresy, morality, unnatural sins, and offences of speech and against women's honour. In short, she was charged with the organisation and supervision of the family order, the religious order, and the moral order of the period. Furthermore, she had the care of that separate ecclesiastical community which, constituted of *tserkovnie liudi* and *bogadielnie liudi* (church officials and church pensioners), was subject to ecclesiastical jurisdiction in all matters, spiritual and temporal. This community included among its members (1) the white and the black clergy, together with the families of the former; (2) lay folk in the service of the Church or in any way acting as ministers to her temporal needs (such as doctors, midwives, makers of wafers, church servants in general, and *zadushnie* or *prikladi—i.e.* slaves bequeathed to the Church by their masters at death or granted their freedom during their masters' lifetime at the instigation of the clergy, and thereafter settled, as semi-free peasants, upon church lands); and (3) poor or homeless pensioners of the Church, such as destitute foreigners, beggars, blind people, and all in general who were incapacitated for work. Lastly, the Church had charge of all spiritual and benevolent establishments in which church folk found shelter—monasteries, hospitals, hostels for foreigners, homes for the aged and destitute. That all the foregoing were departments of ecclesiastical activity we learn from Vladimir's Church Ordinance, in which they are to be found succinctly and clearly enumerated.

We have at our disposal a later and enlarged edition of that Ordinance in the shape of an Ordinance issued by Vladimir's son Yaroslav. This is a much more full and systematic code—the subject matter of Vladimir's Ordinance being tabulated therein in a scheme of sections and articles which constitutes not only a complete system of ecclesiastical penalties, but also a more or less complete guide to the correct procedure in their administration. Both its system of penalties and its system of procedure are based upon the distinction and correlation existing between the theory of sin and the theory of crime. Sin, in the eyes of the Ordinance, was the Church's affair, and crime the affair of the State. Every crime was accounted by the Church a sin, but not every sin was accounted by the State a crime. Sin was a breach of, or negation of, morality—an infringement of the law of God ; while crime was merely an anti-social act—an infringement of the law of man. Sin lay, not only in the commission of a deed involving moral or material injury to a fellow-being, but also in its very *conception*, whereas crime was strictly limited to the commission of the deed. Upon these two basic theories the whole juridical system of Yaroslav's Church Ordinance was built, so that the work constitutes, in fact, a sort of moral catechism, a sort of list of disciplinary injunctions framed from the Church's point of view. Upon her the Ordinance conferred jurisdiction over all Christians with regard to acts of sin, as well as over the separate ecclesiastical community with regard to acts of crime. The matters thus delegated by the Ordinance to the jurisdiction of the Church may be divided into three classes, and described as follows :—

I. *Acts of Sin alone.*—These were subject to ecclesiastical jurisdiction exclusively, and adjudicated upon solely in accordance with the laws of the Church. They comprised all transgressions of the Church's law which did not also come within the purview of the temporal jurisdiction. Those transgressions lay, for the most part, in necromancy, witchcraft, marriage within the prohibited degrees, intercourse with pagans, consumption of forbidden articles of food, and unauthorised divorce by mutual agreement of husband and wife.

II. *Acts involving both Sin and Crime.*—These were subject to the temporal authority in conjunction with the spiritual—the Metropolitan formally determining the penalty, and the Prince's judge confirming and pronouncing the sentence. This class included all matters relating to rape, to desertion or forcible putting away of a wife, to adultery, and to offences in general against women.

III. *Acts of Crime committed by Members of the Separate Ecclesiastical Community.*—Nominally such acts were subject to the jurisdiction of the Church only, but, in practice, the princely power had a consultative voice in the matter, as constituting the actual executor of the sentence. Indeed, in graver cases coming under this head, the Prince usually attended in person, to adjudicate in company with the ecclesiastical judge.

The foregoing classification of acts delegated by the Ordinance to ecclesiastical jurisdiction shows us that the principal aim of the Ordinance was to delimit the spheres of the spiritual and the temporal authorities respectively when the latter were acting apart, and their joint sphere when they were acting in conjunction. The most important point to be noted in this respect is that the Ordinance introduced new features into the jurisprudence of its time. To begin with, it greatly increased the number of indictable offences, by not only extending ecclesiastical jurisdiction to cover all Christians in the land and to embrace both the moral, the family, and the religious life of the people, but also by making provision for dealing with many classes of offences which had not hitherto come within the cognisance of ancient legal custom—offences such as rape, sacrilege, violation of shrines and sacred ornaments, and the calling of a person either a heretic, a "compounder of enchanted philtres," or (in the case of a woman) a whore: the indictment of which forms of verbal abuse represented a first attempt of the Church to arouse newly-converted Rus to a sense of the dignity of the human personality. Equally important as innovations were certain new measures devised by the Ordinance for bringing *moral* treatment to bear upon the criminal. Hitherto ancient legal custom had looked only to the *material* results of crime, and so had exacted only *material* retribution, in the shape of fines and sums in compensation. The view of the Christian jurist, however, went broader and deeper than that, and looked backward from effect to cause—or, in other words, sought to *prevent* crime as well as to punish it, by visiting certain offences, not with the old monetary penalties prescribed by the temporal law (although the Ordinance still preserved them in its general scheme), but with moral-disciplinary treatment, in the form of a term of detention in a "church house" (the detention, in all probability, involving forced labour for the Church's benefit) and penance—*i.e.* either temporary deprivation of church privileges or a course of penitential exercises. For instance, as regards cases of child-murder or assaults upon parents by the children, the Ordinance enacts that "the guilty shall enter into a church house," while for marriage within the prohibited degrees it ordains that, after paying a fine to the Church, the offenders shall "be sundered and undergo penance." Of a form of punishment which, though highly opposed to the spirit of Christian teaching, was nevertheless conceded to the tribunals of the Church, we find no direct mention in the Ordinance. I refer to flogging—a feature borrowed from Byzantine legislation, which had used it to replace maiming, torture, blinding, and other useless legal cruelties of the past. Yet, although, as I say, we find no *direct* mention of this form of penalty, the Ordinance contains an article enacting that a woman found practising witchcraft "shall be

NEW IDEAS 169

stripped and punished," and thereafter made to pay a fine of six *grivni* to the Metropolitan. What that term "punished" implies is made clear to us by one of the Church Rules of the Metropolitan John II. (1080–89), in which he directs that a man or woman found practising sorcery shall first of all be admonished as to his or her evil doings, and then, if such admonition fail in its effect, be "fiercely beaten, yet not unto death, nor even unto the wounding of their bodies."

Such, in the main, were the contents of Yaroslav's Church Ordinance: the new ideas which it imported into primitive Russian jurisprudence and conceptions of law being (1) abrogation of the view of crime as a material injury done only to the community in favour of the view of crime as a moral injury done, not only to the community, but also to the criminal himself; (2) the rendering indictable of a larger number of offences than had hitherto come within the purview of ancient legal custom; and (3) the supplementing of the old monetary penalties by certain moral-preventive measures designed to restore and strengthen the will-power of the criminal—measures such as penance, detention in a "church house," and corporal punishment.

In this manner Yaroslav's Ordinance took the *materialistic* interests and relations of ancient legal custom as its basis for a new system of interests and relations partaking of a *moral* and *religious* character—a system of which the new ecclesiastical courts constituted by the Ordinance were to be the introducers to the Russian community. From this point of view, indeed, the *Russkaia Pravda* would appear to be ending its career at the very moment when the Ordinance was starting out in life: yet, as a matter of fact, consideration of the various stages of juridical development in Rus, as represented by her legal annals, will show us that the two Codes were contemporary examples of legal codification. Moreover (as in the case of the *Pravda*) we need only to glance at the text of the Ordinance and at such of its archæological details as time has spared to us to be able to conjecture with approximate accuracy the period of its composition. As with the *Pravda*, it is the system of monetary penalties observed in the Ordinance which furnishes us with our principal item of evidence in this connection. Yet, at the first glance, that system would seem to be a mere heterogeneous, anomalous medley. For instance, one version of the Ordinance gives "a *grivna* of silver" as the amount of a fine to the Church where another version names a *rouble*, and a third "a *grivna* of silver *or* a rouble"—and this in spite of the fact that the *grivna* and the rouble were non-contemporary units of currency. For another offence one version gives twenty *grivni* as the fine, a second one forty, a third one also forty, and a fourth one a hundred. The reason of these apparent discrepancies is that they represent the same fluctuations of the monetary standard as we noticed in the *Pravda*, except that in the case of the Ordinance the fluctuations are more definitely marked. We have seen that the short version of the *Pravda* gives its penalties in terms of *riezani*, and the full version in those of *kuni*. Similarly we find certain versions of the Ordinance naming sixty *riezani* as the penalty for insulting a "country woman" (*selskaia zhena*), while other versions name sixty *kuni*. The cause of this interchange of monetary units is (as already seen in the *Pravda*) the fact that the *grivna* decreased in weight from, at the beginning of the twelfth century, half a pound to, at the close of that century, a quarter of that amount. As a rule, judicial penalties followed the fluctuations of the monetary standard, but this rule was not invariable, since efforts were sometimes made to preserve the actual *metal weight* of a given penalty, in spite of the decreasing weight of the *grivna*—the method of doing so being either to exact the penalties in "olden" *grivni* [1] or to raise their amounts. Of these two methods, the latter was the one adopted by the ecclesiastical courts, so that the fact that we find one version of the Ordinance naming twenty *grivni* as the fine to the Church for bigamy, and another one forty, merely means that the former version was inscribed during the *first* half of the twelfth century, when the weight of the *grivna* stood at half a pound, and the latter one during the *second* half of that century, when the *grivna* had fallen to a quarter of a pound. But, as said in the last chapter, there was an intermediate period (approximately the portion of the second quarter of the century which followed upon the death of Mstislav in 1132) when the *grivna* weighed about a third of a pound. Of this we have evidence both from written documents and from the fact that ingots of that weight have been discovered in the "hoards" of which I spoke in Chapter IX. Revision of the Ordinance at that period has left its mark upon some of the versions, so that, while certain of them assess the penalty for participating in the rape of a girl at one *grivna*, others name sixty *nogati*—which would be about equal to *three grivni*. Again, in the second quarter of the thirteenth century *grivni* began to circulate of which no fewer than seven and a half went to a pound's weight of silver. That is to say, the *grivna* was now two and a half times lighter than it had been during the third-of-a-pound period. Accordingly, while some versions of the day name forty *grivni* for a certain penalty, others

1 See p. 149.

name a hundred. The truth is that many copyists were prone to incorporate with their own particular version scales of penalties dating from an earlier period, and, placing items calculated according to these obsolete scales beside items calculated according to the scale current in their own day, worked great confusion in the penal system of the Ordinance. Nevertheless, what we know of the history of currency in ancient Rus enables us to overcome, to a certain extent, this difficulty, and to form a conclusion that the oldest versions of the Ordinance date from the beginning of the twelfth century, or at all events from its earlier half. Hence, not only does it follow that the Ordinance and the *Russkaia Pravda* were contemporaries in composition, but further comparison of those two oldest examples of Russian codification makes it clear that they were also (if I may use the term) compatriots. That is to say, they not only sprang simultaneously from, but grew to maturity in, common ground—the ground of ecclesiastical jurisdiction.

The many divergencies between the texts of the various versions of the Ordinance, as well as the evident traces of revision and amplification which they contain, confront the historical critic with two interesting questions—namely, the question of the authorship of the Ordinance, and the question of its original basis. In the brief introduction to the Code (which, again, is given differently in different versions) Yaroslav says that, in accordance with the "bequest" or the "dispensation" of his father, he has "made agreement" with the Metropolitan Ilarion to grant unto the said Metropolitan and the bishops those courts of law which are to be found set forth in the Greek Nomocanon (Rules of the Church) as having jurisdiction over all acts of sin, all acts whatsoever committed by ecclesiastical persons, and certain acts with regard to which the temporal power has joint interest with the spiritual. It is this "agreement," then, between the spiritual power and the temporal for the purpose of delimiting their respective jurisdictions in accordance with the principles of the Greek Nomocanon that we may take to have been the original basis upon which Yaroslav constructed his Ordinance. Indeed, one ancient script—the Script of Archangel—gives the Ordinance in this primal form alone. Later on, however, when the ecclesiastical courts constituted by the "agreement" had become regularly established, their practice was formulated in written articles, and these, again, codified into what, from its origin and contents, is known to us as Yaroslav's Church Ordinance. Thus we see that in those days legislation progressed from practice to codification, and not *vice versâ*, as has since become the custom ; and it was this reverse order of progression which rendered the Ordinance so peculiarly susceptible to those changes which varying conditions of period and locality were bound to bring about in the practice of the spiritual courts.

In explaining the origin of Yaroslav's Ordinance thus, I have also in view the relation in which the Christianising of Russian conditions of life placed the Church to the State. Forced to seek the Church's assistance in organising its social system upon Christian principles, the State entrusted to her jurisdiction all matters and relations of life which sprang directly from the popular adoption of Christianity; while, on their side, the clergy were guided in the regulation of those matters and relations by the Church's rules, reinforced by authority granted them by the temporal power for the taking of such disciplinary and administrative measures as might seem advisable for the adapting of those rules to the existing conditions of Russian life. Consequently, while the ecclesiastical hierarchy was the State's principal coadjutor in the task of regulating the social order, it was by virtue of the State's commission alone that that hierarchy had power to legislate in its allotted sphere. As to the usual circumstances in which the temporal power granted the Church permission to legislate, we have an instance in the preface to the Church Ordinance which Vsevolod, grandson of Monomakh, issued to the Archbishop of Novgorod during his (the Prince's) tenure of rule in that province. In this preface Vsevolod says that hitherto, when called upon to adjudicate in cases of succession in which the children were the issue of one father but of different mothers, he has done so "in accordance with the teaching and tradition of the Holy Fathers"—*i.e.* in accordance with the rules of the Nomocanon ; but that, doubts having arisen in his mind as to his competency to deal with such cases, he now desires that "from henceforth the Archbishop shall judge these suits according to the Nomocanon, and thus remove this burden from my soul." We see, then, that, as soon as a prince's conscience began to trouble him concerning his eligibility to deal with matters which called for canonical authority and erudition, he turned them over to the Church, as a means of relieving himself of the responsibility involved—a responsibility more fitted for the shoulders of those who possessed such knowledge of the Nomocanon as was impossible for a temporal ruler. But to make Byzantine law conform to existing conditions of life in Rus meant revision both of that law and of those conditions—or, in other words, new jurisprudence : wherefore the ecclesiastical hierarchy was entrusted with the task, and the judicial authority of the Church insensibly became converted also into a legislative power.

The foregoing throws considerable light upon the development of law and legal administration in Rus during the eleventh and twelfth centuries. Although the boyar class was the actual instrument of princely rule, its conservative instincts and ideas rendered it incapable of coping with the new problems of law and legal administration which arose in consequence of the broadening of Russian life by Christianity, while its blunders and abuses of authority only "oppressed the spirit of the Prince," as Vsevolod phrases it in his Ordinance. Nevertheless, the princes were anxious to improve the condition of affairs, and therefore sought to define the respective powers of the spiritual authority and the temporal, to set exact bounds to their jurisdictions, to discover new sources of law for their use, and to better the existing methods of making their decrees effective. For all these requirements they had to turn to the ecclesiastical hierarchy, as possessed not only of the necessary moral formulae, but also of the necessary legal erudition, while, in their turn, the ecclesiastical judges and jurists had to set to work to collect such productions of Byzantine Church legislation as bore specially upon judicial procedure and penal administration, to extract from them suitable norms and rules, to refer debateable questions to supreme authorities on ecclesiastical law, and to receive answers to the same in the form of considered pronouncements *ex cathedrâ*. These rules and pronouncements became juridical norms adapted to the peculiar circumstances of Russian life, and, gradually crystallising into articles of positive law according as the new ecclesiastical courts adopted them in practice, were introduced into existing ordinances or tabulated in new digests issued under the Prince's authority. Of this prolonged and laborious task of codification we see fragments preserved in the *Kormtchi* and similar legal compilations, either in the form of complete works such as the Church Ordinances of Vladimir and Yaroslav, or in that of separate documents of unknown date and origin which served as appendices to, or complementary portions of, some complete work. In the main, the process was identical with the one by which the *Russkaia Pravda* was compiled.

Yet, though every version of Yaroslav's Ordinance contains manifest traces of a common origin with the *Pravda*, the express purpose of the former as a code of Church law and discipline caused it to approximate much more closely to its Byzantine sources than did the latter. This will be the more readily understood when we consider that, whereas the *Pravda* reproduced merely the ancient legal customs upon which Russian life was based, with scarcely a tinge of Christian colouring added, the Ordinance sought to instil into those customs a definite measure of Christian doctrine. The fundamental sources of the Ordinance were the two Byzantine codes with which the Ordinance is always to be found bound up in the old *Kormtchi*—namely, the Eclogue and the *Procheiron*—more especially those sections or chapters of them which are headed "Of Punishments." Nevertheless the Ordinance does not merely copy its sources—it also revises them by extending and adapting the norms which it borrows, and by breaking up into detail the general *casus* and propositions of the sources in question. We even find it importing entirely new juridical *casus* into its pages—*casus* suggested to the codifiers by various local phenomena of Russian life. Of these conditions of composition I will cite one instance only, since we have already examined precisely similar conditions in the case of the *Pravda*.

One article of the *Procheiron* enacts that a man who ravishes a married or an unmarried woman of any social standing whatever—even his own betrothed—shall, with any his accomplices, confederates, aiders, or abettors, be subjected to a more or less cruel form of corporal punishment according as he and his accomplices (if any) were or were not armed when committing the misdemeanour. This enactment is amended in Article One of Yaroslav's Ordinance to impose upon the ravisher a *monetary* penalty proportioned to the social status of the woman assaulted according as she chanced to be the daughter "of a greater or of a lesser boyar" (*i.e.* of a member of the senior or the junior grade of the Prince's retinue) or of a member of the burgher class. A certain amount of punishment is also to be awarded to accomplices (if any) in the rape. Subsequently, to this article in the Ordinance was added a clause by which the aforesaid penalties were to be raised if the woman assaulted was unmarried at the time of the commission of the offence and yet did not afterwards become united in Christian wedlock to her ravisher. Presumably, in cases where the act of rape was followed by marriage according to the rites of the Church the culprit was exempted from the prescribed fine to the Metropolitan, and, with the woman, was allotted only a certain amount of penance "in that the twain did not first come together according to the law of God" (as we find it phrased in an old manual of Rules for the Clergy which is usually ascribed to Archbishop John of Novgorod). A further amendment to this article adds to the three social classes which have already been specified in connection with the parentage of the woman yet a fourth class—namely, the common people: which amendment was subsequently amplified further to the extent of making all that had previously been enacted with regard to rape hold good only in cases where the offence was committed with the consent of the woman and without the use of force.   Presumably, then, cases where the element of consent was *absent* were thenceforth treated on a different and more rigorous basis.   This last amendment and its appended clause we find set down in the Ordinance, not with their parent article (article one), but as two separate articles (numbers six and seven); with the result that, at first sight, they are not easy to understand without their context.

I have adduced this instance with the double object of showing, firstly, how a legal *casus* was often worked upon by codifiers of that day until it conformed to local custom, and secondly, what difficulties have to be overcome by those whose business it is to interpret ancient Russian legal records.   Upon the whole, study of Yaroslav's Ordinance reveals to us the fact that at that period both ecclesiastical legal practice and ecclesiastical codification were in a state of immaturity—of hesitating and tentative experiment.   We find one version of the Ordinance roundly and definitely naming a given penalty, and another version putting forward a penalty which is, so to speak, offered only for the *approval* of the ecclesiastical authorities.   Nor does the Ordinance comprise the whole of the ecclesiastical jurisprudence of its period, nor yet make any provision for dealing with offences concerning which the Church of the eleventh and twelfth centuries had already made definite pronouncements. These shortcomings become especially noticeable if we compare the Ordinance either with John of Novgorod's Rules or with the answers given by Bishop Niphont of Novgorod to his questioners.[1]   Nevertheless, Yaroslav's Ordinance remains practically the only general record of the ecclesiastical law of its day, since the Church Ordinances issued by Yaroslav's successors possess only a special or local significance as merely either reproducing Vladimir's Ordinance, amended to suit a given diocese, or confining themselves to an exposition of the financial relations of Church and State in some particular province. Of the first of these two classes of Ordinance the Ordinance given by Sviatoslav at Novgorod in 1137 may be taken as an example, while of the second the Ordinance given by Rostislav at Smolensk in 1151 is typical. Yaroslav's Ordinance, on the other hand, was intended to serve as the official code of the Church in Rus at large.   Moreover, it differed from the rest in making a definite attempt to draw a line of demarcation between the temporal jurisdiction and the spiritual, as well as to establish points of

[1] See p. 155.

contact between them where necessary.   In this regard, indeed, it may be said to stand in close historical and juridical relation to the *Russkaia Pravda*, seeing that, while the latter was designed to be a church code dealing with acts of crime committed by persons subject only to ecclesiastical jurisdiction, the former was designed to be a church code dealing with acts of sin committed by persons subject both to ecclesiastical and to non-ecclesiastical jurisdiction, and that, while the *Russkaia Pravda* was a digest of civil and criminal law adapted to the needs of the Church when adjudicating upon acts of crime committed by members of the separate ecclesiastical community, Yaroslav's Ordinance was a digest of ecclesiastical law concerning acts of sin committed by all Christians without distinction. Again, while the fundamental sources of the *Pravda* were (1) local legal custom and (2) legislation framed by the Princes with the help of Byzantine ecclesiastical law, those of the Ordinance were (1) the Greek Nomocanon and similar works relating to Byzantine Church law and (2) Vsevolod's Church Ordinance—a code based partly upon local legal custom and partly upon legislative enactments of the Princes.   Thus, while the *Pravda* derived its code forms from the same Byzantine sources as did the Ordinance, and the latter derived the basis of its system of penalties and monetary exactions from the same Russian sources as did the *Pravda*, they both of them borrowed from their two Byzantine models (the Eclogue and the *Procheiron*) an identical form of legal tabulation — namely, the synoptical, parallel form.   The general result is that the two codes—the *Russkaia Pravda* and Yaroslav's Church Ordinance—almost appear to be complementary portions of a single comprehensive digest of ancient jurisprudence.

Examination of these old Church Ordinances enables us to form some idea of the influence exercised by the Church upon the Russian community during the early stages of Christianity in Rus.   Included among the Church Rules of John II., Metropolitan of Rus in the eleventh century, we find an injunction which he laid upon an ecclesiastic who sought his advice on matters of church practice.   "Cleave ever unto the law of God—not unto the custom of the land" was John's pronouncement.   Yet neither Russian ecclesiastical legal practice nor Russian legal codification appear quite to have justified this dictum, so far as we may judge from Yaroslav's Ordinance and the *Pravda*, seeing that the Church made no attempt to reconstruct either the form or the bases of the order of state which she found existent in Rus—and that in spite of the fact that, to the newly-arrived hierarchy, accustomed to the strict monarchical rule and political centralisation of Byzantium, the state order of Rus, with its absence of either, must have been anything but congenial. All that the hierarchy attempted to do was to abrogate or to modify some of the worst results of the native system (as, for instance, the princely feuds), and to instil worthier political ideas into the princes' minds by explaining to them what ought to be the true goal of their efforts, and what were the best and most honourable means of attaining it. Nevertheless these efforts were by no means wholly unsuccessful, since they had the effect of bringing about decided improvements in the administrative and legislative practice of the princes, in the generally accepted ideas on law and the functions of a ruler, and in the manner of enacting punishment for civil and criminal offences. Likewise, it was to the Church that Rus owed her first written codes of jurisprudence; so that it is with some reason that a law-writer has ever since been known in our language by the borrowed Greek (*i.e.* Byzantine) term of *diak* or clerk. Nevertheless, the low standard of moral and social feeling yet attained by the Russian princes prevented the Church from introducing as much actual amelioration into the political order as she might otherwise have done. We read that on one occasion, when a feud was impending between two princes, the Metropolitan of Kiev said in expostulation to the would-be disputants: "We pray you that ye do not this hurt to the Russian land. If ye go to war among yourselves, then will the heathen rejoice, and take possession of all this our territory which our fathers and grandfathers obtained for us with so much labour and suffering. Thus the Russian land which our fathers sought through many strange countries will be cast away through your fault." More than this, however, the Metropolitan could not do. Of course, the better sort of princes, like Monomakh and David of Tchernigov, would be amenable to reason when the matter was put to them thus, yet we may take it that, as a rule, things went on in the old traditional manner—the new system of moral principles and the old order of princely relations continuing to develop side by side, yet never converging or displacing one another, except when, upon rare occasions and for a brief period, they met in the person of some exceptional ruler—after whose decease the intrigues of his kinsmen would speedily efface whatever good his isolated efforts had effected. There has come down to us from the twelfth century an eloquent speech delivered by some orator or another in honour of the saintly Princes Boris and Gleb. The panegyric is known as the *Slovo o Kniazach*, or "Oration on the Princes," and has for its *motif* the theme of brotherly love and kindness as opposed to the feuds and dissensions of the reigning princes. "Hear, O ye Princes"—thus runs the crowning passage—"among whom brother fighteth against brother, and raiseth against him a host, and leadeth to his assault the pagans: will not God surely destroy you at the dread judgment? The holy Boris and Gleb did suffer their brother to take from them their rule, and even their life: yet will ye not suffer your brother to speak unto you a word without ye take offence, and conceive a deadly enmity against him, and summon unto your aid the pagans. Feel ye not shame to be at strife with your brother and with those who be of like faith with yourselves?" This stirring appeal throws some light upon the manners of the time, and ought to have had some effect upon them: yet it was not so. The truth is that the system of rule itself was at fault. The princes suffered as much as any one else from the effects of that system, yet were unable to invent one to replace it, or else were unequal to the task of carrying through a revolution. Nor were the ecclesiastical authorities fully possessed either of the necessary authority or the necessary zeal for putting an end to the genealogical rivalries of the. princes, seeing that, as yet, the ranks of the hierarchy were largely filled with Greeks — and not always Greeks of the best stamp. Indeed, some of those dignitaries were more concerned with that remitting of funds to their native country for which we find John of Novgorod reproaching them so bitterly than with caring for the interests and needs of their local dioceses. Already the term Greek had come to be synonymous, in Rus, with the term rogue. "He was full of guile because he was a Greek" is what we find the Ancient Chronicle remarking of one such archbishop.

The hierarchy worked not so much through persons as through the rules and principles which it inculcated—not so much upon the political order of the land as upon private relations, especially those of the family. Without directly shattering rooted customs and prejudices, the Church sought to instil into native conditions of life new ideas and relations born of that change in the manners and outlook of the people which she herself had been the first to set on foot. Thus she continued to insinuate herself more and more into the moral and juridical conceptions of the community, and to pave the way for the reception of new legal forms designed to amend the standard of Russian life. Study of the *Pravda* has shown us that civil rights and qualifications of property divided the people into three political and three economic classes which, superimposed the one upon the other, cut the community horizontally. The Church, however, sought to effect a division in the opposite direction—vertically. The separate ecclesiastical community which she founded was not a solid, homogeneous, permanent class—a class constituting an entirely new popular entity, but a union of persons drawn from *all* classes in the State. Admission to this community went, not by social status, but by misfortune, fortuitous circumstances, or voluntary entry. The destitute man became of necessity a member, and a prince could become so if he desired. Thus Vsevolod's Church Ordinance (based upon that of Vladimir, and issued to the cathedral body of St. Sophia at Novgorod during the second quarter of the twelfth century) adds to the number of "church folk" certain *izgoi*, or persons who, through misfortune or some other chance circumstance, had lost the rights of their class and, so to speak, missed their way in life. Of such *izgoi* waifs and strays the Ordinance names four species—namely, the priest's son who had failed to qualify himself for the ministry, the merchant who had become bankrupt, the slave who had purchased his freedom, and the prince who had prematurely lost his father.[1] Thus side by side with social divisions based upon civil rights and qualifications of property the Church introduced her own demarcation of classes — a demarcation founded upon principles altogether different to those governing the civil system. Her method was to collect members from every social stratum in the State, and to bind them together in a community inspired either by a common *aim*—the aim of religious service, or by a common *sentiment*—the sentiment of Christian charity. Its composition being such, it is clear that the ecclesiastical community was not a new state class with the clergy at its head, but a brotherhood separate from, yet parallel with, the civil community, and having its members all united on a common basis of religious conviction and religious equality.

No less important was the influence of the Church upon the *private* relations of the people—especially upon those of the fundamental popular unit, the family. In this respect she completed that disruption of the pagan clan union which had been begun before the advent of Christianity to Rus and now had left only a few remaining relics (such as blood-vengeance for murder) for the Church to destroy. For instance, one of the distinguishing features of the clan union had been the absence of any system of hereditary succession to property ; yet Oleg's treaty with the Greeks shows us that bequeathal by written will had already become a recognised form of testamentary disposition some three-quarters of a century before the conversion of Vladimir to Christianity—or at all events that it had so become among the classes most in touch with Byzantium. Built as it was

[1] See p. 108.

upon pagan foundations, the clan union was abhorrent to the Church, who began, from the first moment of her entry into Rus, to dissolve its tottering fragments, and to construct in its place a union upon which she could bestow her blessing—namely, the union of the family.   Her chief means of effecting her purpose was by regulating marriage and succession to property. We have seen that the Ancient Chronicle gives the ceremony of bringing the bride to the bridegroom at nightfall as a recognised form of marriage among the Poliani in pre-Christian days,[1] while from John of Novgorod's charge to his clergy we see that, as long as two centuries after the adoption of Christianity, the community was still occasionally resorting to the old pagan *umichka* or marriage by rape, as an alternative to the Christian rite.   All this brought about the presence among the people of so many of those whom the Church looked upon as "unwedded" wives that the ecclesiastical authorities had no choice but to accept the fact, and to recognise such unions as, if not "lawful," at all events "permissible."   We find Yaroslav's Ordinance imposing a penalty upon a husband who should put away his "unwedded" wife without authority, and John of Novgorod instructing his clergy that it is their duty to minister to such wives and their children.   An offence still more heavily punished by the Church than marriage without her benediction was marriage within the prohibited degrees.   John of Novgorod's Rules show us that, in the latter half of the eleventh century, penance was imposed for marriage even between fourth cousins—although at a later period the regulations were relaxed to the extent of permitting third cousins to be joined in matrimony.   Nevertheless, the tendency of the Church was always to narrow the circle of consanguinity within which marriage was permissible, and so to prune the over-luxuriant tree of pagan kinship by lopping off its more outspreading branches.

There can be no doubt that the Church experienced great difficulty in instilling new moral and juridical principles into family relations, seeing that of all relations they would, at that period, be the least susceptible to order and discipline, the least capable of being brought under fixed rules and forms of law.   Based upon inclination and instinct, they confronted the Church with such obstacles as polygamy, concubinage, and the system under which husbands rid themselves of superfluous wives by forcing them to enter a convent.   As a social unit the Christian family was founded by the Church upon mutual agreement of the two parties to live together, and maintained upon the basis of legal equality of husband and wife and of

[1] See p. 47.

mutual endowment with each other's goods. That being so, a necessary corollary was separate property of the wife—a right which we find recognised even in Varangian Rus of the tenth century, since Oleg's treaty with the Greeks stipulated that the goods of a wife were not to be made liable for any misdemeanour committed by her husband. This regulation was supported and confirmed by the Church, while to the clergy Vladimir's Ordinance also entrusted the settling of connubial disputes.

At the same time, the Church's activity with regard to family life was not confined solely to its regulation by formal rules and statutes, for there were other matters connected with it which she entrusted to the purely *moral* influence of her priests. For instance, Yaroslav's Ordinance ordains a penalty for a wife who should assault her husband, but says nothing about the reverse case—leaving it, presumably, to be dealt with by ghostly counsel and reproof. Nor must the priest be overlooked when we are considering the enactments of the various Church Ordinances with regard to the relations to be observed between parents and children. In this connection ecclesiastical law took cognisance only of the simpler breaches of family life; making, on the one hand, the parents responsible for the proper marriage of their children and the chastity of their daughters, and, on the other hand, visiting assaults of the children upon the parents with a double measure of "disciplinary" penalty—*i.e.* with the penalties enacted by the civil, as well as by the ecclesiastical, law. As to the Church's other principal means of influencing family relations—succession to property, she allowed the husband and father the fullest latitude in the bequeathal of his goods to his children; thus differing from the models of Byzantine law upon which she framed her Russian codes. "As a man at death shall divide his substance among his issue, so shall the division stand," was the *Pravda's* formula in this connection, while of collateral heirs the Church took no account whatever so long as there were children; the only exceptions being when the widow remarried during the infancy of the said children, or when the deceased died both childless and intestate.

It should never be lost sight of that this successful displacement of the pagan union of the clan by the Christian union of the family represented—so far as the Church was concerned—merely the completion of a movement initiated, long before her coming, by the influences referred to in Chapters IV. and VI.

CHAPTER XII

The principal phenomena distinguishing the second period—The conditions which brought about the disruption of the social order and economic prosperity of Kievan Rus — The life of the upper classes of the community, and the progress of culture and the civic spirit among them—Position of the lower classes—The development of slavery—The attacks of the Polovtsi—The depopulation of Kievan Rus — The double stream of emigration thence—The western stream of that movement—A glance at the fortunes of South-Western Rus—The question of the origin of the Little Russian stock—Evidence as to the north-eastward exodus from Kiev—Importance of that movement.

NEXT let us turn to the study of the second principal period of Russian history—the period which extends from the beginning of the thirteenth century to approximately the middle of the fifteenth. Two radical changes in Russian life are embraced within that period—namely, the transference of the bulk of the Russian population from the basin of the Dnieper to the region of the Upper Volga, and the substitution of the hereditary prince of the appanage for the great trading town as the chief organising and directing agency of the political and economic orders of the country. Thus the second period brings before us a new historical setting and a new dominant political force. Rus of the Dnieper now becomes Rus of the Upper Volga, and the provincial chief town gives place, as the leading political factor in the community, to its quondam rival the prince. This twofold change gave rise to political and economic orders wholly different to those which had obtained in Kievan Rus; for while, on the one hand, Rus of the Upper Volga responded to the influence of the new political force by becoming divided into princely appanages in place of town-provinces, her population was led by its new environment to replace foreign trade as the prime factor in the popular industry with agricultural exploitation of the land by free peasant labour.

Up to the middle of the twelfth century (*i.e.* up to about the death of Andrew Bogoliubski in 1174) our attention is concentrated chiefly upon the princes of Kiev and their doings; but as soon as ever that point is reached the scene becomes shifted to the north-east—to Suzdal. This change occurs almost too suddenly for us to realise at first whither the old Rus of Kiev has disappeared or whence the new Rus of Suzdal has arisen.   Our best plan will be to seek, first of all, to elucidate the *causes* of this unexpected turn of the historical kaleidoscope, and, in particular, to determine precisely when and how the bulk of the Russian population came to be transferred from the old setting to the new.

Undoubtedly the migratory movement originated in the social disintegration of Kievan Rus.   To that circumstance many and complex factors contributed—factors due both to the internal order of Kievan life and to its external environment.   Of them let us examine the principal.

The middle of the twelfth century saw conditions enter into operation which were bound, sooner or later, to militate against the social order and economic well-being of Kievan Rus.   Hitherto, to judge from the condition of the upper classes, a high level of material affluence, citizenship, and general culture had been attained by the community, since the ruling factor in the popular industry—namely, foreign trade—had served both to preserve the life of the people from isolation and stagnancy and to bring great wealth into the country.   Money circulated in abundance, from the golden *grivna* (an ingot approximately equal in weight to the Greek *litra*) down to minute fractions of the silver *grivna*.   The costly materials and artistic magnificence embodied in such a shrine as Yaroslav's Cathedral of St. Sophia alone show us what pecuniary resources must have lain at the disposal of the princes and the capital towns; while, with regard to the amount of free bullion always ready to a prince's hand, we know that at about the middle of the twelfth century the Prince of Smolensk usually received from his province, in *dan* alone, an annual sum of not less than three thousand silver *grivni*—which, reckoned on the basis of the then market value of that metal, would be about equal to a hundred and fifty thousand roubles of our own day.   Likewise we know that Vladimir once presented to his father, at a single gift, three hundred golden *grivni*, and that in 1144 Vladimirko, Prince of Galicia, sent his Suzerain, Vsevolod, a peace-offering of twelve hundred *grivni* in silver.   Evidence also of great wealth on the part of *private* persons is to be met with.   For instance, a *tisiatski* in the service of Yuri Dolgoruki who wished to present an ornamental railing to the tomb of the Abbot Theodosius found himself able to devote to that purpose no less than five hundred pounds' weight of gold and a like amount of silver.   Again, we see that Yaroslav's Church Ordinance did not consider a fine of three hundred silver *grivni* and five *grivni* in gold at all an extreme penalty to inflict upon a boyar who put away his wife without the Church's authority.   Still further testimony to the general wealth of the community is afforded by documents and inventories referring to the huge establishments maintained by the princes. In those inventories we find slaves numbered by the hundred, horses and *poods*[1] of honey by the thousand, and *korchagi*[2] of wine by tens. Finally, it is recorded of the Prince Igor, son of Oleg, who was slain at Kiev in 1147, that upon his threshing-floor stood no fewer than nine hundred stacks of corn!

Naturally enough, this constant flow of native and foreign wealth to Kiev and other commercial and administrative centres enabled the ruling class to order its life sumptuously, to dress well, and to build itself lordly habitations. For centuries the memory of the Easter festivals given by the Russian princes survived as a source of wonder among the people, and echoes of it are still to be heard in the heroic *bilini* sung by the peasantry of Olonetz and Archangel. All this material affluence found expression also in art and literature, since the wealth of the country attracted many foreign artists and *litterateurs* to its shores. To this day the tumuli and "hoards" of South Russia yield gold and silver articles which, dating from those times, are found, for the most part, to be of the finest craftsmanship; while such fragments of old buildings—churches and shrines, with their curious frescoes and mosaics—of the eleventh and twelfth centuries as still survive in certain of the towns of Kievan Russia strike with admiration and amazement the beholder whose artistic eye has been nourished only on the architecture and colouring of the Kremlin. With all this wealth and artistry—the whole of which was derived from Byzantine sources—went also new moral and intellectual ideas, until in time came Christianity itself, with its literature and jurisprudence, its clergy and monastic orders, its sacred paintings, choral music, and church preaching. The main artery through which this constant stream of moral and material riches entered the country and percolated to Kiev was, of course, the Dnieper. Annals of the eleventh and twelfth centuries make frequent mention of the great knowledge of foreign languages possessed by the Russian princes of their day, as well as of the princes' love for collecting and reading books, their zeal for education, their founding of schools for the teaching of the Latin and Greek tongues, and the attention which they showed to scholars who visited the country from Greece and Western Europe. Nor do those annals refer only to isolated cases, or to such exceptional phenomena as could have no permanent influence upon the standard of Russian culture. On the contrary, they refer to the universal order of things then obtaining. Finally, with the help of the

---

[1] The *pood* = 40 Russian lbs.   [2] Puncheons.

Greco-Slavonic translator, a definite scriptory form of the Russian language was evolved, and an original school of Russian literature founded; until eventually a native manuscript of the twelfth century was able to vie, for scholarship and finish, with the very finest examples of the West.

All this, however, constituted only the *upper* side of the picture. Let us look at the *under* side—at the condition of the lower classes. The economic prosperity of Kievan Rus depended for its maintenance upon slavery—a system which, towards the close of the twelfth century, attained immense proportions. For three centuries the slave constituted the principal article of export to the markets of the Volga, the Black Sea, and the Caspian ; with the result that the Russian merchant came to be known, first and foremost, as a slave-dealer. Eastern writers of the tenth century give a graphic picture of a Russian trader plying his calling on the Volga, as, disembarking at Itil or Bolgari, he erected his stands and booths in the bazaar, and exposed his human wares for sale. Constantinople also was a favourite resort of his, since it was the recognised custom for a Greek needing a slave to repair to the particular market-place reserved for those whom a posthumous work written by Nicholas the Magician at the middle of the eleventh century calls " the merchants who come from Rus to barter with the slave." It was to slavery too (if we may judge from the *Russkaia Pravda*, which, as we have seen, allots its fullest and most detailed section to that subject) that ancient Russian legislation devoted its most particular attention, while it was from the slave-owning system that Russian ownership of land derived its legal and economic origin. Up to the close of the tenth century the ruling class remained exclusively urban by domicile and habit of life. Military expeditions filled its hands full with slaves, so that only a moiety were required for the palaces of the boyars, and the remainder were sent across the sea to constitute, with furs, the principle article of Russian export. In short, the upper class derived such profit from its work of trading and governing that it saw no reason to turn its attention also to landowning. Eventually, however, there came a day when, its position securely consolidated in the great towns of the Dnieper basin, the ruling section of the community began to settle its slaves upon the agricultural portions of the land, and to exchange ownership of human beings for ownership of the soil. Of such private landed proprietorship no evidence is to be found *earlier* than the eleventh century, while the twelfth century is reached before it occurs in any marked proportion. Landowners at that time were drawn exclusively from the upper class, or from the institutions of that class, and consisted of (1) princes and members of the princely house, (2) boyars, (3) ecclesiastical establishments, monasteries, and episcopal sees. It is clear, however, that in each of these cases the original title to the soil was based upon settlement and exploitation of the land by slaves—that, in fact, the slave constituted the indispensable appurtenance of the system, whether his master were an ecclesiastic or a layman, a great proprietor or a small. Hence we may take it that the idea of the right to own land—of competency to hold land as to hold any other article of property—may be looked upon as deriving directly from slave-ownership, and as constituting a further development of the idea of the right to own slaves. "This land is mine for the reason that the human beings who labour upon it are mine"— such must have been the dialectical process by which the theory of right to hold real estate has come down to our day. That is to say, the tenant-slave (or "*stradnik*" [1] as we find him called in the industrial nomenclature of ancient Rus) must have served to transmute the theory from the master to the land—to act as the juridical link between the two, while at the same time serving also as the master's instrument of exploitation. From this originated the old Russian *boyarskaia votchina* or "boyaral manor"—the privileged man-at-arms and merchant-slave-dealer of the tenth century having now become converted into the boyar as the term is applied by the *Russkaia Pravda* to the privileged landowner who constituted the leading economic class in the community.[2] The slave also rose in social value through the process of settling him upon the land (a process continued throughout the eleventh and twelfth centuries), so that, although, before the death of Yaroslav, a freeman might kill a slave other than his own who assaulted him, Yaroslav's successors thought it advisable to repeal that regulation. In short, old ideas and customs with regard to master and slave now gave way to ideas and customs with regard to landed proprietor and free, or semi-free, labourer. Thus we find the *Russkaia Pravda* making frequent mention of a class of persons whom it calls indifferently *roleini*, *naimiti*, or *zakupi*—an order of agricultural workers who, standing in near relation to the *kholop* or absolute slave (though still distinct from him), constituted a class of peasants possessed only of partial rights and bound by temporary contract to work a master's estate with his own stock and implements, while at the same time remaining liable, in case of certain offences such as theft or desertion, to be bound into full slavery or become *obilnie kholopi*. In this

---

[1] Literally, toiler or labourer.   [2] See p. 161.

inferior legal position of the *zakup* we can discern the working of agrarian custom according as the old Russian landed proprietor gradually came to adapt his perspective to the semi-free peasant whom he had formerly looked upon as his absolute property. Indeed, this view led many legal documents of the period to connect the term for a semi-freeman with the term for an absolute slave ; which conjunction of nomenclature helps us to explain a point to be found in a treaty made by Vladimir with the Bolgars of the Volga in the year 1006, and preserved to us only in Tatistchev's *History of Russia*. Under this treaty, Bolgarian merchants visiting Russian towns for purposes of trade were forbidden also to visit the rural districts, or to sell their wares to "*ognevtini* and *smerdini*." Of these two classes, *smerdini* were free peasants settled upon lands belonging to the Prince (*i.e.* to the State), while *ognevtini* were labourers, slave or free, who worked upon lands belonging to a private owner. The mere severity with which ancient Russian law visited a *zakup* for leaving his master's service without previously indemnifying him for his (the *zakup's*) breach of contract (the penalty being, as already stated, conversion into full slavery) bears eloquent testimony both to the master's need of his bondsman's labour and to the eagerness of the latter to escape from his onerous legal position. These peculiar relations arose out of the ruling interests of the period—interests which caused the social status of the individual to be determined by his degree of enrichment or enslavement. In a work by the Metropolitan Clement of the twelfth century we find a picture of a Russian of the period as he rose in the world—of his gradual adding to himself house after house and hamlet after hamlet, together with "all the apiaries, meadows, and *peasantry* thereto appertaining." The inclusion of "peasantry" makes it additionally clear that the social system and economic prosperity of Kievan Rus were maintained only at the cost of the enslavement of the lower classes, and that the amenities of life enjoyed by the upper strata of the community entailed the legal debasement of the lower. This divorce between the upper and the lower strata of society was emphasised still further by wide disparities of property. Of this we find a striking example in the Ancient Chronicle at the point where it relates how, in 1018, the *vietché* of Novgorod decided to raise a fund towards the hiring of a Varangian force to aid Yaroslav in his struggle with his brother Sviatopolk of Kiev. This determination arrived at, the two main orders of the people—the "prince's men" and the "simple men"—contributed each of them their share on the basis of the local assessment of the day ; whereupon it worked out that, whereas "simple men" had to contribute, on the average, four *kuni* apiece, "prince's men" had to furnish eighteen *grivni*! And since at that period twenty-five *kuni* went to the *grivna*, it will be seen that the proportion between the respective contributions worked out at a hundred and twelve to one!

It was this legal and economic disparity between the upper and the lower strata of the community—a feature common enough in communities founded mainly by the efforts of industrial capital—which constituted the first of the conditions disruptive of the social and economic order of Kievan Rus, inasmuch as the social order found no support among the common people, but made itself felt among them only through its disadvantages.

The second disruptive condition was the multitude of the princely feuds. The rota system of rule was unfavourable to the popular industry at large, for the reason that, while the princes had little time, amid their numerous genealogical struggles, to think of territorial acquisition in the sense of enlarging the provinces over which they held temporary rule, they none the less took care to make good any shortage of labour which happened to occur upon their own *private* estates. Their chief method of doing so was by *polon* or capture; which means that they would follow up a victory over a hostile territory by not only laying it waste, but also carrying off as many of its inhabitants as they needed, after which Russian law enabled the captives to be converted into slaves and settled upon the private lands of the Prince and his retainers (for it will be remembered that the former always shared his booty with the latter). Thus we read that, when Vassilko of Terebovl was smitten with blindness,[1] he bewailed himself that his cherished scheme of capturing the Bolgars of the Danube and settling them upon his estates could never now be realised, while a proverb current in the twelfth century concerning Prince Roman of Volhynia (namely, *Tchudim zhiveshi, Litvöu oreshi*, or "When thou art in need, make a raid upon Lithuania") shows us that it was no more than his ordinary custom to recruit his agrarian staff by force from that country. One disadvantage of the system, however, lay in the fact that it provoked the opposite side to reprisals, while a still more disastrous result of it was that the princes gradually came to adopt the same methods in their mutual feuds. Their first care, when attacking a genealogical rival, was to fire his *selo* or country establishment, and to carry off or destroy the whole of his *zhizn* (which might be rendered

[1] See p. 123.

as "stock and store," or cattle, corn, and slaves).   Even Vladimir
Monomakh—the most humane and enlightened of all Yaroslav's descendants—was no stranger to this system of rapine.   In his *Pöuchenie* we find
him relating, for the benefit of his sons, how on one occasion he raided
Minsk and left there "nor beast nor slave."   On another occasion his
son Yaropolk seized the town of Druitsk (also situated in the province of
Minsk), and carried off its inhabitants *en masse* to his own province
of Periaslavl, where he subsequently built them a new town at the point
where the river Suda joins the Dnieper.   More than once, too, the
Ancient Chronicle concludes its story of some twelfth-century raid upon
a foreign territory with the remark that the victorious prince and his force
returned "with great booty of cattle and slaves."   The princes did not
scruple to convert even their own countrymen into slaves when taken in
warfare.   Thus, after the failure of Andrew Bogoliubski's attack upon
Novgorod in 1169, those of his army who were made prisoners by the
enemy were sold in the streets of the city at two *nogati* a man.   The
Polovtsi did the same with their Russian prisoners, and the princes of Rus
retaliated in kind.   Thus converted into a series of mere greedy struggles
for agricultural "hands"—struggles which necessarily brought about a
shrinkage of the free portion of the population—the princely feuds only
aggravated the miserable plight of the lower orders, already rendered
sufficiently wretched by the aristocratic legislation enacted during those
eleventh and twelfth centuries.

To these two conditions disruptive of Kievan Rus must be added yet a
third and an even more potent one.   Let us never forget that, in studying
Russian life at this period, we are observing a drama which had for its
scene the very edge of the world of Christian culture—the edge beyond
which stretched the boundless sea of the European and Asiatic Steppes.
Those desolate wastes and their nomad inhabitants may be said to have
constituted the historical scourge of ancient Rus.   It is true that for some
while after the decisive blow dealt the Pechenegs by Yaroslav in the year
1036 the Russian portion of the Steppes remained more or less clear of
hordes, but with the death of that ruler in 1061 there began a fresh series
of attacks upon Rus—this time from a people named the Polovtsi or
Kumani.   With that barbarian race Rus maintained a stubborn struggle
during the whole of the eleventh and twelfth centuries—a struggle which
has not only served as a favourite subject for subsequent manuscript
tales and heroic *bilini*, but also left at the time some terrible traces upon
the face of the country.   As we read the Ancient Chronicle's record

of those days, there rises before us a vivid picture of the desolation to
which the Steppe regions of Rus became reduced.   Arable lands, we are
told, fell out of cultivation, and became overgrown with grass and bush,
while grazing grounds where formerly herds of cattle had roamed now
harboured only wild animals.   The crafty Polovtsi used to steal up even
to Kiev itself, and in 1096 the Khan Boniak (nicknamed "the Corpulent")
penetrated almost to its very streets.   Failing in this, however, he fell
upon the Petcherski Cloister when the monks were sleeping in their cells
after Matins, and, after doing great damage to the fabric, concluded his
operations by setting it on fire.   Whole provinces, as well as towns, did
these barbarians ravage and denude of their population.   For instance, in
the eleventh century the region of the river Rhos (a western tributary of
the Dnieper, below Kiev) was a populous district from the time of
Yaroslav's death until the Polovtsian raids—its population being a mixed
one consisting of the Lech prisoners of war who had been settled upon the
land there by Yaroslav, of emigrants from Rus, and of a certain number of
friendly Turks, Berendians, and even Pechenegs who had fled from the
Polovtsi to Russian territory and there joined hands with Kiev in the
struggle against that race.   These friendly aliens led a semi-nomadic life—
roaming the neighbouring Steppes in summer, with their herds and tilt-
wagons, and retiring, on the approach of winter, into their fortified
settlements and posts on the Rhos, where they served Rus as an outpost
line against the Steppes.   To distinguish these "friendlies" from the
"wild" nomads the Russians called the former *svoi pogani* or "our own
pagans."   By the close of the eleventh century this region of the Rhos
had become a separate episcopal see from Kiev, with Yuriev on the Rhos
as its cathedral town.   Nevertheless the inhabitants of the district lived
in perpetual terror of the Polovtsi ; so much so, indeed, that when, in
1095, a new attack was threatened from that quarter, the people of
Yuriev left their homes *en masse*, and fled to Kiev, leaving the enemy
to burn the deserted city at their leisure.   Sviatopolk, then Suzerain
Prince of Kiev, built the refugees a new city on the Dnieper, below the
metropolis, and called it Sviatopolch, and later on it became a place
of resort for many other such fugitives from the frontiers of the Steppes.
Owing also to the proximity of the province of Periaslavl to those frontiers,
it too underwent similar vicissitudes.   Indeed, almost every year saw its
territory the scene of a long and bitter struggle between the Russians and
the Polovtsi, until, in the twelfth century, it had become almost a complete waste.   The combined pressure of these perils and of the apprehen-

sion of them, as well as of the ever-multiplying feuds of the princes, caused the foundations of the social order of Kievan Rus to become notably weakened—indeed, momentarily to threaten a cataclysm. At length men began to ask themselves whether life was possible under such conditions, and when, in 1069, Iziaslav (previously dethroned by the Kievans for his want of success against the Polovtsi) returned with Polish reinforcements, and the members of the Kievan *vietché* sent to beg help against him of his two brothers Sviatoslav and Vsevolod, the suppliants could only say to those Princes: " If ye will not do this thing for us, then doth there remain for us nought but to fire the city and to depart unto the Greek land." This intermittent struggle with the barbarian hordes was a constant drain upon the material resources of the country, since no amount of treaty-making could make the Polovtsi curb their inveterate habit of rapine. Monomakh alone—to mention no others—made peace with them no fewer than nineteen times, and surrendered to them, on each occasion, a large amount of cattle and clothing: yet all was to no purpose. Others of the Russian princes tried the experiment of marrying the Khans' daughters, but their new fathers-in-law continued to operate upon the Russian dominions as though nothing had happened. However much Rus might fortify her Steppe frontiers with earthworks, surround herself with a chain of military posts and forts, and make constant sallies from them, the men-at-arms in the frontier provinces had to keep their horses constantly saddled, for fear of being surprised by a new attack. This type of warfare also produced a new type of hero—not the type to be found celebrated in the ancient *bilini*, but its historical original; the type best exemplified by that Demian, son of Kudenev, who appears in the Chronicle at the middle of the twelfth century as dwelling at Russian Periaslavl. Accompanied only by a servant and five other youths, this mighty warrior went out against an entire horde, and put it to flight, while on another occasion he performed the same feat single-handed and clad only in work-a-day attire—*i.e.* without helmet or armour ! Finally, after slaying a great number of barbarians, he himself was severely wounded, and returned to the city more dead than alive. Such heroes were known in their day as " God's men," and constituted at once the direct successors of those old Varangian *vitiazi* (Viking-knights) who had exchanged the row-bench for the saddle and the indirect forerunners of those Cossacks of the Dnieper who subsequently warred both on horseback and in boats with the Tartars and Turks of the Crimea. During the eleventh and twelfth centuries many such heroes arose and fell in the provinces of

Rus adjacent to the Steppes, and one old sixteenth-century treatise on the geography of South-Western Rus describes a spot on the roadside between Periaslavl and Kiev as the burial-place of such men. "There," says that treatise, "do lie buried Russian heroes." Up to the death of Monomakh's son, Mstislav, in 1132, Rus was successful in keeping the Polovtsi outside her frontiers, and even, at times, in making counter-expeditions into the heart of the enemy's country; but with the demise of that active ruler her strength began to fail before the pressure of their attacks, and gradually she was forced to give way. Naturally it was the population of the frontier regions which suffered most from these incursions, and at a princely council held in the year 1103 Monomakh presented a strongly-worded memorial to the then Suzerain Prince, Sviatopolk, on the subject of the life of terror led by the frontier peasantry. "In the spring," said Monomakh, "the *smerd* taketh his horse out to plough; whereupon there cometh to attack him a Polovtsin, who, after that he hath smitten the *smerd* with a dart, goeth his way unto the homestead, and seizeth upon the wife and children and goods of the *smerd*, and setteth fire also unto his byre."

This struggle between the Russians and the Polovtsi—a struggle lasting well-nigh for two centuries—was not without its place in European history at large; for while the West was engaged in crusades against the forces of Asia and the Orient, and a similar movement was in progress in the Iberian Peninsula against the Moors, Rus was holding the left flank of Europe. Yet this historical service cost her dear, since not only did it dislodge her from her old settlements on the Dnieper, but it caused the whole trend of her life to become altered.

From the middle of the twelfth century onwards, then, the three adverse conditions specified (namely, the legal and economic debasement of the lower orders of the community, the feuds of the princes, and the attacks of the Polovtsi) caused Kiev to become depopulated, and the whole region of the Middle Dnieper (which had now attained a high standard of cultivation) to fall to waste. Of this fact we glean our most striking evidence from an episode in the history of the princely feuds. In 1157 the then Suzerain Prince of Kiev—Yuri Dolgoruki, son of Monomakh—died, and was succeeded by Iziaslav, son of David, the senior prince of Tchernigov. In the ordinary course of the rota, Iziaslav ought to have been succeeded, as prince of the *province* of Tchernigov, by his younger cousin Sviatoslav (son of Oleg), then ruler at Novgorod Sieverski, but, instead of that, Iziaslav allowed his junior to assume only the *city* of Tchernigov and seven other towns in the province. Two years later, when Iziaslav was about to undertake an expedition against his rivals, Yaroslav of Galicia and Mstislav of Volhynia, he sent word to his cousin of Tchernigov to come and help him. Sviatoslav, however, refused to do this, whereupon his Suzerain determined to try what a threatening message could do. "Look you, my cousin," he said. "When I shall have gained the mastery in Galicia, blame thou me not if thou shouldst be forced to return to Novgorod Sieverski from Tchernigov." To this menace (and this is the important point) Sviatoslav replied in the following terms: "Sire, surely thou hast seen that I am a man of peace? Did I not forego mine own when, that there might be no spilling of Christian blood, I did resign my full heritage, and did receive from thee naught but the city of Tchernigov and seven others? *Yet are those very cities now desolate, with none to live in them but huntsmen and Polovtsi.*" These last words of Sviatoslav's can only mean that the towns in question had now become deserted by all save menials of the princely courts and friendly Polovtsi who had deserted to the side of Rus. Another startling fact is that among those towns we find the name of one of the richest and most populous centres in all the Middle Dnieper region—namely, Lubiech. *Pari passu* with this exodus of the people from Kievan Rus went a decline of her economic prosperity—the process of her impoverishment keeping pace with her loss of population. The monetary currency of the day confirms this fact. In studying the *Russkaia Pravda* we saw that, in the times of Yaroslav I. and Monomakh, the weight of the silver *grivna* was half a pound, but that from the middle of the twelfth century onwards it began rapidly to decline. This shows clearly that the channels by which the precious metal entered the country were beginning to be silted up, and that silver was rising in value. The real cause of that rise is revealed in the Chronicle's record of the period—the cause being that the foreign trade-routes of Rus were being more and more successfully stopped by the barbarians of the Steppes. Our earliest evidence of this is to be found in words uttered by Mstislav, Prince of Volhynia, when, in 1167, he was attempting to induce his fellow-princes to undertake a fresh expedition against the Polovtsi. "I pray you," he said, "to look upon the Russian land our patrimony, and to behold how each year the pagans do carry away our Christian people in wagons and deprive us of our trade-roads,"—whence he went on to enumerate the various routes of Russian commerce, including "the Greek road." Every year along that "Greek road" (*i.e.* the river-route across the Steppes to Byzantium) the prince

used to set out with an armed escort, for the purpose of convoying outwards or homewards such Russian traders as were journeying to or from
the Greek dominions. This convoying of Russian boat caravans through
the Steppes had always been the subject of the princes' most anxious
solicitude, and the fact of its non-performance—or at all events of its
unsuccessful performance—at this period makes it doubly clear that the
princes and their retinues were becoming powerless in the face of the
barbarian advance, however much they might strive to keep the trade-
routes open.

Such was the series of phenomena which reveals to us both the lack
of cohesion in the structure of the then Russian community (for all its
glittering surface) and the inevitableness of the disasters which overtook
it. Our next task must be to decide whither the population of now
desolate Rus took flight, leaving its ancient habitations on the Middle
Dnieper to be tenanted only by hangers-on of the princes and by Polovtsi
"friendlies."

The exodus from Kievan Rus took two different directions, and flowed
in two different streams. Of these streams, one tended towards the West
—towards the region of the Western Bug, the upper portions of the
Dniester and Vistula, and the interior districts of Galicia and Poland.
Hence a certain proportion of the population of Southern Rus and the
Dnieper returned to the very locality which their forefathers had left
in the seventh century! This westward movement had a marked effect
upon the fortunes of the two most outlying Russian provinces in that
direction—namely, Galicia and Volhynia. Hitherto their position in the
political hierarchy of Russian territories had always caused them to rank
as lesser provinces, but now Galicia—one of the remote districts allotted
only to *izgoi* princes of the house of Yaroslav—rose to be one of the
strongest and most influential in all the south-western region. The *Slovo
o Polku Igorevê* even speaks of the Galician Prince of its day (Yaroslav
the Prudent) as "rolling back the gates of Kiev," while, with the end of
the twelfth century, when Roman, son of Mstislav, had added the province
to his own principality of Volhynia, the combined state waxed so greatly
in population and importance that its princes became sufficiently rich
and powerful to gather into their hands the direction of the whole south-
western region, and even of Kiev itself. In fact, the Ancient Chronicle
goes so far as to describe Prince Roman as "the Autocrat of all the
Russian land." Probably, also, this inrush of Russian refugees into
Galicia and Poland explains the fact that annals of the thirteenth and

fourteenth centuries frequently refer to Orthodox churches as then existing in the province of Cracow and other portions of the South-West.

The same migratory movement may serve to throw light upon a
phenomenon of great importance in Russian ethnography—namely, the
formation of the Little Russian stock.   The depopulation of Dnieperian
Rus which began in the twelfth century was completed during the
thirteenth by the Tartar invasions which took place between the years
1229 and 1240.   For a long period after the latter date the provinces of
ancient Rus, once so thickly peopled, remained in a state of desolation.
A Catholic missionary named Plano Carpini, who traversed Kievan Rus
in 1246, on his way from Poland to the Volga to preach the Gospel to the
Tartars, has recorded in his memoirs that, although the road between
Vladimir in Volhynia and Kiev was beset with perils, owing to the frequency with which the Lithuanians raided that region, he met with no
obstacle at the hands of Russians—for the very good reason that few of
them were left alive in the country after the raids and massacres of the
Tartars.   Throughout the whole of his journey across the ancient provinces of Kiev and Periaslavl (so the missionary continues) he saw count-
less bones and skulls lying by the wayside or scattered over the neighbouring fields, while in Kiev itself—once a populous and spacious city—he
counted only two hundred houses, each of which sheltered but a few
sorry inmates.   During the following two or three centuries Kiev
underwent still further vicissitudes.   Hardly had she recovered from
the Tartar attacks delivered prior to the year 1240 when (in 1299) she
was ravaged afresh by some of the scattered bands of Polovtsi, Pechenegs,
Turks, and other barbarians who roamed her desolate frontiers.   In that
more or less grievous plight the southern provinces of Rus remained
until well-nigh the middle of the fifteenth century.   Meanwhile South-
Western Rus (now beginning to be called in documents of the period
" Malaia Rossia " or " Little Russia ") had been annexed to the combined
state of Poland-Lithuania ; so that of the Empire thus formed the region of
the Middle Dnieper—*i.e.* old Kievan Rus—had now become the south-
easternmost province or Ukraine.   With the fifteenth century a new colonisation of the Middle Dnieper region began, to which two circumstances in
particular contributed : namely, (1) the fact that the Steppes of the South
were becoming less dangerous, owing to the dispersal of the Golden
Horde and the rise of Muscovite Rus, and (2) the fact that the Polish
Empire was beginning to abolish her old system of peasant tenure by
quit-rent in favour of the *barstchina* system, which tended towards serfdom

and therefore filled the oppressed rural population with a desire to escape from the masters' yoke to a region where they might live more freely. These two factors combined to set on foot an active *reflex* exodus from Galicia and the central provinces of Poland towards the south-easternmost borders of the Polish Empire—*i.e.* towards the region of the Dnieper and old Kievan Rus. The chief directors of this movement were the rich Polish magnates, who had acquired enormous estates in that part of the world, and now desired to people and reclaim them. The combined efforts of the immigrants soon succeeded in studding these seignorial domains with towns, villages, hamlets, and detached homesteads ; with the result that we find Polish writers of the sixteenth century at once exclaiming at the surprisingly rapid movement of colonists towards the Dnieper, the Dniester, and the Eastern Bug, and lamenting the depopulation of the central provinces of Poland to which that movement had given rise. All things considered, there can be little doubt that the bulk of the settlers who took part in the recolonising of Southern Rus were of purely Russian origin— that, in fact, they were the descendants of those very Russians who had fled westwards from the Dnieper during the twelfth and thirteenth centuries, and who, though dwelling since among a Polish and Lithuanian population, had, throughout the two or three intervening centuries, retained their nationality intact. The immigrants now returning to what might be termed their own hearths found seated there the remnants of the old Turkish, Berendian, and Pecheneg hordes : and although I do not for one moment mean to suggest that it was from a fusion of those barbarians with the returning settlers that the Little Russian stock originated (a supposition which, in any case, has no adequate historical evidence to support it) or that it was precisely at this period that those peculiarities of dialect arose which distinguish the Little Russian language from the ancient Kievan and Great Russian forms of speech, I none the less venture to assert that the reflex movement from the region of the Carpathians to the Dnieper which was carried out by the same Russians who had been ousted thence during the twelfth and thirteenth centuries had at all events a *connection* with the formation of the Little Russian branch of our people.

With regard to the other of the two streams of emigration which set out from Kievan Rus during the twelfth and thirteenth centuries, its trend was north-eastwards, towards the region of the rivers Ugra, Oka, and Volga. Of this movement we only have scanty information from contemporary observers, since it was a movement which continued quietly and gradually, and among strata of society too far removed below the surface for those standing at a higher level to become readily aware of its progress. Yet that such information is not wholly lacking I will proceed to show, and divide my items, for the purpose, into four sections.

I. Up to the middle of the twelfth century no direct connection is traceable between Kievan Rus and the outlying regions of Rostov and Suzdal: yet Slavonic settlement of that north-eastern corner of Rus had undoubtedly begun long before the period named, while a later wave of colonisation by a Varangian-Russian element had emanated from the North-West—from Novgorod, to which province, under the early Russian princes, Rostov and Suzdal had belonged. Russian towns had arisen in the North-East previous to the twelfth century, and in a few of them (such as Rostov, Suzdal, Yaroslavl, and Murom) we find—even at that early period—Russian princes making an occasional appearance in history. Thus Vladimir's eldest son Boris ruled at Rostov, and his second son Gleb at Murom. Now, it is very important to note that, whenever the princes of those two provinces had occasion to travel southwards to visit Kiev, they invariably made a long *détour*, instead of following the direct line. When, in 1015, Gleb of Murom heard that his father was lying ill at Kiev, and set out to see him, the fact that his horse stumbled and broke a hoof close to the spot where the river Tma joins the Volga[1] reveals to us by what a roundabout route he must have travelled on first starting. Once arrived at Smolensk, he intended to perform the rest of the journey by the Dnieper direct, but was overtaken by emissaries of his brother Sviatopolk, and murdered. Another curious fact is that the absence of any direct road between Murom and Kiev is preserved in one of our popular *bilini*. In the folk-song referred to we are told that once, when arrived at Kiev, Ilya Murometz began to tell the heroes grouped around Vladimir's throne the route by which he had travelled southwards from his city of Murom—declaring that he had taken "the straight-running road." Of this the heroes were incredulous ;—but I will give the lines themselves.

> "I have come by the straight-running road,
> From my capital city, from Murom,
> From my homestead at Karacharóv."
> Then answered the powerful heroes:
> " As the sun is our Vladimir glorious !
> Yet this youth doth but babble in folly :
> For how should he come by the straight road
> Which for thirty long years has been sought for
> By the notable brigand Solóviev ?"

---

[1] The Tma is a small tributary on the *left* bank of the Volga, above Tver.

However, by the middle of the twelfth century we begin to come upon evidence of such a " straight-running road " being opened up between Kiev and the north-eastern regions. Vladimir Monomakh—a tireless traveller, who, in his day, traversed the length and breadth of the Russian land —tells his sons in his *Pöuchenie* (not without a touch of pride in his tone) that he once made the journey from Kiev to Rostov "through the Vatizes." Certain it is that it can have been no easy matter, in his day, to traverse the country lying between Rostov and the Dnieper, seeing that the intervening district (which belonged to the Vatizes, the most outlying, in that direction, of all the original Eastern Slavonic tribes [1]) was covered with almost impenetrable forest—a forest so secluded and secure that it was an habitual place of refuge for the princes of Tchernigov (to whom the Vatizes were subject) when they had had the worst of it in a feud. In fact, in Monomakh's day, the whole territory between the Upper Oka and the Desna and between the town of Karachev and the town of Kozelsk—or, in other words, the greater part of what now constitutes the governments of Orel and Kaluga—was a thickly-wooded wilderness to which Kievan Rus had given the name of Brinski (Brin, it seems, was a *volost* or province which to-day is represented by the canton of Shisdra on the Brinka, in the government of Kaluga). The memory of this wild forest region is to be found preserved in the name of the town Briansk on the Desna (though, perhaps, it should more properly be spelt Debriansk, from *debr*, a ravine). Similarly, the territory of Suzdal was known to Kievan Rus as the *Zaliess-kaia Oblast*,[2] for the reason that the savage country tenanted by the Vatizes formed a kind of forest wall between that territory and Rus. With the middle of the twelfth century, however, this wild region began to be cleared, and although Vladimir Monomakh seems to have had some difficulty in traversing it with only a small retinue at his back, his son Yuri Dolgoruki succeeded in transporting an entire army through its recesses during his stubborn struggle with his nephew Iziaslav of Volhynia (1149–1154). Hence we are justified in supposing that, in the meanwhile, a great movement of population had taken place in that direction—a movement of sufficient volume at all events to clear an open road through the fastnesses of the Vatizes. This constitutes our first item of evidence with regard to the north-eastward exodus from Kievan Rus.

II. Further evidence of that movement is to be found in the fact that at the very time when Southern Rus was being depopulated a great deal of building was going on in the region of Suzdal. Under the Princes

[1] See p. 37.   [2] From *za* beyond or behind, and *liess* a forest.

Yuri Dolgoruki and Andrew Bogoliubski town after town arose there. In 1134 the former built Ksniatin at the point where the Great Norla falls into the Volga, near the present town of Kaliazin, while in 1147 the city of Moscow first begins to come into notice. In 1150 Yuri founded Yuriev v' Polé (*i.e.* Yuriev "in the Field"—whence the name of the modern town of Polski, in the government of Vladimir), as well as removed Periaslavl Zaliesski (founded at the same period) to a fresh site. Next, in 1154 he built Dmitrov on the Yakhroma (called after his son Dmitri Vsevolod, who was born in that year, during the annual *poludie* or governmental tour for the collection of *dan*); while in or about the year 1155 his son Andrew Bogoliubski founded Bogoliubov on the Kliazma, below Vladimir. The growth of these towns was accompanied by a corresponding amount of church-building, the two princes above-named being exceedingly generous donors in that respect. The cities enumerated above comprise all that are to be found specified in the Chronicle, but from other sources we learn that this did not complete the whole of them. Tver, for instance, figures as a well-developed city in the *Skazanie* (Story) of the miracles wrought by Vladimir's image of the Holy Mother—a work composed within the lifetime of Andrew Bogoliubski (*i.e.* at least before the year 1174). Moreover, we have it from Tatistchev that, from the beginning of Yuri Dolgoruki's time, some of his (Tatistchev's) sources (now lost to us) began to mention towns in Northern Rus which had certainly never been known in that region *before* the period in question. Of these may be named Gorodetz on the Volga, Kostroma, Starodub on the Kliazma, Galitch, Svenigorod, and Vishgorod—the last-named of which stood at the junction of the rivers Protva and Oka, below Serpukhov. Andrew seems to have taken a pride in the work of colonisation, for we read that, when debating the possibility of making Vladimir on the Kliazma a rival metropolis to Kiev, he said to his boyars : " Now have I settled the whole of this White Rus " (*i.e.* the Rus of Suzdal) "with towns and large hamlets, and have made of it a populous region."

III. Of the locality whence emanated that migratory movement which gave rise to these towns we have evidence in their very nomenclature. Periaslavl, Svenigorod, Starodub, Vishgorod, Galitch—all of them are South Russian names which occur on almost every page of the Ancient Chronicle when speaking of events in that locality. Of Svenigorods alone there were several both in Kievan Rus and Galicia, while the names of the Kievan brooks Liebed and Pochaina are to be met with again at Suzdal, at Riazan, at Vladimir on the Kliazma, and at Nizhni Novgorod. In the same way, we find the name of the well-known Kievan rivulet, the Irpen (which is a tributary of the Dnieper, and upon whose banks tradition asserts Guedimin of Lithuania to have slain the princes of Southern Rus in the year 1321) reproduced in the Irpen which flows into the Kliazma and is situated in the present government of Vladimir. Nor, indeed, was the name of Kiev itself forgotten in Suzdal, for not only do we find a village named Kievo (in a valley of the same name) mentioned in sixteenth-century documents relating to the neighbourhood of Moscow, but both the river Kievka (a tributary of the Oka, in the present government of Kaluga) and a hamlet named Kievtsi, near Alexin, in the present government of Tula, reproduce the title of the ancient metropolis of Rus. But the most curious feature of all in this migration of geographical nomenclature is to be found in the wanderings of the name Periaslavl. In ancient Rus we meet with no less than three such cities—namely, Periaslavl of the South or Russian Periaslavl (now the capital of the government of Poltava), Periaslavl in Riazan (now the town of Riazan), and Periaslavl Zaliesski (now the capital of the government of Vladimir). All these three towns stood upon a river Trubetza. This transference to Suzdal of the geographical nomenclature of the South can only have been the work of settlers migrating northwards from Kievan Rus, since it is a well-known fact that colonists frequently transfer to their new homes the names of the localities which they have left. An example of this is to be seen in the United States of America, where much of the geographical nomenclature of the Old World is repeated in the New. Further evidence of the movement towards Suzdal is to be gleaned from a comparatively modern source —namely, from the pages of Tatistchev, who says in his History that, when Dolgoruki had begun building new towns in his principality of Suzdal, he contrived to attract population thither by the simple expedient of advancing settlers "a no small loan," and that, in consequence, his towns became the goal, not only of Russians, but of Bolgarians, Morduines, and Vengrians, "so that the confines of those towns did speedily become filled with thousands of people." But how came there to be Vengrians among those thousands? The reason is that, in his feud with Iziaslav|of Volhynia, Yuri Dolgoruki had as an additional antagonist the Vengrian king, and that, consequently, the settlers of that race whom we find assisting Yuri to people his newly-built towns of Suzdal were captives taken in the battles of the South.

IV. Finally, evidence of the north-eastward movement reaches us from a quarter whence we might least have expected it—namely, popular poetry. We know that the cycle of *bilini* treating of the heroes of Vladimir's day was originally composed in Southern Rus; yet those old folk-songs have long ago become extinct in that region, and their places been taken by Cossack *dumi* or legends relating to exploits performed by that people in their wars with the Lechs, Tartars, and Turks.   On the other hand, we find those same heroic *bilini* surviving with astonishing freshness in the North—in the Cis-Ural districts, in the country beyond Lake Onega, and in the governments of Olonetz and Archangel, whence emigrants have carried them even to the remotest corners of Siberia.   In Central Russia also the memory of Vladimir's heroes is still kept green—not in the form of *bilini*, however, but in that of the simple prose tale (*skazka*), since both the art of singing *bilini* and the metrical idiom in which they were composed have died out in that locality.   How comes it, then, that the popular historical epic flourishes where it was never sown, and has passed to regions where it never originally grew?   The reason is that those poetical legends travelled northward with the population which first composed and sang them.   Equally clear is it that that movement must have attained its completion before the fourteenth century—*i.e.* before the appearance of the Lithuanians and Lechs in Southern Rus, since the older of our *bilini* make no reference to those later antagonists of Rus.

These, then, constitute the four items of evidence which lead us to the conclusion that a north-eastward exodus from Kievan Rus took place of similar character to that which set in towards the West.   This dual outflow of population is the central fact distinguishing the beginning of the second principal period of our history, just as the beginning of the preceding period was distinguished by a movement of Eastern Slavdom from the Carpathians towards the Dnieper.   This central fact determined, let us proceed to study its results, but only in connection with the north-eastward stream of emigration.   My reason for thus limiting our scope is that it was the north-eastward movement alone that was responsible for all the fundamental phenomena seen in the life of Rus of the Upper Volga from the middle of the twelfth century onwards, and which constituted the prime cause of all that went to determine the social and political orders of that Rus.   The results of this exodus were exceedingly diverse in their nature, and may be divided into (1) ethnographical and (2) political consequences.

At the same time, all the results in question may be narrowed down to one central, fundamental fact—namely, that the Russian nationality, gradually compounded during the first period of our history, became sundered during the second, according as the bulk of the Russian population was forced to retreat northwards to the region of the Oka and Upper Volga. There, sheltered in the fastnesses of central Rus, it preserved its nationality intact and slowly recovered its strength, until finally it was able to return to the Dnieper and the South-West, there to rescue from foreign influence and the foreign yoke the small remnant of Russian population which had remained behind.

CHAPTER XIII

Ethnographical results of the Russian colonisation of the Upper Volga—The question of the origin of the Great Russian stock—The Finnish tribes formerly inhabiting the region of the Oka and Upper Volga, and the traces now left of them—Relations of the Russian settlers to the aboriginal Finnish tribes of Suzdal—Traces of Finnish influence upon the Great Russian physical type, form of town-building, popular beliefs, and social composition—Influence of the natural features of the region of the Upper Volga upon the industry of Great Rus and the racial character of the Great Russian stock.

THE *ethnographical* results of the colonisation of North-Eastern Rus may be summed up in one central fact—namely, the formation of the Great Russian stock. To estimate the importance of that fact in our history we need but to remember that, of the three main branches of our race, the Great Russian stock stands to the Little Russian in the proportion of three to one, and the Little Russian to the White Russian in a similar ratio ; so that of the population at large the first-named stock constitutes nine-thirteenths, or rather over two-thirds.

The conditions under which the Russian settlers colonised the region of the Oka and Upper Volga may be studied under two heads—namely, *ethnographical* conditions, or those which arose out of contact of the Russian immigrants with the Finnish natives, and *geographical* conditions, or those which arose out of the physical features of the country. In other words, the Great Russian stock was evolved through the action of two factors—namely, racial fusion and natural environment.

The native inhabitants of North-Eastern Rus were Finnish tribes— tribes of the race described in the Chronicle as neighbours of the Eastern Slavs from the moment of their first entry into the Russian plain. Nevertheless those Finnish aborigines had made their homes in the swamps and forests of Northern and Central Rus long before any Slavonic element becomes traceable there. As early as the sixth century Jornandes knew of their existence, for he includes among the population of Hermanric's Gothic kingdom both Estians (Esthonians), Wesses, Meres, Morduines, and Tcheremissians. The three tribes inhabiting the immediate region of the Oka and Upper Volga during the eleventh and twelfth centuries were the Finns of Murom, the Meres, and the Wesses. Their local distribution is indicated in the Chronicle with sufficient clearness to show us that the Finns of Murom dwelt upon the Lower Oka, the Meres in the swamps around Periaslavl and Murom, and the Wesses in the region of Bieloe Ozero. No remnants of those tribes now remain in Central Russia, but their memory still survives in its geographical nomenclature. The extensive area between the Oka and the White Sea furnishes us with thousands of non-Russian names derived from that aboriginal race—names of which the lingual uniformity makes it clear that the same tongue was spoken throughout the whole of that region, and that it was a tongue closely akin to the one now in use among the native population of Finnland and the present-day Morduines and Tcheremissians of the Middle Volga. For instance, we find scores of names of rivers ending in *va* (*va* in Finnish means water) such as the Protva, the Moskva, the Silva, the Kokva, and so on, while the name of the Oka itself is of Finnish origin, since it is only a Russianised form of the Finnish word *joki*, of which the general meaning is river. Nor have the tribal names of the Meres and Wesses altogether died out from Central Russia, seeing that many villages and minor rivers are to be found called after them, and if we take the distribution of those names as a guide to the former habitat of the tribes we shall find that they occupied an area embracing the great part of the northern portions of the present governments of Kaluga, Tula, and Riazan. Thus we see that the north-eastward direction taken by the Russian immigrants brought them in contact with Finnish aborigines almost at the exact centre of what now constitutes Great Russia.

Two questions next arise: namely, what was the manner of the meeting of the two racial elements, and how did they react upon one another? Speaking generally, their meeting was of a peaceful character, since neither in our written annals nor in our popular traditions is there to be found recorded any general or prolonged struggle between them. The very nature of the Finns would contribute to such a peaceful *rapprochement*, seeing that from the very first moment of their entry into European history they have always been noted for their love of peace—it might almost be said for their subservience and docility. Tacitus remarks in his *Germania* that the Finns are a surprisingly poor and uncultured people, possessing neither houses nor *weapons*, while Jornandes declares them to be the meekest of all the inhabitants of northern Europe. The same impression of Finnish mildness and docility was produced upon the

Russians, who knew those tribes under the generic name of Tchudes. There can be no doubt that, from their first encounter with them, the Russians realised their superiority over the Finns. The irony expressed in all Russian words derived from the root *tchud* (such as *tchudit, tchudno, tchudak*,[1] and so on) bears this out, and the impression is still further strengthened by the history of the Finns on European soil. In past ages those tribes spread far to the southward of the line of the rivers Moskva and Oka, and covered an area where now not a trace of them remains, but at length the migratory movements of population in Southern Rus forced them backwards towards the North, where they continued gradually to give way, or else became incorporated with stronger neighbours. This process of their extinction is in progress to this day. On the other hand, the Russian colonists were no more desirous of picking a quarrel than were the natives, seeing that the majority of the newcomers belonged to a peace-loving rural population which had fled from the South-West only to escape from the ills which oppressed them there, and now sought among the wilds of the North, not booty, but habitations where they might pursue their industrial and agricultural avocations in peace. Settlement, there-fore, was what took place, not conquest. True, at times there may have been neighbourly feuds and dissensions, but our annals say nothing about expeditions for aggrandisement on the one side or revolutionary risings on the other. Further evidence that such were the character and method of the Russian colonisation is to be seen in a feature of Great Russian geographical nomenclature—namely, the feature that Finnish and Russian names do not occur in compact strips of country, but alternating and intermingled with one another. This means that the Russian settlers did not invade the territory of the Finns in large masses, but, percolating thither in thin streams, took possession of such extensive areas dividing the scattered settlements of the natives as chanced to be unoccupied. This system of distribution would have been impossible had the colonists been engaged also in a violent struggle with the natives. It is true that certain traditions of Great Russia retain dim recollections of local fights between Russians and Tchudes, but it is rather of *religious* contests than of *racial* that those traditions speak. The trouble arose, not out of the actual shock of contact between settler and native, but out of attempts on the part of the former to impose his faith upon the latter. Traces of those religious differences are to be met with in two ancient biographies of ecclesiastical dignitaries who laboured for Christianity

Meaning, respectively, to be uncouth, uncouthly, and an uncouth person.

in Rostov during the latter half of the eleventh century — namely, Bishop Leontius and the Archimandrite Abraham. From the life of the former we learn that the inhabitants of Rostov were so bitterly opposed to Christianity that they expelled the first two bishops of the see, Theodore and Ilarion, and murdered the third—Leontius himself; while Abraham's biography (issued soon after that of Leontius) makes it clear that, even after Leontius' day, the inhabitants of one of the wards in the city of Rostov, called the Ward of the Tchudes (a sign that the majority of the townspeople were Russians), remained pagans, and worshipped an image of the Slavonic "Cattle God" or Volos. Hence, even before the introduction of Christianity to that region, the local Meres had adopted the *heathen* beliefs of the Russian Slavs; and, inasmuch as we have seen also that the pagans of the city offered continual and uncompromising resistance to Christian missionaries, it may be assumed that they were joined in so doing by the *Russian* pagan element. Likewise we have a legendary tale of the seventeenth century to the effect that, to escape from "*Russian* baptism," a portion of the pagan Meres of Rostov migrated to the kingdom of the Bolgars on the Volga, where the newcomers joined their kinsfolk the Tcheremissians. All this means that at different periods and in different localities there occurred disturbances, but that, as already said, the trouble invariably arose out of religious, not racial, differences — differences, that is to say, between Christian and pagan, not between immigrant and native, Russian and Tchude.

The question of the respective influence of the Russian and Finnish elements upon one another—of their mutual gains and losses through contact—is one of the most curious and perplexing problems in our history. Seeing, however, that the process ended in the complete absorption of the one element by the other, the really important question for us becomes the influence of the Finns alone; in which regard the ethnographical point chiefly to be decided is the manner in which the fusion of the Finnish and Slavonic elements (the latter, of course, predominating) gave rise to the Great Russian stock. Finnish influence affected the Russian settlers in two ways. In the first place, owing to gradual diffusion of the latter among the native Tchudes, intimate association and common conditions of life among them were bound to result in an adoption by the Russians of Finnish manners and customs; while, in the second place, the gradual Russification of the Finns tended to introduce the physical and ethnographical peculiarities of the latter—their racial type, their language, morals, and beliefs—into the composition of the Russian nationality.

Thus the Russian element became imbued in two ways with the moral and physical characteristics of the Finnish leaven present in its midst.

Likewise there can be no doubt that the Finnish element played a part in the formation of the *facial* type of the Great Russian, since his physiognomy does not by any means reproduce every one of the features generally characteristic of the Slav. The high cheek-bones, the dark hair and skin, the squat nose of the Great Russian all bear credible witness to the influence of a Finnish admixture in his blood.

However, the nature of the relations between Finn and Slav at that period will best be understood if we turn to the realm of religious beliefs. Here we see a marked process of exchange in progress, especially from the Finnish side, and to this day the popular customs and beliefs of the Great Russians retain traces of their partially Finnish origin. At the time of their first encounter with the Russians the Finnish tribes then inhabiting (and, to a certain insignificant extent, still inhabiting) the central and north-eastern portions of European Russia seem to have been only in the primitive stage of religious growth, since their mythology had not even arrived at anthropomorphism. Though worshipping forces and objects of external nature, they did so without *personifying* them. That is to say, the Morduine or Tcheremissian deified rocks, trees, or the earth *themselves*, but recognised therein no symbol of superior beings. In fact, his cult was a sort of rude fetichism, and it was not until later, when Christianity had begun to assert its influence, that the elements became peopled with spirits. Among the Finns of the Volga in particular there flourished a cult of water and forest, of which certain features passed wholesale into the mythology of the Great Russians. On their Olympus, as on that of the Finns, appears the Forest God, who was the guardian of trees, roots, and herbage, and had a bad habit of bursting out into childish shouts and laughter —a proceeding which often scared or misled travellers. As for the Water God, the Kalevala (an epic current among the Finns of the Western Baltic, who had attained to a higher standard of culture) gives an actual picture of him. He was an old man who, wearing a beard of seaweed and a cloak of foam, ruled the waves and the winds, lived at the bottom of the sea, and loved to raise storms and cause shipwreck. Likewise he was an amateur of music, so that when Kalevala, the hero of the epic, let fall his harp into the sea the Water God at once annexed it for his own amusement in his submarine kingdom. These characteristics vividly remind us of the King of the Sea in the well-known Novgorodian *bilina* which tells of Sadka, the rich merchant and harp-player, who plunged, harp and all, into the domain of the watery God, and there so delighted the latter with his playing that his Majesty cast all royal dignity to the winds and fell to dancing. Now, the physiognomy of the god described in the Novgorodian *bilina* is precisely the same as that attributed to the deity of the Kalevala, and although other regions of Rus possessed a Water God, the particular myth just referred to was peculiar to Novgorod. This permits us to suppose that the Novgorodians borrowed it from the Baltic Finns, not the Baltic Finns from the Novgorodians. Finally, traditions concerning the lives of certain of the Great Russian saints furnish us with traces of the survival of rock and tree worship even in their day, although that cult was concealed beneath Christian forms and is nowhere to be met with in Southern or Western Russia.

Under date of 1071 the Ancient Chronicle gives two legends which may enable us to understand still better the attitude adopted by the Russians towards the heathen beliefs of the Finns and the light in which, in their turn, the Finns regarded the Christianity which they saw practised by the Russians. In brief the two legends—or rather, the versions of them given in the Chronicle—are as follows. Once upon a time, when a famine was ravaging the region of Rostov, two soothsayers set out from Yaroslavl to ascend the Volga, saying: "We know who they be that are holding back the harvest." Arrived at a certain *pogost*,[1] they ordered the chief women to be brought to them, saying: "Some of them are holding back the grain, and some the honey, and some the fish." Thereupon one man brought to them his sister, and another man his mother, and a third one his wife, and so on, and the soothsayers stabbed the women in the back, and took out of them grain or fish. Then, having given the women their final dispatch and annexed their property, the soothsayers proceeded onwards to Bieloe Ozero. Now, it so happened that Yan[2] (then a boyar in the service of the Suzerain Prince of Kiev, Sviatoslav) had just arrived at Bieloe Ozero for the purpose of collecting taxes, and as soon as he heard that the soothsayers had been slaying women on the rivers Sheksna and Volga he commanded the townspeople to seize the culprits and bring them before him. "Otherwise," he threatened, "I will not depart from you for the space of a year" —meaning thereby that he and his men-at-arms would remain in the town during that period at the townspeople's expense. Thereupon the inhabitants of Bieloe Ozero hastened to bring the soothsayers before him. "Wherefore are ye slaying so many of the womenfolk?" Yan asked of them; to

---

[1] Market centre. See p. 53.   [2] See p. 15.

which the soothsayers replied : " For the reason that they are withholding the harvest. If we do slay them, then will the famine cease. If thou commandest us, we will take from them grain, fish, and other things before thine eyes." To this Yan retorted : " Ye lie! God made man of the earth, so that he doth consist of bone, sinew, and blood. Of aught else is there naught within him. God alone knoweth the manner of his making." " Nay, but we also do know it," replied the soothsayers. " How, then, is it done?" asked Yan. "God," said the soothsayers, "did wash Himself, and wipe Himself with a napkin, and cast the napkin down to earth ; whereupon Satan did begin to contend with Him as to which of them should create of the napkin a man, and the Evil One did create the body of the man, and God did breathe into that body the breath of life. Wherefore, whensoever a man dieth, his body goeth back unto the earth, but his soul returneth unto God." These soothsayers were Finns of the Meres of Rostov, and the legend which they retailed to Yan still survives among the Morduine peasantry of Nizhni Novgorod. Nevertheless, it does so in a more extended and intelligible form than that given by the Chronicler, who probably had it from the lips of Yan himself,[1] and so received it touched with a strong Christian colouring. The real form of the myth is as follows. The Morduines have two principal gods in their mythology—the good Tchampas and the wicked Shaitan (Satan). Of these, it was the last-named who first conceived the idea of creating man ; to which end he took clay, sand, and earth, and began to fashion of them man's body, but without succeeding in producing the exact shape he desired. First of all, the mould brought forth the form of a pig, and then that of a dog, whereas Shaitan's aim was to make man godlike both in form and appearance. Thus the evil god wrestled and wrestled with the problem. At length he summoned to his aid the flying-mouse (for mice still flew in those days), and bid her fly to heaven, build herself a nest in Tchampas' towel, and bring forth her young there. This the flying-mouse proceeded to do; whereupon the weight of her newly-arrived little ones caused the towel to fall to earth, where it was immediately seized upon by Shaitan, and used by him to clean his mould. This had the desired effect, and lo ! there issued therefrom the godlike body of a man. Next, Shaitan found himself hard put to it to instil into his cast the breath of life, and, after many unsuccessful attempts, was just about to break his handiwork in pieces, when Tchampas appeared, and said : " Hence into the abyss of fire, cursed Shaitan, while I create man without thee !" " Nay," objected Shaitan. " Grant

[1] See p. 15.

me, I pray thee, that I may abide here and see how thou dost put the breath of life into this man whom I have wrought. Inasmuch as it is I who have fashioned him, surely thou wilt be doing a wrong unto me and a shame unto thyself if thou dost not grant me a share in him." Thus they disputed and disputed, until at length they agreed to divide the man —Tchampas taking the soul, and leaving Shaitan the body. To this Shaitan was forced to consent, since Tchampas was immeasurably the stronger of the two. Wherefore, when a man dies, his soul returns in its godlike image to Tchampas, while his body, divorced from the soul, loses that image, falls into corruption, and returns to the earth and Shaitan. Tchampas also visited the presumption of the flying-mouse by depriving her of her wings, and giving her a long tail and paws like Shaitan's: since which time mice have ceased to fly. The Ancient Chronicle's version of the legend concludes by relating that to Yan's question, "In what god do ye believe?" the soothsayers replied: "In anti-Christ." "And where sitteth he?" pursued Yan. "He sitteth in Hell," answered the soothsayers. "A god, forsooth, to sit in Hell!" was Yan's scathing retort. "Rather is he a devil, seeing that God sitteth in *Heaven*, where He reigneth upon the Throne."

The other of the Ancient Chronicle's two stories runs thus. Once upon a time a Novgorodian took a journey into the country of the Finns, where he visited a seer to have his fortune told. The seer began to invoke demons, according to the custom of his kind, while his visitor sat and waited upon the threshold of the hut. Presently the seer subsided into a trance, and, while lying in that condition, was struck by a demon. Thereupon he rose up, and said to the Novgorodian: "My gods say that they cannot come hither, since there is that upon thee which affrighteth them." Then the Novgorodian remembered that he was wearing a little cross; so he took it off, and laid it outside the hut. Then the seer began his incantations again, and after suffering some little mauling and buffeting at the hands of the demons, was able to transmit from them the information required. Finally the Novgorodian said to the seer: "But wherefore do thy gods shun the Cross?"; to which the seer answered: "Because it is the sign of the Heavenly Gods—the Gods of whom our gods do stand in fear." "And where dwell your gods, and what manner of gods be they?" "Our gods are black, with wings and tails, and live in Hell, whence they do fly to and fro upon the earth in subjection to *your* Gods; for your Gods do live in Heaven, and when one of your people dieth, they carry him thither, but when one of our people dieth, he is delivered over to our gods in Hell."—"And of a surety it is so," adds the Chronicle on its own account. "Sinners do abide in Hell, awaiting eternal torment, but the righteous do abide in Heaven, consorting with the companies of angels."

These two stories exemplify at a glance the exchange of religious beliefs which took place between the Russian settlers and the Finnish natives—a process in which the association between the two parties was as peaceful as in their adjustment of social relations. The hostility, the immeasurable incompatibility, between their respective creeds was never felt on either side. Of course it will be understood that I am not now speaking of Christian or non-Christian *theology* so much as of the *popular religious ideas* held by the Russians on the one hand and the Finns on the other. Each race could always find room in its mythological purview for a fresh article of faith, whether Finnish or Slavonic, pagan or Christian; with the result that the two sets of gods shared the general stock of beliefs among them in amicable fashion—the Finnish deities sitting down below, in Hell, and the Russian deities up above, in Heaven. Thus they lived long and friendlily together, and even came to feel a certain mutual respect for each other, seeing that, once the Finnish gods had acquired the Christian name of devils, they took advantage of the fact to make good their footing in the Russo-Christian cult, and, thus becoming Russian themselves, shed, in the eyes of their new worshippers, much of their former alien character. In fact they repeated very much the same process which we have observed in the case of their Finnish devotees when the latter first came in contact with the Russian immigrants. That is why the writer of that part of the Ancient Chronicle which records events of the eleventh century gives not a hint, in his references to soothsayers, customs, or beliefs manifestly Finnish, that it is of an alien race, of the Tchudes, that he is speaking. To him paganism, whether Russian or Finnish, was all one, and he took no account of racial origin or ethnographical differences when writing of heathen beliefs.

It is clear, then, that, in proportion as the two races drew nearer to one another, their differences of belief tended to disappear. To illustrate this community of religious creeds I will adduce a brief legend—unique of its kind in form and contents—which is to be found set forth in a manuscript preserved at the Monastery of Solovetski. In it we see described, in guileless fashion and in the half-light of legendary atmosphere, the building of the first church at Bieloe Ozero, at a spot on the banks of the Sheksna where formerly there had stood a pagan place of prayer—presumably

Finnish. The particular tribe inhabiting the district was that of the Wesses, among whom rocks and birch-trees were the peculiar objects of religious veneration; yet the legend gives not a hint that the same form of worship was not participated in by the Russian settlers in the locality.

"Formerly," says the legend, "the men of Bieloe Ozero lived as heathens, but after that they had learned that it was meet to be baptized and to become of the Christian faith, they built them a church there, though not knowing to what saint they builded it. On a certain morning, therefore, they did gather themselves together and go unto the church, that they might sanctify it and name thereunto a saint. And when they had come to the church, behold, there was upon the river, beside the church, a small boat, and in the boat a stool, and on the stool an *ikon* of the Great Vassili,[1] and before the *ikon* the Host. Then did they raise up the *ikon*, and name the church in the name of the Great Vassili. And an unbeliever did seize upon the Host, and would have eaten it, but that something from it smote him, and the Host itself became as stone. Thus, when the church was sanctified, they sang the Mass. And when they had begun to read the Gospel, behold, there came as it were a great and terrible thundering, so that all the people were affrighted, thinking that the church was falling, and did leap and gaze around them; for in former times there had stood behind the sanctuary a place where the heathen did pray unto a birch-tree and a rock, but the birch-tree had been rooted out of the earth, and the rock also, and the rock cast into the river Sheksna, and sunken. Thus the first church of the Great Vassili was builded in Bieloe Ozero, from the time when the faith first began."

So far, then, from rooting up the heathen beliefs of the natives, Christianity, as received by the Tchude from the Russian, served merely to impose a layer of Christian dogma upon a foundation of pagan superstition. To the mixed Russo-Finnish population Christianity and paganism represented less two religions opposed to and negative of one another than two creeds supplying each other's deficiencies and relating to two different orders of life, two different worlds—a world above, in Heaven, and a world below, in Hell. Indeed, the popular beliefs and religious rites which were to be found until quite recently among the Morduines and certain affiliated Russian colonies in the governments of the Volga show us at a glance how those relations originally arose—show us that the religious process initiated when Eastern Slavdom first came into contact with the Tchudes was continued, with no essential change in its working,

[1] Saint Basil.

through all the centuries needed for the Russification of the Eastern Finns. Thus the Morduine festivals of to-day—the great *moliani*—can be traced back to the Russian popular or church festivals of the Ascension, Trinity-tide, Christmas, and the New Year. First of all, in proportion as the Morduine adopted the Russian tongue, Russian *phrases* crept into the prayers which he addressed to the Supreme Creator (Tchampas), to the Mother of the Gods (Angi Patiai) and to her children. Of this an instance is to be seen in the fact that the Morduine formula *Viniman mon!* ("Have mercy upon us!") soon became supplanted by the Russian *Davai nam dobra zdorovia* (literally, "Grant us good health"). This exchange of phrases was followed by an interchange of religious *personalities*. Thus Tchampas began to be addressed in prayer as "Almighty God," Angi Patiai as "Mother of God," and Nishkipas, her son (*pas* in Finnish means God), as "Saint Ilya" or "Elijah." Again, on New Year's Day an extra title began to be inserted into the petition usually addressed at that season to the Morduine god of swine—as follows: "O Taünsiai, *Great Vassili*,[1] grant unto us swine's flesh, black and white, such as thou thyself lovest"; until finally this truly pagan prayer became perfected into the Russian formula: "Holy Mother, shed thy blessing upon us Christians." Next, pagan *symbols* began to be Christianised, so that, instead of the chaplet of birch-leaves, hung about with rags and linen, which had hitherto adorned the *peredni ugol* or front corner of the hut, there became installed in the place of honour the Russian *ikon* with a wax candle constantly burning in front of it, while Morduine devotees addressed to the great emblem of our Christianity prayers intended for Tchampas or Angi Patiai, but borrowed from the Russian ritual and tongue for the reason that the old Morduine precatory forms were now forgotten. Lastly, observing how much Russian and Christian phrasing and ceremonial there had come to be employed at the public prayer-meetings of the Tchudes, their Russian neighbours began first of all to attend those gatherings, then to take part in them, and finally to repeat at their own services certain of the rites they had witnessed there, as well as to sing the accompanying chants. The result of it all was that neither side could say with certainty to which set of religious customs and ritual it adhered. Yan, when told by the soothsayers that their god sat in Hell, scornfully remarked that, if so, he must be a devil, while, on the other hand, the Finnish seer consulted by the Novgorodian did not hesitate to give his deities wings and a tail—a description clearly borrowed from the Russian

[1] Saint Basil.

ikons, upon which were usually carved figures of devils. Again, in 1636 a Tcheremissian of Kazan answered a question put to him by Olearius [1] as to whether he knew who had created the heavens and the earth by saying (according to Olearius's own account): "Tzort sneit." From this it would seem that the Morduine pagan thought highly of the "Russian gods," but feared the Russian devil; which impression is further confirmed by the fact that the Jesuit missionary Avril records that, when leaving Saratov on Saint Nicholas' Day 1680, he saw heathen Morduines drunk in the streets, and thereby scandalising their Russian neighbours.

There can be no doubt that this mutual adoption of the religious beliefs of Tchudes and Russians had its share in contributing also to an assimilation of racial customs and characteristics, as well as actually to the progress of Christianity among the Finnish people, since, on the one hand, the exchange permitted of the Tchude passing the boundary-line between paganism and Christianity without abandoning altogether his former gods, and, on the other hand, it enabled the Russian to imitate the heathen customs and beliefs of the Tchude without ceasing conscientiously to look upon himself as a Christian. This explains later phenomena which might otherwise have seemed unintelligible, such as the fact of a sixteenth-century Morduine *bearing a Christian name*, yet addressing to a monastery an application to be admitted as an inmate, and being told, in reply, that he must *first of all be baptized*, as well as present a donation to the monastery's funds. Yet such extraordinary interweaving of wholly contrary ideas imported great confusion into the religious sphere—confusion which manifested itself in more than one untoward phenomenon in the moral-religious life of the people. Indeed, the adoption of Christianity proved not so much a passage from darkness to light, from the false to the true, as what I might call a transference of jurisdiction from the gods below to the gods above, seeing that the deities superseded were not wholly abolished as inventions of superstition, but retained as realities of religion, albeit negative ones. Already the confusion bound to arise out of a development of pagan mythology into Christian demonology had made itself felt in Rus during the eleventh century, and might very well be called, according to the apt expression applied by Abbot Theodosius of Petcherski to persons who practised both their own and an alien religion, "*dvoeviera*" or "double faith," while there can be little doubt that, if only that prelate could have foreseen the manner in which Finnish paganism was destined later to join hands with Russian,

[1] Ambassador to Russia from the Duke of Holstein.

he would have called such a nondescript religious system "*troeviera*" or "*triple* faith."

Lastly, we must take into consideration the influence exercised by the native Finnish element upon the *composition* of the community thus created by the Russian colonisation of the Upper Volga. For the most part, the natives occupied the *rural* districts of Suzdal. The biography of the Archimandrite Abraham has shown us that, in the eleventh century, only one ward of the city of Rostov was tenanted by Tchudes—or at all events, that only one ward of it bore their name. Moreover, the Russian titles of most of the ancient towns around Rostov show either that they were founded by Russian immigrants or that they had not arisen when the latter first made their appearance in the region. In any case those titles are proof that the Russian element predominated among the townsmen. On the other hand, we can see no signs of any social graduation, any division into upper and lower classes, among the Finnish people, who appear, on the contrary, to have formed a compact, homogeneous whole : and since we have seen also that Russian colonisation of the region of the Oka and Upper Volga introduced thither a purely rural population, we may take it, on the whole, that the Russo-Finnish people was less urban in character than the unmixed population of Kievan Rus had been.

We have now answered the two questions propounded earlier in the chapter—namely, the question of the manner of the meeting between the Russian settlers and the Finnish natives in the region of the Upper Volga, and the question of the nature of the mutual reaction of the two sides. We have seen that from that meeting no bitter struggle arose, whether racial, social, or religious, and that the meeting bred none of that sharp antagonism or contrast—moral, political, or ethnographical—which usually follows the conquest of one people by another. On the contrary, from the meeting there sprang a threefold blending —namely, (1) a religious assimilation which became the basis of the mythological outlook of the Great Russian stock, (2) a racial fusion which gave rise to the type of the Great Russian, and (3) a social amalgamation which gave the agricultural classes a decided preponderance in the composition of the community.

It now remains for us to note the other chief factor in the formation of the Great Russian stock—namely, the influence of the natural features of the country upon the mixed population evolved through Russian colonisation of the Upper Volga. The term "Great Russian stock" includes, not only a definite ethnographical entity, but also an original economic movement and a special national character. Upon that movement and that character the natural features of the country exercised a formative influence.

To this day the region of the Upper Volga—the region which constitutes the exact centre of Great Russia—is distinguished from the region of the Dnieper by certain physical peculiarities, and six or seven centuries ago it was still more so. Its most notable features are the extent of its swamps and forests, the prevalence of a clayish loam in the composition of its soil, and the tangled network of its streams and rivers. These features had a great influence upon the industrial life and racial character of the Great Russian type of our people.

In Kievan Rus, the chief spring of the popular industry—namely, foreign trade—gave rise to a multitude of towns serving as larger or smaller centres of commerce, but on the Upper Volga—a region remote from the great maritime markets—it was impossible for foreign trade to resume its former rôle as the chief driving force of the industry of the people. That is why, in the fifteenth and sixteenth centuries, we see comparatively few towns in that part of Russia, and even those few inhabited chiefly by a population engaged in agricultural pursuits. Moreover, not only did rural settlements predominate, but they differed sharply in character from those of old Kievan Rus. In the latter the never-ceasing pressure of external perils, added to an insufficient water supply in the open Steppes, compelled the greater portion of the population to group itself into those large masses, those settlements numbering their thousands of inhabitants, which constituted the distinguishing feature of Southern Rus. On the other hand, the first difficulty which confronted the Russian settler among the forests and marshes of the North was to find a spot dry enough to afford him a secure and suitable site for the erection of a hut. Such dry spaces and non-submerged plateaus were like scattered islands amid a sea of timber and swamp, and, for the most part, only afforded room for one, two, or at the most three, homesteads on each. That is why hamlets of one or two dwellings only continued to be the ruling form of settlement in Northern Russia until well-nigh the close of the seventeenth century. The settler's next difficulty was to find sufficient cultivable land around his homestead to win him a subsistence, since suitable plots were few and far between, and needed to be cleared before cultivation could be begun. This work of clearing plots was an exceedingly arduous task, since, first of all, the timber covering the ground had to be burnt off, then the stumps pulled out, and finally the rough ground broken up. That done, the great distance from the chief foreign markets, added to insufficiency of transport, afforded little encouragement to the settler to extend the area of the spaces exploited with such labour; and although any cultivation of a soil such as the loam of the Upper Volga would ensure him the bare necessaries of life, we must not let the comparative paucity of settlers in proportion to the superabundance of unoccupied land lead us to suppose that the Great Russian agriculturist of the sixteenth or seventeenth centuries was able to farm on any a larger scale than the peasant of the nineteenth century or of to-day. The very conditions of husbandry at the period of which I am speaking were all against it, since they communicated to that industry a character insensibly unsettling and nomadic, owing to the fact that the preliminary burning off of the timber for the clearance of the land rendered the soil, for the time being, doubly fertile—the manuring effect of the wood-ashes ensuring bumper crops for at all events the first few seasons. This fertility, however, was only of a spasmodic, transient order, and in six or seven years' time the soil was so exhausted that the settler had no choice but to give it a long rest in fallow. When, therefore, matters reached that point he was frequently tempted to move to a new location, where he could make another clearing, and break fresh ground again. This process of land-exploitation tended to convert the Great Russian into a wanderer, but always in a north-eastward direction, until he had arrived at the natural boundaries of the Russian plain on that side—namely, the Ural range and the White Sea. If at any time he desired to supplement the bare subsistence which he won from the clay of the Upper Volga he had to turn his hand to extraneous rural industries—for which, however, the forests, rivers, lakes, and swamps of the region offered abundant material. It is in this last circumstance that we see the source of the peculiar feature which, from time immemorial, has distinguished the industrial life of the Great Russian peasant—namely, the minor rural industries known as *kustarnie bromisli* or "hand-labour industries." Bast-making, twine-weaving, the trapping of wild animals, bee-keeping (of the wild variety—the variety which nests in hollow trees), fishing, salt-mining, resin-gathering, iron-mining—each and all of these pursuits have long served as the basis, the foster-mother, of the industrial life of whole districts of Great Russia.

Such were the peculiar features communicated to Great Russian industry by the influence of the nature of the country. Briefly recapitulated, those features were (1) sparseness of settlement and predominance or small habitations or hamlets; (2) pettiness of cultivation and limited dimensions of homesteads and plots; (3) mobility of agriculture (*i.e.* prevalence of transient or migratory husbandry); and (4) rise and growth of small rural industries, and consequent exploitation of forest, river, and other natural resources.

The physical features of the country likewise influenced the *racial character* of the Great Russian. Everywhere the swamps and forests of Great Russia of the thirteenth, fourteenth, and fifteenth centuries confronted the settler with a thousand unforeseen risks, difficulties, and hardships. Consequently he learnt to watch nature very closely ("to keep an eye open on both sides of him," as the saying is), to scan and probe the ground on which he walked, and never to attempt the passage of a strange river where there was not a ford. All this bred in him resourcefulness in the face of minor perils and difficulties, and inured him to patient wrestling with hardship and misfortune. No people in Europe is so unspoiled, so handy, so taught not to wait upon nature or fortune, so long-suffering under adversity, as the Great Russian. The peculiar features of the country caused its every hole and corner to beset the settler with some new and difficult industrial problem to solve. Wherever he thought of establishing his homestead he had first of all to study the locality and its conditions, that he might know what it had to offer in the way of profitable resources. Hence originated the extraordinary faculty of observation which we see disclosed in the Great Russian *primieti* or popular nature-sayings—sayings in which we see caught with astonishing fidelity all the characteristic, yet frequently most elusive, phenomena of nature's yearly round in Central Russia. In them we see noted her multitudinous phases, both climatic and industrial, and the entire annual routine of the rural homestead sketched. The seasons of the year, the months—nay, almost every day of every month—find their place in this series, with their several climatic and industrial features duly distinguished. Moreover, these observations of nature not only give us a clear picture of the physical phenomena described, but also furnish us with a portrait of the observer himself. We can see him contemplating his surroundings, and thinking how best he can identify them with the names and festivals of his saints, since it was the Church's calendar which served him both as note-book of nature-observation and diary for the register of his thoughts concerning his daily toil. The Church, too, it was which first taught him, not only to use his powers of observation, but also to reckon time by fasts and festivals; with the result that he came to connect those fasts and festivals with all the natural objects by which he found himself surrounded.

These popular *primieti* well reflect the rugged, wayward character of the physical features of Great Russia. Nature there so often makes sport of even the best-laid agricultural plans that the Great Russian peasant soon grows inured to disappointment, and even comes to take a pleasure in pitting himself against her whims, on the off chance of beating her. This characteristic *trait* in the psychology of the Great Russian is summarised in his oft-repeated catchword *yavos*—" perhaps." About one thing, however, he is never in doubt, and that is, that, come what may, he must make the most of his short summers, seeing that even their brief span may be cut short at any moment by inclement weather. This has made the Great Russian peasant work hard—made him attempt to do as much as possible in the short time at his disposal, ere the autumn and winter (when no work whatever is possible) be upon him. Thus rendered active, alert, and capable of concentrating his whole energies upon the task of finishing his labour while the weather remains open, he has not his equal in Europe for accomplishing so much in so short a time. Yet it must also be confessed that in no quarter of Europe is there to be found so much hopeless incapacity for *long-sustained, systematic* toil as in that same Great Russia.

We have seen that the natural features of the country influenced the distribution of Russian settlement, and led to the adoption of habitation in small, isolated hamlets. Naturally, this lack of social intercourse did not teach the Great Russian to act in large unions or compact masses. The scene of his labours lay, not in the open field, in the sight of all men, as did that of the inhabitant of Southern Rus, but in the depths of the primeval forest, where, axe in hand, he waged a strenuous war with nature. It was a silent, secluded struggle in which he was engaged— a struggle with the elemental forces, with the forest and the wild morass— a struggle which left him no time to think of the community, nor yet of his feelings and relations towards his fellow men. This made him self-centred and retiring, cautious and reserved, diffident in public, and non-communicative of speech. To this day he is happier when facing a difficult problem alone than when he has solved that problem and has thus drawn upon himself the unwelcome attention of his fellows. Hope of success arouses all his energies, but attainment of success leaves him cold again. To overcome obstacles and perils comes easier to him than to wear his well-deserved laurels with tact when he has done so. In short, the Great Russian belongs to that type of humanity which deteriorates from the moment that it first becomes aware of its own powers, and is seen to greater advantage in the individual than in the mass.

We may with reason suppose that every nationality derives from the world around it certain definite impressions which cause it to produce certain definite types, just as a process of grafting produces from a plant flowers of more than one colour. In this evolution of types the physical features of a given region undoubtedly play their part. In the case of the Great Russian, the impossibility of seeing far ahead of him, of formulating any definite plan of action against unforeseen perils or invariably taking the nearest road to a desired point, is strongly reflected in his psychology and modes of thought. The changes and chances of life early taught him to look back whence he had come rather than forward whither he was going. Sudden blizzards or thaws, unexpected August frosts or January mildness, have made him observant rather than provident, attentive to consequences rather than to their prevention, careful of sums-total rather than of their constituent amounts. By some observers he is accused of lack of straightforwardness and sincerity. That is a mistake. True, he often takes two views of a question, but this seeming double-mindedness arises from the fact that, though his mental process leads him to make straight for his goal (ill-considered though the goal often be), he does so looking to either side of him as he goes, even as his ancestors scanned the surrounding fastnesses which they were forced to traverse. " Beware lest thou strike thy forehead against a wall : none but crows fly straight," says a Great Russian proverb. Circumstances and the forces of nature have combined to teach the native of Great Russia to try all roads when making for a given point, and to think and act as he goes along. A symbol of this is to be seen in the ordinary Great Russian country road. What in all the world could be more dilatory and tortuous in its progress than it ? Yet, try to go straighter than it does, and you end either by losing your way altogether or by finding yourself back in its sinuous windings.

Such, then, was the influence exercised by the natural features of Great Russia upon the industrial life and racial character of the Great Russian type of our nationality.

CHAPTER XIV

Political results of the Russian colonisation of the Upper Volga—Prince Andrew Bogoliubski —His relations with Kievan Rus—His attempts to convert the patriarchal rule of the Suzerain Prince of Rus into absolute rule—His policy in Rostov—His relations with his kindred, with the older towns, and with the senior grade of his retinue—The princely and social feud which arose in Rostov at his death—Opinion of a chronicler of Vladimir upon that feud—Supremacy of Northern Rus under Vsevolod III.—Effect of the political achievements of Andrew and Vsevolod upon the community of Suzdal—Summary of the foregoing.

TURNING, next, to the *political* results of the Russian colonisation of the Upper Volga, we must constantly bear in mind the fact that, in studying them, we are studying the first bases of the order of state which became established during the period now confronting us. Let me specify those bases (which are two in number), so that we may then proceed to follow their elaboration and development into the new order of state referred to. The first of them was the permanent establishment upon the Moskva of the governmental centre of the Upper Volgan region—of the centre which hitherto had fluctuated between Rostov, Suzdal, Vladimir, and Tver ; while the second basis was the new type of ruler which now arose—the type in which, in the person of the Muscovite Prince, the joint power of the multitudinous princes of the northern appanages became concentrated. The Muscovite type of ruler who now replaced his Kievan prototype was an hereditary, immoveable, pan-territorial prince, and destined to become the fundamental and most active element in the future Muscovite state. For that reason let us examine the various other factors amid which the two bases of the new order of state were laid—the bases represented by the Muscovite type of ruler and the Muscovite centre of government.

The political results of the Russian colonisation of the Upper Volga first became apparent during the time of Andrew Bogoliubski. His father, Yuri Dolgoruki, a younger son of Monomakh, was the first of an unbroken line of princes who ruled Rostov after that province had been created a separate principality (hitherto it had been a mere appendage to the province of Periaslavl in the South). In this newly constituted principality there was born, in 1111, Prince Andrew Bogoliubski—a typical chieftain of the North in his habits, ideas, and political upbringing. Appointed in infancy by his father to be governor of the newly-arisen, insignificant town of Vladimir on the Kliazma, he retained that post for the first thirty years of his life without ever once going southwards to visit Kiev; with the result that it is not until 1146, when the great feud between his father and his cousin Iziaslav of Volhynia arose, that chroniclers either of the South or the North make any mention of him. In 1149, however, he makes his first appearance in the South, on the conclusion of the great feud and the assumption by his father of the Kievan throne, and from that moment the South rings with his name. The Ancient Chronicle alone furnishes such a wealth of stories as enables us to form a vivid picture of his personality. The peculiarities of his personal character and political relations to Southern Rus soon brought him into prominence from among the general mass of Kievan princes of that day. In warlike prowess he seems to have been not inferior even to his father's redoubtable rival Iziaslav, since he not only performed wonders in the way of pillage and slaughter, but would hurl himself, helmed or bareheaded, against the most impregnable of ramparts. Of course there was nothing unusual in all this, since the constant pressure of external perils, added to the constant waging of feuds, did at least breed *physical* courage in the princes of that day. What marked him out from all his contemporaries was his faculty of swift recovery from a bout of military intoxication, so that no sooner was the torch of war extinguished than he became once more a sane and enlightened politician, as well as a provident administrator. Everything, with him, was always in order and to hand—it was impossible to take him unawares, for the reason that amid the general confusion he never lost his head. Indeed, his habit of constantly looking to the future, added to his faculty of producing order out of chaos, caused him greatly to resemble his grandfather Vladimir Monomakh. Moreover, in spite of his valour he had no real love for war, but, on the contrary, was always the first after a successful battle to beg his father to make peace with the vanquished foe. This *trait* in his character is noted with astonishment by the Chronicle, which adds : " Andrew loved not to be commended for his warlike prowess, but looked only for praise from God." Furthermore, he did not share his father's passionate devotion to Kiev—being indifferent alike to Southern Rus in general and to "the Mother of Towns" in particular. When, in 1151, it came to his father's turn to be defeated by his old rival, Iziaslav, Yuri shed bitter tears at the thought of having to leave the city, but Andrew only remarked: " Now doth there remain nought for us here, my father. Come, let us depart hence while the season is yet open," (it was then early autumn). On Iziaslav's death in 1154, Yuri finally established himself upon the Kievan throne, and held it until his own death in 1157. To Andrew, as to the most promising of his sons, he assigned Vishgorod, near Kiev, but Andrew could not rest quietly in Southern Rus. Without asking permission of his father, he one day arose, and returned to his native Suzdal in the North, taking nothing with him from Vishgorod but a Greek-made *ikon* of the Holy Mother: and from that time onwards she became the patron saint of Suzdal under the name of Our Lady of Vladimir. One of the later Recueils explains Andrew's conduct thus : " Prince Andrew was vexed in his heart when he saw the divisions among his brethren, his nephews, and all his kinsfolk, for they were continually at war among themselves through seeking to attain the Suzerain throne, and were never at peace the one with the other. Hence the principalities did fall to waste, and entice the Polovtsi continually to enter upon them from the Steppes. Thus, Prince Andrew being grieved in his heart, he spake no word unto his father, but resolved to return privily unto his own country of Suzdal and Rostov, where there was greater peace." After Yuri's death, several princes succeeded each other in rapid succession upon the Kievan throne, until at length it was filled by Mstislav, son of Yuri's former rival Iziaslav of Volhynia; whereupon Andrew, conceiving himself to be the senior of Mstislav, waited only for a favourable moment to send his son southwards with a force from Suzdal, and to this force other princes who were opposed to Mstislav soon joined themselves. The allies took Kiev "with spear and shield "—*i.e.* by storm, and sacked the city so thoroughly that the Chronicle declares that neither churches nor women nor children were spared when they fell into the victor's hands. " Then was there among the people of Kiev anguish and wailing—grief that would not be comforted and tears without ceasing." Yet, despite the success of his troops, Andrew did not come southwards in person to assume the Suzerain throne, but delegated it to his younger brother Gleb, while his victorious son first installed his uncle upon the Kievan throne, and then returned home to his father in the North—"with honour and great glory," as a northern chronicler expresses it, and "with a curse upon him," as a more pro-Kievan writer of the South declares.

Never before had such a calamity befallen " the Mother of Russian Towns." That she should be sacked by her own countrymen was indeed a striking revelation of her decline as a territorial and cultural centre, and it is clear that the tide of her political influence was fast ebbing in proportion to the outflow of her population. This blow which the northern prince had dealt to the old ideas and relations inherited by the southern princes from their fathers and grandfathers made itself felt in the life of the entire country; with the result that a rift opened in the common nationality, and the estrangement between the settlers of the North and the Kievan region whence they hailed became permanent. On the death of his brother Gleb, Andrew deputed the government of the region of Kiev to his three nephews the Princes of Smolensk (of Rostislav's line), the eldest of whom—Roman—took Kiev itself, and his two younger brothers, David and Mstislav, the adjacent towns of Bielgorod and Vishgorod. Yet it was Andrew who, though residing and ruling at Suzdal in the North, now held the title of Suzerain Prince, and on one occasion when his nephews proved disobedient to him he sent them the following threatening message: " If thou, O Roman, and thy brethren walk not in my will, of a surety shalt thou depart from Kiev, and David from Bielgorod, and Mstislav from Vishgorod. Yea, ye shall all of you return to Smolensk, where ye may apportion yourselves as ye will." Thus for the first time we see the Suzerain Prince of Rus—the ruler who hitherto had stood to his younger kinsfolk in the relation of "father"—addressing his juniors in a strain neither paternal nor fraternal. This innovation in inter-princely relations was felt with especial bitterness by the youngest and best of the line of Rostislav — Mstislav the Brave. Accordingly, when Andrew sent a second threatening message, Mstislav retorted to it by cutting off the messenger's beard and sending him back with the reply: " Hitherto, O Andrew, we, of our love, have acknowledged thee in place of father, but inasmuch as thou hast now sent unto us words not meet to be spoken unto princes, but only unto underlings and simple men, thou mayest do what thou proposest, and God be judge between us." This, then, was the first occasion on which the term " underling " had arisen in the princely circle—the first occasion, that is to say, on which an attempt had been made to exchange the old indefinite, voluntary system of princely relations based upon kinship for an obligatory subordination of the junior members of the princely house to the senior member and for their political degradation to the rank of " simple men " or commoners.

Such was the series of novel phenomena disclosed in the relations of Andrew Bogoliubski with Southern Rus and his brother princes. Hitherto the title of Suzerain Prince had always gone with the throne of Kiev, while the prince recognised as senior had usually held that throne, and the prince holding that throne had usually been recognised as senior. Such had been the regular, accepted system. Now, however, Andrew threw seniority completely out of gear by proclaiming himself Suzerain Prince of the Russian land without at the same time leaving his old province of Suzdal and migrating southwards to Kiev to ascend there the throne of his father and grandfather. Indeed, we see Iziaslav's well-known saying concerning "a head going to a place" receiving an unexpected application at this juncture, since, instead of the usual circumstance of a junior ruler aspiring to succeed to a senior post, we have the case of a senior ruler voluntarily remaining in a junior one. Thus princely seniority was displaced, and, by acquiring a personal, individual significance, may have given rise to the first dim idea of the concentration of the supreme power in the person of one ruler alone. The position of Suzdal among the rest of the Russian provinces also underwent a change, as did the relation of its Prince towards his domain. Hitherto the prince recognised as senior and permitted to ascend the Kievan throne had usually been followed in his late province by the prince standing next to him in order of seniority, since each province was merely the temporary, vacateable holding of its ruler—the property of the princely family as a whole, not of any individual member of that family. When, however, *Andrew* became Suzerain Prince he still remained resident in his old province of Suzdal; with the result that it lost its family significance, and, acquiring the character of personal, inalienable property belonging to one prince alone, dropped out of the rota of provinces governed in order of princely seniority. Thus Andrew's policy towards Southern Rus and his brother princes constituted virtually an attempt to revolutionise the whole political organisation of the Russian land. At all events that is the light in which his policy appeared to the ancient annalists, who may be taken as voicing the view of Andrew's contemporaries generally. According to that view, the Suzerain throne (hitherto exclusively Kievan) now became divided, since Andrew and his Rus of the North separated themselves from the South, and formed in Suzdal a second Suzerain Principality, with the town of Vladimir as its federal capital.

Scrutiny of events in Suzdal during the time of Andrew, as well as after his death, reveals to us traces of a second revolution—this time a revolution in the internal organisation of the province. At home, also, in his own peculiar domain, Andrew disregarded all precedent in his methods of governing. A custom first established when the princely stock became divided into lines and had the common rotation of its rule interrupted required that the senior prince of a given line should share the government of the province peculiar to that line with his nearest junior relatives, by appointing them *posadniki* of the lesser towns in the province. In Rostov, however, the migratory habits adopted by the Russian settlers confused and upset all established customs and relations. Yuri Dolgoruki desired that after his death the province should pass to his younger sons, while the two senior towns of Rostov and Suzdal had sworn to him upon the cross (though such was not the usual custom in such cases) that they would faithfully observe his wishes. Yet no sooner was he dead than they invited his eldest son—Andrew—to assume the reins of government. Andrew, indeed, held his father's memory in dutiful respect, but self-interest proved the stronger, and he acceded to the invitation of the perjured townsmen. Nevertheless he refused to share his newly-acquired province with his kinsmen, and drove them out of the country as potential rivals for the power which he had thus usurped. As we know, the old original town-provinces of Rus were governed by a dual aristocracy—an official and an industrial, of which the former served as the prince's instrument of rule, and the latter as his advisor or coadjutor. The official aristocracy consisted of boyars and princely retainers generally, while the industrial aristocracy was formed of that upper stratum of the non-official population of the great towns which bore the name of " *liuchshie muzhi* " or " *liepshie muzhi* " (*i.e.* " best men " or " gentle men ") and administered the populations of their several provinces through the medium of town *vietcha* elected on a democratic basis. Both these two classes of aristocracy are to be met with in Rostov in the time of Andrew's father Yuri, but when Andrew himself became ruler trouble ensued, since he and his two upper classes could never agree. The established system required that the reigning prince should sit and rule in the capital town of his province, in harmony and co-operation with the local *vietché*. The province of Rostov contained two such capital towns—namely, Rostov and Suzdal, but Andrew had no love for either of them, and resided at Vladimir on the Kliazma, with which he had been associated from his earliest youth. There no *vietché* held its sessions, but all the duties of fortifying and embellishing the place devolved upon Andrew himself. This was to him a labour of love, and the Chronicle tells us that he " builded strongly," and erected, among other things, a magnificent Cathedral of the Assumption, dedicated " to the wonder-working Mother of God of the golden locks " (meaning thereby the miraculous *ikon* of the Virgin which he had brought with him from Vishgorod). For the carrying out of his schemes of town-building he imported (so we are told by one of the Recueils) artisans, mechanics, and handicraftsmen generally. Such an unprecedented removal of the princely throne from the capital city to a lesser town displeased the inhabitants of Rostov and Suzdal, who began to murmur, saying : " Behold, we are the capital towns, whereas Vladimir is but a *prigorod.*"[1] In the same way, Andrew had no love for the senior grade of his retinue, and even went so far as to exclude it from his diversions. In the matter of hunting, for instance, he would bid his boyars (in the words of the Chronicle) "fashion their sport separately, wheresoever it might please them," and then betake himself to the chase with only a few *otroki* (pages) in attendance. At length, determined to rule unhampered, he banished all his "greater boyars" from the country as he had already banished his brothers and nephews—this conduct of his being attributed by the Chronicle to a desire to make himself "autocrat over all the land of Suzdal." Yet for these contraventions of precedent he paid, in the end, with his life. His high-handed action in executing a boyar named Kuchkovitch—a brother of his first wife's and a notable member of his court—led to the brother of the murdered man joining with other courtiers in a conspiracy, and Andrew fell beneath the hand of the assassin in the year 1174.

The whole figure of this ruler breathes the spirit of innovation. Yet not all of that innovation was good, seeing that with the liberal spirit went a grim, relentless bent which impelled him always to act independently and in defiance of established custom and tradition. This dual tendency in him—this mixture of strength and weakness, of orderliness and caprice —was duly noted by his contemporaries. "Though prudent in all things and valiant," says the Chronicle of him, " Prince Andrew did undo his own purposes with his own intemperateness "—*i.e.* with his want of self-control. In spite, too, of the well-deserved reputation for military courage and political acumen which he won in early manhood in the South, he was guilty of many egregious acts at a later period when he was leading his sedentary life at Vladimir. From his dim stronghold on the Kliazma he organised and dispatched expeditions against both Kiev and Novgorod— thus seeking to throw the net of his ambitious schemes over the whole of Russian territory. Yet to order affairs so badly that a force of no fewer than seven thousand men of Suzdal should be put to flight at Bieloe Ozero by four hundred Novgorodians, or that a second expedition

[1] A lesser or attached town.

should result only in prisoners of the attacking force being sold in the streets of Novgorod for a third of the price of a sheep, or that, after banishing all his "greater boyars," he should surround himself with a gang of courtiers capable of requiting his lordly favours with assassination and the pillaging of his palace, were all of them things scarcely worthy of Andrew's great abilities. On the other hand, he was consistent in his piety and personal asceticism, built numerous churches in the province, made a practice of going personally to light the candles for Mass in the Cathedral, and frequently caused food and drink to be served to the sick and needy in the streets. Moreover, he had for his town of Vladimir an almost paternal tenderness, and endeavoured by every means to make it another Kiev, a second Russian metropolis. To this end he set up in its cathedral the famous Golden Gates, and designed to have them opened on the Feast of the Assumption. "All men will then be coming hither for the festival," he said to his boyars, "and they shall see the Gates." Unfortunately the mortar used in the work failed to set firm by the appointed day, so that, just when the people were gathering for the festival service, the Gates collapsed, and crushed in their fall twelve onlookers. Thereupon (so the story continues) Andrew flung himself upon his knees before the sacrosanct *ikon* of the Holy Mother, and besought her, saying : "Save these our people, or of their death shall I, a sinner, be guilty." Then the Gates were raised, and behold! from beneath them came forth the twelve victims, alive and well! The city was by no means ungrateful for all Andrew's care and protection. Indeed, the panegyric with which the weeping citizens greeted the funeral procession of the murdered prince partakes almost of the nature of a *bilina* in honour of a deceased hero. After his death, however, the organisation of the province which he had built up with such care during all those twenty years of sedentary life which elapsed between his flight from Vishgorod and his death developed into something very like anarchy. Everywhere murder and robbery were rife, and many *posadniki*, *tiuni*, and other government officials were assassinated. Never before in Rus had the demise of a prince been accompanied by such shameful scenes. The cause of them lay in the general atmosphere created by Andrew's self-will, lack of discrimination, and contempt for old customs and traditions. Even his own wife,[1] who came of the Bolgars of the Kama, took part in the conspiracy against him, in revenge for all the cruelty he had shown to her people; so that the Chronicle gloomily remarks, *à propos* of the disunion to be seen in Andrew's family

[1] *i.e.* his second wife.

circle: "Even his own household did hate him, and there was sore dissension in the land of Rostov and Suzdal."

In Andrew his contemporaries were inclined to see a veritable pioneer of new governmental ideas, yet his actual policy compels us to wonder whether it was really by systematically thought-out principles of responsible sovereignty or whether only by an instinct for autocracy that he was guided. In any case, it was in his person that the Great Russian first entered upon the historical stage, and that entry cannot be deemed a happy one. Certainly, at moments of stress Andrew could develop immense force of character, yet in his calmer, leisured years he relapsed into sheer error and folly. It can hardly be that every feature in his policy was a chance phenomenon, the mere fortuitous outcome of his personal character and exceptional temperament: rather is it likely that his political ideas and administrative methods were derived from the social *milieu* amid which he was born and amid which he played the greater part of his rôle in life. That *milieu* was the town of Vladimir, and in it he spent the major portion of his existence. The lesser towns of Suzdal formed a world of their own —a world created by the Russian colonisation of the region and by the consequent rise of new ideas and relations of a kind unknown in the original provinces of Rus. Upon that world the events which followed upon Andrew's death throw a vivid light.

No sooner was he dead than there arose in Suzdal a feud which, as regards its origin, bore a strong resemblance to the feuds of old Kievan Rus, seeing that the cause of dispute was the question of the relative seniority of younger uncles and older nephews. In this case it was Andrew's younger brothers, Michael and Vsevolod, who fell out with their nephews, Mstislav and Yarapolk, sons of a deceased elder brother, and it was a struggle in which the people were afforded, for the first time, an opportunity of taking sides. The senior towns of Rostov and Suzdal, together with the boyars of the province of Rostov, had elected to be governed by Andrew's nephews, but the townsmen of Vladimir (now become the actual seat of the princely throne) summoned Andrew's brothers, Michael and Vsevolod, to be their rulers. That was how the feud arose. From the first the nephews had the best of the struggle, so that the elder of them succeeded in establishing himself at the capital city of Rostov, and the younger one at Vladimir. After a while, however, the townsmen of Vladimir rose against the nephews and their allies the capital cities, and sent for the uncles, who this time got the better of their rivals, and shared the land between them—though taking the lesser towns of Vladimir and Periaslavl Zaliesski for their respective capitals, and not the older towns of Rostov and Suzdal. On the death of the elder uncle, Michael, the feud broke out again between the younger uncle, Vsevolod (to whom the townsmen of Periaslavl, as well as those of Vladimir, had sworn allegiance), and the eldest of his nephews, Mstislav, who had at his back the chief men of Rostov and the boyars. This time Mstislav had to give way, after being beaten in fights, first at Yuriev, and then on the river Koloksha; with the result that Vsevolod was left master of the whole of the Suzdal region. All this took place during the years 1174–1176. Though similar in its origin to the bygone feuds of the South, this northern quarrel differed from them in the actual manner of its progress, since it included phenomena altogether unknown in the genealogical contests of old Kievan Rus. Usually the non-official portions of the southern population had remained passive spectators of the princely quarrels— only the princes themselves and their actual retainers taking part in them, not provinces or entire provincial communities (though occasionally, and here and there, one might become partially involved). In Suzdal, however, the local population took active sides in the disputes of their local princes; the cities of Rostov and Suzdal ranging themselves against the lesser town of Vladimir, and so forth. In all the other provinces of Rus the *vietcha* of the capital towns had long ago arrogated to themselves the right to nominate *posadniki* to govern the lesser towns, so that we now find the *vietché* of Rostov saying with regard to Vladimir: "The town is our *prigorod*. Come, let us burn it if we may not send thither our own *posadnik*. In it do abide none but masons and slaves." Clearly the *vietché* was referring to the artisans imported thither by Andrew. Vladimir did not stand alone in the feud, but was joined by one or more of the lesser towns of Suzdal. "The men of Vladimir," says the Chronicle, "were of one heart with the men of Periaslavl." Another newly-arisen town which was inclined to take the same side and only restrained by fear of the nephews was Moscow. Nor was territorial hostility strictly confined to the capital and junior towns, for it went deep enough to embrace practically the whole community from top to bottom. On the side of the nephews and the capital towns stood the boyars of Suzdal, while even those of Vladimir (to the number of fifteen hundred) answered the call of the magnates of Rostov to join the capital cities against the princes whom their (the boyars' of Vladimir) fellow townsmen were supporting. Yet, though the upper classes, even in the lesser towns, sided with the capitals, the inferior population of those capitals certainly sided with the opposite party. After the first success gained by the uncles over the nephews we find the common people of the city of Suzdal sending a deputation to Michael with the message : " O Prince, we did not join Mstislav against thee.   It was our boyars alone.   Therefore be not thou vexed with us, but come and be our ruler." Such were the terms employed by the *prostonarodie*[1] of the city of Suzdal ; whence it follows that the whole local community was involved in the struggle, and that it was divided in its sympathies, not vertically, but horizontally.   On the one side stood the two classes of the aristocracy of the capital towns, and on the other side the lower orders of the capitals and the whole population of the lesser towns.   Direct evidence of this social division in the feud is to be found in a message sent by Vsevolod to Mstislav on the eve of the battle at Yuriev.   Vsevolod hoped to be able to settle the affair without bloodshed, and therefore sent to say to his nephew : " My brother, although the boyars be for thee, return thou unto Rostov, that we may make peace together.   On thy side hast thou the chief men of Rostov and the boyars, but on our side do stand both God and the men of Vladimir and Periaslavl."

Thus we see that the feud revealed the different elements in the local community, as well as their mutually hostile relations.   That is to say, we see the uncles opposed to the nephews, the senior towns to the junior, and the upper classes of society to the lower.   Yet at the bottom of this three-fold struggle there lurked one general cause of territorial enmity.   To understand its origin we must remember that the senior cities of Rostov and Suzdal owed their rise and growth to the old-established Russian population which a wave of colonisation had wafted thither before Yuri Dolgoruki's time, and that that population had since been used to take the lead in the local community.   Later, with Dolgoruki's tenure of rule (*i.e.* with the opening of the twelfth century), there came the boyars of his retinue to constitute a second old-established ruling class, and to join hands with the mercantile magnates of Rostov and Suzdal in opposing the growth of the younger towns.   Of these towns the population consisted wholly of colonists from Southern Rus—men derived, for the most part, from the lower classes of the region whence they had come, both urban and rural.   On reaching Suzdal, these immigrants came in contact (as we have seen) with the native Finnish population (itself a lower stratum of the local community), and the process of colonisation thus gradually communicated to the common people, urban and rural, a decided preponderance in the composition of the population of Suzdal at large.

[1] Populace.

Indeed, an old heroic *bilina*, in which we hear re-echoed the ideas and relations of bygone official and aristocratic Kievan Rus, had some reason for describing the inhabitants of Rostov as the "beyond-the-forest peasants"[1] and Ilya Muromets (the principal hero of that region) as "the peasant's son." This preponderance of the lower classes altogether upset—so far as the North was concerned—that balance of the various social elements which, in the South, had preserved the social system intact. We have seen that that Southern system bore the aristocratic stamp—that it favoured the political supremacy of the upper classes, but oppressed the lower, and that while, on the one hand, it enabled foreign trade to maintain the social position of the industrial aristocracy, on the other hand it caused the continual pressure of external perils and internal feuds to strengthen the power of the military-official class. In the North, however, the situation was different. There the sources of the two classes of the aristocracy soon became dried up, since the colonising movement sundered tradition, and so freed the settlers from the ties and customs which had served as the basis of social relations in the older-settled locality of Kiev. In fact, it was due to a social cause, and not to a racial or territorial, that that friction arose between the North and the South which became such a marked feature during the twelfth century—the cause of it being the vexation felt by the aristocracy of Kievan Rus at the fact of their *smerdi* and *kholopi* escaping from their clutches and betaking themselves to the North. Naturally enough, the fugitives cherished similar sentiments with regard to the boyars and *liepshie muzhi* both of the South and their new country. In this manner the political supremacy of the upper classes in Rostov lost its moral and material supports, and was therefore bound, in view of the influx of peasant colonists and the resultant changes in the former relations and conditions of local life, to evoke only antagonism between the upper and the lower strata of the community. It was this antagonism, then, which served as the mainspring of the feud between the brothers and the nephews of the deceased Andrew. Consolidated through fusion with the Finnish element, the lower orders were, for the first time, roused to action by the princely dispute, and, arming themselves against their superiors—against the original, time-honoured rulers of the local community—converted the princes whose cause they espoused into a means of attaining their end. Thus the struggle was not only a feud of princes, but a war of classes, and the revolution in the internal organisation of the community which overthrew the two local

[1] See footnote to p. 198.

aristocracies was as intimately bound up with the colonisation movement as was the revolution in the external position of the province—the revolution which involved the abrogation of the rota system of rule.

Of this feud we have a description written by a contemporary chronicler who, as a citizen of Vladimir, was naturally on the side of the uncles and the lesser towns. The great success achieved in the struggle by his native town is ascribed by him to the miraculous aid of the Holy Mother, whose wonder-working *ikon* stood in the local Cathedral. After relating the history of the first victory of the uncles over the nephews and the triumphant return of Michael to Vladimir, this historian turns annotator, and interlards his narrative with such quaint moralising as the following : " And there was great joy in Vladimir when it saw again in its midst the Suzerain Prince of all the Russian land. For this new miracle let us give thanks unto the great and Orthodox Mother of God, in that She hath saved Her city from calamity and hath made Her citizens strong. God did so preserve them from faintheartedness that they feared not even the two Princes and their boyars, and paid no heed unto their threatenings, but placed their trust only in the Holy Mother of God and their own right. The men of Novgorod, Smolensk, Kiev, Polotsk, and all the other chief towns of provinces are wont to assemble themselves together to take council in their *vietcha*, and by that which the chief towns decide do the lesser towns abide ; but here, in our own chief towns of Rostov and Suzdal, have the boyars attempted to establish their own law rather than to fulfil the Law of God, saying : ' As it shall please us, so will we do, seeing that Vladimir is our subject town.' Yea, they have gone against God and against the Holy Mother of God and against the Law of God, and have hearkened unto evil men and disturbers who wished to do us no good thing, by reason of their envy of this town and of them who dwell in it. Not knowing, therefore, how rightly to fulfil the Law of God, the men of Rostov and Suzdal did conceive that, inasmuch as they be the elder towns, they should do all things according to their own fashion : but we, the newer and younger men of Vladimir, did understand wherein lay our right, and have stood strongly to uphold it, and have said unto ourselves : ' Either will we have Michael for our prince, or we will give our lives for the Holy Mother of God and for Prince Michael.' And behold! God and His Holy Mother have comforted us, and the Orthodox men of Vladimir have stood up before the whole world for their right—God being their helper." This makes it clear that the chronicler in question saw in the feud, not so much a quarrel between princes, as a struggle between the various elements of the local community—a revolt of the "newer and younger men" against the upper classes and the ancient directors of local life, the official and the industrial aristocracies.   Thus one of the results of the Russian colonisation of the region of Suzdal was that the lower strata of the local community gained the ascendancy over the upper : whence it will be foreseen that from that moment the community began to develop on more democratic lines (comparatively speaking) than Kievan Rus had ever done, and that this new tendency favoured the resurrection of the princely power which we have seen decline in the South through the feuds, as well as through the position of dependency upon the *vietcha* of their towns into which the princes had drifted.   This revolution found detailed expression in the great feud of Suzdal above-mentioned.   On the death of the elder of the two uncles, Michael, the people of Vladimir lost no time in swearing allegiance to his younger brother, Vsevolod, and not only to him, but to his sons as well.   This meant that they established among themselves hereditary succession of the princely power in the descending line, in contravention both of the old rota system and of that claim of the older towns to choose between the various competing princes which had gradually arisen out of the system in question.

Taking another step forward, we come upon a second new factor—namely, the marked domination of Suzdal over all the other provinces of the Russian land.   After vanquishing his nephew in 1176, Vsevolod III. ruled Suzdal until 1212 ; his tenure of power being largely a continuation of the internal and external policy of Andrew Bogoliubski.   Like the latter, again, Vsevolod enforced his recognition as Suzérain over the whole of the Russian land without, however, proceeding to Kiev to ascend the actual throne of his father and grandfather.   Ruling Southern Rus from the banks of the far-off Kliazma, he permitted the Suzerain Princes of Kiev to ascend their thrones only by his authority —to hold office, as it were, only on sufferance and as his "underlings." Thus there came to be *two* Suzerain Princes—one sitting at Kiev, and the other one at Vladimir, or a senior and a junior, a real and a nominal. Vsevolod's nephew, Rurik of Smolensk (of the line of Rostislav), was an "underling" Suzerain of this kind, and on one occasion we find him saying to his father-in-law, Roman of Volhynia : "Thou thyself knowest that the will of Vsevolod must be obeyed, and that without it we can do nothing.   All our brethren have yielded unto him seniority in the line of Vladimir."   This political supremacy of Vsevolod's was felt as far away as Galicia, the extreme south-westernmost province of the

Russian land, as is shown by the fact that, after assuming his father's throne there with the help of Poland, the Galician Prince Vladimir (son of Yaroslav the Prudent) found it advisable to lose no time in placing himself under the protection of his uncle in distant Suzdal. "O father and lord," was his message, "hold thou Galicia under my feet, and of a surety will I be God's and thine for ever, together with all my province, and will alway walk in thy will." Likewise Vsevolod's neighbours, the princes of Riazan, felt his heavy hand so effectually that they "walked alway in his will," and sent their troops to join those of Suzdal on expeditions whenever ordered to do so. In 1207, however, Vsevolod became aware that certain of these princes were intriguing against him, and therefore had them seized and brought to Vladimir. Appointing *posadniki* of his own to the towns of Riazan, he then ordered the inhabitants to give up all their remaining princes and princesses (whom he held captive until his death), and appointed his son governor of the province. When, also, at a later period "the rude and turbulent men of Riazan," as the Chronicle of Suzdal calls them, had been pardoned by Vsevolod, but had followed that up by banishing his son, the masterful Prince of Suzdal at once gave orders for all the townsmen of the city of Riazan to be seized, together with their families and the local bishop, and, distributing them among the other towns of the region, burnt their city to the ground, conquered its attached province, and added the same to Suzdal. Others too of his neighbours had reason to remember him. For instance, we find the Prince of Smolensk humbly begging his pardon for some offence or another, and Vsevolod appointing his own nominees to Novgorod, violating its most cherished traditions, and putting its citizens to death without reason given. His very name (so says the Chronicle) "made all lands to quake," and his fame spread far and wide. Even the author of the *Slovo o Polko Igorevé*—a South Russian poet and writer of the later twelfth century—had heard of the political power of this mighty Prince of Suzdal, for, in describing the misfortunes which overtook the Russian land after the defeat of its Northern heroes in the Steppes, he addresses to Vsevolod the following appeal: "O Suzerain Prince Vsevolod, come thou from afar and protect thy father's throne of gold—thou who canst divide the waters of the Volga with thine oars and empty the river Don with the helmets of thy soldiers!" In short, by the opening of the thirteenth century, Suzdal, which, at the beginning of the twelfth century, had been a remote, barbaric region of the North, had now become a principality supreme over the rest of Rus, and the political centre of gravity had shifted from the banks of the Middle Dnieper to those of the Kliazma. This was the second direct political result of the outflow of Russian population and energy from Southern to Northern Rus.

A third arresting phenomenon which we see disclosed at this period is the growing indifference both of the community and the Princes of Suzdal to Kiev, the beatific vision of the earlier princes, and, consequently, to Kievan Rus as a whole. This indifference first becomes noticeable in Vsevolod, and subsequently and to a still greater extent in his sons. On Vsevolod's death there arose a new feud among those sons—the immediate cause of it being the irregular treatment of one of them by his father. It seems that, shortly before his decease, Vsevolod fell out with his eldest son, Constantine, and transferred the latter's right of seniority to his (Vsevolod's) second son, Yuri. Thereupon Mstislav the Bold (son of Andrew's old antagonist, Mstislav the Brave, of the line of Rostislav) espoused the cause of the injured son, and, invading Suzdal with troops drawn from Novgorod and Smolensk, joined issue with Vsevolod's three younger sons, Yuri, Yaroslav, and Sviatoslav. Now, on the eve of the decisive battle on the Lipetza which ended the feud in favour of Constantine and Mstislav, Vsevolod's younger sons indulged in a feast with their boyars, and began parcelling out the Russian land among themselves as their certain booty of war. The eldest of the three, Yuri, asserted his right of seniority by allocating to himself the best province—namely, that of Rostov and Vladimir, while the second brother, Yaroslav, declared that he would take Novgorod, and the youngest one that Smolensk should be his portion. As for Kiev—"Well," said they all, "such a desolate land may pass to one of the Princes of Tchernigov." This shows us that it was the northern provinces of Rostov and Novgorod—the provinces which, but a century and a half ago, had figured in Yaroslav's deathbed division of Rus as mere appendages to the senior provinces of the South—that had now come to be looked upon as the senior and best, as well as that a change had taken place in the organisation of the local community, and that the heretofore "insignificant men of Vladimir" had reached the position of being able to look down upon the other provinces of the Russian land. At the same feast before the battle an old boyar advised the younger brethren to make peace with their senior, seeing that the latter had with him so great a *vitiaz*[1] as Mstislav; whereupon another boyar—a younger

[1] Knight or warrior.

man and, in all probability, one even more intoxicated than the first—
began to protest against that advice, saying to the Princes : " Neither
in the time of your grandfather nor in that of your father was it the
custom for any man to lead an army into the strong land of Suzdal
and to come out thence unscathed, even though he had brought with
him thither the whole of the Russian land—both Galicia and Kiev and
Smolensk and Tchernigov and Novgorod and Riazan. Never can
these companies that now be gathered together against us withstand our
strength, but we will roll them from their saddles and beat them with
our fists." This speech pleased the princes mightily : yet within twenty-
four hours the boasters had sustained a terrible defeat and lost in the
battle over nine thousand men! The words of the younger boyar make
it clear that the growing contempt of the Princes of Suzdal for Kiev
was accompanied by a corresponding conceit on the part of the community at large: which form of pride owed its rise and growth to those
political achievements of the Princes Andrew and Vsevolod which had
first enabled the community to feel its own strength and the importance
of its province in Rus.

Thus, in studying the history of the Rus of Suzdal from the middle of
the twelfth century up to the death of Vsevolod III., we find ourselves
confronted, at almost every step, with new and unexpected factors. Developing on parallel lines, these factors caused Suzdal to acquire an unusual
position in the Russian land, seeing that, while certain of them altered
its relation towards the other provinces of Rus, others of them brought
about changes in the internal organisation of the Principality. Those
factors may be recapitulated as follows.

To begin with, the Princes Andrew and Vsevolod made several attempts
to separate the title of Suzerain Prince from the Kievan throne, and to convert Suzdal into a permanent domain of their own by detaching it from the
rota of provinces governed in order of princely seniority. Andrew also
made a first attempt to replace the old princely solidarity based upon kinship with compulsory subordination of the younger princes to the eldest
member of the family, as "underlings" subject to an autocratic sovereign.
With Andrew's death, also, the political supremacy of the senior towns and
the two upper classes of the local aristocracy came to an end, while the junior
town of Vladimir (already the seat of the suzerain throne) became, through
its feud with the senior towns, the capital of an independent, heritable
province. Under Vsevolod that province acquired a decided supremacy
over the rest of the Russian land, and its Prince made a first attempt to

detach by force yet a second province from the rota, and to add it to the domain already under his rule. With this went a gradual realisation of their own strength on the part of the Princes and community of Suzdal, and, consequently, a growing contempt for Kiev and a permanent estrangement from the territory subject to the Kievan throne. These combined developments led inevitably to a rupture of the ties by which the northern portion of the Russian land had formerly been bound to the ancient centre of the country.

Such were the factors of which the Russian colonisation of the region of Suzdal was the direct or indirect source.

CHAPTER XV

Survey of the position of the Russian land during the thirteenth and fourteenth centuries— The appanage system of princely rule under Vsevolod's successors—The princely appanage—The chief items of evidence with regard to the appanage system—The origin of that system—The idea of separate, devisable rule among the princes of the South—Conversion of Russian princes of provinces into princes subject to the Lithuanian Empire— Strength of the clan tradition among the senior lines of Yaroslav's stock—Relations between the princes of the Upper Volga and the princes of Riazan at the close of the fifteenth century—Fundamental features of the appanage system—Causes of its successful growth among Vsevolod's successors—Absence of impediments to that system in the region of Suzdal.

THE political results of the Russian colonisation of the Upper Volga described in the last chapter gave rise to a new order of social relations in that region. As we proceed with our history of the Rus of Rostov and Suzdal we shall trace the development of the two bases of the new state order which became established during the times of Yuri Dolgoruki and his successors, and in so doing must remember that during the period (the thirteenth and fourteenth centuries) when the reorganisation of social relations was pre-eminently in progress not a vestige survived of the historical setting in which, and through which, the rota system of rule had hitherto been maintained. The Rus of Yaroslav I. and Monomakh had altogether come to an end—had been torn in pieces by the Lithuanians and Tartars, while the stock of St. Vladimir which formerly had served to unite the country into something like a political whole had seen its senior lines either die out or enter, with the remnants of their ancestral domains, into the composition of the Lithuanian Empire, and there become subject to new and alien political relations and cultural influences. The common cause and common interests which had bound those lines together no longer existed, nor yet did their old reckonings of seniority, genealogical disputes, and turns of rule. When Kiev, the fundamental knot of princely and popular relations (as well as of economic and religious interests) in the Russian land, reared her head once more after the passing of the Tartars she found herself the outermost Steppe frontier town of a new state, and a town hourly expecting to have to defend herself from the violence of her new conquerors. Alien and unfamiliar conditions of life had invaded the half-ruined, deserted haunts of ancient Russian activity, and the forces of old Kievan Rus which were destined later to rehabilitate and carry on the national cause had fled for temporary refuge to the Finnish wilds of the Oka and the Upper Volga.

The direction of the new Russian community in the region just named fell to the lot of three junior branches of the princely stock—namely, the Princes of Riazan (of the line of Yaroslav of Tchernigov), the sons of Vsevolod of Suzdal, and the sons of Theodore of Yaroslavl (of the Smolensk branch of Monomakh's stock). These were the sole remnants of St. Vladimir's once abundant posterity of which the new Rus could boast—the sole survivors of the posterity which once had made the care of Kievan Rus "its chief work." Hence, although the old order was able to provide the new region neither with a genealogical nor a geographical basis for the building of a new state system, such a system had at least no living survivors of the *ancien régime* to contend with.

At the same time, the political results of the Russian colonisation of the Upper Volga were not solely confined to the factors which we have studied, since examination of phenomena consequent upon the death of Vsevolod reveals to us yet another one—one even more important than the others, seeing that it was the result of their accumulated action.

The old system of princely rule in Kievan Rus was based upon order of seniority, but, in Suzdal, Vsevolod's transference of seniority from his eldest to his second son shows us that seniority had now lost its true genealogical meaning, and acquired only a conditional significance; that, in fact, it had become not so much a birthright as an honorary title to be granted or assumed at pleasure. When, too, we take into consideration the subsequent inter-relations of Vsevolod's sons it becomes additionally clear to us that a new order of princely rule had arisen which was altogether unlike to what had gone before. In studying the rise and growth of that new order we may leave out of account the fact that the first generation from Vsevolod had not wholly disappeared from the scene before Rus underwent conquest by the Tartars, since all the phenomena observable after that event derived directly and without a break from conditions operative as long before the Mongolian invasion as the twelfth century. Thus, although the twelfth century had not closed when Kiev lost its last shred of importance as a pan-territorial centre, its final downfall did not come until the Tartar inroads were a thing of the past and Vladimir on the Kliazma had become the seat of the senior Suzerain throne, the political metropolis of Northern Rus (Kiev itself remaining only—and that only for a short time—the headquarters of the ecclesiastical administration).

In general, Vsevolod's successors followed the old order of seniority —Constantine recovering the place in it of which he had been deprived by his father, and being followed in regular succession by his brothers Yuri, Yaroslav, and Sviatoslav. This sequence was repeated also in the case of Vsevolod's grandsons. Since all the sons of the two elder brothers, Constantine and Yuri, had fallen in battle with the Tartars, the throne next passed to the sons of the third brother, Yaroslav—first to the eldest, Alexander Nevski, then to the third son, the Prince of Tver (the second son, Andrew, had been banished by the Tartars), and lastly to the fourth son, Vassilii, Prince of Kostroma (1276). Thus the old system of princely rule was observed on the throne of Vladimir up to the final quarter of the thirteenth century. Nevertheless there were certain deviations from it, just as had occurred in ancient Kiev, since, in addition to the senior province of Vladimir, which continued to be governed according to the old order of seniority, there became formed in Suzdal various minor provinces governed *in the descending line*, not the collateral, by the younger princes of Vsevolod's house. That is to say, those provinces passed continuously *downwards* —from eldest brother to youngest, from youngest uncle to eldest nephew, and so on. Of course such a system of rule altered the whole juridical character of the minor provinces in question. In the South, the principalities collectively (save those allotted to *izgoi* princes) had constituted the common heritage of the princely house at large, and their rulers had held temporary sway over them according to order of seniority. In the North, however, each of the minor provinces above-mentioned became the separate and permanent property of a given prince—became his own personal possession, and devisable from father to son either through testamentary disposition of its ruler or according to accepted custom. From this change in the juridical character of princely rule there arose a new nomenclature. In old Kievan Rus the various portions of the Russian land had been known as the *volosti* or *nadielki*[1] of the princes, in token of their temporary tenure, but the new minor provinces which became formed in Suzdal during the early thirteenth century came to be known, first as *votchini*, and subsequently as *udieli*,[2] in token of each of them being the separate, permanent, devisable property of a given prince.

---

[1] Provinces or allotments.
[2] Respectively, " patrimonies " and " appanages."

This latter system of rule, therefore, may be termed the *udielni poriadok* or appanage system, in contradistinction to the old rota system of Kievan Rus, while its first appearance may be assigned to the early thirteenth century, under the sons of Vsevolod.

The appanage system of rule was the fundamental and initial factor to which all the subsequent phenomena in the history of Rus of the Upper Volga were due, and upon which all the political conditions in force there up to the middle of the fifteenth century were based. Two signs in particular point to the establishment of that system. In the first place, the movement of princes from province to province came to an end. They became stationary rulers, living and dying in the capitals of their appanages, nor leaving them even when it came to their turn to fill the Suzerain throne. In the second place, the system of princely succession —the means through which a province passed from one ruler to another —underwent a change. In old Kievan Rus a prince had had no power to bequeath his province by personal disposition—even to his own son— unless the latter would in any case have succeeded him in the natural order of seniority, but in the North a prince of the thirteenth and fourteenth centuries was permanent ruler of his own particular domain, and could therefore devise it at will to his sons, or, in the absence of such, to his wife, daughter, or any relative, however distant. In annals of the centuries in question we come upon several instances of such arbitrary devisings of provinces in the absence of direct heirs. Thus in 1249 Vassilii of Yaroslavl, grandson of Vsevolod, died, leaving behind him only a daughter, the Princess Maria, who thereupon succeeded to the province, and, through marrying Theodore of Mohilev, caused the latter to become the founder of a new line of princes. Again, Yaroslav, Vsevolod's third son, bequeathed his appanage (to which he had added also the province of Periaslavl Zaliesski) to his eldest son Ivan; but, inasmuch as the latter had no issue, he (Ivan) re-devised the domain at death (in 1302) to his neighbour, Daniel of Moscow. Finally, in 1353, the then Suzerain Prince of Moscow, Simeon Gordii, left his appanage to his wife, who, in her turn, bequeathed it to her late husband's brother, Ivan.

Next let us examine the historical origin of the appanage system of rule. In tracing the progress of princely relations in Northern and Southern Rus during the eleventh, twelfth, and thirteenth centuries, we notice one marked discrepancy between the relations obtaining in Suzdal and those which had obtained in Kiev. In the latter region the idea of the indivisibility of princely rule had always been looked upon as the one standard or basis of all state relations, even between princes so widely removed from one another by birth as the second and third cousins of Yaroslav's house, so that never once had the princely family lost sight of the fact that they were members of one ruling stock, grandsons of one grandfather, who must govern their heritage in common and in strict order of seniority. No trace of this idea, however, appears in Vsevolod's successors, even between nearest relatives, but, on the contrary, only a desire to divide the common heritage as speedily as possible into separate, devisable lots. In fact, Vsevolod's grandsons seem to have forgotten the founder of their house even sooner than those of Yaroslav had forgotten theirs. What, then, was the cause of this hasty adoption of separate rule by Vsevolod's successors? What conditions gave rise to that mutual estrangement of the northern princes which led them to rule their territories in disregard of their (the princes') close mutual relationship? Before answering that question we must first of all establish its *actuality*, just as we did in the case of the question with regard to the origin of the rota system of rule.

The princely appanage was the devisable *otchina* of its prince. The term *otchina* had been known also to the earlier princes of South-Western Rus, though with a different meaning attached to it. With them the whole of the Russian land had been accounted the *otchina i diedina* ("paternal and grand-paternal heritage") of the princely stock at large, though frequently a given province was recognised as the peculiar *otchina* of the line which it maintained, and still more frequently a given prince came to look upon the principality in which his father had sat, and no other, as his true *otchina*, even though intermediate rulers had intervened between the father and the son. None of these meanings, however, contained any trace of the idea of permanent, personal, devisable possession of the *otchina*. Yet such an idea of possession had not been altogether a stranger to the minds of those South-Western princes. In 1289 Vladimir of Volhynia, son of Vassilkov, died without issue, and, before doing so, executed a written will to the effect that his principality should devolve at death to his younger cousin Mstislav, son of Danilov, and not to Mstislav's elder brother Lvov. The question, therefore, arises—Was the will of the testator always accounted the sole and sufficient source of the right of possession? We read that in this case the inheritor, Mstislav, deemed it necessary to assemble the boyars and chief burghers of the town of Vladimir [1] in the local cathedral, and there to read to them the will of his dying cousin.

---

[1] Vladimir in Volhynia.

Yet not a word is vouchsafed us by the Chronicle in explanation of the legal significance of this solemn proclamation of the testator's wishes—the Chronicle merely saying that the reading was listened to by "all, from lesser to greater." Was, then, the consent of the boyars and burghers *necessary*, or was the ceremony merely held for their private information? We read, further, that the town of Beresti declined to respect the wishes of its late Prince, and took an oath of allegiance to his nephew Yuri; whereupon the rightful inheritor treated the townsmen's offence as *kramola* or treason against the State, and Yuri's father threatened both to deprive his son of his seniority and to bequeath his own principality to his (the father's) brother (the Mstislav above-mentioned) unless Yuri previously abandoned Beresti. All this contains nothing of the idea of rule by rota of seniority. Nevertheless these phenomena do not altogether justify us in assuming that the appanage system, in the true meaning of the term, was in force in Volhynia in the thirteenth century, since we see Vladimir's testamentary disposition needing to be confirmed by the voluntary assent of Lvov, Danilov's dispossessed eldest son; Danilov's sons addressing Vladimir as the local Suzerain Prince; the younger of Vladimir's cousins and his nephew telling him that they honour him as a father; and Lvov and his son requesting Vladimir to assign them to Brest—to "apportion" them, in fact, even as in former days the Suzerain Princes of Kiev "apportioned" their various younger kinsmen. The act of bequeathal, therefore, does not seem to have been a one-sided exercise of will on the part of the testator, but rather a *riad* or agreement between him and the selected heir. In short, the whole transaction reads like a survival of the old Kievan system of princely relations. Tatistchev cites in his "History" the text of a circular letter addressed to the various local princes by Roman (grandfather of the above Vladimir) after his taking of Kiev in the year 1202. In this letter Roman proposes, among other things, that the existing system of refilling the throne of Kiev should be exchanged for "such a fashion as doth exist in other well-ordered states," and that, instead of dividing their provinces among *all* their sons, the local princes should assign their throne to the eldest son only, while granting to the younger sons a town or a district each for their maintenance. "Thus shall the whole of them subsist under the authority of the elder brother." However, the princes did not accept the proposition, for the reason that at that period (the early thirteenth century) bequeathal of a principality in the descending line was, as yet, neither a common fact nor a commonly accepted proposition, and the idea of it must have reached

Roman from the feudal West. Nevertheless this shows us that the theory of a principality being the personal possession of its prince had at least *awakened* in the minds of those South-Western princes, though, as yet, only in the guise of a revolutionary pretension, a threatened calamity to the Russian land. In the *Slovo o Polku Igorevé* the following remarkable passage occurs: "The warring with the pagans by the princes did become weakened, in that brother said unto brother, 'This is mine, and that also is mine,' until for even a small thing the Princes did begin to speak high words, and to conceive rebellion one against the other. Thus did the pagans come from all sides with victory upon the Russian land."

In Western Rus the theory was prevented by circumstances from developing into a system; yet it is difficult to say whether, even had circumstances been different, such a development could ever have taken place. At all events, subjection to the Lithuanian Empire brought princely relations under the influence of conditions which imparted to them a special direction. In the first place, decentralisation proceeded too slowly in that Empire for the appanage stage ever to be reached. The Suzerain Prince of Lithuania ruled supreme over the local princes, and not as a mere senior among other princes of appanages, as did the Suzerain of the other half of Rus. When conferring a principality upon a given prince, he did so either "in perpetuity" or for the time being, as he saw fit ("at the master will of the Suzerain" is the phrase used). The former of those two acts would annul the rota system (or, at all events, presume its absence), while the second one denied the very basis of the system of appanages, and both of them degraded the assignee of a given province to the level of a "servitor" prince subject to the obligation expressed in the Suzerain's phrase: "And henceforth he shall be unto us truly a servitor." Yet their juridical status in itself precluded the idea of either a prince of the kinsman-coadjutor species or a prince of the appanage order becoming a "servitor" ruler: for which reason the local princes of the Russo-Lithuanian Empire of the fourteenth and fifteenth centuries can scarcely be looked upon as appanage princes, except in a very conditional sense of the term, and in default of one which expresses more correctly the peculiar relations which had become established there.

Within that Empire, however, there was a corner where the exceptional conditions of life enable us to gain a very good idea of the manner in which the Princes of South-Western Rus would have organised themselves had they been left free to do so. The corner in question was the little province of the Upper Oka, ruled by the descendants of St. Michael of

Tchernigov (the Princes of Bieloi, Odoiev, Voronezh, Mtzensk, and other petty principalities). At the middle of the fifteenth century they became subject to Lithuania, yet still continued to avail themselves of their outlying position to serve two masters at once—namely, Lithuania and Moscow. Secure, through their very insignificance, from all external interference, they retained their ancestral seats up to the very close of that century, nor did they ever cease to dispute in the old traditional manner concerning "which of them should hold the Suzerain Province, and which an *appanage*." This shows us that their rule over their "appanages" or diminutive lesser principalities must have been defined, not by any law of succession, but by some agreement establishing a rota of kindred (natural or arbitrary) such as had obtained in Kiev during the twelfth century. The real fact was that those Princes could not adapt their actual position to the ideas which they had inherited from a bygone age. That is to say, circumstances impelled them towards divided rule, yet could not wholly extinguish their hereditary instinct for chattering and quarrelling "about birth and about seniority"—*i.e.* about what was, to all intents and purposes, the old rota system of rule. Thus they continued the policy of their remote ancestors, and supported the tottering *régime* which had descended to them from antiquity by means of "agreements"—a means which, while underpinning the system, abolished also its natural basis.

Another example may be cited to show the innate political conservatism of the older lines of Yaroslav's stock. The Princes of Riazan—a branch of the line of Tchernigov which governed a province at once outlying and separated from the general rota of rule—resembled the Princes of Galicia in that they succeeded in envisaging the idea of separate, devisable rule at an earlier date than did the princes adhering to the old rota system. Indeed, their feuds were distinguished by such extraordinary animosity, even for South Russian descendants of Rurik, that not a vestige of the theory of joint brotherly government of a common *otchina* could possibly have survived such contests. At length, in Vsevolod's time, this Principality of Riazan found itself at close quarters with, and often hardly pressed by, the neighbouring Principality of Vladimir, in the first instance, and that of Moscow later; in both of which States the appanage system was firmly established. At the close of the fifteenth century the Princes ruling Riazan were two brothers—Ivan and Theodore, sons of Vassilii; of whom the former, as senior, was styled the Suzerain Prince, and the latter, as junior, the *Udielni Kniaz* or Appanage Prince. These two brothers concluded a mutual agreement that their respective Principalities should be distinct from one another, and pass at death in the direct descending line. Likewise they made provision for the eventuality of one of the two brothers dying without issue, as I will briefly explain.

The working of the rota system precluded all possibility of a princeship becoming extinct, since the shoes of a prince who died without issue could always be filled by the *collateral* heir next upon the rota. With the substitution, however, of the appanage system, extinct princeships inevitably evoked misunderstandings and disputes. According to the theory of appanage law, a childless prince was none the less absolute owner of his province, and could therefore devise it at death to any favourite kinsman, however distant from the testator. At the same time, near kinsmen had a natural interest in preventing any portion of their common heritage from passing out of their own immediate circle, and so were inclined to oppose to the strict right of possession the moral need for solidarity of kindred. The clashing of the theories of two such widely differing systems aroused in Vsevolod's stock—especially in the branch of it which held Tver—exceedingly bitter feuds over the question of extinct princeships. On the other hand, we see Dmitri Donskoi of Moscow meeting the situation with a scheme based upon the composition of the family which was to be left behind him. In the event of his sons having no issue they were to be precluded from all right of disposing of their possessions at death—the appanage of the eldest son, the Suzerain Prince, passing, with the Suzerainty, to the next elder brother, and the junior appanage of all (becoming, of course, in this case, "extinct") being divided among *all* the surviving brothers of the deceased, at the discretion of the widow-mother. This substituted scheme of Donskoi's was not so much a *variant* of common rule by a princely stock as a complete *negation* of it, and a very cunning negation too, seeing that it made the passage of an appanage out of his family forever impossible, through the simple fact that it sundered all dynastic ties connecting the family with the rest of their kindred.

Our two Princes of Riazan, however, proceeded on wholly different lines to those followed by Donskoi a century earlier. If either of them died childless and intestate, his appanage was to pass, in the natural order, to the surviving brother or to his children. Nevertheless, mutual coldness and suspicion moved the two Princes to fear lest, if one of them died childless, he should leave his portion of the common *otchina* to a *collateral* relative; wherefore in 1496 they bound themselves by a further agreement that, should either of them prove childless, the one denied issue should undertake "by no cunning device" to devise his province away from the surviving brother. Neither of them, however, foresaw—or, if they did foresee, they declined to recognise—the possibility of one of them being granted issue, yet predeceasing a childless brother. True enough, as things turned out, the elder of the two died first, leaving behind him an only son ; whereupon the childless Theodore availed himself of the lack—perhaps the calculated omission—of foresight in the agreement to devise his appanage to the Suzerain Prince of Moscow, his maternal grandfather, instead of to his brother's orphaned son. Thus we see a case of appanage law of bequeathal indirectly supporting the solidarity of family rule. Kinship on the mother's side exercised greater weight in the execution of Theodore's last will and testament than did either kinship on the father's or the principle of bequeathal in the direct descending line—simply through the fact that between the Princes of Riazan and those of Moscow there was a common bond as members of one Russian ruling stock. Had Theodore's mother been a sister, not of Ivan of Moscow, but of Casimir of Lithuania, he would probably have acted otherwise.

I have adduced these instances in order to point out the more clearly the political break which began in the two halves of the Russian land just when the first period of our history merges into the second. The testamentary disposition of the Prince of Riazan above referred to reminds us of the procedure of Vladimir of Volhynia in devising his personality to a younger cousin instead of to that cousin's elder brother. In Southern Rus of the thirteenth century the right of devising a family domain by personal disposition was, as yet, only a claim—an act of arrogation. Vladimir, however, concealed his exercise of personal will beneath the forms of the old-established system. That is to say, he concluded an agreement with the dispossessed heir, and obtained the consent of the other near relatives, as well as of the boyars and chief burghers of his capital town. Thus Claim, advanced as Right, grew to Precedent, and acquired sufficient force, not only to override, but altogether to alter such Right; until, decaying slowly and surely, the old rota system of the South expired, and was reborn in the form of a new order of *devisable* rule. Yet the process of that rebirth was not yet completed when it was interrupted and diverted by the Lithuanian power—although even had such *external* pressure been absent, it is doubtful whether, in South-Western Rus, the new system would ever have escaped opposition from the *internal* social forces of the day—from the boyars, from the chief towns, and from the numerous princes with whose interests it clashed. Both the boyars and the chief towns had long been accustomed to have their say in the ordering of princely relations, and, aware of their own importance in the body politic, had so shaped the latter to their ends that they had become as conservative in their political views as the majority of the Princes themselves.

In Northern Rus thought and action moved more swiftly. Yet even there they could not wholly shake themselves free of old Kievan methods, and for a considerable period the Province of Vladimir continued to be, for Vsevolod's successors, much what Kiev had been for those of Yaroslav—namely, a common heritage ruled in order of seniority. When, however, the gradual ramification of Vsevolod's stock caused the appanages formed by his descendants to become combined into large groups, there arose new Suzerain Principalities of Tver, Nizhni, Novgorod, and Yaroslavl, under local Suzerain Princes ranking with the Prince of Vladimir. Further than this, however, the precedent of Kiev did not go, since, as a rule, but a few disputes and changes of ruler sufficed to make those Suzerain thrones the permanent seats of the senior lines of the princely stock, with the right of bequeathing their appanages in descending succession. In fact, matters in Kiev and in the North progressed in exactly opposite directions; for while, on the Dnieper, it was the senior principalities which imposed the rota system of rule upon the junior provinces, in the region of the Upper Volga it was from the junior provinces (or appanages) to the senior principalities that the system of separate, devisable rule first spread. This difference entailed a sharp break in the law of princely rule—a marked change both in the subject of the law and in the system or means of carrying it out. Formerly the Russian land had been accounted the common *otchina* of the whole princely stock, which, in its turn, had been the collective wielder of the ruling power in that *otchina*, while the individual princes, as *participators* only in the collective ruling power, had been *temporary* holders only of their provinces. Yet that power had never contained the least trace of the idea of a prince's right to own territory *as* land—of such a right, that is to say, as would naturally accrue to the private owner of an estate. Ruling their principalities either in order of seniority or by agreement both among themselves and with the provincial capitals, the princes had always exercised supreme rights of *government* in their domains; yet neither they as a body nor any of them as an individual had ever applied to their provinces those means of disposing of the same which would have accrued to them had they possessed any actual right of *ownership*. That is to say, they had never proceeded to sell, mortgage, give away in dowry, or bequeath, their temporary spheres of rule. In the North, however, although the region of Rostov was the common *otchina* of the whole of Vsevolod's stock, it did not remain their *collective, joint otchina*, but became split up into a number of principalities altogether separate from and independent of one another—territories which were looked upon as the personal and devisable property of their several rulers, who governed the free population therein as overlords, and administered their territories as private owners possessed of all the rights of disposal of the same which would naturally arise out of absolute ownership. Such rule as that was appanage rule in its purest form and most complete development: which form and development were attained only in the *otchina* governed by Vsevolod's successors during the thirteenth, fourteenth, and fifteenth centuries. Thus, in the appanage system, the wielder of the governing power was the *individual*, not the *stock*, while princely rule became divided, and, losing none of its ancient supreme rights, acquired also such rights as would attach to private, personal ownership. It is in that combination that we must seek for an explanation of the fact that local conditions contributed both to this division of princely rule in the *otchina* of Vsevolod's successors and to the rise of the idea of an appanage being the personal property of its ruler.

The local conditions referred to were due, in the first place, to the nature of the country where the system in question became established. In Kievan Rus too it was to the geographical features of its material environment that the family solidarity of princely rule owed its existence, since there the land constituted a compact area embracing the basin of a single great river—the Dnieper, the former great highway of Russian industrial traffic—and so had had its constituent portions knit together in a natural manner by threads geographical, economic, juridical, and religious. Upon such a physical basis had the economic and political organisation of old Kievan Rus rested. Next let us picture to ourselves Northern Rus as it existed in the thirteenth century. There, first and foremost, we see a complicated network of rivers and streams, all flowing in different directions, with a population following their devious courses, and becoming equally complicated in the varied currents of its settlement. Such a diffusion of the people forbade the establishment at that period of any permanent centre in Suzdal, whether political or economic. Centrifugal attraction was too strong for the formation of conditions favourable to centralisation. According as the population spread along the river-ways, it was forced, first and foremost, to seek dry spots upon their banks; which gave rise to the settlement of long strips of country wherein the areas actually inhabited stretched like a chain of little islands amid a sea of forest and swamp. Thus colonisation of the country resulted in the formation of small river provinces separated from one another by almost impassable wilds, and serving as ready-made frames for division of the region into appanages, as well as for the subsequent preservation of their boundaries. When the prince of such an appanage came to apportion his *otchina* among his heirs, the geographical diffusion of the population afforded him a ready-made basis for division and subdivision of his territory into the required lots. Of course this process of settlement gave rise to lack of association—a lack which led also to political disintegration. In its final form a political system expresses the sum and common character of the various private interests and relations which it maintains and by which it is maintained. Thus the appanage system was the expression and, in part, the product of that condition of detachment in which the immigrant Russian population found itself when seeking new habitations before it had become assimilated either with the novel conditions or the native inhabitants of the country. It follows, therefore, that the system of individual princely rule which arose in that region did so in close correlation with the geographical diffusion of the population, and that such diffusion was governed, in its turn, by the natural features of the country and by the manner of the country's colonisation. The general order of life born of those conditions, with its sluggish industrial traffic, its shattered and, as yet, unrestored interests and relations, and its relaxed social organisation, was bound to weaken the sense of solidarity of kinship in the first generation of Vsevolod's successors. This was the *geographical* basis of the appanage system—a basis which helped less to strengthen the new order of life than to destroy the old one.

It is in quite other conditions (albeit conditions evoked by the same process of colonisation) that we must look for the source of the actual *idea* of the appanage as the private, personal property of its ruler. Colonisation placed the princes of the North in a different relation to their principalities to that which had obtained in old Kievan Rus. Upon their arrival in Kiev the early princes had entered into a ready-made social organisation which arose before their time, and their rule of the Russian land had been confined to its defence from external foes, to the maintenance of the existing social order, and to its completion in the sense of adaptation of its details to the requirements of the day. Yet they could not have laid claim to being the founders of that order, nor yet have called themselves the creators of the community which they ruled. That community was older than its princes. It was altogether a different view of themselves, as well as altogether a different relation to the community which they governed, that the princes of Northern Rus were led to adopt through the circumstances of North Russian colonisation. Here the rule was that when the first prince of a newly-constituted appanage entered upon his province he found there no ready-made community to govern, but only a desert wild just beginning to be settled, and needing to be opened up and organised before any such community would be possible. From the first the virgin region was developed under the immediate eye of the prince, who saw to the clearing of the fastnesses for the accommodation of the settlers, to the starting of new agricultural works and industries, and to the imposing of new taxes for the benefit of the princely treasury. All these things were superintended by him in person, and so came to be looked upon by him as the work of his own hands, his own personal creation. Consequently, colonisation in this form caused a whole series of princely generations to adopt one and the same idea of their relation to their appanages and of their governmental status in them. Yuri Dolgoruki began the work of organising the land of Suzdal, and his son Andrew continued that work—boasting (not without reason) that he had "settled all the country with towns and large hamlets," and thus made of it a populous region. Indeed, in speaking of his father's labours and his own subsequent efforts, Andrew might well have said : "We two have fashioned the Rus of Suzdal, and in it have created a community." Practically this view was the prime cause of Andrew's estrangement from Southern Rus, and of his desire to make his own northern province as unlike it as possible. Conscious of being absolute master in his own house, he had no wish to share that dwelling with others by joining it on to the general rota of princely rule. His younger brother and successor, Vsevolod, adopted a similar view, and the form of their joint policy and ideas devolved as an heirloom thenceforth. In short, "Hoc meum quia ipse feci " was the political view inculcated in the early princes of Northern Rus by the process of colonisation, as well as the maxim which lay at the root of the idea of an appanage being the personal property of its ruler, the idea which passed from father to son and became an hereditary family tradition among Monomakh's posterity in Suzdal, and the theory which guided the latter both in the organisation of their *otchini* and in their bequeathal of the same at death. This was the *political* basis of the appanage system — a basis which, constituted of the idea of personal, devisable rule, first arose out of that relation of ruler to the ruled which became established on the Upper Volga during the thirteenth and fourteenth centuries as a result of the process of colonisation.

Thus we see that the appanage system rested upon two bases—a geographical and a political. That is to say, it was created by the joint action of the nature of the country and of the process of colonisation. Let us sum up those factors. (1) The physical features of the region caused the process of colonisation to give rise to small river provinces, isolated from one another, and serving as a ready-made basis for political division of the land—*i.e.* for its disintegration into *appanages*. In other words, the appanages of the thirteenth and fourteenth centuries were river basins. (2) Colonisation of the country usually brought the first prince of an appanage face to face, not with a ready-made community, but with a desert wild which needed settlement and organisation before it could contain one. Hence, the idea of a prince as the personal owner of his appanage was the juridical outcome of his significance as its first settler and organiser.

That is my explanation of the historical origin of the appanage system of princely rule which came into being in Northern Rus during the thirteenth century.

To the above it should be added that, in the North, the new system had no opposition to contend with such as was offered in the South to the first faint struggles for existence of the idea of separate, devisable rule —an opposition which came from the boyars, from the numerous old and influential towns, and even from some of the princes themselves. In Rostov and Suzdal the strength of the boyars (never at any time very great), as well as that of the two capital towns, had been utterly shattered by the great social feud which arose through the colonisation of the country by the Southerners, while the thirteenth-century princes of the locality were all of them chips of the Vsevolod block in their customs and ideas of government. Lastly, the scattered and ever-moving population had not had time to become firmly established in its forest settlements or to form large unions, and, being dependent for everything upon the local prince-proprietor, was wholly under the thumb of Vsevolod's house, and so formed a readily yielding soil for political exploitation.

CHAPTER XVI

Observations on the importance of the appanage period in Russian history—Results of the appanage system—Questions preliminary to their study—The process of territorial subdivision into appanages—Impoverishment of the appanage princes—Their mutual estrangement—The status of an appanage prince—His juridical relation to private landholders in his appanage—Comparison of appanage with feudal relations—Composition of the community in an appanage—Decline of local patriotism and the territorial sense among the appanage princes—Results of that decline.

IT now remains for us to study the *results* of the appanage system of princely rule. Before doing so, let us glance once more at the cause of which we are about to observe the effect.

After touching upon the fortunes of South-Western Rus at this period we dismissed them temporarily from our purview, that we might the better concentrate our attention upon that north-eastern portion of the Russian land where the successors of Vsevolod of Suzdal ruled their hereditary *otchini* on the Upper Volga. Such an occasional limitation of our field of vision is an inevitable concession to the conditions of our task, seeing that we can only follow the leading movements in our history—can only, so to speak, sail its main current, and must forbear turning aside into backwaters near the banks. It was in the region of the Upper Volga that the most potent of the popular forces of Rus became concentrated during the thirteenth century, and therefore it is to that region that we must turn for study of the bases and forms of popular life which afterwards acquired a ruling importance. Already we have noted the direction in which the social life of the people began to be directed in consequence of the trend of popular forces towards this portion of Rus. The old régime had undergone disruption, while, in the new setting of affairs, the pressure of fresh external difficulties was bringing about a general tendency towards localisation and self-centrement. Broad social ties were being snapped, substantial interests shattered, and relations of all kinds restricted. The community was becoming dissolved into small local communes—each man departing to his petty plot of land, to confine his ideas and relations to his own narrow interests or to such ties as chance and his nearest neighbours imposed upon him. A state relies for its support upon lasting common interests and broad social ties, and therefore either becomes impossible under such a disintegrated, relaxed order of life as I am now describing or adopts forms and methods of action foreign to its nature. With the population, it becomes divided up into small units, in whose organisation the elements of a state order find themselves inter-mingled, in happy promiscuity, with the norms of private right. In Western Europe such a condition of society gave rise to feudalism. On the Upper Volga it provided the basis of the appanage system.

In the study of history it is always difficult to rivet the attention upon periods which have little instruction or interest to offer to the mind. To Karamzin the three hundred years or so which followed upon the death of Yaroslav appeared a season " devoid of deeds of glory, but abounding in the petty quarrels of numberless princelings, whose shades, red-splashed with the blood of their miserable subjects, flit dimly through the gloom of those far-off ages." Soloviev too experienced the feeling of *ennui* which oppresses the mind of every historian as he studies the tedious, colourless annals of the thirteenth and fourteenth centuries—a feeling which, in Soloviev's case, found vent in the following pithy, clear-cut characterisation of the period in question. "The players in the scene act in absolute silence. Neither in war nor in peace do they utter a word, and the chronicler can only record that they waged the one or preserved the other. In the city and in the Prince's palace not a sound is to be heard. Every-thing is still. Every man seems to be sitting close behind his shutters and thinking his own thoughts to himself. A door opens, and figures come out and move upon the stage, but it is all done in silence, in absolute silence."

Nevertheless, though tedious to study and, apparently, barren of history, such periods have their historical importance, and that not a small one. They constitute those so-called "transitional epochs" which frequently stretch in broad, dim patches between two more clearly-defined periods, and allow of the ruins of a fallen system being worked up into the elements of the one which is to follow. Such a transitional epoch, such a temporary historical landmark, was the period of appanages—the importance of which lay less in itself than in its results.

The appanage system of which we are about to study the results was itself an outcome of the Russian colonisation of the Upper Volga. The process of colonisation introduced thither precisely the same social elements which had made up the community of Kievan Rus. The princes, their retinues, the urban industrial class, the mixed population of the rural districts—all were there.   The question, therefore, arises: What correlation was established between those social forces under the appanage system, and what part did each of them play in the working of the new political form?   Let us make that question our guide in studying the results of the appanage system, but at the same time confine our investigations to the appanage *in detachment*, and leave the appanage in its relation to its fellows to be touched upon when we arrive at the period of the great Principality of Moscow.

The results of the appanage system first made themselves apparent during the thirteenth century, and still more so during the fourteenth. First of all we see the system causing an ever-increasing disintegration of Northern Rus into small appanages—a sort of ever-increasing process of detrition.   In old Kievan Rus the number of provinces was strictly proportioned to the number of eligible adult princes and a few minors, and this proportion was preserved through each successive generation.   Now, however, with the disappearance of the rota system, that mode of apportionment came to an end.   The members of a princely line which multiplied greatly could not occupy vacant thrones in principalities other than their own, and so were forced to go on dividing and subdividing up their common hereditary *otchina*.   In certain cases the excess of heirs caused a principality to become broken up into well-nigh microscopical fragments.   Let me sketch in outline the process as it occurred under the first two generations of Vsevolod's house.   On the death of that ruler his *otchina* was apportioned among his five sons.   That is to say, within the confines of the main, the senior, Principality of Vladimir (which was accounted the common heritage of the whole of Vsevolod's stock) there appeared four appanages—those of Rostov, Periaslavl, Yuriev, and Starodub on the Kliazma.   When Vsevolod's *grandsons* succeeded to their fathers' shoes the land became still further divided up.   The senior Principality of Vladimir still continued to descend in order of seniority, but with three additional appanages cut out of its bulk—namely, those of Suzdal, Kostroma, and Moscow.   The same process, again, was applied to the appanage of Rostov, with the result that there became formed of it the two lesser appanages of Yaroslavl and Uglitch.   Next, Periaslavl was treated in the same way, and gave birth to the appanages of Tver and Dmitrov-Galitch.   Thus, of the four original portions allotted to Vsevolod's four younger sons there now remained undivided only those of Yuriev and Starodub; the reason being that their first princes had left only *one* son apiece behind them. Thus the region of Suzdal, originally apportioned into five lots only, under Vsevolod's five sons, had now become parcelled out into twelve, under his twelve grandsons; and the same process of division and subdivision was continued under further generations of the stock. To gain an idea of the final result, let us take the case of Restov—the senior of the original four appanages which were cut out of the senior Principality of Vladimir. First of all, as already stated, there became separated from it the appanages of Yaroslavl and Uglitch. Next, the remainder of Rostov was divided into the appanage of Rostov proper and the appanage of Bieloe Ozero. Finally, during the fourteenth and fifteenth centuries, the last-named principality became broken up into a score or so of little appanages, all named after the various rivers of the region. A similar process was applied to the main appanage of Yaroslavl.

This result of the appanage system was closely bound up with another result—namely, the impoverishment of the majority of the petty appanage princes. In proportion as certain of the lines of Vsevolod's stock increased in membership, the various heirs began to receive from their fathers an ever-decreasing portion of the family *otchina*. Consequently most of the appanage princes of the fourteenth and fifteenth centuries appear in circumstances not a whit more affluent than those of independent owners of private estates in the latter part of that period. For instance, one of the appanages cut out of Yaroslavl was the petty principality of Zaozersk, which, situated on the north-eastern shores of Lake Kubin, belonged, at the opening of the fifteenth century, to a Prince Dimitri Vassilievitch. One of that ruler's sons went and became an inmate of the Kamenni Monastery,[1] situated on an island in the middle of the lake, under the name of Brother Josephus, and in an old biography of the prince-monk we find an illuminating picture of the official residence of his father, the Prince of Zaozersk. His capital, we read, consisted only of the princely palace itself, which stood where the river Kubin flows into the lake of the same name. Beside this princely establishment stood a church dedicated to St. Demetrius—evidently built by the Prince in honour of his patron saint, while at a little distance from it stood a scattered hamlet named Tchirkovo, which served as the church's parish. That was all that the official residence, the headquarters, of an appanagal "*derzhavetz*" or "sovereign" of the early fifteenth century consisted of!

The very nature of the appanage system tended also to bring about grave *estrangement* among the Northern princes—such estrangement as had

---

[1] *i.e.* Monastery of the Holy Sepulchre.

never existed among the princes of Kievan Rus. The calculations and disputes of the latter concerning seniority and turns of rule had served, if anything, to maintain among them a close solidarity, since all their relations had been based upon the one idea that each prince was dependent upon the rest. Hence had originated their custom of acting in common, so that even their rivalry for the Suzerainty of Kiev served rather to draw them together than to drive them apart. On the other hand, the appanage princes of Northern Rus had nothing to do with one another. The individualism of the system precluded all possibility of any strong common interest connecting them all, and each prince, secluded in his *otchina*, acted independently, and for his own hand alone. The only occasions, indeed, when he paid any heed to his neighbour and kinsman were when the latter seemed to be threatening an attack, or when he himself saw an opportunity of doing his neighbour a bad turn. This mutual lack of association rendered the princes powerless to combine together in large political unions, while the princely councils which had been so frequent a feature of the twelfth century became much rarer during the thirteenth, and almost extinct during the century following.

The individualism of rule peculiar to the appanage system also tended to diminish the princes' *political importance*. The political importance of a ruler is customarily determined by the degree to which he makes use of his supreme rights for the furtherance of the public weal and the protection of the common interests and social order of the community. In old Kievan Rus the importance of the Prince was based, first and foremost, upon the fact that he was the guardian of the external security of the Russian land and the armed watchman of its frontiers. Yet the merest glance at the social relations which obtained in the North will make it clear to us that the status of an appanage prince was of a very different order to this. The moment that the idea of the public weal becomes extinct in a community, at that moment does the idea of its ruler as an all-compelling power become extinct also. The appanage contained no feature to prevent such a result from happening, seeing that it was a union neither of kindred nor territory. In fact, it was not a community at all, properly speaking, but only a fortuitous conglomeration of individuals of whom no more could be said than that they happened to find themselves within the borders of a district owned by such and such a prince. In the absence, therefore, of any common connecting interest, the prince ceased to be a sovereign in the essential meaning of the term, and became a mere landowner or seignior, while the population of his appanage became converted into its unattached, temporary inhabitants only—inhabitants bound together by no tie save that of propinquity, even though some of them might remain there for several successive generations. The only persons territorially bound to the appanage were the prince's own personal slaves—the free population being bound to him only by, at best, *temporary*, personal ties. Such free population was divided into two classes—" *sluzhilie liudi* " and " *tchernïe liudi.*" Of these, the former consisted of boyars and " *slugi volnïe*," or free servitors who took personal service with the prince under the terms of a written agreement, and recognised his authority only so long as they were in his actual employ. That employ they could leave at any time, and depart to take service under another prince, without the act in any way constituting treason against their late employer. This was made possible through the fact that appanages were not water-tight political compartments, possessed of permanent, immoveable frontiers, but units which contracted or expanded as parts of a broken, yet surviving, whole ; while the population which wandered over them took little reck of boundaries, seeing that its wanderings never led it outside the Russian land, or from among its own people, or out of the jurisdiction of the same Russian princes. It was long before the latter could bring themselves to insert into agreements with their servitors the necessary clauses for doing away with this last remaining relic of Russian unity—a relic which, though no longer a political factor, still continued to constitute a popular sentiment or tradition. Consequently, for the present, change of service did not cause a *volni sluga* or member of the free servitor or retainer class to lose his right to any lands which he had acquired in his late principality. Similar relations obtained between the prince and the *tchernïe liudi* or state tenant class. Just as the relations of the *sluzhilie liudi* to the local ruler were those of personal service, so the relations of the *tchernïe liudi* to that ruler were those of personal land-tenure. A *tcherni*, urban or rural, recognised the prince's authority and paid him rent-dues only so long as he (the *tcherni*) was tenant of the prince's land. Immediately that the local conditions of such tenancy became inconvenient to him he could move into another appanage, and all ties between him and his late landlord would come to an end. Thus it follows that the *sluzhili* was practically the indentured retainer of the prince, while the *tcherni* was his agrarian tenant. This enables us to form an estimate of the real status or importance of the prince in the community, and to see that, properly speaking, he was not so much the *ruler* of his appanage as the *sole proprietor of its soil*. Consequently, he did not *govern* it—he only *exploited* and *developed* it. The person, however—the free individual—did not come juridically under that proprietorship. A *sluzhili* or a *tcherni* could settle in an appanage, engage in official service or agricultural enterprise there, and depart again, without constituting a political unit in the community, but only an economic accident in the appanage. The prince did not look upon him as his subject in our meaning of the word, for the reason that he did not regard himself as a sovereign.[1] No such ideas, indeed, nor their resultant relations, found a place in the appanage system. In those days the title "*hosudar*"—"overlord" or "sovereign"—connoted only the authority of the free man over the slave, and the appanage prince was therefore "overlord" only of his own slaves, just as was any other private landowner.

Yet, though not a "*hosudar*" in our modern sense of the word, the appanage prince was more than a private landowner, for he enjoyed certain supreme rights within the appanage. Those rights did not arise out of his sole proprietorship of the appanage, nor were they the source of such proprietorship. They were a bequest, rather, from those forefathers who, as princes of the old rota system, had looked upon themselves as *temporary* rulers only of their provinces, yet participants, one and all, in the supreme power appertaining to Yaroslav's posterity at large. When, later, the unity of the princely stock became dissolved, the sovereign rights of the appanage princes lost none of that dynastic support which had become a political custom and acquired popular recognition. Only the *importance* of those rights and the *view popularly adopted of them* underwent a change. The appanage prince still continued to be looked upon as wielder of the supreme power by virtue of his *origin*— by virtue of the mere fact that he was a *kniaz* or prince; but it was only as a ruler specifically appointed to his particular sphere of rule through the personal dispensation of his father, brother, or other near relative, and not as a participant in any pan-territorial power belonging to the princely stock as a whole, that he governed his appanage. His inherited authority, therefore, could not find a new and purely political basis in the idea of a ruler as overseer of the public weal, seeing that such an idea was inherently impossible in a state where the social order was organised in the private interest of the prince-proprietor, and where the relations to him of the free population were determined, not by any general, compulsory law, but by personal, voluntary agreement alone. Therefore, when the idea of an appanage as the personal property of its prince became crystallised into an actual *right* to possess it, the supreme ruling

---

[1] In the primal, not the monarchical, sense of the term.

power became added to that right, and, gradually blending with it, entered into the general mechanism of the prince's appanagal administration. Thus there resulted a combination of relations possible only where no exact boundary runs between public and private right. The supreme rights of the prince as inheritor of the appanage were looked upon as lucrative assets appertaining to the property which he inherited, and, consequently, as conferring upon him full liberty to use or dispose of the same at will, whether by subdivision, alienation, bequeathal, or otherwise. Government dues were assigned him for his temporary use and maintenance, or else to be let on lease by him or to be sold as he saw fit. Thus the prince's private right of possession of an appanage became the political basis of his ruling power, while the only juridical instrument through which that power touched the free inhabitants of the appanage was voluntary agreement. A prince of the *twelfth* century who found himself without a province was none the less not deprived of all "share in the Russian land"—of all right whatsoever to rule a portion of the *otchina* which was partially his due by virtue of his membership of the princely stock. The appanage prince of the *fourteenth* century, however, who lost his *otchina* lost also his governmental rights, since the appanage princes, though still kinsmen, did not constitute a *clan*, a *union* of kindred. All that a prince left without an appanage could do was to enter his father's service or that of the Suzerain Prince of Lithuania.

The status of an appanage prince as the personal proprietor of his appanage, as well as the nature of his rights of rule, are also to be seen shown forth in his relations to the three classes of lands which composed his *otchina*. Those classes consisted respectively of court lands, leasehold lands, and boyaral lands—the last-named comprising all lands belonging to private owners, whether ecclesiastical or lay. The distinctions between these several species arose out of a purely agrarian source—out of the fact that they were exploited by the prince through the agency of three different methods of tenure. Court lands represented, in the scheme of princely estate-management, what seigniorial glebe represents in the *ménage* of a private proprietor. That is to say, their produce was set apart exclusively for the use of the princely court, and their exploitation carried out either by the forced labour of *stradniki* (*i.e.* court slaves settled upon the cultivable portions of the land), or by the free labour of *krestiané* or peasants, who were bound to make over a certain tithe of the grain, hay, fish, and other produce, to the court. This rendering of tithe (*izdielie*) in return for the use of these lands constituted the prime distinguishing feature of

the category to which the lands belonged. The second class of lands—
tchernia zemli, or leasehold lands—were let out on lease or quit-rent, either
to individual *krestiané*, or to associated bodies of such tenants, as well as,
occasionally, to members of other social classes (as was done also by
private owners). All such leaseholders were known as *obrokhnïe* or rent-
payers. The relations of the prince to the third class of lands in his
appanage—the boyaral class—were rather more complicated. The whole
of the soil of the appanage was his hereditary property, yet its actual
possession he shared with certain other—private—inheritors. Let me
explain this. To begin with, when the first prince of an appanage
entered upon his province he usually found in possession certain private
landowners, both ecclesiastical and lay, who had penetrated thither before
the region became a separate principality. Subsequently, to such of those
persons or ecclesiastical institutions as rendered him special services he
allotted lands as their *otchini* or heritable estates. Thus the prince's
main *otchina*, the appanage at large, came to include within its boundaries
a number of lesser *otchini* of private persons. This juxtaposition of the
rights of several different landowners in one appanage was rendered possible through the fusion of the rights of ruler and of sole owner of the soil
in the person of the prince alone. Though resigning all rights of *private*
disposition of the *otchini* of private proprietors, he reserved to himself
his *supreme, official* rights over the same ; and, inasmuch as those supreme
rights of his were essentially proprietorial in character and formed part of
his juridical title to sole ownership of the appanage, the acquisition of
land therein by private owners in no way affected his position in that
regard, seeing that he still retained the supreme rights in question. This
led to a similar idea obtaining with regard to the relations between him
and the *persons* of the private owners. Occasionally the prince would
confer upon a boyar possessing an hereditary *otchina* in his appanage not
only an absolute title to that *otchina*, but also a portion of his (the
prince's) supreme rights over it. From this circumstance arose relations
reminding one, to a certain degree, of the feudal systems of Western
Europe. Yet the two phenomena were by no means identical with one
another—only parallel, since in the relations of the boyars and free servitors of the prince to their master much was lacking that was needed
to complete the identity of the two systems. Indeed, those relations
lacked two of the fundamental features of feudalism—namely, (1) combination of relations of service with those of land-tenure, and (2) hereditary
devolution both of the one and the other. In the appanage the agrarian

relations of the prince's free servitors were strictly distinguished from their relations of service, and we find this distinction running through all the agreements made between princes and servitors during the fourteenth century. Boyars and free servitors could pass at will from the service of any prince to the service of any other; they could serve in one appanage and possess an *otchina* in another; and change of service in no way affected their rights with regard to an *otchina* acquired in the appanage which they had just left. Moreover, a free servitor serving where he pleased escaped payment of land-dues in the locality where he owned estates, while the princes were bound to see to the interests of servitors other than their own who possessed lands in their (the princes') appanages as though those servitors were under contract to themselves. These various relations were all of them summed up in the one general condition inserted into agreements between princes and servitors—"The boyars and servitors who dwell among us shall be at liberty to come and to go." The feudal stage, then, is to be seen only in the juridical status of the prince himself, who in his person united both the ruling power and the supreme ownership of the soil. Thus he approximated closely to the seignior, except that his boyars and servitors were freemen, not vassals.

Western feudalism was constructed, so to speak, from both ends— through processes which met half-way. On the one hand, rulers of provinces in a given state took advantage of the weakness of the central authority to make themselves owners of the territories which they governed, and thus to become absolute, hereditary proprietors of those territories; while, on the other hand, great landowners who had been rewarded for their services by being appointed the sovereign's vassals availed themselves of a similar weakness to acquire or to appropriate a portion of the chief power in the state, as its hereditary plenipotentiaries. Both these processes, by dividing up and localising the supreme power geographically, helped to disintegrate the state into large seigniories, in which sovereign prerogatives became fused with rights of private landownership. Through a like process, again, the seigniories became divided up into large baronies, with secondary vassals of their own—*i.e.* vassals bound in hereditary fealty to their particular baron; until, finally, the whole of this military agrarian hierarchy rested upon a fixed basis formed of the rural population or "villeins," who were either bound to the land or at all events hereditarily attached to it by long residence. In ancient Rus, however, things worked out differently. The old provinces of Kievan Rus, ruled by rota, gave place (as we have seen) to the appanages of the North; which, again, in the fourteenth century and under a Khan ruling upon the far-distant Lower Volga, became independent of their local Suzerain Princes. The prince of a larger appanage governed his territory through his boyars and free servitors, to whom he apportioned, for their "maintenance" and for purposes of tax-administration, certain towns, town-districts, rural communes, hamlets, and other taxable units, as well as plenipotentiary powers of rule over them and legal and financial administration of the same. In some cases, also, those boyars and servitors possessed *otchini* within the appanage, and if so, the prince conferred upon such estates certain exemptions or immunities, in the shape either of freedom from dues or of certain legal and financial rights. Nevertheless, districts administered by these plenipotentiaries never became their actual *landed* property, any more than rights of administration conferred upon privileged inheritors of private *otchini* ever became their *hereditary* rights. Consequently neither lands conferred upon servitors nor *otchini* granted to boyars ever developed into baronies. True, we see from the history of the Principality of Moscow during the fifteenth century that some of the Suzerain Princes of the day attempted to place their appanage princes in a sort of position of vassalage to themselves, yet this did not denote any attempt to effect feudal division of the supreme power, but merely a preliminary to and means towards its state centralisation. Although not a few juridical and economic features resembling feudal relations are discoverable in the appanage system, feudalism rested upon an altogether different social basis to the latter—namely, the fixed rural population, and so formed different combinations, as well as constituted a stage of an entirely different process. The marks of mere *similarity* between the two do not render them *identical* with one another, since the similar elements in them both did not combine in identical fashion (particularly in the early part of the process), and formed, in the final result, two entirely different social structures. The scientific interest, then, to be derived from them is afforded, not by the elements themselves, but by the properties of the respective formations to which they gave rise. In the structure of feudalism we see something like our own *kormlenia* or grants of districts to plenipotentiaries, as well as like our exemptions of boyaral *otchini* from land dues: yet neither the one nor the other class of concession ever developed (as they did in the West) into *permanent* social institutions, but remained always more or less temporary, fortuitous rewards for personal service. In the West a freeman secured his freedom by confining himself strictly within a ring of permanent, inherited relations—relations which permitted of his making himself the centre of the lower social forces in his locality, and thus creating around himself a little world of which he was both the director and the supporter. On the other hand, the free servitor of the Russian appanage could find, in the ever-shifting local community, none of the elements necessary for a durable environment of that kind, and therefore sought to secure his freedom by the conclusion of a personal, temporary agreement with his prince, with the right of at any time tearing it up and departing into service in some appanage to which he was not bound by any ties consolidated through lapse of time.

This comparison of the feudal with the appanage system helps us to picture to ourselves the form assumed by the community under the latter. Our attention is arrested, first of all, by the boyars and free servitors who formed the retinue of the appanage prince. They constituted a class which appears largely in the light of a social and political anachronism when seen against the general community of the fourteenth-century appanage. Their social position, in particular, offers more than one feature little in keeping with the then system of government or with the general tendency of appanage life. The strict separation of the *official* relations of the prince's servitors to their master from their *agrarian* relations to him—a separation emphasised in all the prince-and-servitor agreements of the fourteenth and fifteenth centuries—did not by any means coincide with their natural desire to combine personal service of their employer with landownership in his appanage—with their desire to strengthen the former tie with the latter, and so to secure satisfaction of the paramount requirement of a government—an armed force. Moreover, the power of a free servitor to combine service in one appanage with landownership in another clashed with the princes' tendency towards individualism of rule. As regards that power, indeed, the boyars and free servitors appear in sharp distinction from the civil community of the appanage, since the social position of all other classes was determined solely by their agrarian relations to the prince as hereditary owner of the soil. Yet, though the social position of the boyars also was beginning to become more and more based upon landownership, they alone of the community continued to maintain purely personal relations with the prince— relations arising out of their mutual agreement of service with him, and dating from the period when the social status of the official classes possessed no agrarian basis at all. These peculiar features in the position of the princes' servitors cannot have arisen out of the appanage system of the thirteenth and fourteenth centuries, but must have been relics of an earlier day, when neither the princes nor their retinues were connected with their local communities by any *permanent* ties. Such features were altogether out of place in Northern Rus, where the process of disintegration into small appanages was growing with each successive generation. Moreover, the right of the boyars and free servitors to select the locality of their service—a right which represented a political form surviving from the territorial unity of old Kievan Rus—was equally unsuited to the times, since, in Northern Rus, that class constituted only a peripatetic representative of a political system which had quite passed away, and continued to serve as a connecting link between portions of a country which no longer constituted a political whole. The Church's admonitions of the fourteenth century summed up the general view of their time when they urged the boyars to remain faithful to one prince and not to transfer their services from appanage to appanage, seeing that, in the Church's eye, such mobility constituted treason, however old-established the custom might be. However, the same prince-and-servitor agreements which had formerly recognised the right of a retainer to serve in appanages other than the one in which his lands were situated begin eventually to confront us with a clause wholly at variance with the foregoing—a clause indicating that appanage policy was now beginning to set its face against ancient custom. The clause in question not only throws difficulties in the way of princes or boyars acquiring lands in appanages other than their own, but expressly forbids them to raise mortgages on such lands or to let them out on quit-rent. In other words, the clause forbids the inhabitants of a given appanage to enter into personal or material dependence upon a prince or boyar belonging to another one. On the other hand, life in those northern appanages of the fourteenth century presents phenomena altogether different to those seen under the courts of the former princes of the South. The course of affairs now offered few opportunities for the military-official class to win honours for itself and glory for its prince. True, the princely feuds of the appanage period bore almost as hardly upon the peace-loving common people as those of olden days had done, yet the former no longer partook of a military character, and called rather for sheer barbarism than soldierly skill. Nor did the external defence of the land afford the same opportunities to the military class as formerly, seeing that it was not until the middle of the fourteenth century that any serious attack came from the Lithuanian frontier, while the Mongolian

yoke had long ago relieved the princes and their retinues from the obligation of guarding the far south-eastern regions—the regions which once
had served the southern princes as a training ground for their warriors.
Indeed, even after the great battle of Kulikovo [1] had taken place, it continued to be tribute rather than troops that had to be dispatched thither.
The real factor which broke down old-established customs and ideas was
the brute force of existing conditions. We know that in the twelfth
century the princes' retainers were paid a fixed salary—a sign that foreign
trade swept large stocks of ready cash into the princes' hands. In the
North, however, the following century saw that source of boyaral income
come to an end, and exploitation of natural resources begin once more to
constitute the popular industry. In the fourteenth century, again, we see
the appanage princes making the grant of judicial and administrative functions their chief means of recompensing their servitors, and by studying
the organisation of the Principality of Moscow at that time we see how
complex was that system of administration, and for what an enormous
number of persons it provided a living. Yet those administrative functions
did not altogether constitute a *dependable* livelihood, but shared in the
general insecurity of the political and economic institutions of the time.
In fact, the princes' circumstances were undergoing a rapid change, and,
with few exceptions, a change for the worse. Some of the princely establishments were carried on only with difficulty, while others had already come
to utter ruin, and not a single one of them stood upon a secure footing or
possessed a source of income which could be looked upon as trustworthy.
This general change of social positions led the princes' servitors and boyars
to turn their thoughts to an economic source which at least promised
better things than the rest, however much, like the others, it was feeling the
effects of the disorganisation of the social system. I refer to landowning—
a resource which was at least likely to place the boyar in a position
of less dependence upon the moods and caprices of his prince than a
salary and grant of administrative functions had ever done. Thus the
servitor or official class in the North adopted the interest most dominant in
the civil life of the appanage, and set about converting itself into an order
of seigniors, acquiring landed property, and clearing and settling waste
areas. For success in this enterprise four things were necessary—namely,
enslavement of agricultural hands, the establishment of slave settlements
(*i.e.* colonies of *stradniki*) upon the estates, a grant of exemption for the
latter from land dues, and the inducing of free *krestiané* to help in

---

[1] In which Dmitri, son of Ivan II. of Moscow, defeated the Khan Mamai in the year 1380.

the scheme. Members of the retainer class who owned lands were not unknown even in old Kievan Rus, and, in fact, it was there that the original type of boyar-landowner arose whose fundamental features survived sufficiently long to exercise a marked effect upon the growth and character of the serf laws of later days. In all probability, however, landownership by Kievan boyars never attained notable dimensions, since it would be too much overshadowed by other interests of the military-official class for it ever to exercise any great influence upon their political rôle. Now, however, in Northern Rus, landownership assumed an important political significance in the fortunes of the upper class, and gradually effected a change in its position, both at court and among the local community.

The remainder of the Northern community also differed largely from that of ancient Kievan Rus. To begin with, it was poorer than the latter had ever been. The industrial capital which had been created and maintained by the active and long-continued foreign trading operations of the Southern community shrank, in the North of later days, to such insignificant dimensions that it ceased to have any notable effect upon the industrial and political life of the people. Proportionately with this there took place a diminution of the sum of that popular labour which, evoked by the movement of abundant capital, had communicated to the towns of the Dnieper and its tributaries their great industrial activity. This curtailment of commercial traffic showed itself, as we have seen, in the gradual enhancement of the value of currency. In fact, the agrarian industry, with its offshoots the small rural *promisli*, was now left, if not the only economic force in the country, at all events a force more dominant than it had ever been before. Yet for a long while it remained only a mobile, semi-nomadic industry— an industry *na novi*, or always working fresh land, and passing from one scarcely developed spot to one altogether untouched. Indeed, as a rule, an entire series of generations of settlers was required to cut down and burn the timber off the land, to plough up the rough soil, and to thoroughly manure it, before a tilth suitable for permanent, systematic husbandry was formed out of the clay of the Upper Volga. The industrial change from foreign trade to agrarian exploitation explains, I think, a phenomenon upon which we touched during our examination of the *Russkaia Pravda*,[1] and which seemed difficult to account for. In moneyed Kievan Rus capital was none the less exceedingly dear, so that for long-date loans the law of Monomakh allowed interest at the rate of forty per cent., and, in practice, the lenders exacted far

[1] See p. 163.

more. In appanage days, however, the Church inculcated the exaction of "light" interest—that is to say, interest at the rate only of from twelve to fourteen per cent. We may therefore suppose that, in reality, this cheapening of capital was due to the great fall in the demand for it which occurred when agrarian industry once more entered the field as the leading industrial factor.

At the same time there dropped out of the ranks of the social forces of the North a class whose labour had turned wholly upon capital— namely, the class of old-established industrial workers in the two ancient capitals of Rostov and Suzdal. That class had never prospered since the day when the tide of immigration first set in from Kievan Rus, and its decline was hastened by the fact that the two cities named never achieved a thorough economic recovery from the *débâcle* suffered by them in their feud with the "newer and younger men."[1] Yet for a long while none of the more recently arisen towns took the place of those ancient capitals in the political and industrial life of the country or became independent territorial centres and directors of the local community. This was because none of those towns possessed *vietcha* or the necessary seniority for imposing their will upon the junior townships attached to them. This makes it clear that, in Northern Rus of the thirteenth and fourteenth centuries, those sources had become dried up whence the capital town of each province had formerly derived its economic and political strength. With the disappearance of the provincial capital from among the number of the effective forces of the community there disappeared also from the round of social life those interests which had been based upon the relations of the inhabitants of the provincial capitals in question to the other social forces of the community. In short, the influence of the general process of colonisation caused the community of the thirteenth century to become at once poorer and less complex in its composition.

Finally, the decline in the political importance of the appanage prince was equalled by the deterioration in his standard of culture. A faulty social system levels *down* the morals and ideals of its community much more easily than it itself is levelled *up* by them. Personal interest, therefore, and personal contract of service—the two main bases of the appanage system—would be but sorry preceptors in this regard. In fact, it was the appanage system which brought about the decline of territorial consciousness and local patriotism in the princes, just as it was the appanage system also which extinguished the idea of the unity and integrity

[1] See p. 233.

of the Russian land—the idea of a common popular weal—in the community at large. From such a world-outlook as that even the limited *Russkaia zemlia* of St. Vladimir and Yaroslav would have been a step upward! Indeed, the term *Russkaia zemlia* seldom occurs in the Chronicle's record of appanage days. Political disintegration inevitably led to a fining down of the political sense and a cooling of the territorial sentiment. Brooding persistently upon their petty territorial nests, whence they flew abroad only in search of plunder, the princes grew more and more impoverished and more and more barbaric with each successive generation, until in time they had come to be incapable of any thought beyond the mere care of their fledgelings. The onerous external conditions and individualism of princely rule caused each prince to act more and more on the principle of self-preservation. While less pugnacious than his Kievan predecessor, he was, for the most part, more barbaric in his ideas and form of policy. These characteristics enable us to understand the exhortations addressed to him by the chroniclers of his day when they urged him not to allow himself to be led away by the vainglory of this world, nor to despoil his neighbour, nor to play false with his brother princes, nor to wrong his junior kinsmen.

Such were the principal results of the appanage system. They may be summed up by saying that the working of the system caused Northern Rus to undergo ever-increasing political disintegration and to become bereft even of her former slender ties of political unity; that that disintegration, in its turn, rendered the princes continually more and more impoverished; that, in proportion as that occurred, they shut themselves up more and more in their *otchini*, and became estranged from one another; and that, in proportion as they became estranged from one another, they converted themselves, according to their several ideas and interests, into private rural seigniors, and, losing altogether their rôle of overseers of the public weal, lost also their territorial sense. These results of the system were of great importance in the subsequent political history of Northern Rus, for they paved the way for conditions favourable to political reunification. When at length a strong ruler arose from among the mass of petty, impoverished appanage princes, he encountered among them, it is true, a total absence of support for his unificatory ideas, and so was forced to take advantage of their mutual estrangement and incapacity for common action in order to subdue them each in turn: yet, on the other hand, the prince-unifier found in the local communities at large such utter indifference to the petty, semi-barbarous rulers with whom those communities were connected by only the slenderest of ties that he was able to annex them, one by one, without evoking in them any rising in support of their respective princes.   All this helps us to determine the importance of the appanage system in our political history, and to show us that it was through its own results that the downfall of the system came.   Its very nature, indeed, rendered it less capable of self-defence than its predecessor, the rota system, had been, and therefore the more easy to destroy in order to rear upon its ruins a unified state.   Hence the appanage system of rule represents, in our history, a transitional political form which enabled the Russian land to pass from mere *national* unity to *political* unity.   The story of that passage is the story of the Principality of Moscow : for which reason let us turn, next, to the study of Muscovite fortunes.

CHAPTER XVII

Moscow begins to combine the appanages into a single great principality—Early references of the Chronicle to Moscow—The original area of the Kremlin—Economic advantages of Moscow's geographical position—The city as the meeting-place of three great roads—Traces of early settlement of the region—Moscow as the ethnographical centre of Great Russia—The river Moskva as a trade route—Political results of the geographical position of Moscow—Moscow as the junior appanage—Influence of that circumstance upon the external relations and internal policy of the Muscovite Princes—Political and national achievements of those Princes up to the middle of the fifteenth century—Summary of the foregoing.

Two processes took place in Northern Rus during the period of the appanages. Of these, we have seen that the first broke up the country into a number of small hereditary *otchini* held by the house of Vsevolod : and it was to a branch of that house that it fell to initiate the second and reverse process—the process of collating the various disunited territorial fragments into something like a political whole. Of the state thus formed Moscow became the centre.

The Chronicle gives Moscow in its list of new towns which arose in Rostov during the times of Yuri Dolgoruki. It is curious, however, to note that the name makes its first appearance in the Chronicle's record as a mere spot on the boundary-line between the northern province of Suzdal and the more southern one of Tchernigov. To this spot, in 1147, Yuri Dolgoruki invited his neighbour Sviatoslav, Prince of Novgorod-Sieverski: which constitutes the first actual mention of the name of Moscow to be found in the Chronicle. Evidently the place was then only the Prince's country palace—or, to be more correct, a half-way villa where the Princes of Suzdal halted during their journeys to and from Kiev and the South. Yet the villa must have had a considerable establishment attached to it, since we read that on the day after Sviatoslav's arrival his host arranged "a mighty dinner" in his guest's honour, as well as entertained the guest's suite right handsomely. To do this he must have had extensive supplies and house-room at his disposal, even though Sviatoslav is said to have come "among a small retinue." Nine years later (according to the Chronicle) Yuri "laid the town of Moskva" at a point below the confluence of the river Moskva with the Neglina brook. This means that he built a ring of wooden walls around his villa, and converted the enclosure into a town. That enclosure constituted the great Kremlin of Moscow in its original form, and occupied (according to Zabielin's *History of Moscow*) that particular western corner of the Kremlin hill where a steep spur runs down to the mouth of the Neglina and the Borovitski gate now stands (the name of the latter recalling the *bora* or pine forest which at one time covered the hill). Nevertheless, the portion of ground (triangular in shape, according to Zabielin) which Yuri enclosed occupied only a third, or, at most, a half, of the present-day area of the Kremlin.

Moscow arose midway between Rus of the Dnieper and Rus of the Upper Volga, and in later annals also we find it accorded a similar importance as the frontier-most town of Suzdal. I have spoken of the fierce struggle which arose between Andrew Bogoliubski's younger brothers and his nephews at his death. In 1174 the uncles worsted the nephews, and then sent to Tchernigov for their (the uncles') wives, who had repaired thither for refuge. Oleg, a son of the Prince of Tchernigov, escorted the women homeward, and, after depositing them safely in Moscow, "returned unto his own province of Lopasnia." Now, Lopasnia is a village situated only some seventy versts to the southward of Moscow, on the road to Serpukhov; which shows us how near, at that time, the frontier of Tchernigov approached to the town of Moscow and the territory of Suzdal. The same account shows us that Moscow bore a yet earlier name of Kutzkova—a name derived from a local seignior, whom tradition asserts to have been named Stepan (Stephen) Kutzek or Kutchek, to have been a boyar and *tisiatski* of Suzdal, and to have owned all the hamlets and homesteads in the region of Moscow. It might be mentioned, in passing, that the name of this boyar long survived in that of the quarter of Moscow formerly known as "Kutchkovo Polé" or "Kutchek's Plain"—the quarter now occupied by Srietenka and Lubianka Streets.

The political fortunes of Moscow were closely connected with the period of its rise, as also with its geographical position. As a town newly founded and far removed from the two chief centres of Suzdal (Rostov and Vladimir), Moscow became the capital of a principality at a later date than its fellows had done, and so was assigned to a junior line of princes. In fact, the greater part of the thirteenth century saw no permanent princeship there at all. Princes made an occasional appearance in the city, but only for a short time, and were all of them younger

sons of their fathers.   The first of such transient rulers was Vladimir, a
younger son of Vsevolod's.   Next came another Vladimir—this time one
of the younger sons of the Suzerain Prince Yuri, and a grandson of
Vsevolod's.   It was this Vladimir who was captured by the Tartars at the
taking of Moscow in the winter of 1237-38.   Later on, Moscow fell to
one of the younger sons of Vsevolod's son Yaroslav—Michael Khorobriti
(*i.e.* "the Bully"), but upon his death in 1248 the town seems again
to have remained several years without a ruler.   At length, in 1263, on
the death of Alexander Nevski, his youngest son Daniel, a minor, was
created Muscovite Prince, and from that date onwards the town was the
capital of a permanent principality.   Thus Daniel was the original founder
of the princely house of Moscow.

That is as far as our early information concerning the town goes, nor
would it have been easy to guess from it to what a height the later
political fortunes of Moscow were destined to raise the city.   Similarly, later
generations of Northern Russia were accustomed to ask themselves in
amazement how Moscow ever contrived to rise so rapidly and to become the
political centre of North-Eastern Rus.   We find that perplexity expressed in
one of the many popular tales which have for their subject the early vicissitudes of Moscow and its Princes.   The tale in question (written in the
seventeenth century, and reminding one, by its semi-rhythmical diction,
of the old-time *bilini*) begins something after this fashion : " What man
ever thought or divined that Moscow would become a Kingdom, or what
man ever knew that Moscow would be accounted an Empire?   Once by
the river Moskva there stood only the goodly hamlets of the boyar, of the
worthy Stepan Kutchek, of the son of Ivan."   The reason why Moscow's
early progress remained such an enigma to later generations lies in the fact
that the ancient chroniclers failed to take due note of the early stages of its
growth—to note the very considerable acquisitions added to the town during
the initial period of long-continued, though inconspicuous, effort.   Nevertheless, we have preserved to us certain *indirect* evidence of the secret
historical forces which paved the way for the rise of the Principality, and
paved it from the very first moment of the Principality's existence.   The
working of those forces is to be seen best in the economic conditions
which aided the city's growth—conditions of which the city's geographical
position in relation to the Russian colonisation movement in Northern Rus
was the principal creating factor.

It is clear that the earliest and most vigorous phase of colonisation
took place along the two great rivers enclosing the Mezhduriechïe (*i.e.* the

region enclosed by the courses of the Upper Volga and the Oka). Up to the coming of the Tartars the general lines of those rivers were marked by two long chains of towns—the one chain following the Upper Volga from Rshev to Nizhni Novgorod, and the other chain the Middle Oka from Kaluga to Murom. The first of those chains (the principal links of which were the old-established Russian settlements of Yaroslavl, Riazan, and Murom) represented a current of colonisation wafted from Great Novgorod in the North-West and Smolensk in the West, and the second chain a like current from the region of the Dnieper and the Upper Oka. After the two outer rivers of the Mezhduriechïe had been settled, a similar process took place with regard to their inner tributaries—*i.e.* such of their tributaries as intersected the Mezhduriechïe (though, be it noted, there were already established here the two ancient centres of Rostov and Suzdal). Most of the towns comprised in the two chains arose at about the middle of the twelfth century, or a little earlier. The appearance of a town on an inner tributary meant that a large body of colonists was massed along the main, the outer, river, and needed, therefore, an in-lying fort of refuge. The geographical distribution of the towns founded in the Mezhduriechïe during the twelfth and thirteenth centuries shows us that the immigrant population settled in regular strips along the tributaries. Those strips were divided from one another by wide spaces of forest and swamp, so that the settlements or embryo towns which arose at the ends of the narrow " portages " connecting the various tributaries with one another acquired great importance as strategical points in the general system of land and river communication. In this regard the geographical position of Moscow offered especial advantages. To begin with, the Istra, the highest tributary of the Moskva, connected the latter very closely with the Lama, a tributary of the Sosh ;[1] and inasmuch as the Sosh itself fell into the Volga, the " portage " between the Istra and the Lama brought the Moskva into direct communication with the Upper Volga on the one side and the Middle Oka on the other. Again, Moscow arose just where the Moskva bends southwards and almost comes in contact (through its small tributary the Yausa) with the Kliazma, along the banks of which, at that period, ran a great highway which passed east and west through Moscow. Along that highway travelled Andrew Bogoliubski when, accompanied by the miraculous *ikon* of the Holy Mother, he was returning to his native Vladimir from Vishgorod (1155). A second highway—"the great road to Vladimir "—left Moscow by way of the " Kutchkovo Polé," and an old

---

[1] Not to be confounded with the greater Sosh, a tributary of the Dnieper.

manuscript has an account of how, in 1395, the citizens of Moscow went out along that road to meet another *ikon* of the Holy Mother which was approaching the city. Finally, there ran north and south through Moscow a highway from Lopasnia and the Kievan country to Periaslavl Zaliesski and Rostov. Thus Moscow arose at the point of intersection of three great land roads — a geographical position which conferred important economic advantages upon the city and its neighbourhood.

To begin with, the position of Moscow contributed to a comparatively earlier and denser colonisation of its region than was the case elsewhere. Arising on the border-line between Northern and Southern Rus, its neighbourhood was the first locality in which colonists coming from the South and South-West found themselves landed after passing the Ugra. Consequently it was the region where, as their first halting-place, they settled in the largest numbers. Faint traces of this active precipitation of the colonising element upon the Moskva are to be found in the old genealogical traditions of the region. The ancestral records of the ancient boyar families which gradually became founded in Moscow usually begin with the story of how and whence the founders of those families entered the service of the Muscovite Prince. By collating these various family records we obtain a solid and important historical fact— namely, that, even before the opening of the thirteenth century, and long before Moscow had begun to play any considerable rôle in the fortunes of Northern Rus, boyars had begun to drift thither from every quarter of the land—from Murom and Nizhni Novgorod and Rostov and Smolensk and Tchernigov—nay, even from Kiev and Volhynia. Among other magnates there migrated thither, as early as Daniel's time, the great Kievan boyar Rodion (the original founder of the Kvashnin family), who brought with him the whole of his establishment of seventeen hundred retainers—enough with which to garrison a fairly large fortified town. Boyars always followed the currents of popular migration, so that their genealogical records are evidence that at that period the general trend was towards Moscow. This steady influx into the city, as into a central reservoir, of all the Russian popular forces threatened by external foes was primarily due to the geographical position of Moscow.

Moscow is frequently spoken of as the geographical centre of Russia. Yet, if we take the country in its present limits, the statement is incorrect both in a physical and an ethnographical sense, since, to be really the geographical centre of Russia, Moscow should stand a little further to the south-east. If, however, we consider the distribution of the bulk of the Russian population (that is to say, of the Great Russian stock) during the thirteenth and fourteenth centuries, we shall see that at that period Moscow was more or less the *ethnographical* centre of the country. The process of colonisation caused the Russian population to become chiefly massed in the region between the Oka and the Upper Volga—namely, in the Mezhduriechïe, where it remained for a long period without a chance of issuing thence in any direction. Settlement of the country to the northward, beyond the Volga, was debarred to South Russian immigrants by an intersecting stream of colonisation from Novgorod—a stream which intimidated the peaceable population of the Mezhduriechïe with its bands of half-colonists, half-freebooters. Moreover, the rapacious gangs of *ushkuiniki*, or canoemen, whom the great free city of the North-West sent foraging along the Volga and its tributaries were sufficient to deter any peace-loving population from penetrating into the country northward of that river. The son of Yaroslav of Zaozersk to whom I have already referred as becoming a monk of the Kamenni Monastery [1] of Kubin must have had those thirteenth and fourteenth centuries in his mind when, in the following century, he wrote in his chronicle that only a small proportion of the Trans-Volgan country contained any baptized persons ; by which he meant to say that only a small proportion of *Russian* Christians had yet penetrated thither. As for the North-East, the East, and the South, they too were debarred to the Russian immigrant population of the Mezhduriechïe by the alien peoples who dominated those regions—namely, the Morduines, the Tcheremissians, stray bands of Vatizes who roamed beyond the Volga in quest of plunder, and, finally, the Tartars ; while, with regard to the West and South-West, the Russian population was denied access to that quarter by the now united Lithuanian-Polish Empire, which was getting ready for its first onslaught upon Eastern Rus. Thus for a long period the bulk of the Russian population was confined within the Mezhduriechïe, without any opportunity of emerging thence, and inasmuch as it was in the midst of that population, *which constituted the Great Russian stock*, that Moscow arose, the city might then have been considered, if not the geographical, at all events the *ethnographical*, centre of Rus, as constituted in the fourteenth century. Moscow's central position was a protection to the city on every side from external foes. Blows from without might fall upon neighbouring principalities — upon Riazan, Nizhni Novgorod, Rostov, Yaroslavl, and Smolensk, but they seldom reached as far as Moscow. Thanks to that protection, the Muscovite

---

[1] *i.e.* the Monastery of the Holy Sepulchre. See p. 257.

Principality became a refuge for the surrounding Russian population, which everywhere was suffering from alien pressure. For more than a century between the burning of the city by the Tartars in 1238 and Olgerd's [1] first attack upon it in 1368 Moscow was probably the only point in Northern Rus which suffered no injury at the hands of an enemy, or only very little. At all events, with the exception of the Tartar raid in 1293, we find no mention of any such occurrences happening during the period named. This immunity from attack, so rare in those days, caused the eastward movement of Russian colonisation to become reversed. That is to say, settlers began to flow back from the old-established colonies of Rostov to the unoccupied lands of the Principality of Moscow. This constituted the first condition which, arising out of the geographical position of Moscow, contributed to the successful settlement of the Muscovite region.

Another condition which, arising out of the geographical position of Moscow, contributed to the growth of the Principality was the fact that Moscow stood upon a river which had always—even from the most ancient times—been possessed of great commercial importance. Bisecting the Muscovite State diagonally from north-west to south-east, it formed a waterway connecting the system of the Middle Oka with the system of the Upper Volga. In fact, it formed a chord between the two ends of the broad loop of river communication of which the two sides constituted the principal trade-routes of the Mezhduriechïe. Of this commercial importance of the Moskva we have evidence in the fact that at a very early period a town arose on the "portage" between Moscow and the Upper Volga—namely, the town of Volokolamsk, which, built by the Novgorodians, served as their central trade depôt in their commerce with the basin of the Oka and the region of the Middle Volga.

By thus making Moscow the point where two great popular movements intersected one another—namely, a movement of colonisation north-eastwards and a movement of commerce south-westwards, the city's geographical position conferred great economic advantages upon *the Muscovite Prince*. A large population attracted to his appanage meant a large number of direct taxpayers, while the movement of a large volume of commercial traffic on the Moskva meant a stimulation of popular industry in his dominions and a large flow of transit-dues into his treasury.

With these *economic* results of the geographical and ethnographical position of Moscow went an important series of *political* results arising

1 Of Lithuania.

out of the same source. To begin with, the geographical position of the city was closely bound up with the *genealogical position* of its Prince. As a new and outlying appanage, Moscow fell to one of the junior lines of Vsevolod's stock ; wherefore the Muscovite Prince could scarcely hope ever to attain to the highest rung of seniority and to occupy the Suzerain throne. Conscious of having, as it were, no part nor lot among his fellow kinsmen and princes, nor yet any customs and traditions of antiquity to fall back upon, he found himself forced to secure his position by other means than genealogical relations and the rota of seniority. Consequently, at an early period the Muscovite rulers elaborated a policy of their own, and began, practically from the very first, to carry it out in defiance of ancient precedent, to depart more readily and more thoroughly out of the beaten rut of princely relations than any of their fellow princes had done, and to tread new paths regardless of old political customs and traditions. This policy is to be seen illustrated both in their dealings with other princes and in their conduct of the internal affairs of their appanage. Always quick-witted observers of what was going on around them, and ever ready to make the most of their opportunities, the earlier Muscovite Princes were none the less robbers of the most unblushing type, and it was by no mere chance that one of their number—Michael, the son of Yaroslav—has come down to us as "Khorobriti" or "the bully." He it was who, in 1248, set about his uncle Sviatoslav, then Suzerain Prince of Vladimir, and drove him, in defiance of all right, from the senior throne. In the same way the Chronicle relates how the first Prince of Alexander's stock, Daniel, wantonly attacked his neighbour Constantine of Riazan, and, having defeated him "by certain cunning" (*i.e.* by a stratagem), took him prisoner, and deprived him of Kolomna. In 1303, again, Daniel's son Yuri made an unprovoked onslaught upon his neighbour the Prince of Mozhaisk, cast him into prison, and annexed his appanage—following this up by the murder of his late father's prisoner, Constantine, and the permanent annexation of Kolomna. Thus henceforth the river Moskva was Muscovite to its mouth. Of each and every Suzerain Prince the Prince of Moscow was the sworn foe. It seemed, indeed, as though the very soil of the city bred in its rulers a contempt for old-established ideas and relations of seniority. Daniel fought long and stubbornly with his two Suzerains, although in each case they were his own elder brother. First of all he tried conclusions with Dmitri, and then with Andrew. Nevertheless, on Dmitri's death, Daniel made friends with the latter's kindly son Ivan, and became so intimate with him that Ivan (who died childless) bequeathed to him his appanage instead of devising it to his senior kinsmen. Thus, though sworn foes to seniority, the Muscovite Princes were invariably opportunist in their statecraft. When circumstances changed they could change their policy accordingly. For a long period —in fact throughout the entire thirteenth century—the Tartar raids plunged the industry of the population of Northern Rus into utter confusion, but, with the coming of the fourteenth century, civil relations originally disorganised by the Tartar flood began to readjust themselves, and popular industry to return to something like order. From that time onwards the Muscovite Princes, who had begun their career with shameless acts of brigandage, continued it only as peaceable stewards, economists, and domestic organisers of their appanage. They strove to introduce into it a durable system, and to settle their towns with industrial workers and artisans whom they invited thither from other principalities. Likewise they ransomed thousands of Russian prisoners from the Great Horde, and settled them and other agriculturists upon free lands, where new villages, hamlets, and households soon arose. From the opening of the fourteenth century onwards we can follow this setting of the Muscovite house in order by means of the long series of State documents which begins with the wills (two in number) executed by the third Prince of Alexander Nevski's line—Ivan Kalita. These documents help us to explain how it was that, until the middle of the fifteenth century, the community of Northern Rus looked upon the Prince of Moscow as a model ruler, and upon his Principality as the best-ordered appanage in Rus. In one of the State documents in question—written at the middle of the fifteenth century, and consisting of a genealogical list of the Russian princes, from Rurik onwards—we read that Vsevolod begat Yaroslav, Yaroslav Alexander the Great (or the Brave), Alexander Daniel, and Daniel Ivan Kalita, "who did free the Russian land of robbers." This shows us that to the community of Northern Rus of that day Kalita appeared in the light of a reformer strong enough to rid his territory of bad characters and introduce therein public security. This view of him is confirmed by further evidence, for in a preface to an old manuscript written at Moscow towards the end of Kalita's tenure of rule we find his love of justice eulogised " in that he did grant unto the Russian land great peace and a court of laws." Moreover, the well-known writer on canonical jurisprudence, A. S. Pavlov, attributes to Kalita the introduction into Rus of the "Law of Landowners"—a Byzantine code of agrarian criminal enactments which is supposed to have been drawn up by the Iconoclastic Emperors during the eighth century.

If that is so, it would seem that Kalita paid special attention to the organising of the *rural* population in his domains. In short, the genealogical position of the Muscovite Princes—their consciousness of being more or less outcasts among their kinsfolk—caused them early to elaborate a form of policy based rather upon skilful adaptation of circumstances to the passing moment than upon tradition or precedent.

Thus the conditions primarily conducive to the rapid growth of Moscow were two in number—namely, the geographical position of the town and the genealogical position of its Prince. The first of these conditions entailed economic advantages which placed great material resources at the disposal of the Prince, while the second showed him how to make the most use of those resources, as well as helped him to elaborate an independent form of policy based, not upon ties and traditions of kindred, but upon skilful exploitation of opportunities. The fact that the Princes availed themselves of their resources and held fast to their policy when adopted enabled the Muscovite rulers of the fourteenth century and the first half of the fifteenth to achieve some important political results. They were as follows :—

I. *Extension of Muscovite Territory.*—Judicious use of the resources at their disposal enabled the Princes of Moscow gradually to extend their Principality far beyond its original narrow limits. At the opening of the fourteenth century Moscow was probably the most insignificant appanage in all Northern Rus, since its borders did not coincide even with those of the present-day government of Moscow, nor include, of the towns now comprised within that government, either Dmitrov, Klin, Volokolamsk, Mozhaisk, Serpukhov, Kolomna, or Verea. Indeed, before Daniel seized Mozhaisk and Kolomna, his appanage occupied only what now constitutes the middle portion of the government of Moscow. That is to say, it was limited to a strip which, following the course of the Middle Moskva and extending eastward along that of the Upper Kliazma, ended like a wedge between the two appanages of Dmitrov and Kolomna. Moreover, within that petty domain of Daniel's there stood only a couple of towns — Moscow and Svenigorod, since, as yet, Ruza and Radonetz seem to have been rural districts. Indeed, of the thirteen cantons composing the present government of Moscow, not more than four can have been included in Daniel's ancient territory — namely, those of Moscow, Svenigorod, Ruza, and Bogorod, as well as a portion of that of Dmitrov. Even when Ivan Kalita—the third Prince of Alexander Nevski's line — became Suzerain Prince, the appanage of Moscow still

remained an insignificant one.   In the first of Kalita's two wills (made in
in 1327) we find a list of his hereditary possessions, which consisted
merely of five or six towns and their districts—namely, the town-districts
of Moscow, Kolomna, Mozhaisk, Svenigorod, Serpukhov, Ruza, and
Radonetz (of which even the two last-named may then have been rural
districts only, not urban).   Of Periaslavl no mention whatever is made.
These town-districts comprised fifty-one rural communes and about forty
"court" villages.[1]   That comprised the whole of Kalita's possessions even
after he had become Suzerain Prince!   Nevertheless he had abundant material
resources at his disposal, and he made the most of them.   The then
onerous conditions of land tenure in Rus gradually compelled many proprietors to sell their hereditary estates, so that a long-continued glut in the
market ended by rendering land cheap.   Accordingly the Muscovite Prince
(who always had plenty of ready cash at his disposal) seized the opportunity
to buy up estates, both from private owners and from ecclesiastical institutions—from the Metropolitan, from monasteries, and from princes of other
appanages.   This purchasing of lands and villages in appanages other
than his own enabled Kalita to get three entire town-districts into his
possession—namely, those of Bieloe Ozero, Galitch, and Uglitch, although
for the time being he arranged to leave their heretofore rulers undisturbed.
The same process was continued by his successors, so that in each successive inventory of the Muscovite State we find districts and settlements
enumerated which have not figured in the preceding list.   Indeed, the
new acquisitions bob up in these documents in the most surprising
fashion, as though they were being forced to the surface by some ceaseless, unseen process which worked on no visible plan and seldom
disclosed the means by which the new additions were obtained.   For
instance, we read that Dmitri Donskoi acquired Medyn from *Smolensk*:
yet whence he also acquired Verea, Borovsk, Serpukhov, one half of
Volokolamsk, Kashira, and a score or so of settlements scattered over the
Suzerain Province of Vladimir and several other appanages, is left unspeci-
fied.   In the times of Kalita and his sons territorial acquisition was always
effected through private, friendly negotiation—usually purchase, but, later on,
that peaceful method became reinforced by seizure, with or without Mongol
assistance.   Thus Dmitri Donskoi seized Starodub on the Kliazma, Galitch,
and Dmitrov, and expelled therefrom the rightful princes, while his son
Vassilii "did induce" the Khan and his Murzas [2] "by gifts" to sell him,

---

[1] *i.e.* settlements of court slaves engaged in working lands directly exploited by the Prince.
See p. 261.   [2] Tartar nobles.

"for much gold and silver," a *yarlik* or firman making over to him Murom, Tarusa, and the whole of the principality of Nizhni Novgorod. That done, he either dislodged the rightful princes or returned them their *otchini* under certain contingent conditions of service. After the close of the fourteenth century, however, a definite plan—though possibly a self-originated one—becomes noticeable in the seemingly promiscuous, haphazard process of extending Muscovite territory. By seizing Mozhaisk and Kolomna the Muscovite Prince got the whole course of the Moskva into his hands, while subsequent seizure of the Suzerain Province of Vladimir, and next of Starodub, gave him the command also of the whole course of the Kliazma. Next, the acquisition of Kaluga and Meshtera by Donskoi, and of Kozelsk, Lichvin, Alexin, Tarusa, Murom, and Nizhni Novgorod by his son, placed all those portions of the Oka between its junction with the Upa and Kolomna and between Gorodetz and Nizhni Novgorod under Muscovite rule, so that the principality of Riazan soon found itself enclosed on three sides by the combined provinces of Moscow and Vladimir (the latter Muscovite from the time of Kalita onwards). Similarly, the acquisition of Rshev, Uglitch, and Nizhni Novgorod by the same princes and of Romanov by Vassilii the Dark combined with the permanent possession of Kostroma (now an appendage of the Suzerain Province of Vladimir) to make the greater part of the Upper Volga Muscovite property, as well as to cause the principalities of Tver and Yaroslavl to become almost entirely enclosed by Muscovite land. This would seem to show that the Princes of Moscow sought, first and foremost, to get hold of the chief river-ways, inner and outer, of the Mezhduriechïe. Finally, the acquisition of the two principalities of Bieloe Ozero and Galitch opened up a broad field for Muscovite agrarian enterprise in the regions beyond the Upper Volga. There the Muscovite Prince of the day found his task an easy one. The wide, secluded stretches of forest which covered the basins of the Sheksna and Upper Sukhona and the banks of the rivers discharging into Lakes Bieloe and Kubin were at that time (the early fifteenth century) divided among the numerous princes of Bieloe Ozero and Yaroslavl. Weak and impoverished as they were, as well as growing ever more so through frequent subdivision of their *otchini* and through Tartar exactions (so much so, indeed, that sometimes four or five princes would share a single township, or even a single rural district), they were in no position to maintain either the governmental rights or the governmental establishment of an appanage prince, and so gradually descended to the level of small private landowners. To get them under his thumb the Muscovite Prince needed neither an armed force nor money, since they soon made voluntary submission to him, and, like the princes of Murom, Tarusa, and Nizhni Novgorod, had their appanages restored to them under certain contingent conditions. Vassilii the Dark acted similarly with the *otchini* belonging to the princes of Zaozersk, Kubin, and Bochtuza.

Extension of Muscovite territory in this direction was largely assisted by the popular movement which now set in. The increasing strength of Moscow had caused the region of the Upper Volga gradually to become more secure from attack, both on the Novgorodian side and on the Mongolian. This enabled the pent-up surplus of population in the Mezhduriechïe to begin to discharge itself across the Volga into the wide forest spaces of the Trans-Volgan territories. To this movement missionaries from the central monasteries—notably from the Troitski Monastery of St. Sergius—acted as an advance guard. Penetrating into the wooded fastnesses of Kostroma and Vologda, they settled along the banks of the Komela, Obnor, Polshma, Avnega, and Glushitsa, and founded there cloisters which became rallying points for the immigrant settlers. In a few years' time, indeed, there had arisen on each of those rivers a province of similar name, in which stood many scores of settlements. The fact of these provinces being settled by emigrants from the region around Moscow entitled the Muscovite Prince to look upon them as his own, especially since he already shared Vologda with the Novgorodians, as well as had an undoubted right to Kostroma by virtue of his Suzerain Princeship.

Thus there were five principal methods employed by the Muscovite Princes for the extension of their dominions—namely, purchase, seizure by armed force, diplomatic acquisition (with or without Mongol assistance), treaty with princes of appanages on the basis of contingent service, and colonisation. The will of Vassilii the Dark (executed about 1462) shows us the fruits of a century-and-a-half's sustained effort on the part of the rulers of Moscow. In that document we see the Muscovite domains, whether original settlements or newer acquisitions, figuring, for the first time, as a single Suzerain Principality, and only a few fragments of Tver and Yaroslavl, with half of Rostov (the other half had been purchased by Vassilii the Dark), remaining as non-Muscovite portions of the Mezhduriechïe. Indeed, Muscovite territory now extended far beyond the limits of the Mezhduriechïe, since, southwards, it ran with the course of the Upper Oka, while, northwards, it reached to Ustiug—which first became Muscovite property at the close of the fourteenth century. Thus, while Daniel's original appanage cannot have comprised, at the most, more than five hundred square miles (the present government of Moscow covers about five hundred and ninety), a sketch of Muscovite territory as we find it defined in the will of Vassilii the Dark would show us that that territory would need to be reckoned at about *fifteen thousand* square miles. Such were the territorial acquisitions of the Muscovite Princes—the acquisitions which, by the middle of the fifteenth century, had given Moscow an immense preponderance over all the rest of Rus.

II. *Acquisition of the Suzerain Throne.*—Availing themselves of their resources, and pursuing a connected policy, the rulers of Moscow gradually emerged, during the fourteenth century, from their original position of rightless princes. Though juniors of the princely stock, they were wealthy, and so did not hesitate to challenge their senior relatives for the Suzerain throne, for which their principal rivals were the Princes of Tver. For a long time those of Moscow, though representing might against right, were unsuccessful in the struggle, which began with Yuri of Moscow defeating his uncle Michael of Tver, and then being defeated by Michael's son. Nevertheless the final victory was bound to fall to Moscow, since the resources of the two contending parties were unequally matched. To the personal valour and right of seniority possessed by the Princes of Tver the Muscovite Princes could oppose money and the wit to make the most of their opportunities. In other words, resources moral and juridical had to give way to resources material and practical. Never at any time, indeed, did the Princes of Tver possess the gift of grasping the true state of affairs at a given juncture. For instance, at the opening of the fourteenth century we find Alexander of Tver—another son of the Michael above-mentioned—conceiving resistance to the Tartars to be still possible, and exhorting his fellow princes of Rus "to stand as friend beside friend and brother beside brother, nor to yield unto the Tartars, but to withstand them, and to defend the Russian land and all Orthodox Christians." At the time that he sent this message he was in hiding at Pskov, after being goaded by Tartar exactions to join his citizens (of Tver) in massacring some Mongol emissaries who had arrived in the city on a mission. The Muscovite Princes, however, looked at things differently. They never dreamt of resisting the Tartars, since they perceived that the Horde could more easily be dealt with by "peaceful cunning"—*i.e.* by complaisance and money—than by force of arms. Consequently they paid assiduous court to the Khan, and made him the instrument of their schemes. No prince more often went to pay his respects to the Mongol potentate than did Ivan Kalita, nor was he ever aught but a welcome guest on his arrival, seeing that he took care never to come empty-handed. Already it was an accepted axiom among the Tartars that a visit from the Muscovite Prince meant "much gold and silver" for the Khan, for his favourites, and for his leading Murzas. In fact, it was through such subserviency that the Prince of Moscow, though the genealogical junior of his brother princes, at length acquired the Suzerain throne of Rus. The Khan entrusted Kalita with the chastisement of Tver for certain resistance, and Kalita executed the commission with such thoroughness that he and his Tartar force laid the entire principality in ruins. "To speak in simple words," adds the Chronicle, "they did make all the Russian land desolate"—though, of course, leaving Moscow untouched. In return for this service Kalita received the Suzerain throne of Rus, which from that date onwards (1328) never again passed out of the hands of the Prince of Moscow.

III. *Arrest of the Tartar Raids and Formation of a Union of Princes.* —The acquisition of the Suzerain throne by Moscow was attended by two very important results for Rus; one of which we might call the *moral* result and the other the *political* result. The *moral* result lay in the fact that, once become Suzerain, the Prince of Moscow was able to effect a deliverance of the Russian population from that torpor and dejection into which it had become plunged by its external misfortunes. A model organiser who knew how to enforce peace and security in his dominions, the Muscovite Prince lost no time in taking advantage of his Suzerain status to make the advantages of his policy felt elsewhere in North-Eastern Rus: by which means he laid up for himself widespread popularity—and therefore ground for further achievements. The Chronicle tells us that, from the moment when the Prince of Moscow obtained the Suzerainty from the Khan, Northern Rus began to be relieved of the Tartar raids which had hitherto been its constant lot. Again, in speaking of Kalita's return from his profitable visit to the Khan in 1328, the Chronicle adds: "Thenceforth there was great quietness for forty years, and the conquests of the Russian land by the Tartars did cease." Clearly these were the words of an observer living in the latter half of the fourteenth century—of an observer who, glancing back over the last forty years, was fain to remark the extent to which Muscovite rule had made itself felt in Northern Rus during the four decades reviewed, and to decide that for the period of rest thus accorded Rus between the years

1328 and 1368 (the latter the date of Olgerd's first attack upon Rus) the Russian population had Moscow to thank. Moreover, those forty years of peace allowed time for two whole generations to be born and grow up whose nerves had not been inoculated with that unreasoning terror of the Tartar with which their fathers and grandfathers had been filled—generations which went out boldly to the field of Kulikovo.

As for the *political* result of the acquisition of the Suzerain throne by Moscow, it lay in the fact that, once become Suzerain, the Muscovite Prince was able to begin an emancipation of Northern Rus from the condition of political disintegration into which the country had fallen through the appanage system. Hitherto, though kinsmen, the appanage princes had remained solitary, mutually estranged rulers, but afterwards, during the times of the Suzerain Princes Dmitri and Andrew (elder sons of Alexander Nevski), certain alliances became formed among the appanage princes against both the one and the other of these Suzerains, while princely councils also began to be held for the decision of disputed matters. Nevertheless, these alliances were mere haphazard, passing attempts to re-establish unity of kindred and rule, and, inasmuch as they were always directed against the Suzerain Prince—who, as theoretical "father," was supposed to unite his juniors—they weakened rather than strengthened the blood tie among Vsevolod's posterity. On the death of Kalita a union of princes became formed on more lasting foundations, and was directed by the Suzerain Prince in person. At first it was a union of finance only. After their conquest of Rus the Tartars were at first accustomed to collect their exactions themselves, for which purpose they thrice during the first thirty-five years of their supremacy made a *tchislo* or numbering of the Russian people (the clergy alone excepted) through the agency of Mongol *tchislenniki* or census-takers; but in later days, the Khans began to entrust the collection of the "*ordinski vichod*" or "Tartar impost" to the Russian Suzerain Prince—the first such princely commissioner being Daniel's son Ivan, and from that time onwards the duty of gathering in the *vichod* and transmitting it to the Khan became, in the hands of successive Suzerain Princes, a potent instrument for the reunification of the appanages. If unable or unwilling to castigate a junior with the sword, the Suzerain of Moscow could now castigate him with the rouble. Thus the union of princes, originally only one of finance, assumed a wider basis, and acquired political significance, while from simple tax-gatherer on behalf of the Khan the Prince of Moscow became the Khan's plenipotentiary as regards the direction and judicial regulation of the Russian princes. The Chronicle tells us that when Kalita died in 1341, and his sons went to pay their respects to the Khan Uzbek, they were received by the latter with great honour and friendliness, by reason of the respect and affection which he had borne their father, and granted an assurance that the Suzerain throne of Rus should pass to Moscow above all other claimants. The eldest son, Simeon, therefore, was nominated to the office, as well as had placed " under his hand " the whole body of appanage princes; the Chronicle going on to state that "all the Princes of Riazan and Rostov—nay, even those of Tver—were so obedient unto him that they did perform everything accord- ing to his word." Simeon, for his part, knew how to make the most of his position, as well as how to make the other princes conscious of it—as his nickname of Gordii or "the Proud" testifies. On his death in 1353, his brother and successor, Ivan, acquired from the Khan a further addition to his Suzerainty in the shape of *judicial* authority over the princes of Northern Rus, whom the Khan enjoined to obey him and to be judged by him in all things, but, in case of dispute, to lodge an appeal with himself. During the time of Ivan's son, Dmitri, the union of princes under Moscow—a union ready at any moment to become converted into a Mus- covite hegemony over the other princes—became still further widened and strengthened, until it had acquired a national significance. In the same Prince's time the struggle was renewed between Moscow and Tver, and inasmuch as Michael Alexandrovitch, Prince of Tver, resorted for help both to Lithuania and the Tartars, he completely destroyed the popularity which the Princes of Tver had hitherto enjoyed among the population of Northern Rus. Accordingly, when, in 1375, the Muscovite Prince again took the field against Michael's principality, no fewer than nineteen other princes joined his standard. True, many of those princes were either old-established or recent dependents of Moscow, yet there can be no doubt that others of them acted out of purely patriotic motives; the reason of their enmity against Michael being that he had more than once sought to incite Lithuania—Lithuania the oppressor of Orthodox Russian Christians—against Rus, as well as had actually united himself with the pagan Khan Mamai. Finally, the whole of Northern Rus took its stand with Moscow on the Kulikovo Polé, and, under the Muscovite standard, gained its first victory over the Tartars. This invested the Prince of Moscow with the significance of *national leader* of Northern Rus in its struggles with external foes, so that the Golden Horde actually became the blind instrument which created the Russian political and popular forces which were arrayed against itself.

IV. *Removal of the Metropolitan Cathedra to Moscow.*—This was the supremely important political achievement of the Muscovite Prince—an achievement to which the geographical position of the city once more contributed. Tartar incursions had laid Kievan Rus in ruins—had done so, in fact, by the middle of the twelfth century, and the flight of the Kievan population northwards had carried with it the supreme dignitary of the Russian Church, the Metropolitan of Kiev. This we know from the Chronicle, which tells us that in 1299 the then occupant of the *cathedra*, Maximus, became so alarmed at the violence of the Tartars that, leaving Kiev with all his train, he withdrew to Vladimir on the Kliazma. "Thereupon," adds the Chronicle, "all the city of Kiev did flee also" (meaning thereby its inhabitants). Yet the disturbed state of the times rendered care of the South Russian pastorate as necessary as ever, or even more so, so that the Metropolitan had to make frequent journeys to the southward to visit his Kievan bishoprics. During those expeditions he was accustomed to halt at the half-way city of Moscow, for an old biography of Maximus' successor, Peter, informs us that, "when travelling to and fro in Rus and passing by many towns and places, he did often halt and make a long sojourn in Moscow." This gave rise to close friendship between Peter and Ivan Kalita, who, even in the time of his elder brother Yuri, was frequently vice-governor of Moscow during that brother's absence. These two—Peter and Kalita—joined together in founding the Usspenski Sobor, or Cathedral of the Assumption, in Moscow—though whether with an idea already forming in the mind of the churchman of one day removing the Metropolitan *cathedra* from the banks of the Kliazma to those of the Moskva is not certain. Moscow formed part of the see of Vladimir, of which the archiepiscopate had become merged in the office of Metropolitan since the transference of the ecclesiastical headquarters from Kiev. At first, when visiting Moscow, Peter used to stay with Kalita, though maintaining his own permanent residence[1] at Vladimir, but, later on, he moved into a hospice near the site where shortly afterwards the Usspenski Cathedral was founded. Now, it so happened that it was during one of his sojourns in Moscow that Peter died (in 1326), and the circumstance was interpreted by subsequent Metropolitans as a sign. His successor, Theognostes, had already taken a dislike to Vladimir, and therefore lost no time in establishing himself permanently in the new hospice built beside the miraculous tomb attached to the Usspenski Cathedral in Moscow. Thus the latter city became the ecclesiastical capital of Rus long before it became the political

---

[1] Dolgoruki's old palace,

capital. The threads of church life which radiated far and wide over the Russian land from the Metropolitan *cathedra* now began to draw the various portions of the country towards Moscow, while the abundant material wealth in the hands of the Church also tended to gravitate towards the city, and so contributed to its enrichment.   Even more important was the *moral impression* produced upon the population of North Rus by this translation of the Metropolitan *cathedra*, since the people now treated the Prince of Moscow with a respect commensurate with the supposition that all he did was done with the sanction of the head of the Russian Church.   A trace of this popular impression is to be seen in the remark of the Chronicle *apropos* of the translation of the *cathedra* : " Many others of the princes would have been right glad if haply they could have had the Metropolitan of Moscow dwelling in their midst."   In annals of a later date this impression is still more noticeable.   The Metropolitan Peter may be said to have died a martyr for his country, since he undertook many a journey to the Horde on behalf of his flock, and suffered many a hardship in ministering to its needs.   The Russian Church, therefore, added him to the roll of our patron saints, and the fourteenth century had not closed before the Russian people had begun to invoke his name in prayer.   Now, in a biography of the holy man, compiled by his friend and contemporary, Prochorus, Bishop of Rostov, we find given, in brief and simple language, an account of Peter's death at Moscow *during the temporary absence of* his friend Ivan Kalita : yet we also find that at the close of the fourteenth century or at the beginning of the fifteenth one of Peter's successors, the Serb Cyprian, wrote a rather more florid biography of the Saint, in which an altogether different account is given of the latter's decease.   This version says that Peter died *in the presence of* Ivan Kalita, and that before his death he earnestly charged the Prince to complete the building of the Cathedral of the Assumption which they had jointly founded—uttering at the same time the following prophecy : " My son, if thou shouldst hearken unto me, and shouldst build the Church of the Holy Mother, and shouldst lay me to rest in thy city, then of a surety wilt thou be glorified above all other princes in the land, and thy sons and thy grandsons also, and this city will itself be glorified above all other Russian towns, and the Saints will come and dwell in it, and its hands will prevail against the breasts of its enemies.   Thus will it ever be so long as my bones shall lie therein."   This episode, though apparently unknown to Prochorus, was evidently borrowed by Cyprian from popular legend compounded under the influence of the events of the fourteenth century, and affords evidence of the sympathetic relations into which the ecclesiastical community had now entered with the Muscovite Prince in consequence of his intimacy with the head of the Russian Church. Probably it was these sympathetic relations which helped, more than anything else, to consolidate the national and moral position of the Prince of Moscow in Northern Rus.

Traces of cordial relations between Church and State are to be found also in another, though somewhat later, work. About the middle of the fifteenth century the monk Paphnuti Borovski—one of the strongest and most original characters known to us in ancient Rus—began an active Christian work in the monastery which he had founded. This good man used to be fond of telling his pupils all that he had seen and heard during his lifetime, and these stories of his, taken down by his auditors, have descended also to us. Among other things, he used to relate how, in 1427, a great pestilence swept the country, in which people died of "an aching sore." Probably it was the black death. Now, a certain nun (he used to say) died of the disease, but came to life again, and recounted whom she had seen in Paradise and whom in Hell: and whatsoever she reported of those persons was found, on reference to their previous earthly lives, to have been true. Among other people whom she met in Paradise was Ivan Kalita—doubtless sent thither (so Paphnuti used to add) because of his charity, since on earth he had always carried a purse (*kalita*) at his girdle from which to give alms to any beggar who stretched out his hand for them.[1] One day, however (so Paphnuti would continue), a beggar approached the Prince, and received from him a dole. The beggar approached him a second time, and received from him a second dole. Thereupon the beggar could not refrain from approaching him yet a third time, and although he duly received a third dole, it was accompanied by the furious words: "Here, take it, thou never-satisfied one!" "Nay, but it is thou thyself that art the never-satisfied one," retorted the beggar; "seeing that thou rulest in this world, yet dost desire to rule also in the world to come." This was merely faint praise put in a rather rude form. What the beggar meant to say was that the Prince's charity and kindness to the poor were chiefly designed to win for him the kingdom of heaven. "It is manifest, therefore," Paphnuti used to comment, "that the beggar was sent of God to try the Prince, and to show him that whatsoever be done for God should be done again,

1 Possibly later generations invested with a kindly significance a nickname which had been given to the Prince by his contemporaries only in irony.

and yet again." Now, another personage whom the nun met in the next world—this time in Hell—was (so said Paphnuti) the Lithuanian Prince Vitovt, whom she saw as a gigantic man into whose mouth a fearsome black devil kept stuffing red-hot ducats with a pair of tongs and repeating : "There, take thy fill, thou villain!" The naïve humour of these stories leaves us in no doubt as to their popular origin. Nor must the student be dismayed at their chronology, nor boggle over the statement that the nun met Vitovt in Hell in 1427 when he only died in 1430. Popular legend has its own chronology and pragmatics, its own conception of historical phenomena. In this case legend forgot chronology in its desire to draw a contrast between the Lithuanian Prince, the foe of Rus and Orthodoxy, and Ivan Kalita, the friend of his poorer and humbler brethren —and that although Kalita was the *great-grandfather* of the Prince (Vassilii Dmitrievitch) who actually repelled the terrible onslaught of the Lithuanian ruler upon Orthodox Rus. That the popular mind noted the close relations existing between the two principal powers in the State, the princely and the ecclesiastical, is shown still further by another of Paphnuti's brief, but expressive, stories—a tale in which those two powers are embodied in the persons of Ivan Kalita and St. Peter of Moscow respectively. Once upon a time Kalita saw in a dream a lofty hill covered with snow. Presently the snow melted away, and the hill itself disappeared. Kalita went to St. Peter and asked him to interpret the dream. "The hill," replied the Saint, "was thyself, O Prince, and the snow upon it was I, the old man. The vision signified that I shall die before thee." The strong ecclesiastical colouring with which these stories are tinged affords evidence that the clergy, as well as the popular mind, had a hand in their com- position, and that the political achievements of the Muscovite Princes were hallowed in the popular imagination by the supposed co-operation and blessing accorded to them by the supreme ecclesiastical authority in Rus. Thanks to this popular idea, those achievements, though not always accomplished by the cleanest of methods, became permanent assets of the Muscovite ruler.

Combining the various factors described, we are now in a position to form an idea of the relations which became established during the fourteenth century between the population of Northern Rus and the Prince and Principality of Moscow. Events of the century in question caused that population to take three separate views of the Muscovite ruler and his domain. In the first place, the people came to look upon the Prince as a model steward and administrator, as well as a man capable of maintaining territorial peace and civil order in his dominions, and upon his Principality as the source whence a new system of territorial relations originated of which the first outcome was the establishment of absolute internal and external security. In the second place, the people looked upon the Muscovite Prince as their popular leader in the struggles of Rus with external foes, and upon Moscow as the source of the first popular victories gained over the treacherous Lithuanians and the " raw-flesh-eating " Tartars. Lastly, Northern Rus saw in the Muscovite Prince the "eldest son " of the Russian Church—the closest friend and coadjutor of the supreme Russian hierarch, and in Moscow the city upon which rested the special blessing of the first saint in the Russian calendar—the city which had bound up with it all the moral and religious interests of Orthodox Russian Christians. Such, at the middle of the fifteenth century, was the status finally acquired by the ruler who, but a century and a half ago, had begun his career as a petty robber waiting to despoil his neighbours from the vantage-ground of a petty corner of Rus.

CHAPTER XVIII

Mutual relations of the Muscovite Princes—System of Muscovite succession—Absence of any
juridical distinction between moveable and immoveable property in appanages—Relation
of the system of Muscovite princely succession to the juridical custom of ancient Rus—
Relations of the Muscovite Princes with regard to kinship and rule—Rise in importance
of the senior inheritor—Forms of subordination of appanage princes to their Suzerain—
Influence of the Tartar yoke upon the relations of the Princes—Establishment of succession of the Suzerain power in the direct descending line—Coincidence of the
family aims of the Muscovite Princes with the popular needs of Great Rus—Importance
of the Muscovite feud under Vasilii the Dark—Character of the Muscovite Princes.

WE have now studied the territorial acquisitions of Moscow during the
fourteenth century and the first half of the fifteenth, as well as the national
and political status of the Muscovite Princes during the same period. Yet
that extension of Muscovite territory and Muscovite influence was only
one of the processes through which the greatness of Moscow was created,
for with it went the political advancement of one of its princes—of the
prince who, bearing the title of Suzerain, was looked upon as the senior of
the Muscovite princely family. While the Principality of Moscow was
absorbing into itself the various disjointed portions of the Russian land,
the actually or theoretically senior prince was collecting into his hands the
various scattered elements of the supreme power : and just as the former
process converted the Principality of Moscow into a national Russian state,
so the result of the latter process was to convert the Suzerain Prince of
Moscow—senior only by title over the other appanage princes—into an
autocratic Russian sovereign. While Moscow was emerging from obscurity
and swallowing up the other Russian principalities, its ruler was attaining
the point of placing in subjection to himself all his fellow-princes of the
Muscovite appanages. Such subjection was rendered possible by the fact
that the external achievements of the Principality of Moscow had added
by far the largest share of territory to the Suzerain Prince, seeing that,
among other things, they had united the Suzerain Province of Vladimir to
his original appanage of Moscow. It is this second process—the process
envisaging the *internal* political achievements of the Muscovite Principality—that we now have to study. To understand it the better, let us

once more picture to ourselves the system of princely rule then operative in Moscow and the other principalities of Rus.

Although we can trace the rise of the Principality of Moscow first and foremost to the policy of its Suzerain Prince, he was not the *only*, merely the *senior*, Muscovite Prince. The *otchina* of Daniel's posterity was not a solid, homogeneous unit of rule, but, like the *otchini* of the other princely lines, a group of independent appanages. At the time when Moscow began to play its unificatory part, the old appanage relations still held good among the Muscovite princely family. In proportion, however, as the dominions and external importance of Moscow increased, the internal relations subsisting between the Suzerain Prince and his junior kinsmen of the other appanages underwent a change—a change all in favour of the former. To study thoroughly the course of that change let us examine, first of all, the system of succession operative among the Muscovite princely family up to the middle of the fifteenth century, and thereafter the mutual relations which obtained among the various co-inheritors with regard to rule.

The system of succession operative among the Muscovite Princes during the fourteenth and fifteenth centuries can be gathered from the long series of their wills which has come down to us. Beginning with Kalita, and ending with Ivan III., almost every Muscovite ruler left such a will behind him—some of them two or three, so that for the period now under study we have at our disposal no fewer than sixteen. This affords us ample material for studying the system of princely succession which obtained in Moscow. Indeed, the very existence of those wills adumbrates the character of the system. Methods of succession ordinarily number two—namely, succession by law or custom, and succession through bequeathal. The former of those methods is based upon rules establishing a uniform, obligatory transference of property irrespective of the personal views of the testator, or even against his wishes. Since, then, the princely wills above-mentioned show us that, in every instance, Muscovite succession was determined by *bequeathal*, it follows either that no rules of law or custom on the subject then existed, or that new rules contravening such law or custom had become established. Thus the juridical basis of the system of succession which obtained among the Princes of Moscow was the *personal will* of the testator, even as it was also among the other lines of Vsevolod's house. This basis fully harmonises with the juridical character of appanage rule, since that rule rested, as we know, upon the idea of a prince's appanage being the personal property of its ruler. Inasmuch, then, as the prince was the sole personal proprietor of the appanage which he governed, succession thereto could be determined only by his personal wishes. Nevertheless the system was applied only to the *original* common *otchina* of the Muscovite Princes, as well as to such later territorial acquisitions as had become divided up into appanages. That is to say, it was not applied either to the Trans-Volgan colonies or to the Suzerain Province of Vladimir, which latter old custom had always assigned to the senior prince, who now was he whom the Khan chose to recognise as such. The princely wills above-mentioned show us that the sons of the testator ranked first as inheritors, then his brothers, and finally his wife—whether alone, or with daughters, or with the sons and brothers of the testator. Ivan Kalita, for example, divided his *otchina* into four parts, of which he left one to each of his three sons and the fourth to his second wife and her daughters—one of which latter, when the mother died, assumed possession of the mother's share of the common appanage. Again, Kalita's son Simeon, who died childless, passed over his brothers, and bequeathed his appanage intact to his wife. In fact, these wills furnish us with frequent instances of widows of princes partaking in the succession, though not in quite the same manner as the more direct heirs, since they received from the testators, their husbands, *two* species of property—namely, *oprichnini*, or possessions absolutely their own, and *prozhitki*, or possessions to be held for life only. This frequent participation of princes' widows in the succession constituted the second feature in which the system harmonised with the juridical character of appanage rule, since appanage rule was synonymous with personal ownership of the territory governed. This private-proprietorial character of appanage tenure can be seen from the manner in which a prince apportioned his various properties when making his will. The *otchina* of the testator was never divided up into compact allotments, but, on the contrary, subjected to a curious process of disintegration into strips. The Principality of Moscow was composed of four different classes or sections of property—sections which differed from one another either in their productive value or in their historical origin. In Dmitri Donskoi's will we find these several classes or sections set down in the following order: (1) the township of Moscow, court lands attached to the same, and court lands situated in appanages other than the appanage of Moscow, as well as in the province of Vladimir; (2) other towns and rural districts in Muscovite territory; (3) the old original lands of Moscow; and (4) the newer, extra-Muscovite territorial acquisitions. Of each of these several classes of property each heir was allotted a portion, as he was also in each several class of the moveable property of the testator.   Each son, for instance, received a cap, a fur coat, a *kaftan*, and a girdle from his father's domestic effects, in the same way that each inheritor, male or female, received a portion respectively of the township of Moscow, of the court lands belonging to the same, of the original Muscovite territories, and of the newer acquisitions.   Thus the Muscovite dominions came to be greatly cut up into strips.   This uniform method of apportioning both moveable and immoveable property constituted the third feature wherein these princely wills harmonised with the juridical character of appanage rule. The testator seems to have divided his possessions into the various classes specified less out of considerations of state than out of considerations of agrarian utility—less in the interests of society at large than in those of his family alone.   He looked upon his domain merely as an article of property, and not as a community to be governed by him for the public weal.   Moreover, the very form of these wills approximates closely to that of private wills of the same period.   Take, for example, the will of the second Suzerain Prince, Ivan Kalita, which was executed about 1327 at a time when he was preparing to lead an expedition against the Horde. It begins thus : " In the name of the Father and of the Son and of the Holy Ghost.   I, the sinful, miserable servant of God, Ivan, do write this my Testament before setting forth against the Horde, and do declare that I am constrained to do so by no man, and that I am of whole mind and in the possession of my corporal faculties.   Before God who judgeth of my life I do hereby make bequest unto my Sons and to the Princess.   To my Sons I do bequeath my *otchina* of Moscow, together with what share apart I have already unto them committed." [1]   Upon that follows a list of the towns, villages, and districts which were to constitute the appanage of each son.   Moreover, just as the wills of private persons were executed in the presence of witnesses, and confirmed by the authority of the Church, so the wills of the Muscovite Princes were written in the presence of "*posluchi*" [2] (usually some of the attendant boyars), and signed by the Metropolitan of Moscow.   Thus the fundamental features of the system of succession observed among the Muscovite Princes were (1) the personal wishes of the testator as the sole basis of the system, (2) the participation of *all* the members of the testator's family in the succession (including even his wife and daughters), and (3) the absence of any visible

[1] *i.e.* " To all my sons *jointly* do I bequeath the township of Moscow, over and above whatsoever I do bequeath unto them *severally*."

[2] Literally, ear-witnesses.

juridical distinction between moveable and immoveable property—between domestic effects and territorial possessions.

Consideration of these three fundamental features of the system might lead some to suppose that the third and last of them indicates bluntness of the social sense during this period. Yet we must look with extreme caution at the documents in question if we wish to avoid falling into error as to the intelligence of those who executed them. Even the earliest of those testators—Kalita—understood that possession of Moscow and its population was not the same thing as possession of a coffer and its contents. To us the comprehension of such a fact seems such an essentially simple matter that to deny it to any one else, even to persons of the fourteenth century, would appear out of the question. Kalita distinguished clearly between himself as proprietor and himself as sovereign—between himself as landlord and himself as ruler. Although he accounted the soil of Moscow, together with the right of erecting buildings on it, of exploiting it through trade and industry, and of taking tolls therefrom, as so much personal property of his own, so that he disposed of those assets in his wills much as he did of his clothing and silver-ware, he none the less realised that he was also judge and executioner of the inhabitants of Moscow, whose suits he had to decide, to whom he had to issue statutes for the preservation of social order, and upon whom it was his to impose taxes for the public needs, as well as that all those duties arose, not out of his proprietorship, but out of his office of ruler sent by God " to restrain his people from untoward habit." [1] For that reason, therefore, Kalita omitted from his wills all reference to his rights as *ruler*, seeing that those wills were *private testamentary dispositions* only, and not territorial ordinances. For the same reason, also, it is not until Dmitri Donskoi and his successors had begun to assume rights of *otchina* (in addition, that is to say, to rights of *rule*) over the Suzerain Province of Vladimir that that portion of the Muscovite domains begins to figure in the wills of the Muscovite Princes. Personal effects, as well as the use and ownership of them, were bequeathable, but not persons, nor yet communities or political unions, which, even in those days, were distinct from proprietary articles. There are two reasons, however, why examination of the wills of the Princes leads us to regard those rulers as sovereigns in the essential sense of the word. In the first place, the area of the Principality of Moscow ranked as

---

[1] This is a phrase used at a later date by the Abbot Cyril of Bieloe Ozero, in a letter which he wrote to one of the Muscovite appanage princes.

their personal *otchina*, and not as territory of state; and in the second place the Prince's rights of rule which jointly went to make up the supreme power could be divided or alienated by will equally with the *otchina*, just as also could material effects. The Princes were not lacking in state ideas, but their state ideas had not yet assumed forms and modes of action corresponding to their nature. Thus the absence from these wills of any distinction between moveable and immoveable property is not so much indicative of the social sense of the Princes as of their governmental customs, which had not yet rid themselves of that confusion between ownership and rule which was, above all things, the distinguishing feature of the appanage system.

Since, then, the private proprietor overshadowed the ruler in the Muscovite Prince of the fourteenth and fifteenth centuries, we might naturally ask: "What was the relation of the system of succession established by the wills of the Princes to the juridical custom operative in the private social life of ancient Rus in her citizen grades? This we could have estimated best by reference to cases of ordinary legal succession in the princely house of the period, had there been any such cases extant of which the details were set forth with sufficient clearness: but unfortunately there are none. In the princely wills at our disposal we meet both with agreements with and with departures from old juridical custom. On the one hand, we find that, over and above property bequeathed to them by their husbands, widows of princes received, for their lifetime, the use of certain portions of their sons' appanages—an arrangement in full accordance with the *Russkaia Pravda*, wherein it was enacted that "widows shall receive of their sons a portion " (the words " for life," of course, being understood), and that of such property as should come to a widow from her husband she should be "*hospozha*"—*i.e.* full mistress. Again, these Muscovite wills furnish not a single instance of brothers succeeding in the presence of sons—which also was in accordance with old Russian custom, whereby collateral heirs were considered inadmissible where direct heirs were extant. On the other hand, these wills furnish us with more than one instance of wives and daughters participating in the succession (sometimes with absolute proprietorial rights) where nevertheless there were sons and brothers of the testator extant: which, of course, was flat contrary to old Russian custom. This shows that the system of testamentary succession observed among the Muscovite Princes was not on all fours with *legal* succession. Possibly that fact is explainable on the ground of family considerations—of such considerations as prompted the Muscovite Princes to contravene the appanage principle of strict individualism of rule by bequeathing the township of Moscow to *all* the sons of the princely family, instead of to the eldest son only, though at the same time keeping their individual shares apart. In all probability this was done because, in view of the general tendency of appanage princes to shut themselves up and become estranged from one another, the fathers desired that their sons should meet more frequently in the family nest and beside the tombs of their parents, and not forget that they were children of one father and one mother.

Next let us see what relations became established between the various princely inheritors after that they had entered into possession of their several portions of the paternal *otchina*. Those relations can best be studied from the treaties between appanage princes which have come down to us (to the number of several scores) from the fourteenth and fifteenth centuries. According to those treaties, each princely co-inheritor became absolute owner of the appanage allotted to him—he ruling it independently, as his father had done the common *otchina* before him. As a formula expressive of that independence we have the words of Dmitri Donskoi in the treaty which he made with his cousin Vladimir of Serpukhov in 1388 : "Thou shalt know[1] thine own *otchina*, and I will know mine." This formula constituted the whole basis of the relations of rule observed among themselves by the princely co-inheritors. Each Prince was bound to refrain from meddling in the affairs of other appanages, as well as from acquiring land in an appanage not his own, nor even passing through any part of such an appanage, without first obtaining the permission of its owner and ruler. Nevertheless, the system by which *otchini* were allotted often combined with the facilities always at the disposal of the princes for acquiring land to cause a prince to become the owner of villages and settlements in an appanage not his own. Such properties then had, as it were, two proprietors—a territorial and a personal, and their position was defined in a clause in inter-princely treaties which bears all the appearance of having been the stereotyped rule. This clause stipulates that properties of this kind should be judicially subject to, and pay direct land tax to, the local territorial ruler in whose appanage they were situated, and not to their *actual* proprietor, whose income from them was to be limited to private *obroki* or dues. At the same time, this clause allowed of exceptions, since there were cases in which princely lands situated in a

[1] *i.e.* keep to.

"strange" appanage paid land-tax to the local territorial ruler, but, as regards judicial administration, were subject oniy to their *de facto* proprietor. Thus each appanage prince was the independent owner of his own appanage.

At the same time, it will readily be understood that the appanage princes of a given line could not well be rulers wholly estranged from one another, seeing that they were also near kinsmen—usually brothers and cousins, or an uncle and nephews. Consequently, nearness of kinship tended to establish among them certain involuntary ties, and in obedience to this force they usually bound themselves in their mutual treaties "to be the one for the other for life." The father's will, also (as we have seen), constituted the eldest son the guardian "before God" of his juniors, and required the younger appanage princes to bind themselves to respect him as a father, while the senior brother, in his turn, was required to bind himself to maintain his juniors in the brotherhood, to see that they sustained no wrong, and to take care of their children if the latter should become orphaned. The status of the widow-mother in the family also acquired great importance through the supersession of clan relations by those of the family: wherefore testators instructed their children to obey her in all things, to contravene her will in nothing, and to honour her as a father. Yet it is plain that these relations were relations of kinship rather than of rule—moral covenants or pious promises rather than actual political obligations; and although, in the same way, kinship tended to form proprietorial relations, so that the life property of the widow-mother passed, at death, to her sons or grandsons, while mothers-in-law usually bequeathed their *oprichnini*[1] to their daughters-in-law, and mothers theirs to their sons, and so on, these also were none the less private, civil, non-obligatory relations. The question, then, arises: Did any *obligatory* relations exist with regard to rule—any relations partaking of the direct nature of political ties? The princely treaties of the fourteenth century and early half of the fifteenth show us that the senior Suzerain Prince (for there was now more than one in Rus) no longer possessed, through the mere fact of his seniority, any permanent, binding authority over his junior kinsfolk, and so had no power to "apportion" or to "adjudge" them unless they were his own sons. As already said, there was now more than one Suzerain Prince in the land, since the growth of the appanage system of rule had caused the office to become divided. The princes who ruled Northern Rus belonged to several princely lines, the majority

[1] See p. 296.

of which derived their origin from Vsevolod.   According as each of these
lines separated from the rest, it set up a Suzerain Prince of its own—of
Tver, of Rostov, of Yaroslavl, of Riazan, and so forth.   True, the Suzerain
Prince of Moscow was the superior of them all—the senior of seniors,
as it were—for the reason that, from Kalita's time onwards, he exercised
unbroken sway over the Suzerain Province of Vladimir, which Province,
during the thirteenth century, had been the common heritage of all
Vsevolod's stock, and had always passed from one Suzerain to another;
but with the coming of the fourteenth century the working of the appanage
system of rule gradually caused even that last territorial relic of the
indivisibility of princely rule to lose its old clan character, and to be
added by Dmitri Donskoi's grandson, Vassilii the Dark, to his appanage
of Moscow.   To judge, then, from the treaties of the Muscovite Princes,
no permanent political ties of rule existed between the Suzerain and his
juniors in a given line—the only ties so formed being temporary family
ones, such as common guardianship of the widow-mother during her lifetime, and so forth.   True, Dmitri Donskoi's will made shift to establish
a certain solidarity of rule among his sons, but it was only a casual
solidarity—a kind that went no further than interdicting a childless
son from disposing of his appanage at death, as well as directing that the
appanage thus "extinct" should be divided among the surviving brothers
of the deceased at the discretion of the widow-mother—the sole exception being that the appanage of the *eldest* son, now become Suzerain
Prince, should, in such a case, pass undivided to the next brother,
while the latter's appanage should be divided by the widow-mother among
the rest of the adult brothers.   Similar casual and temporary ties arose
out of the necessity for common defence against external foes, as well
as out of the relations existing between Rus and the Horde.   Thus,
in the interests of external security, bands of princely kinsmen (usually
near relatives) frequently formed offensive and defensive unions among
themselves.   Consequently we find junior appanage princes saying
to their Suzerain in treaties with him: "Thou shalt be[1] with us,
and we will be with thee."   On the same principle, a Suzerain was
debarred from concluding any treaties without the knowledge of his
juniors, and *vice versâ*, since Suzerain and juniors were supposed to have
the same friends and foes.   The phraseology used in this connection by
a Suzerain when making a treaty with his juniors ran: "When I do
mount my charger,[2] than shall ye also mount your chargers; and when I

---

[1] *i.e.* stand,   [2] *i.e.* set forth on an expedition.

go not out myself, but do send you, then will it be for you to go without disobedience." These again, however, were only *temporary* agreements, such as might be concluded between independent rulers under international law : which is why the conditions of such documents changed with each successive generation of princes, and even with each alteration either in the *personnel* of the princely union or in the circumstances of the moment. In fact, it is to that same mutability of princely relations that we owe the fact that so many of these copies of inter-princely treaties have come down to us. Vassilii the Dark concluded no less than seventeen such treaties with his cousins Ivan and Michael of Mozhaisk alone, not to speak of an even greater number with his Uncle Yuri of Galitch and with his (Yuri's) two sons, Vassilii the Squint-eyed and Dmitri the Handsome. Another class of relations among the princes arose out of the dependence of the latter upon the Horde. As already stated, the Khan began by collecting his Russian tribute through the agency of Tartar emissaries, but subsequently found it more convenient to entrust the work to the Suzerain Princes of Rus, each one of whom gathered in the "*ordinski vichod*" from the appanage princes of his own particular line, and then transmitted it to the Horde (Kalita alone being entrusted to collect it from princes of other lines than his own). This commission enabled the Suzerain Princes to acquire a great hold over their juniors of the appanages, and was therefore so much valued by them that they did all they could to prevent those juniors from entering into independent relations with the Horde. This aim of the Suzerain Princes is well summed up in the words which a Suzerain always addressed to a junior in a treaty : "It shall be for me to know [1] the Horde, but not for thee." This *financial* dependence of the appanage princes upon their Suzerain was bound, sooner or later, to develop into *political* dependence. Yet the princes clearly understood that such political dependence was a tie imposed upon them from without, and that, with the disappearance of that external force, there would disappear also the tie which it imposed. That is why the treaty of Donskoi with the appanage prince of Serpukhov already referred to contains the following condition : "Should God deliver us and set us free from the Horde, then shalt thou" (the appanage prince) "retain in thy hands thy two portions of the Tartar impost, and I" (the Suzerain Prince) "my three portions of the same." This shows us that the Muscovite Princes took it for granted that, as soon as ever the Tartar yoke should fall, there would fall with it the financial

---

[1] *i.e.* hold dealings with.

dependence of the appanage princes upon their Suzerain. In short, we see that the inter-princely treaties of the fourteenth and fifteenth centuries furnish no trace whatever of the existence of any *permanent* political tie placing the appanage princes in subordination to their Suzerain. The question, therefore, arises : By what means did the political dependence of the former upon the latter arise? The answer to that question must be sought in the process through which the supreme power in the Principality of Moscow became created.

For the student desirous of studying the mutual relations of the Muscovite Princes during the fourteenth and fifteenth centuries these treaties constitute a deceptive source, seeing that their conditions, as described above, did not correspond to the actualities of their time. Indeed, those treaties were, in a sense, an historical anachronism, seeing that they reproduced princely relations which, though undoubtedly operative during the early stages of the appanage system (*i.e.* during the thirteenth century and the first part of the fourteenth), were operative no longer. In fact, from the moment when Moscow began to acquire a decided supremacy over the other principalities of Rus, those conditions in the treaties to which I have referred began to grow obsolete, and were only repeated in successive treaties and agreements because the intellects of the scribes who drafted the documents were not sufficiently adaptive to keep pace with the changing times. This shortcoming on the part of the official *diaki* or clerks was shared also by the Princes. In these treaties—documents in which we see Idea so widely divorced from Reality—we hear the Northern Princes of the fourteenth century making use of the same archaic phraseology as their Southern forefathers of the *eleventh* and *twelfth* centuries had employed for the defining of their mutual relations. Yet those terms and expressions of kinship had only a conditional meaning. According to them, the stripling whom some aged appanage prince was supposed to address as an elder brother might be only his mere boy of a nephew—yet also his Suzerain, since degrees of kindred formed the standard which determined power and authority. For the newer relations, however, no suitable terminology had yet been found, since they were relations arising out of ideas of the day—*i.e.* out of conditions operating without the knowledge of the persons affected by their action.

From the time of Dmitri Donskoi, however—indeed, even from the times of his immediate predecessors—the relations of the Muscovite Princes began to be established on other lines. Under cover of the old terminology of conditional kinship there began a gradual conversion of the appanage princes from independent rulers into rulers in the service of their actual or conditional senior and kinsman, the Suzerain Prince. We have seen that for some time past the Suzerain of Moscow in particular had been acquiring an ascendancy over his juniors of the appanages, and it is curious to note that this ascendancy, though destined later to shatter the appanage system, was created out of the system's very conditions. The Muscovite wills have shown us that the order of succession observed in the princely circle was determined solely by the personal wishes of the testator. Nevertheless, certain permanent rules for the guidance of testators in the testamentary disposition of their property had gradually been framed and adopted. Kalita's first will makes it clear that as early as his day there was a tendency on the part of such testators to divide their *otchini* into unequal portions, of which the dimensions varied with the respective degrees of seniority of the inheritors to whom they were assigned. The older the heir, the larger the share of patrimony which he received. Clearly this inequality of apportionment indicates some dim recollection of the old system of rule according to rota of seniority. Even in this case, however, ancient tradition was adhered to only because it chanced to co-incide with family considerations—only because, since the eldest son was supposed to become " father " to his juniors, he therefore required to be rendered stronger than they. Owing, then, to the custom of unequal division thus gradually adopted by the Muscovite princely testators, the senior inheritor (the eldest son of the testator) received a larger share of the paternal *otchina* than his younger brethren and co-inheritors. At first the excess granted him by right of seniority was only a small one—a few extra towns or villages, or a few allotments of extra taxes ; but with Dmitri Donskoi's will the excess assumed considerably greater proportions. Under that will the testator's possessions were divided among his five sons, and the income of each such appanage duly specified. The testator also named the proportion per thousand of roubles which each inheritor was to contribute to the Tartar impost: whence it will be seen that in each case the contribution was proportioned to the income of the appanage, and that, in consequence, the eldest son, the Suzerain Prince Vassilii, had to con-tribute to each thousand of roubles, not a fifth part, but three hundred and forty-two roubles, or a little more than a *third* of the whole sum. From Donskoi's time onwards the excess of heritage allotted to the senior in-heritor continued to increase still further with each generation. Let us take, for instance, the will of Vassilii the Dark, executed in 1462. In this case, again, it was among five sons that the testator divided his *otchina*.

To his eldest son, the Suzerain Prince Ivan, he allotted an excess of fourteen of the most important towns and their districts, although to all his other four sons combined he left only eleven or twelve minor ones. The better to understand the growth of the process let us pass beyond the limits of the period now under study, and look at the will of Ivan III., executed about the year 1504. Here again we have a case in which the testator devised his *otchina* among five sons. To his eldest son, the Suzerain Prince Vassilii, he left sixty-six towns and their districts, while to all his other heirs combined he left but thirty! Moreover, in this case, as in Donskoi's, the testator named the contribution per thousand roubles which each inheritor was to contribute to the Tartar impost: whence we see that the share of the Suzerain Prince, as senior inheritor, amounted to no less than seven hundred and seventeen roubles per thousand—*i.e.* about three-fourths of the whole sum, or a third more than the contributions of all his other four brethren put together! Such was the final result of the process first initiated through the action of the Muscovite Princes in breaking through the custom of equal apportionment and allotting such an ever-increasing excess to the senior inheritor as to confer upon him, by the beginning of the fifteenth century, a very decided material ascendancy over his juniors. Nevertheless, these testatators did not invest their eldest sons with any corresponding excess of *political rights*, nor did they place the younger sons in direct political dependence upon their elder. All that the testators did was gradually to concentrate in the hands of the eldest son such a stock of the *means* of ruling as enabled him, even without extra *rights*, to engineer his juniors into a position of subordinacy. This purely material, propertied ascendancy of the Muscovite Suzerain Prince or senior inheritor served as the foundation of his subsequent *political* authority, while the excess of territorial heritage thus allotted him placed it in his power—even without an excess also of political privileges—to convert himself into a sovereign ruler over, not only the inhabitants of the appanages of Moscow, but also the appanage princes themselves. Thus the political authority of the Suzerain Prince of Moscow which subsequently put an end to the appanage system of rule arose out of certain of the system's very conditions, aided by the right of princely testators to dispose of their *otchini* as they individually saw fit.

The aggrandisement of the eldest son through testamentary bequest was accompanied, in Moscow and Tver, by a general tendency of the Suzerain Princes to place their weaker appanage brethren in a position of subordination to themselves. Different circumstances caused this subordination to assume different forms, and to attain different degrees of dependence. In its simplest form it amounted only to an agreement of personal service between the two parties—a form to be met with in the treaty made by Donskoi in 1362 with his cousin Vladimir of Serpukhov. Under this treaty, Vladimir, though still to be left independent ruler of his own appanage, was to perform certain stipulated services for his Suzerain, and to receive therefor a certain stipulated recompense. In this case the obligation of service involved no dependence of rule. A second form of subordination is to be seen in the position of "*okupnie*," or "bought out" princes—princes who had had their appanages purchased from them by their Suzerain, but had been left in possession of the same on condition of performing certain obligatory services. Such was Kalita's method of dealing with the princes of Bieloe Ozero and Galitch, as well as that of Vassilii the Dark with the princes of Rostov. In this case the obligation of service derived its origin from the dependence of rule. A similar position was that of princes who were deprived of their appanages by the Suzerain, and received into his service, but subsequently rewarded for such service by the return of their appanages or a portion of them. This was the treatment accorded to the princes of Starodub by Donskoi, and to those of Tarusa and Murom by Donskoi's son, Vassilii. Finally, Suzerain Princes often endeavoured to bring about the desired subordination by propounding the principle that appanage princes were subject to their Suzerain through the mere fact of their being appanage princes, while at the same time the Suzerains would demand that that subjection should be secured on the warranty of their (the juniors') appanages. The most emphatic expression of this demand is to be found in a treaty made in the year 1427 between Boris Alexandrovitch, Suzerain Prince of Tver, and Vitovt, Prince of Lithuania. According to this treaty, all the princes of Tver— uncles, brothers, and nephews of the Suzerain Prince of that principality—were to be bound into obedience to him, while he was to be at liberty to punish or to reward whomsoever he pleased. Furthermore, if any one of their number entered the service of any other Suzerain Prince, the delinquent's appanage was to be forfeit. Similar conditions, with but a few slight changes, attended the subjection of the princes of Suzdal by Vassilii the Dark. In this case, however, the appanage princes had their *otchini* neither annexed nor purchased, but, instead, made voluntary cession of them to the Suzerain, and had them returned in reward for services performed —the case being distinguished from the second form of subordination (*see above*) by the fact that the obligation of service became the source of the dependence of rule, as well as from the first form by the fact that the agreement of service was secured upon the servitor's appanage, and that the relations of service were linked with the relations of rule. In the Principality of Moscow these two last-mentioned forms of subordination were applied with such success that, by the end of his tenure of office, Vassilii the Dark could boast to the authorities of free Novgorod that authority had been granted him over all the Princes of Rus.

We have now traced the two processes through which the political and national importance of the Principality of Moscow and of its Suzerain Prince became created, and have seen that, while the one process brought about the extension of the territory and external influence of the Principality, the other process concentrated the elements of the supreme power in the person of the Suzerain Prince of Moscow alone. To these results certain conditions favourable to the Princes and tending to reinforce the action of the causes to which Muscovite growth was primarily due contributed in a very considerable degree. Those conditions may be described as follows :—

I. *Influence of the Tartar Yoke.*—Many of the difficulties which the Princes of Northern Rus created for themselves and their fatherland were to a certain extent removed or lightened by the relations in which the Tartars stood to the country. The Khans imposed no governmental system of their own upon Rus, but remained satisfied with the collection of tribute from it, or with only a very small participation in the existing system. Indeed, extensive participation in that system would have been impossible, seeing that, as a matter of fact, the relations of the Russian Princes to one another at that period scarcely amounted to a system at all. In this respect Vsevolod's descendants of the Upper Volga stood upon a far lower plane than their forefathers, Yaroslav's descendants of the Dnieper, had done, since the conceptions of the former never rose above the most shadowy of ideas on the subject of seniority and duty to a common fatherland—ideas so imperfect as to play but a small part in the influencing of action. Few of Vsevolod's thirteenth-century successors gave a thought to old clan or territorial traditions, while still fewer of them honoured them, seeing that those successors were lacking in all sense of kinship or duty to society at large. Yuri of Moscow shocked even the Tartars with his indifference when the mutilated corpse of his kinsman, Michael of Tver, was thrown down naked before his tent. Social consciousness of so atrophied a kind was incapable of rising beyond the mere instincts of self-preservation and plunder.   Only in Alexander Nevski did there lurk any detestation of the barbarism and fratricidal enmity which too often possessed the rulers of Rus, whether brothers or cousins, uncles or nephews.   Indeed, had those rulers been left to themselves, they would soon have torn their patrimony of Rus into petty shreds of appanages between which the sword was never sheathed.   Fortunately the principalities were not independent units, but *ulusi*[1] paying tribute to the Tartars—*ulusi* whose princes were the " *slaves* " of the "free lord," as the Khan was then known in Rus.   At the same time, the Khan's authority invested those various petty, mutually hostile appanages with at least a *semblance* of unity, and although Sarai on the Volga was not exactly the place where strict justice reigned (it was the scene, among other things, of a shameless buying and selling of the Suzerain throne of Vladimir—the whole nefarious transaction being covered with a *yarlik*), it not infrequently happened that a Prince, when wronged, appealed to the Khan, and sometimes with success.   More than once the threat of that potentate's wrath served to deter squabbles, or his discretion to forestall or arrest a disastrous feud.   In fact, the Khan's authority was the blunt Tartar knife which cut the knots of the tangled skein in which the stupidity of Vsevolod's posterity frequently enravelled the affairs of the country ; so that the old Russian chroniclers had some reason for dubbing the Mongols the " *Bozhi batog*," or " cudgel of God," appointed for the correction of sinners and their turning back into the paths of repentance. Those who made the most successful use of that cudgel were the Suzerain Princes of Moscow, and the most striking instance of this occurred when Moscow's one feud—a dispute raised during the Suzerainty of Vassili the Dark—was threatening.   The dispute in question arose out of a claim by Yuri of Galitch (Vassilii's uncle) to occupy the Suzerain throne in place of his nephew.   Relying upon his seniority in years, and citing in his support the will of his father, Dmitri Donskoi, Yuri declined to recognise his ten-year-old nephew as his theoretical elder, and set off to the Horde to lay the case before the Khan.   Had Yuri's claim been admitted, it would have meant the transference of the Suzerainty to another line of the Muscovite princely house, and thus the shattering of the system now established in Moscow for a century past and the stirring up of endless feuds. The Khan, however, cut the Gordian knot.   Bewildered by the halffawning, half-sneering eloquence of the crafty descendant of Vsevolod as he strove to convince the potentate that the true fount of justice lay in his

---

[1] Literally, nomad camps.

(the Khan's) wisdom, and not in old manuscripts or long-defunct deeds (whereby he meant Donskoi's will), the Khan then and there decided the matter in favour of Vassilii.

II. *Establishment of the Succession in the Direct Descending Line.*— Throughout, the importance attained by the Principality of Moscow was due chiefly to the policy of its Suzerain Prince, but more especially to his adding the Suzerain Province of Vladimir to his own appanage of Moscow. For a hundred years after Kalita's death the Suzerain Prince of Vladimir was invariably the eldest son of his predecessor, owing to that predecessor seldom having any younger brothers extant at the time of his death. Moreover, the princely house of Moscow was fortunate in never ramifying into collateral lines, owing to the fact that the junior uncles of the house always disappeared from the scene, and so left the way clear for the senior nephews. Consequently it was not until the death of Kalita's grandson, the Suzerain Prince Vassilii (son of Dmitri), that the question of succession to the Suzerain throne evoked any dispute among the Muscovite Princes, or caused the Princes of the two lines rival to their own—namely, those of Suzdal and Tver—to interfere with Muscovite succession to the Suzerainty. Repetition of a given case becomes precedent, which, in its turn, is converted, through the force of custom, into obligatory demand, or rule. Thus, repeated and undisputed passage of the Suzerain power downwards through several generations of fathers and sons became—to borrow the Chronicle's phrase—*otchestvo i diedstvo*, or a custom hallowed by so many instances of fathers and grand-fathers succeeding one another that eventually the community took it to be the regular system, and forgot all about the old system of succession according to order of seniority. This is very clearly seen in the Muscovite feud above-mentioned. Continued, after Yuri's death, by his sons, it set the whole of the Russian community by the ears—the ruling classes (*i.e.* the clergy, the princes, the boyars, and other official personages) being all of them for Vassilii. Everywhere in Moscow the princes of Galitch were greeted as aliens and usurpers, and found themselves surrounded on every side with mistrust and ill-will. At length, when Yuri's son Shemiaka (who became heir to his father's claim after the father's death) broke his treaty [1] with Vassilii, the latter appealed to the spiritual authorities, and in 1447 a board of five bishops and two or three archimandrites (at that particular moment Rus lacked a Metropolitan) addressed a menacing injunction to the treaty-breaker, as well as delivered a judgment on

1 *i.e.* the usual treaty of an appanage prince with his Suzerain.

the subject of what the board regarded as the rightful order of succession in the land. Utterly rejecting the claim put forward by Shemiaka's deceased father, the spiritual judges assigned the exclusive right to the Suzerain throne to Yuri's nephew, the eldest son of the late Suzerain, and even compared Yuri's pretensions to the sin of our forefather Adam in listening to the Serpent's suggestion that he should make himself equal with God. "For all that thy father did strive," wrote the judges, "and for all that Christendom hath suffered much tribulation at his hands, the Suzerain throne was not his to receive, seeing that it had not been given unto him of God *nor of the ancient custom of this land.*" Thus the only system of succession recognised as regular by the spiritual authorities was succession in the descending line, not succession in order of seniority ; the authorities even going so far as to flout history and call their system the "ancient custom of this land." The new order, then, paved the way to the establishment of monarchical rule by strengthening the position of one direct and senior line only—that of Moscow, and thus setting aside and weakening the claims of its collateral juniors. True, the feud did not end there, but at least the chief of the Russian Hierarchy had proclaimed the exclusive legal right of the Suzerain Prince of Moscow to exercise monarchical power—had voiced an accomplished fact before which the entire community of Rus, both princes and commoners, must bow. In his well-known encyclical of the following year we find the newly-con-secrated Metropolitan John inviting all Princes, *pani,*[1] boyars, *voievodi,* and other folk of Russian Christendom to do homage to their sovereign lord the Suzerain Prince Vassilii, and to submit themselves to his will: adding that whosoever should not do so, but should aid Shemiaka in renewing the feud, would be accounted guilty of shedding Christian blood, recognised by none as Christians, ministered unto by no priest, and shut out of all God's churches in the land.

It was in the active support shown by the community, during this feud, to the new system of succession of the Suzerain power that lay the condition which, more than all else, served to confirm the national and political progress of the Muscovite Principality. No sooner did there arise from among the appanage princes a ruler possessed of the means and aspirations which pertained to and inspired the now hereditary line of Muscovite Suzerain Princes than there began to group themselves around him all the political schemes and popular interests of the community of Northern Rus. For such a leader the people had been waiting, and its

[1] Nobles.

expectation had found voice in the feud.   In the struggle which then arose the family strength and resources of the Muscovite Suzerain Princes met and coincided with the popular needs and aspirations, for, although the prime motive-spring of the Princes' policy was the dynastic interest which aimed at both the external aggrandisement of the Principality and the internal concentration of the supreme power in the person of one ruler alone, this family interest—self-interest, rather—was nevertheless actively taken up by the whole of the North Russian population, with the clergy at its head, as soon as ever it became aware that that self-interest coincided with "the common weal of all our Orthodox Christendom " (as the Metropolitan John phrases it in one of his encyclicals).   This combined popular support is explained by the unseen rise of a new factor—a factor from which attention had been diverted by the clash and shock of the princely feuds and Tartar irruptions.   We have already noted the circumstances which compelled the bulk of the Russian population to migrate from ancient Rus of the Dnieper to the region of the Upper Volga.   Confronted there with new conditions, an unaccustomed setting, and an alien native population, the settlers from the South found themselves unable either to re-establish their old social system or to set up a new one, and so became more and more divided up among the innumerable little appanages which I have described. Yet the settlers did not confine themselves to self-contained, mutually hostile communes as did the princes to their appanages.   On the contrary, the popular migratory movement still continued, and was, if anything, increased by the princely feuds.   In fact, in one passage the Chronicle specifically tells us that the disputes of the Princes of Tver with their fellows compelled the inhabitants of their principalities perforce to depart to more peaceful regions.   After the close of the fourteenth century, however, there set in that active colonising movement across the Volga which we have already noted.   Settling in the Trans-Volgan territories in small colonies which for more than two centuries worked in isolation from one another, yet under identical economic and juridical conditions, the immigrants gradually began to develop identical social types, to associate together more freely, to form definite mutual ties and relations, to adopt common modes of life, manners, and systems of industry, and to assimilate the surrounding natives of the country.   Thus by the middle of the fifteenth century there began to arise amid the political chaos of the appanages a new national formation, a product of ethnographical elements formerly scattered and distinct.   In short, born of toil and tribulation there became evolved the Great Russian stock.   During the period

1228–1462 Northern Rus suffered no fewer than ninety internal feuds and a hundred and sixty external wars, so that, reared amid perils from without and disasters from within which often annulled in a moment the fruits of years of patient industry, the Great Russian people at length realised the need of concentrating its disorganised forces in some durable political and governmental system if ever it was to rid itself of chaotic appanage rule and Tartar enslavement. This need served as a new and subtle, though none the less a potent, factor in the aggrandisement of the Muscovite Suzerain Prince—the other factors being, as already explained, (1) the *economic advantages* conferred upon Moscow by its geographical position, (2) the *ecclesiastical importance* attained by the Principality through the aid of the same condition and of other circumstances of the times, and (3) the *form of policy* adopted by the Muscovite Princes as the result of their genealogical position.

The same need, again, explains the unlooked-for and extremely important result of the Muscovite feud. Entering upon his princeship when little more than a child, Vassilii might have been thought to be altogether too meek and mild a youth for the warlike rôle which he was destined to play. Yet, though more than once defeated, despoiled of his possessions, and banished (as well as, finally, stricken with blindness), he none the less issued from his nineteen years' struggle with acquisitions which threw into the shade those won by the continuous efforts of his father and grandfather. When he ascended the disputed throne the *otchina* of Moscow was divided into fully half a score of appanages, but when he came to write his will he was in possession of the whole of that *otchina* except half of one appanage—the Verea half of the appanage of Mozhaisk. Moreover, the principality of Suzdal was now his (its late princes had either entered his service or fled the country), Muscovite *posadniki* sat in the various towns of Riazan, and Novgorod the Great and Viatka had made complete submission to him. Finally, he not only felt himself strong enough to nominate to the Suzerainty his eldest son—a thing which his father before him had hesitated to do—but also to include in the inventory of his devisable property the Suzerain power itself. All these achievements of his became possible through the fact that all that was most influential, thoughtful, and statesmanlike in the Russian community stood for him and for the succession of the Suzerain power in the descending line. His adherents allowed his rivals no rest, but persecuted them with continual complaints, protests, and intrigues. In short, they exerted on his behalf every means, moral and material, which lay at their command.

Into this fortunate position—a position not created, but only acceded to, by him—Donskoi's grandson fell through the fact that it was one in which the ends and means of action were so clearly designated, the forces so well directed, the resources so ready to hand, and the arms so perfectly adapted and tried, that the machine was able to work automatically, and without the help of the chief mechanician. The moment that the population of Northern Rus realised that Moscow was capable of becoming a political centre around which it could group its forces for the struggle with external foes, and that the Prince of Moscow was competent to act as its leader in the struggle, a change took place in the ideas and relations of Rus of the appanages—a change which sealed the fate of the appanage system. All those hitherto suppressed or dormant national and political aspirations of the Great Russian race, all those forces which had for so long and so unsuccessfully sought a *point d'appui*, hastened to ally themselves with the dynastic policy of the Suzerain Prince of Moscow, and to raise him to the height of national sovereign of Great Rus. Thus we complete our task of defining the chief stages in the political growth of the Principality of Moscow.

It is usual to ascribe the chief credit for the rise of Moscow to the personal qualities of its Princes. In concluding, therefore, our survey of the political growth of Moscow it might be well to estimate the importance of those qualities in the history of the State. There is no need to exaggerate it unduly, nor to look upon the national and political greatness of the Principality as the sole work of its Princes—the outcome of their personal creativeness and talents alone. Unfortunately, annals of the fourteenth and fifteenth centuries furnish us with no data for reproducing personal likenesses of those princes, but only present the rulers of Moscow as a series of pale phantoms succeeding one another on the Suzerain throne under the names of Ivan I., Simeon, Ivan II., Dmitri, Vassilii I., and Vassilii II. As we gaze at them we soon realise that it is not a series of original personalities which is passing before our eyes, but a mere series of repetitions of a single family type. All the Muscovite Princes, down to Ivan III., are as like one another as a string of peas, so that the observer is often puzzled to decide which of them is, say, Ivan, and which Vassilii. Their *policies*, it may be, present certain individual peculiarities, but those peculiarities are attributable rather to differences of age or to the exceptional external circumstances in which some of the Princes became placed. In any case, such peculiarities do not go beyond an occasional change of policy on the part of the same individual, so that, as we look at the series of

Suzerain Princes who suceeeded one another upon the Muscovite throne, we can detect in them only typical family features, while their likenesses hardly seem to be living presentments at all, nor yet portraits, but rather automata whose attitudes and costumes, indeed, afford material for study, but whose faces contain not a particle of expression.

To begin with, Daniel's descendants were remarkable for their consistent mediocrity, for their never exceeding or falling short of the mean. Vsevolod's stock in general was not resplendent for abounding talent (with the exception, perhaps, of Alexander Nevski), and Daniel's descendants in particular did not reach even the front rank of that stock. They were Princes devoid of all brilliancy, of all signs of moral or heroic greatness. In the first place, they were very peace-loving men—men who seldom entered into a fight, or, if they did so, generally lost the day. True, they knew how to withdraw behind the wooden (after Dmitri Donskoi's time, stone) walls of the Kremlin when an enemy was approaching, but they none the less preferred, when the enemy was near at hand, to remove to Periaslavl or some more distant spot, taking their troops with them, and leaving their wives and children and the Metropolitan of Moscow to defend the city. Remarkable, therefore, for no great talents and no great valour, these Princes were remarkable also for no great vices or passions. This made them, in many respects, absolute models of temperateness and precision—even their tendency to get drunk after dinner never being carried to any very great lengths. In short, these mediocre men of ancient Rus were chronological marks (so to speak) rather than actual historical persons. Perhaps their best family description is to be found in a character-sketch of Simeon Gordii given in one of the later Recueils. "The Suzerain Prince Simeon was surnamed the Proud in that he loved not falseness nor sedition, and did punish all such as were guilty of the same; in that he drank of mead and wine, but drank not unto drunkenness, nor would suffer other drunkards to do likewise; and in that he loved not war, but did alway hold his army in readiness." Of the six generations, Dmitri Donskoi alone stands out at all prominently from the dead level of his predecessors and successors. His youth (he was only thirty-nine when he died), the exceptional circumstances which placed him on a war-horse at the age of eleven, the fourfold struggle in which he was engaged simultaneously with Tver, Lithuania, Riazan, and the Horde—a struggle which filled with clamour and alarms the whole of his thirty years of rule—and, above all, his great victory on the Don, shed upon him a clear reflection of Alexander Nevski; so that the Chronicle says of him, with notable enthusiasm, that he was "strong, and as a man, and very wonderful to behold," while a contemporary biographer, in noting other and more peaceful qualities of his (such as piety, virtue, and so forth) adds the statement that, "although he was not learned in books, he did none the less carry the sacred tomes in his heart." With this one solitary exception, the artist of lofty themes would find little material for his brush in the Muscovite Princes. At the same time, though not resplendent for actual accomplishments, those Princes could boast of several, if less valuable, at all events more *profitable*, qualities. For one thing, they were liberal towards all who stood in need of assistance. Again, and above all things, they lived on friendly terms with one another—kept strictly to the father's injunction "to live at one." During the four generations between the death of Daniel and the death of Dmitri's son Vassilii the Principality of Moscow was, perhaps, the only one in all Northern Rus which did not suffer from the feuds of its Princes. Indeed, the Muscovite rulers were sons of such filial piety, and held the memory and injunctions of their parents in such respect, that it was not long before they had amassed an hereditary stock of ideas, rules, and customs with regard to their princeship which, eventually taking rank as family custom and ancestral tradition, superseded individual princely initiative, just as, among ourselves, academic precept not infrequently supersedes independent thought. It was from this that there originated the Muscovite Princes' unswerving continuity of policy, in which they acted rather according to rote—according to rules ready-made for each occasion or inculcated by their fathers—than by the light of personal reason. Thus they played what is called a "steady game"—a game free from interruptions and invariably a winning one. Work, in their hands, pursued the even tenour of its way very much as did the thread in the hands of their wives as it answered to the movements of the spindle. A son took up his father's task, and carried it as far as his strength allowed him. Yet occasionally their cold, formal wills warm to a touch of generous piety. "This word do I write unto you"—so runs the concluding testamentary charge of Simeon Gordii to his younger brethren—"that ye suffer not the memory of our Grandfather nor of our parents to cease, nor yet our own candle to wane." In what, then, lay this family tradition, this inherited policy, of the Muscovite Princes? Simply in their excellence as petty stewards and economists. It was not without reason that one of them who attained exceptional success in this somewhat unlovely phase of the struggle became known to posterity as Kalita or "the Purse." When dictating their wills to a clerk, in preparation for appearing before the Throne of the Supreme Judge, how attentive were these rulers to every petty detail of their property, how mindful of every item! They forgot neither their fur coats, their flocks and herds, their golden girdles, nor their treasure chests. Everything was written down, everything accorded its place, by these testators. To preserve intact their fathers' goods, and to add to them something new (from a fur coat to a village)—that, apparently, was the chief aim and object of those rulers' ambitions, to judge by their wills. Yet it was those very qualities which contributed so much to their political success.

Every period produces its heroes in keeping with itself, but, in general, the thirteenth and fourteenth centuries were a time of degeneration in Rus—a time of petty sentiments, petty interests, and insignificant characters. External and internal misfortunes had caused men to become timid and low-spirited, to give way to despondency, to abandon high aims and ambitious aspirations. In the Chronicle's record of those centuries we hear none of the old talk about "the Russian land" or the necessity of guarding it from the pagans and preserving intact the language of the South Russian princes and chroniclers of the eleventh and twelfth centuries. Men shut themselves up in a narrow circle of their own private interests, and issued thence only for the purpose of taking advantage of their fellows. When, in a community, public interests fall into abeyance and the aspirations of its directors become confined to their money chests, the guidance of affairs usually falls into the hands of those who with the most energy pursue their *private* interests—persons who are seldom the most gifted of individuals, but more often those who are the most threatened, those to whom the lapse of public interests would entail the most loss. This was the case with the Muscovite Princes. Though rendered, through their *genealogical* position, the most rightless and rankless of all the Russian Princes, they were enabled by the conditions of their *economic* position to acquire abundant means for promoting their personal ends. Consequently they were better able than their fellows to adapt themselves to the character and conditions of their times, and so to act the more decisively in their private interest. They were like business men whose calling develops commercial acumen and dexterity at the expense of other and higher qualities and aims. The more energetically a merchant applies himself to his trade and forgets all other interests, the more does he prosper. At the same time, I ought to say that the family character of the Muscovite

Princes must not be reckoned as one of the fundamental conditions which ensured their success, but rather as the *product* of that success, seeing that their family peculiarities did not create the national and political greatness of Moscow, but were themselves the work of the historical forces and conditions which created that greatness. That is to say, they were a secondary, derivative cause of the rise of the Principality of Moscow, even as (for instance) was the help of the Muscovite boyars, who, attracted to Moscow, in the first instance, by its convenient position, subsequently, and more than once, rescued their Princes at difficult moments. Thus frequently are the conditions of life so capriciously compounded that great men of the stamp of Andrew Bogoliubski are thrown away upon small deeds, while small men of the stamp of the Princes of Moscow are fated to perform great ones.

CHAPTER XIX

The Free Town Commonwealths—Novgorod the Great—Its situation and plan—Division of
its territory into *piatini* and *volosti*—Conditions and development of Novgorod's freedom—Treaty relations of Novgorod with its Princes—Its administration—The relations
of its *vietché* with its Princes—Its *Posadnik* and *Tisiatski*—Its judicial system—Its Council
of Magnates—Its provincial administration—Its minor towns, and their relation to the
capital—Conclusion.

In completing our study of the appanage system of rule, as well as of
the process by which one appanage raised itself above the rest and ended
by absorbing the majority of its fellows, we stopped at the middle of the
fifteenth century, at the moment in the history of the Muscovite Principality
when Moscow was preparing to complete the process by absorbing the few
remaining independent principalities in Northern Rus.   Yet the Principality of Moscow was not the only political form of its time in Rus, since
contemporary with it were two forms in which the social elements coalesced
in a combination altogether different.   Those two forms were (1) the
Cossack State, and (2) the Free Town Commonwealths.   Although, at the
middle of the fifteenth century, the first-named form was only in process of evolution, the second had completed its first hundred years of
existence.   To conclude, therefore, our study of the structure of the
Russian land during the appanage period, we should do well to glance at
the history and organisation of the great Town Commonwealths.   They
were three in number—namely, Novgorod the Great, Novgorod's "younger
brother" Pskov, and the Novgorodian colony of Viatka, founded during
the twelfth century.   Instead, however, of going into the history of each
of them in turn, let us confine ourselves to the fortunes of the oldest—
namely, Novgorod, while touching also upon the more important features
in the life and organisation of Pskov, of which, with Viatka, Novgorod the
Great was the founder and representative type.

The political organisation of Novgorod the Great—*i.e.* of the capital of
the territory of that name—was closely bound up with the situation of the
city.   Novgorod stretched along the banks of the river Volkhov, at a point
close to where the river issues from Lake Ilmen.   At that time it consisted

of a number of suburbs (*slobodi*) or settlements (*sela*) which, though formerly independent communities, had gradually become combined into one large township. Traces of the former independent existence of those constituent portions of Novgorod survived to a later date in the distribution of the *Kontzi* (Ends or Quarters) of the city. Novgorod was divided by the Volkhov into two halves or sides (*storoni*)—an eastern and a western, of which the former was known as the *Torgovaia Storona*, from the fact of its containing the principal market or *torg*, and the latter as the *Sophiskaia Storona*, from the fact of its containing the Cathedral of St. Sophia, built at the close of the tenth century, at the time when Novgorod first adopted Christianity. The main connection between these two halves or sides of the city was by a bridge, which, situated near the market, was known, in contradistinction to smaller ones, as the *Veliki Most* or Great Bridge. Adjoining the market was a square known as the *Yaroslavovi Dvor* or *Kniazhi Dvor* (*i.e.* Yaroslav's Court or the Prince's Court, for the reason that it was the site of an old palace tenanted by Yaroslav when he was *Posadnik* of Novgorod during his father's lifetime), and, in the middle of the square, a *stepen* (rostrum or platform) from which the Novgorodian dignitaries addressed the people when assembled in *vietché*, while, close by, stood a tower containing, in its upper portion, the great bell for summoning the people to *vietché*, and, in its lower storey, the *vietché* offices. The other side of the city (the *Torgovaia* side) was made up of two *Kontzi* or Ends— the *Plotnitski Konetz* towards the north, and the *Slavenski Konetz* towards the south. Of these, the latter derived its title from an old settlement named Slaven, which had become incorporated with Novgorod, while for the same reason the *Torgovaia* side of the city was sometimes known as the *Slavenskaia Storona*. In the *Slavenski Konetz* stood both the principal market and the Square of Yaroslav. On the other, the *Sophiskaia*, side of the river, and immediately at the end of the Great Bridge, lay the *Dietinetz* —an enclosed space having in its middle the Cathedral. This side also of the city was divided into *Kontzi*—namely, the *Nerevski Konetz* on the north, the *Zagorodski Konetz* on the west, and the *Goncharski Konetz*, or *Liudin Konetz*, on the south, near the lake. These two names, *Goncharski* and *Plotnitski*,[1] bear witness to the former industrial character of the suburbs out of which these *Kontzi* subsequently became formed, and prove that the Kievans of the eleventh century had some reason for their gibe when they dubbed the Novgorodians of their day " a contemnable small company of *plotniki*." Beyond the rampart and ditch which

---

[1] *Gonchar* means a potter and *plotnik* a carpenter.

encircled all these five *Kontzi* lay the numerous outlying suburbs and establishments attached to monasteries which made up the rest of the township and surrounded it like a belt. Of the total population of the city we can form an approximate estimate from the fact that in the portion of it destroyed by fire in the year 1211 there had formerly stood 4,300 houses.

Novgorod, with its five *Kontzi*, was the political centre of extensive territories attached to the city. These were composed of two classes of provinces—namely, *piatini*[1] and *volosti ;* the *piatini* being apportioned as follows. North-westwards from Novgorod, and between the rivers Volkhov and Luga, lay the *piatina* of Vodi, which derived its name from the Finnish tribe of the Vodi or Voti which inhabited that region. North-eastwards from the city, and to the right of the Volkhov, lay the *piatina* of Obonezh, which enclosed Lake Onega and extended almost to the White Sea. Southeastwards from Novgorod, and enclosed by the rivers Msta and Lovat, stretched the *piatina* of Dereva, and south-westwards from the same point, and enclosed by the rivers Lovat and Luga, lay the *piatina* of Shelon—so called because it comprised the entire basin of the Shelona river. Finally, behind the two *piatini* of Obonezh and Dereva stretched, in an easterly and south-easterly direction, the *piatina* of Biezhesk, which derived its name from a colony of emigrants from Biezhesk—a town now included in the government of Tver. This last *piatina* embraced what now constitutes the northern portion of the government of Tver, the western portion of the government of Yaroslav, and the south-eastern corner of the government of Novgorod. Although this system of division of Novgorodian territory into *piatini* appears in state documents of Novgorod after the city's subjugation by Moscow, it is nowhere to be found in Novgorodian annals belonging to the period of Novgorodian freedom (*i.e.* the period previous to the close of the fifteenth century). Such annals always speak of Novgorodian territory as divided, not into *piatini*, but into *zemli* or *volosti* of identical names with the foregoing, or, during the twelfth century, into *riadi*. At the same time, a trace of something like division into *piatini* obtaining some fifty years before the city's fall is to be found in a biography of the Abbot Varlaam—a work written at the end of the sixteenth century. In it we read that " at that time " (the writer is referring to the year 1426, or thereabouts) " Great Novgorod was divided into lots called *piatini*." Probably Moscow was unwilling to intrude upon old local custom, and so retained Novgorod's system of territorial division intact. A peculiar feature

[1] Fifths.

of this division into *piatini* lay in the circumstance that every one of them, with the exception only of the *piatina* of Biezhesk, started either from the city itself or from a point close to it, so that they radiated outwards in strips. In the *piatina* of Obonezh, for instance, the nearest *pogost* or market centre to Novgorod lay only two versts from the city, while the farthest one from it lay quite seven hundred versts to the northward.   Only in the *piatina* of Biezhesk was the nearest *pogost* as far distant from Novgorod as a hundred versts.   This would seem to show that the districts which at some time or other acquired the name of *piatini* originally consisted of small lots which, at first lying close in to Novgorod, gradually became further and further extended outwards.

Other and more outlying territories of Novgorod were there which it acquired at a later date than the *piatini*.   Consequently these newer territories never entered into the system of division just described, but formed a series of *volosti* or *zemli* occupying each of them a special position.   Thus the towns of Volokolamsk, Biezhichi, Torzhok, Rshev, and Veliki Lugi, with their districts, did not belong to any particular *piatini*, but were in the peculiar situation of being shared with princes of other states—the three first-named with the Suzerain Princes of Vladimir (subsequently, of course, with those of Moscow), and the two last-named with the Princes of Smolensk (subsequently with those of Lithuania, after Smolensk had undergone conquest by that state). Of the other *volosti*, that of Zavolochïe or the Dvina lay behind the two *piatini* of Obonezh and Biezhesk, and stretched in a north-easterly direction from them.   It derived its name of Zavolochïe from the fact that it covered the *volok* or broad watershed which divided the basins of the rivers Onega and Northern Dvina from that of the Volga.   Next, along the river Vitchegda and its tributaries stretched the *volost* of Permia, while beyond it, again, lay that of Petchora, enclosing the river of the same name. Further northwards, in the direction of the Ural range, lay the *volost* of Ugra ; while, finally, the *volost* of Trei or Ter comprised the regions bordering the northern shores of the White Sea.   All these *volosti* were distinct from the *piatina* system.   Nevertheless they must have been acquired at an early date, since even in the eleventh century we find Novgorodians levying tribute beyond the Dvina, and even northwards towards the Petchora, while, in the following century, we see them penetrating to the White Sea itself.   The principal method of extending Novgorodian territory was through military-industrial colonisation, *i.e.* colonisation by companies of armed workmen and traders from Novgorod, who spread along the rivers in different directions, but more especially towards the Finnish North-East, and, founding scattered settlements here and there, proceeded to levy tribute upon the conquered natives, and to engage in forest and other industries.

Next let us study the conditions and development of Novgorodian freedom. At the opening of our history we see the territory of Novgorod organised on precisely similar lines to those of other provinces of the Russian land, and its relations to its princes differing but little from those of other capital towns of provinces. When, however, the early princes of Rus deserted Novgorod for Kiev the former became tributary to the latter, until finally, on Yaroslav's death, the province was united to the Suzerain Principality,[1] the ruler of which usually sent his son, or some other near relative, to govern Novgorod in conjunction with a *Posadnik*. Up to the second quarter of the twelfth century, Novgorodian conditions of life furnish no trace of any special political features distinguishing it from the life of other provinces. It is only *after* that period that we find the Novgorodians referring (in their treaties with their Princes) to charters granted them by Yaroslav on condition that they paid tribute to the Suzerain of Kiev—charters which were merely written specifications of financial relations which, in the case of other chief towns of provinces, it was usual to establish *orally* between the local princes and the *vietcha* of their respective capitals. After the death of Vladimir Monomakh the Novgorodians proceeded apace with the acquisition of those privileges which, later, were destined to become the basis of their freedom ; which successful development of the city's political differentiation was largely contributed to by conditions coalescing to place the fortunes of Novgorod in a wholly different combination to that seen in the case of any other province of the Russian land. Some of those conditions were closely bound up with the geographical features of the region, while others of them arose out of the historical setting in which Novgorod moved—in fact, out of its external relations. First of all let me point out the geographical conditions. To begin with, Novgorod was the political centre of what then constituted the far north-western corner of Rus—a position which removed the province altogether out of the circle of those Russian territories which served the Suzerain Princes and their retinues as their principal arena. This circumstance relieved Novgorod of any direct pressure at the hands of those Princes, and so allowed of Novgorodian life developing more

[1] Kiev.

freely and fully than could otherwise have been the case. Secondly, Novgorod was the economic centre of a region covered with forests and swamps, in which agriculture could never become the prime basis of the popular industry. Thirdly, the city lay close to the principal river basins of the Russian plain—to those of the Volga, the Dnieper, and the Western Dvina, while the Volkhov also connected it directly with the Gulf of Finland and the Baltic Sea. Thanks to this propinquity to the great river trade-routes of Rus, Novgorod was drawn at an early period into the vortex of the commercial traffic of the land; with the result that manufactures and barter soon became the prime bases of the popular industry. Equally favourable to the development of Novgorodian independence were the city's *external* relations. Throughout the twelfth century the feuds of the princes gradually tended to weaken the authority of the latter, and so to enable the local communities to treat more independently with their rulers. Of this facility Novgorod took every possible advantage. Situated at the extreme edge of Rus, confronted on more than one side by hostile aliens, and engaged principally in foreign trade, the city stood in constant need of a prince and his retinue to defend its frontiers and trade-routes. Yet it so happened that during the twelfth century—the very time when the genealogical calculations of the Princes had become most entangled and their authority most weakened—Novgorod needed such protection less than it had ever done before, or than it was ever destined to do later. Later, indeed, two dangerous enemies arose on the Novgorodian frontiers—namely, the Livonian Order of Swordbearers[1] and united Lithuania; but, as yet, neither of those foemen menaced the State, seeing that the Order of Swordbearers was only founded at the opening of the thirteenth century, and the unification of Lithuania did not begin until its close. The united action of all these favourable conditions determined, not only the relations of Novgorod to its Princes, but also its administrative organisation, its social tendencies, and the character of its political life. Let us glance at the history of the city in connection with each of these particulars.

During the tenth and eleventh centuries the Princes thought little of the Novgorodian province, since their interests were more bound up with the South. Thus we read that, when Sviatoslav was dividing his dominions among his sons before setting forth on his second expedition against the Bolgars, the Novgorodians came to him to beg for a prince; whereupon (so says the Chronicle) Sviatoslav answered: "Who, forsooth, would

---

[1] A German militant religious order, founded ostensibly to spread the Catholic faith.

go unto such as ye?" This contempt for any town lying remote from Kiev was one of the reasons why Novgorod never became the heritage of any particular branch of Yaroslav's stock, although its citizens, weary of constant changes of ruler, petitioned again and again for a permanent prince of their own. Another reason was that, on Yaroslav's death, the province of Novgorod did not become a separate principality, but only an appendage to the Suzerain province of Kiev, and so shared the mutable fortunes of that common *otchina* of Yaroslav's stock. In later days the Princes came to pay more attention to this wealthy city, since, no sooner was Monomakh dead and his heavy hand removed, than circumstances permitted of Novgorod attaining important political privileges. The feuds of the Princes entailed frequent changes on the Novgorodian throne, and, through taking advantage of these feuds and changes, the Novgorodians succeeded in introducing into their political organisation two important principles destined to develop into the prime guarantees of their freedom —namely, the right of electing the heads of the local administration, and the right of making treaties with their Prince before he assumed office. Novgorod's frequent changes of ruler were accompanied also by changes in the *personnel* of the local administration. The Prince ruled the city and its attached territories with the help of two Kievan officials nominated either by himself or by the Suzerain Prince—namely, a *Posadnik* or civil governor and a *Tisiatski* or military prefect, and when the Prince elected or was forced to leave the city his *Posadnik* usually resigned office, seeing that the new Prince would bring with him, or else appoint, a *Posadnik* of his own choosing. In the interval, however, the people of Novgorod were left without chiefs of administration, and consequently fell into the habit of electing a temporary *Posadnik*, and requesting the incoming Prince to make the appointment permanent. This was the beginning of Novgorod's right to elect its own *Posadnik*—the first instance of this occurring in the year 1126, after the death of Monomakh, when, to quote the words of the Chronicle, " the men of Novgorod did award the office of *Posadnik* unto one of themselves." The custom gradually became permanent, and was much valued by the citizens for the fact that the office was now awarded in the public Square instead of in the Prince's palace, and that, from being the representative of the Prince and the Prince's interests in the presence of Novgorod, the *Posadnik* now became the representative of Novgorod and Novgorod's interests in the presence of the Prince. Subsequently the important office of *Tisiatski* also became subject to election. The local Bishop was another leading member of the administration. Up to the middle of the twelfth century he was always consecrated by the Metropolitan at Kiev, in presence of convocation of bishops, and therefore under the eye of the Suzerain Prince; but during the latter half of the century the Novgorodians took to electing their own Bishop from among the local clergy, and *then* sending him to Kiev to be consecrated by the Metropolitan. The first Bishop so chosen was Arcadius, a monk belonging to a local monastery, who was elected in the year 1156, and from that time onwards the Metropolitan of Kiev retained only the right of *consecrating*, not of *selecting*, the candidate sent to him from Novgorod. Thus the second and third quarters of the twelfth century saw the three principal heads of the Novgorodian administration become elective. At about the same period the citizens began to make more stringent terms with their Princes, since the princely feuds now made it possible to choose among rivals, and thus to impose upon the selected Prince a number of obligations limiting his powers—a custom usually unopposed even by the princes themselves. With the growth of Novgorod's freedom the social life of the community took on a more restless, a more clamorous, tendency, which rendered the position of the local Prince so increasingly insecure that more than once a ruler-designate declined office, or, having done so, left the city by night. Thus we find one prince of the twelfth century saying to another one who had been invited to go and rule on the Volkhov: " Talk not to me of Novgorod. Let it rule itself as best it may, and seek itself princes where it listeth." Vsevolod made no ceremony about abolishing the privileges which the city had acquired : yet even he occasionally conceded the citizens permission to choose their own Prince, and in 1196 came to a permanent agreement with the other princes of Rus that the Novgorodians should thenceforth be free "to take unto themselves a Prince wheresoever it might seem unto them good"—*i.e.* to select a ruler from any princely line they chose.

The *riadi* or treaties by means of which Novgorod imposed its conditions upon its Prince defined also his status in the local administration. Only faint traces of such treaties being made and sworn to on the cross appear during the first half of the twelfth century, but, later on, we see them distinctly referred to in the Chronicle's pages. In 1209 the Novgorodians gave Vsevolod their active support in his campaign against Riazan, and in return for this assistance were granted " full freedom in the ordinances of the old Princes." Likewise (says the Chronicle) Vsevolod added to that the charge : " Love ye them who do good unto you, and punish the evil." This means that he re-established certain statutes made by former Princes for the defining of the rights of the Novgorodians, as also that he granted the city independent jurisdiction in criminal matters. Again, in 1218, when Mstislav (son of Mstislav the Bold, and Prince of Torepetz) left Novgorod and was succeeded by his kinsman Sviatoslav of Smolensk, the latter demanded the retirement of Tverdislav, the elected *Posadnik* of Novgorod. "But wherefore?" inquired the Novgorodians. "Wherein hath he offended?" "In nought," answered the Prince. Thereupon Tverdislav turned to the assembled *vietché*, and said: "Right glad am I that I have offended in nought: yet remember ye, my brethren, that ye are free both in *Posadniki* and Princes." This was a sufficient hint for the citizens, who closed the matter by saying to the Prince: "Thou, forsooth, wouldst deprive a man of his office, even though thou hast sworn to us upon the Cross that thou wouldst deprive no man without cause." From the above instances we see that, as early as the thirteenth century, it was the custom for the Princes of Novgorod to confirm certain rights to the citizens by oath; and the condition that no official should be dismissed without cause—*i.e.* without trial—figures in all treaties of the citizens with their Princes as one of the guarantees of Novgorodian freedom.

It is from copies of these treaties that we glean all our information concerning the privileges acquired by the Novgorodians. The three earliest copies of such a treaty which lie at our disposal date from the latter half of the thirteenth century, and contain the conditions under which Yaroslav, son of Yaroslav of Tver, was to rule Novgorodian territory. Two of these copies were written in the year 1265, and the other one in 1270, and, with a few slight alterations and additions, all subsequent treaties repeat the conditions contained in this one made with Yaroslav. From the copies in question we see clearly what were the bases of Novgorod's political organisation, and what were the principal conditions of the city's freedom. The citizens begin the treaty by binding Yaroslav to kiss the self-same cross upon which their fathers and grandfathers, as well as his own father, had always sworn their oaths. Thence they go on to name as the principal social obligation to be imposed upon the Prince the undertaking that he will rule "and maintain Novgorod according to the custom of ancient times." From this it follows that the conditions set forth in the treaty were not mere innovations, but bequests handed down from antiquity. The treaty defines (1) the judicial-administrative relations of the Prince to the city, (2) the financial relations of the city to the Prince, and (3) the relations of the Prince to Novgorodian commerce.

Under this treaty the Prince was to be the supreme judicial and administrative authority in Novgorod, the arbiter of private civil relations as regulated by local law and custom, and the ratifier and maintainer of contracts. Yet all these judicial and administrative functions were to be performed by him, not alone or at his personal discretion, but in company with, and with the consent of, an elected *Posadnik*. "Without the *Posadnik*, O Prince, shalt thou hold no courts, nor bestow *volosti*, nor grant charters." For such lesser administrative posts (the "*volosti*" mentioned in the above clause) as did not require election by the *vietché*, but only nomination by the Prince, he was to select officials from among the Novgorodian community itself, and not from among the ranks of his own retinue : all such appointments, however, to be subject to the approval of the *Posadnik*, as well as to the condition that the Prince might not cancel them (nor, indeed, any other appointment, whether elective or nominated) without trial. Likewise he was to perform all his judicial and administrative duties *in person* at Novgorod, and not from Suzdal, where his *otchina* was situated. "Not from the land of Suzdal shalt thou administer Novgorod nor apportion *volosti*." Thus all the Prince's judicial and administrative work was to be performed under the constant and watchful supervision of the people's representative, the *Posadnik*.

In this treaty, too, we find the *financial* relations of the citizens with their Prince defined with jealous minuteness, as intended in every possible way to tie his hands with regard to his income from Novgorodian territory. From those provinces which formed no part of the original possessions of Novgorod (such as Volok, Torzhok, Vologda, Zavolochïe, and so on) he was to receive "*dar*" or tribute, as also (in instalments) from the citizens of Novgorod *so long as he was present in the city*, but not during his absences from it. Likewise fear of his seizing Zavolochïe or inducing it to secede led the Novgorodians to employ every possible means to prevent him from holding communication direct with that large and important province. To this end we find inserted in the treaty a demand that the Prince should either let his Zavolochian dues to citizens of Novgorod or have them collected by an official from the city, who, instead of taking them direct to Suzdal (where the Prince's *otchina* lay), should convey them first to Novgorod, whence they would subsequently be handed over to the Prince. This procedure was designed to enable Novgorod to keep a tight hold over the transaction. After the Tartar invasion Novgorod was forced, like the rest of Rus, to furnish its quota of "Tartar impost"—the Khan entrusting the collection of the tax (locally known as the "*tcherni bor*" or poll-tax) to the Suzerain Prince of Vladimir, who at that time was usually administrator also of Novgorod. The Novgorodians, however, collected the tax themselves, and dispatched it to the Suzerain, who, in his turn, transmitted it to the Horde. In addition to the above-mentioned dues, Prince Yaroslav was to have the use—when in Novgorodian territory—of certain judicial and transit fees, as well as of tolls upon fishing, crop-cutting, wild bee-keeping, and hunting. Nevertheless these sources of income were only to be enjoyed by him in agreed proportions and in accordance with exact rules framed for fixed periods, while he was also expressly forbidden to possess any sources of income *of his own* in Novgorodian territory—*i.e.* any sources which were altogether independent of Novgorod. Above all things the citizens desired to prevent him from forming, in Novgorodian territory, any such direct juridical or industrial ties as might enable him to override the elected authorities of Novgorod and so to obtain a permanent footing in the place. To that end they inserted into the treaty a special clause binding the Prince, his wife, his boyars, and his courtiers not to acquire or lease any village or settlement whatsoever in Novgorodian territory, nor yet to grant any Novgorodian a loan—*i.e.* not to place any Novgorodian subject in a position of personal dependence upon Novgorod's ruler or his *entourage*.

Similar precision of detail marks the defining of the Prince's relations to Novgorodian commerce. Trade, both domestic and foreign, was the life-blood of the city : consequently Novgorod needed a Prince both to defend its frontiers and to safeguard its trade interests. Under the treaty in question Prince Yaroslav was bound to guarantee safe conduct to all Novgorodian traders in his Principality,[1] as well as to admit all other merchants to the same as "sojourners without hindrance." Likewise the treaty defined exactly what tolls he was to take of each boat-load or wagon-load of Novgorodian merchandise in his dominions. Foreign traders began to settle in Novgorod at an early date, for even about the middle of the twelfth century we find merchants there who had come from Visbi, on the Isle of Gothland—then the centre of Baltic trade. These Gothlanders built an exchange and church on the *Torgovaia* side of the river, and dedicated the church ("the Varangian temple," as the Novgorodians usually called it) to the Scandinavian saint, Olaf. Later on, some merchants from German towns who likewise had formed a trading company on the Isle of Gothland came and built an exchange beside that of the Scandinavians, and added thereto, in 1184, "the German temple," —*i.e.* a German church dedicated to St. Peter. With the growth of the

---

[1] *i.e.* the Principality of Suzdal.

Hanseatic League the Germans gradually squeezed out the Gothlanders from Novgorod, and began to use the Scandinavian exchange as well as their own; which development was followed by the removal of the headquarters of the German-Novgorodian trading company from Visbi to Lubeck, then the chief city of the Hanseatic League. The Novgorodians set great store by their Baltic commerce, and granted generous exemptions to the two foreign trading companies, although the corporate constitution and carefully elaborated business system of the oversea merchants must have enabled the latter to extract far more profit from Novgorod than ever Novgorod succeeded in extracting from them. Finally, this treaty with Yaroslav stipulated that the Prince should participate in the city's commerce with foreign merchants only through the agency of Novgorodian merchants, as well as be debarred from closing the German exchange or from appointing to it officials of his own. This was designed to safeguard Novgorod's foreign trade from falling into the Prince's hands.

It cannot be said that the treaty defines the Prince's relations to Novgorod with absolute fullness and from every aspect. One of the chief purposes, if not *the* chief purpose, for which Novgorod required a Prince was to defend its territory from external attack—and of this the treaty with Yaroslav of Tver says nothing, while even later treaties say no more than that, in the event of a rupture with the Germans or the Lithuanians or any other people, the Prince was to "aid Novgorod without cunning." The Prince's status is not made clear by these treaties for the reason that his commission was not clear, so far as can be gathered from his rights and obligations. Those rights and obligations are not directly specified, but only adumbrated, since the wording of the documents formulates only the limits of the one and the results of (*i.e.* the remuneration to be awarded for the fulfilment of) the other. Indeed, the suspicious, scrupulously detailed specification of the *korm* or sources of such remuneration occupies by far the greater part of these treaties between Novgorodian Princes and people. If in this connection, however, we recall the status of the Prince and his retinue in the old trading towns of Rus of the ninth century, it will be remembered that in those days he was the guardian of the town and its trade; and it was a precisely similar position that the Prince of Novgorod occupied in the appanage period also. An excellent definition of that position is to be found in the Chronicle of Pskov where it dubs one of the Novgorodian Princes of the fifteenth century "the war-making, *kept*[1] Prince alongside

[1] *Kormlenni*—literally, fed.

of whom the citizens may stand and fight." This status of their Prince (*i.e.* that of a hired fighter) was strictly maintained by the Novgorodians (a people ever true to their traditions) down to the very close of their independence. Their fathers and grandfathers had always looked upon him as such, and consequently neither they nor their children could or would do otherwise. Unfortunately this view which Novgorod took of its Prince during the appanage period by no means coincided with the view which the Prince took of Novgorod.

Now let us pass to the organisation of the Novgorodian administration and judiciary. These were based upon the exact definition of the relations of the city to its Prince—a definition which was secured, as we have seen, through treaties. Yet, inasmuch as the other provincial capitals of Rus had been accustomed thus to define their relations with their Princes at a period as early as the twelfth century, it follows that Novgorod of appanage times had only just developed an order of political relations which had been the rule throughout the rest of Rus at a much earlier stage. That order, however, had proved a failure in the other provinces, whereas in Novgorod it had had time to develop into a complex system of administrative rules. Therein lay at once Novgorod's similarity to the other provincial capitals of Kievan Rus and its dissimilarity from them. Let us glance at the bases of the system in question.

Novgorod never possessed any permanent Princes of its own. Though theoretically the common property of the princely stock at large, and therefore to be ruled in order of seniority by the senior members of that stock (*i.e.* by the Suzerain Princes), it was, in practice, a no-man's land, and, through selecting its Princes at random, on mere terms of remuneration and maintenance, always remained as much a stranger to them as they to it. In proportion, therefore, as it established relations with its Princes more and more by treaty, the more did the ruler of Novgorod cease to be bound by any organic ties to the local community. In fact, he and his retinue mingled with it only in mechanical fashion and as an extraneous, temporary force, since the Prince's residence (the Gorodistché as it was generally known) lay some distance outside the city. Hence the centre of gravity in Novgorod was bound in time to become shifted from the Prince's palace to the actual hub of the local community—namely, the Square where the *vietché* met in council. That is why Novgorod of the appanage period constituted a self-governing Commonwealth in spite of the fact that it possessed a Prince. In it we meet also with the same quasi-military organisation as had distinguished the other provincial

capitals of Rus in the era before the Princes. The city as a whole
constituted a *tisiach*—*i.e.* a regiment under the command of the *Tisiatski*,
and this, again, was subdivided into a *sotnia* or "hundred" for each ward
of the city. Each such *sotnia*, with its elected commander or *sotski*,
constituted a separate commune possessed of given powers of self-government and of its own meeting-place and *vietché*. During war-time, therefore,
the *sotnia* formed a military company, and, during peace-time, a political
faction. Nevertheless the *sotnia* was not the smallest administrative unit
in the city, since it was further subdivided into *ulitzi* or streets, of which
each one, with its elected commander or *ulitski*, constituted a special
local *mir* or lesser commune possessed of certain powers of self-government.
On the other hand, the *sotni* were grouped into the larger unit of the
Konetz—two to each *Konetz*, with an elected *kontchanski* who superintended the current affairs of his unit. This, however, he did, not alone,
but with the help of a board of the leading men of his district, who constituted its administration in so far as executive functions were concerned,
but always remained in dependence upon the deliberative body, the local
vietché of the *Konetz*. Finally, the whole five *Kontzi* combined to form
the *Obstchina* (Commonwealth) of Novgorod the Great. Thus Novgorod
represented a many-graded union of large and small local communes, of
which the larger were made up of combinations of the smaller.

The joint will of these several communes of the city was voiced in the
general *vietché* of Novgorod. In origin this *vietché* was precisely similar
to the *vietcha* of other chief towns in Rus; and although so extensive
a political area as Novgorod might have led one to suppose that its
assembly would assume some form more elaborate than the one here
seen, the old Chronicle of Novgorod shows us that that magnitude of
political area led to nothing more than the possession by its *vietché* of
greater prestige and greater independence than was the case elsewhere.
Yet up to the very fall of Novgorod's independence there remained some
notable blanks in the organisation of the city. The *vietché* was sometimes
convened by the Prince, but more often by one of the city's two chief
dignitaries, the *Posadnik* and the *Tisiatski*—or even, in times of faction
wars, by private persons. It was not a body constantly operative, but one
convened only when occasion arose and for no fixed term of session.
The citizens assembled to the sound of the great bell which I have
referred to—a sound which every ear in Novgorod could easily distinguish
from the tones of the church bells of the city; and although, on ordinary
occasions, the *vietché* assembled in the Square known as Yaroslav's Court,

it was accustomed, when the business was the election of a new Bishop of Novgorod, to repair to the Square of the Cathedral of St. Sophia, in which edifice the voting urn was placed on the episcopal throne. Nor was the *vietché*, by its constitution, a *representative* body, a body of deputies, but every man repaired to the Square who considered himself a citizen of full rights. Usually only citizens of the capital repaired thither, but at times inhabitants of two minor towns of the province—namely, Ladoga and Pskov—also attended. Such inhabitants were either commissioners from their respective towns who had been sent to be present at the *vietché* when some question was on foot which concerned their particular town, or chance visitors from the same to whom an invitation had been extended to be present on a given occasion. In 1384, when some citizens of Oriekhov and Korela visited Novgorod for the purpose of laying a complaint against the salaried governor (Prince Patricius of Lithuania) who had been set over them by the ruling city, we find *two vietcha* convened—one to hear the Prince, and the other one to hear the visitors. This, however, was a mere application for redress at the hands of the ruling city, and not in any way a participation by the visitors in the legislative or judicial authority of the *vietché*. Questions calling for the consideration of the *vietché* were laid before it from the *stepen* or rostrum—either by the Prince or by the *Posadnik* or the *Tisiatski*. Within the purview of the assembly lay the whole field of legislation, all questions affecting external policy and internal organisation, and adjudication upon political questions and such of the graver criminal offences as entailed the two extreme penalties—namely, death, and exile accompanied by confiscation of property (the "*potok i razgrablenïe*" of the *Russkaia Pravda*). Likewise the *vietché* established new laws, summoned a new Prince or banished the old one, elected and judged the principal officials of the city, decided official disputes with the Prince, determined the question of peace or war, and so on. In all this legislative work the Prince had a share, but the competition between the two authorities makes it difficult for us to distinguish exactly between their *regular* relations and their *actual*. Under the treaties the Prince was not to declare war "without the word of Novgorod": yet we meet with no condition preventing Novgorod from declaring war without the consent of the Prince, even though the external defence of the country was his especial function. Also, the treaties debarred the ruler from assigning salaried posts (*volosti i kormlenia*) without the consent of the *Posadnik* : yet in practice it usually worked out that the *vietché* did the assigning independently of the Prince. Again, the latter was not to deprive any official of his office "without offence given," but to lay the "offence" of the person concerned before the *vietché*, which would then proceed to hold a court of discipline on the accused: yet we sometimes find the rôles of prosecutor and judge reversed, and the *vietché* summoning a defaulting provincial governor to appear before the Prince. Lastly, the treaties forbade the Prince to dispense with the co-operation of the *Posadnik* when granting charters of rights to any private or official person: yet it not infrequently happened that such charters were issued by the *vietché* over the Prince's head—even without his authority attached, and it was only by a crushing defeat of the Novgorodian garrison that (in 1456) Vassilii the Dark compelled the citizens to forego their practice of granting "charters of *vietché*."

The very composition of the *vietché* forbade of any regular decision or resolution ever being arrived at, since the issue went rather by weight of shouting than by majority of votes. When those present were divided into two parties the issue might even go by *force*—*i.e.* by a faction fight, in which the winning side was recognised as the majority. Of course this was merely a peculiar form of the *polé* or "judgment of God," [1] just as the throwing of accused persons from the Great Bridge by order of the *vietché* was a survival of the old trial by water. Sometimes the entire city was "split asunder" between the two contending factions; whereupon two *vietcha* would assemble simultaneously—one at the usual spot (which lay on the *Torgovaia* side of the river), and the other on the *Sophiskaia* side. These, however, were intestine feuds rather than normal *vietché* debates. More than once the affair would have ended in the two rival *vietcha* taking up arms, meeting on the Great Bridge, and beginning there a battle royal, had not the clergy intervened and parted the combatants. The importance of the Great Bridge as the accustomed scene of Novgorod's faction fights is referred to in a legend introduced into certain of our Russian chronicles, as well as into copies of a foreign one written by Baron Herberstein, [2] who visited Rus at the beginning of the sixteenth century. According to Herberstein's version, the Novgorodians of St. Vladimir's time threw their idol of Perun [3] into the Volkhov; whereupon the enraged god swam to the Bridge, and, laying upon it his staff, uttered the words: "This do I leave with you, O

---

[1] See p. 129.

[2] Ambassador from the court of the German Emperor.

[3] The Slavonic god of thunder.

THE EXECUTIVE AGENTS 335

Novgorodians, that ye may remember me." From that time onwards the Novgorodians always assembled, on a given date, on the Bridge, and set about one another with staves like men demented.

The executive agents of the *vietché* were the two chief elected officials of the city—namely, the officials who, carrying on the current work of civil and legal administration, were known respectively as the *Posadnik* and the *Tisiatski*. So long as they held their posts they ranked as *stepennïe*, *i.e.* men entitled to occupy the *stepen* or rostrum, but when they resigned office they became known as *starïe*—*i.e.* retired officials. To determine their respective departments is no easy task, since not only did both *stepennie* and *starie Posadniki* command the Novgorodian troops in time of war, but the *Tisiatski* likewise performed certain functions in conjunction with the *Posadnik*. However, it seems certain that the *Posadnik* was, first and foremost, the civil governor of the city, and the *Tisiatski* its military and police prefect. Both officials received their commissions for an indefinite period, so that some held their posts for a year, others for less, and others for as much as several years. Not until the fifteenth century, apparently, was any fixed term established for the tenure of those offices. At all events we find the Flemish traveller, Guillebert de Lannoy, who visited Novgorod early in that century, saying of the *Posadnik* and the *Tisiatski* that they were officials appointed *annually*. Both the *Posadnik* and the *Tisiatski* did their work with the help of a staff of subordinate agents—*pristavi, birichi, podvoiski, pozovniki,* and *izvietniki,* who performed various legal, administrative, and police functions, such as proclaiming the decrees of the *vietché,* summoning persons to court, laying information concerning crimes committed, holding inquests, and so on. In remuneration for their services both *Posadnik* and *Tisiatski* received a land-due known as the *poralïe* (from *ralo,* a plough).

In addition to matters of a purely administrative character, the *Posadnik* and the *Tisiatski* took an active share in the *legal* work of the Commonwealth. Of Novgorodian tribunals we find a description given in a portion of the Charter of Law (*Ustav*), composed and promulgated by the local *vietché* towards the close of the city's freedom. The sources of that document were the juridical custom and old-established judicial practice of Novgorod, the decrees of the *vietché,* and the treaties made with the Princes. The first feature in Novgorodian legal administration to strike the attention is the multitude of minor courts. Instead of constituting a department to itself, legal administration was divided up among the various other departments of government—to each of which it was a necessary source of income. The Archbishop had his own court, as also had both the Prince's Representative, the *Posadnik*, and the *Tisiatski*. The rise of these various tribunals imported an increasing element of complexity into legal procedure. Under the treaties the Prince could adjudicate only in the company of the *Posadnik*, while the Charter of Law above-mentioned enacted that the *Posadnik* should sit with the Prince's Representative, but should not be competent, in his absence, to "*end*" a case—merely (presumably) to begin it. In practice this joint jurisdiction of the *Posadnik* and the Prince's Representative worked out thus. The accredited agents of them both—agents known as *tiuni*—sat "in chambers" as we call it, and made a preliminary investigation into each case, with the assistance of two *pristavi* or assessors chosen by the two parties to the suit. These *tiuni*, however, could not finally decide a given case, but were bound to remit it to the court of further instance—either for *doklad* (final judgment) or *peresud* (revision and confirmation of the preliminary proceedings so far as they had gone). This supreme court of judgment or revision consisted jointly of the *Posadnik* and the Prince's Representative, together with ten sworn *dokladchiki* or assessors, drawn from the Prince's boyars and the burghers of each *Konetz* of the city. These ten assessors constituted a permanent panel, and were bound to assemble three times a week in "the Bishop's chambers" of the archiepiscopal palace, on pain of a monetary fine for non-appearance. In time legal procedure became still further complicated by combinations of different jurisdictions in mixed cases—that is to say, in cases involving coadjudication by members of different departments of the judiciary. In suits between a member of the separate ecclesiastical community [1] and a layman one of the city's judges sat either with a representative of the Archbishop or with one of his *tiuni*, while suits between a member of the Prince's *entourage* and a citizen of Novgorod were tried at the Gorodistché by a special commission of two boyars—a Prince's boyar and a Novgorodian, who, if unable to agree upon a common judgment, had to remit the case to the Prince himself, to be adjudicated upon by him in company with the *Posadnik* when he (the Prince) next visited Novgorod. As for the *Tisiatski*, he appears to have dealt with matters of a purely police character, as well as to have been president of the board of three merchants which stood at the head of the local mercantile community and held its sittings near the church of St. John the Baptist—its chief function being to assist the *Posadnik* in deciding suits between Novgorodian merchants and merchants

[1] See p. 166.

belonging to the German exchange in the city. A system of legal procedure so carefully graduated ought to have ensured due justice and social tranquillity in the land ; yet, as a matter of fact, those articles in the Charter of Law which prescribe enormous fines for robbery, for trespass on disputed lands, and for *navodka* or incitement of the populace to assault a judge, produce upon us a very different impression. Such marked stringency of legislation in support of the social order can hardly imply that the social order enjoyed by the community was one of a very satisfactory character.

The *vietché*, then, was the legislative body, and the *Posadnik* and the *Tisiatski* its executive agents as regards administration and law. Yet the very composition of the *vietché* forbade of its formulating any regular decision on any question submitted to it, and still more so of its raising any question or possessing any kind of legislative initiative. All that it could do was to give a plain *answer* to a given question—a plain yea or nay. For that reason a special body was necessary to work out a preliminary abstract of a given legislative *casus*, and to furnish the *vietché* with ready-made plans of all proposed laws and decrees. Such a preparatory and formulative body was provided in the Novgorodian Council of Magnates—the *Herrenrath* of the Germans, and "the Magnates," pure and simple, of Pskov. This Novgorodian Council of Magnates really consisted of the old-time Prince's council of boyars, with the addition of the chief citizens of the place. We meet with such a Prince's council of boyars in the Kiev of St. Vladimir's time. For the decision of questions of more than ordinary importance the Novgorodian Princes of the twelfth century sometimes invited the *sotskie* and *starosti* of the city (the latter the heads of *ulitzi* or streets) to join the boyars on the Council. In proportion, however, as the Prince gradually lost all organic ties with the local community, he and his boyars became more and more squeezed out of the Council of which we are speaking. At that time the permanent president of the body was the local Archbishop, in whose "chambers"—*i.e.* palace—the Council was accustomed to meet; but, later on, the Council came to be composed of the Prince's Representative, past and present *Posadniki* and *Tisiatskie*, and the various *kontchanskie* and *sotskie* of the city. The presence of an inordinate proportion of retired *Posadniki* and *Tisiatskie* on the Council is to be explained by the frequent changes which took place in their respective offices through the struggle of contending parties—changes so frequent that, shortly before the loss of the city's freedom, the Council numbered over fifty members, of whom all, with the exception of the president, bore the honorary title of boyar. As already stated, it was the function of the Council to prepare and present to the *vietché* all questions calling for legislation, and also drafts embodying the same, but not to have an actual voice in any legislation which might follow. Nevertheless, the nature of the socio-political organisation of Novgorod conferred upon the Council a much greater importance than that. Consisting solely, as it did, of representatives of the upper class—a class possessed of great influence in the city at large, this preparatory body frequently pre-decided the very questions which it afterwards formally submitted to the *vietché*, and moved the citizens to give the answer to them which the Council itself desired. For this reason the Council of Magnates was of far greater importance in the history of Novgorod's political life than the *vietché*, which usually constituted merely its obedient instrument. In short, the Council was the hidden, yet exceedingly active, spring of Novgorodian administration.

The central authority of the legal and political administration of Novgorod was a dual one—namely, the *vietché* and the Prince, while the administration of the territory attached to the city was distinguished by duality of *principles*—namely, centralisation and local autonomy. Novgorod was the ruling centre of an extensive area; yet to the component parts of that area it conceded a considerable measure of self-government. The mutual antagonism between the two principles above-named gave rise to a singular relation between the provincial administration and the central. Certain traces of evidence—albeit faint ones—point to the fact that the fundamental areas of territory which later figured as *piatini* were originally assigned among, as well as administratively dependent upon, the five *Kontzi* or wards of Novgorod. As one of our authorities for this we have the Baron Herberstein already mentioned, although his testimony on the point is far from clear. He relates that, some forty years after the fall of Novgorod, he was informed in Moscow that Novgorod had formerly possessed extensive territories divided into five portions, each of which was subject, in public and private matters, to the ordinary, accredited authority of its particular portion of the city ("quarum quaelibet pars non solum de publicis ac privatis rebus cognoscendis ad ordinarium ac competentem suae partis magistratum referebat"). Likewise he states that the inhabitants of those five portions could conclude contracts only with fellow inhabitants of the same portion, and were forbidden to have recourse, in any matter whatsoever, to the administrative authority of a portion other than their own. Evidently what Herberstein meant, or what he was told, was, that each *rural* portion of the Province of Novgorod was subject, in administrative matters, to a *portion of the city*—*i.e.* to a *Konetz* or ward. A similar relation of rural portions to corresponding portions of an urban area obtained also in the case of Pskov, where the *prigorodi* (which locally corresponded to the Novgorodian *piatini*) were divided among the wards of the town on their first creation in 1468—two to a ward. Of the administrative dependence of the Novgorodian *piatini* upon their respective wards there is evidence in Novgorodian documents, since written folios of the end of the fifteenth century show us that holders of suburban estates in the *piatina* of Voti paid socage or rates to the *Nereva Konetz* of the city, to which those lands were adjacent. Again, the Novgorodian Charter of Law describes certain persons in minor *volosti* as *kontchanskie* and *ulitskie* whom it was the duty of the *urban kontchanskie* and *ulitskie* to summon to court when suits were pending against them. Nevertheless the *piatina* was not a self-contained administrative unit, and possessed no local administrative centre of its own, but was divided up according to its *prigorodi*,[1] to which were attached portions of territory originally known as *volosti*, but, during the Muscovite period, as *uezdi* (cantons) or *peresudi* (governments—literally, jurisdictions). Each such *volost* had its own *prigorod* as its administrative centre, so that the only tie uniting the *piatina* into an administrative whole was the central administration of the corresponding *Konetz*. In short, the *prigorod* and its *volost* formed a self-governing commune very similar to the *Konetz* or *sotnia* of the city, and, like them, had its own local *vietché*. Over that *vietché* presided the local *Posadnik*, who was usually appointed from the capital: and it was in the appointment of such local officials by Novgorod that the first of the forms of the political dependence of the *prigorodi* upon the capital consisted. A second of those forms is to be found indicated in the story of Pskov's acquisition of its independence from Novgorod. Up to the middle of the fourteenth century, Pskov was only a *prigorod* of Novgorod, but in 1347 it received a charter of freedom from the capital city, and became known as Novgorod's "younger brother." Under that charter the Novgorodians resigned the right of sending a *posadnik* to Pskov or of summoning Pskovians to Novgorod for trial before the civil or ecclesiastical courts. Instead, the Archbishop was to appoint a representative of himself in Pskov who should act as local ecclesiastical judge and always

---

[1] Minor or attached towns.

be a native of the town. From this we may take it that the legal institutions of the capital served as courts of higher instance for the *prigorodi*. The treaties between Princes and people stipulated that in no court should *sotskie* and *riadovichi* adjudicate without the *Posadnik* and the Prince's Representative : which implies that, like the Novgorodian *tiuni* of the two officials last-mentioned, the authorities of the outlying towns and villages could only *open*—that is to say, make a preliminary investigation into—a case, but for final decision must remit it to the court of *dokladchiki* or assessors in Novgorod. The third form of political dependence of the *prigorodi* upon the capital lay in the right of the latter to tax the former's population. Moreover, Novgorod could assign to its Princes *prigorodi* for those Princes' "maintenance," while in time of war outlying townships likewise had to furnish contingents at Novgorod's bidding, and those contingents were sometimes commanded by Novgorodian *voievodi*. In cases of disobedience to the capital the *prigorodi* could be punished with a fine, or even with *kazn*—which meant military execution of the inhabitants, as well as burning of villages in the *volost* attached to the offending *prigorod*. In 1435 we find Rshev and Veliki Lugi being punished in this manner for refusing to pay *dan* to Novgorod. Nevertheless the political dependence of the *prigorodi* upon the capital was never, for all its variety of form, anything but very slight, for we find *prigorodi* declining to accept *posadniki* appointed from the capital ; Torzhok more than once revolting against Novgorod, and setting up a Prince of its own in opposition to the rightful one ; and (in 1397) the entire *volost* of the Dvina acceding to the first overture which came from Vassilii, Suzerain Prince of Moscow, and swearing allegiance to his rule. In general, the administration of Novgorodian territory presents clear traces of the influence of forces which, acting outwards, paralysed the working of the political centre.

In beginning this chapter I said that the organisation of Novgorodian territory during the appanage period was a further development of the principles underlying the social life of the provincial capitals of old Kievan Rus. Nevertheless it was a development governed by local conditions. It is true that both in Kievan Rus and in Novgorod we meet with duality of authority—namely, the *vietché* and the Prince, as well as with similar treaty relations between them, but in Novgorod those relations were elaborated and defined in greater detail than ever they had been in Kiev, and cast in the stereotyped formulae of a written treaty, while Novgorodian administration was a graduated one, and woven into a complex—not to say complicated—system of regulations: the whole—both relations and regulations—being aimed against the Prince, with whom, nevertheless, the great free city could not well afford to dispense. That is to say, the Prince was required to stand *by* Novgorod, even if not *over* it. For the Commonwealth he represented either a mercenary servant or a foe. If the latter, then the Novgorodians sent to his Gorodistché, as to the palace of a hostile ruler, an ultimatum written on parchment and "setting forth all his fault," with the concluding words: "Else depart thou from us, and we will devise us another Prince." Yet, since the Prince was the sole centralising force which could unite and direct the various individual and associated interests of the locality for a common end, the weakening of his authority only helped a mass of contradictions and causes of dispute to creep into the social life of Novgorod. The vital elements of Novgorodian territory were compounded in a combination which made of that territory an aggregate of large and small local communes which, built on the model of their centre, had either gained or been conceded a greater or less share of autonomy. This aggregate was internally unstable, and united in mechanical fashion only by the threat of external perils, so that the land stood in need of some internal moral force to give it the requisite stability. That force we will seek in the social composition of Novgorod.

CHAPTER XX

Classes of the Novgorodian community—The Novgorodian order of boyars and its origin—
Zhitïe liudi—Merchants and *tchernïe liudi*—*Kholopi, smerdi*, and *polovniki*—Origin and
status of the class of *zemtsi*—Basis of class division in the Novgorodian community—
The political order of Novgorod—Origin of the princely and people's parties, and their
mutual rivalry—Character and importance of the Novgorodian factions—Peculiarities of
the political organisation and life of Pskov—Differences between the political systems of
Novgorod and Pskov—Faults of the Novgorodian political system—The general cause
of the fall of Novgorodian independence—Prophecies concerning the event.

HAVING now completed our study of the political forms of Novgorod the
Great, let us enter into the life of the city, and touch, first, upon the composition of the local community.

The Novgorodian Charter of Law—the document in which we see the
high-water mark of Novgorodian juridical thought—enacted, in its first
article regarding the ecclesiastical court, that "all men shall be judged
equally, both boyar and *zhiti* and *molodchi*," and in a treaty with Casimir of
Lithuania we see that article made applicable also to the joint court of the
Posadnik and the Prince's Representative. Consequently we may suppose
that this formula of equality of persons before the law expressed the final
development of the Novgorodian community in the direction of democracy.
Yet, if so, Novgorod must be regarded as unlike communities of a similar
age to itself—communities, for instance, such as the provincial capitals
of old Kievan Rus, wherein social life was remarkable for its aristocratic
and patrician character.

First of all, we must distinguish the *urban* classes of the Novgorodian
community from the *rural*. The former consisted of boyars, *zhitïe liudi*,
merchants, and *tchernïe liudi* or *molodchi*.

At the head of the community stood the order of boyars. We have
seen that, in other provinces of Rus, this order was based upon free service
of the Prince. In Novgorod, however, the Prince and his retinue represented an extraneous, adventitious force only—a force which did not
enter organically into the composition of the local community. How was
it, then, that an order of boyars could arise in Novgorod where there was
not present the root from which that class had sprung in other provinces

of Rus ? In answering that question we must recall how, until the coming of the Princes, the great trading towns of Rus were administered by a military governor elected from among the ranks of the local industrial class; and it was from the same class that the Novgorodian order of boyars subsequently became formed. In other provinces of Rus the coming of the Princes caused the military-industrial class to become supplanted in the administration of the towns by the Princes' retinues, but in Novgorod various circumstances combined to preserve to that class its administrative functions, even under the Princes. As early as the eleventh century we find the rulers of Novgorod appointing members of the local community to local posts of administration, so that Novgorodian administration became native in its *personnel* even before it became elective. Next, by the opening of the twelfth century the system had given rise to an influential circle or class of leading families—a class exercising a dual function in the government of the local community, since its members not only occupied the chief administrative posts in the city, on the nomination of the Prince, but also headed the city against the Prince whenever the two came to loggerheads. Thus nominated by the Prince to posts which, in other provinces, were assigned only to the Prince's boyars, the Novgorodian ruling class gradually assumed the same name and status as the latter. In the Church Ordinance issued by Vsevolod to Novgorod in 1135 we find him referring to the Novgorodian *sotskïe* as " my men "—and " prince's men " in those days meant boyars. Thus it will be seen that the Novgorodian order of boyars sprang from the same political source as the boyars of other provinces in the Russian land: which source was service to the Prince through nomination by him to the higher administrative posts of the city. Once the name of boyars had been adopted, the local administrative class retained the title even after administrative officials had come to receive their commission, not from the Prince at all, but from the *vietché*.

The class next on the social ladder of Novgorod—the class of *zhitïe liudi*—stands out less clearly in Novgorodian annals, yet sufficiently so to show us that its status approximated to that of the local boyars rather than to that of the two lower strata of the population. Its position, in fact, depended to a certain degree upon the *economic* part played by the boyars. In addition to being elected by the *vietché* to the administrative posts of the city, the leading social class directed the industry of the people. Consisting as it did men who were at once large landowners and capitalists, it played a double part in commerce, since it used its extensive agrarian properties as sources of industrial material rather than as cultivable estates, and so constituted the class which supplied the Novgorodian markets with the commodities—furs, hides, wax, resin, alkali, building-timber, and so on—which formed the principal articles of Russian export. As middlemen between that class and the foreigner stood the Novgorodian merchant class. Instead of employing their capital in independent trading operations, the boyars invested it in credit operations—either as direct loans to merchants, or to finance commercial enterprises carried on through the instrumentality of merchants. Consequently Novgorodian annals and traditions usually present the local boyar in the guise of a moneylender or financier. An instance of this occurs in a passage in which we read that a popular raid made upon the house of a *Posadnik* in the thirteenth century brought to light "money-tables" containing records of loans "without number." This *indirect* participation of the boyars in commerce explains the absence of a boyar from the presidency of the council of the association of merchants which became established in 1135 at a hospice attached to the church of St. John the Baptist. The *zhitie liudi* appear to have been a moderately rich class which, as "*serednïe zhiletskïe*" (the "intermediate householders" of the social terminology of Moscow), stood halfway between the boyars and the *molodchi* or *tchernïe liudi*. They took a more direct share in trading operations than did the boyars, and, with the *tchernïe liudi*, were represented on the council of the mercantile association by the *Tisiatski*. Capitalists of a secondary order and permanent householders in the city, they were also landowners, and frequently on a large scale. De Lannoy (the Flemish traveller already quoted) wrote that, besides boyars, Novgorod contained *gorozhané* or *bourgeois*, who were possessed of great wealth and influence. Evidently he meant the *zhitie liudi*. The fact of the latter being, first and foremost, personal landowners led Moscow (which transported them in thousands to its own provinces after the fall of Novgorod) to rank them, not with urban dwellers or merchants, but with the official class which possessed also landed property. Thus personal land-ownership caused the *zhitie liudi* to approximate closely to the boyars, yet without including them in the close circle of leading families whence the Novgorodian *vietché* was accustomed to select its higher administrative officials, or bringing them into direct administrative association with the boyars (beyond sharing with the latter certain diplomatic and other functions as heads of *Kontzi*).

The third class consisted of those actually engaged in trade—the *kuptzi* or merchants. Standing nearer to the great mass of the *tchernie liudi* than did the two upper classes, the *kuptzi* worked with the aid of boyar capital—either through loans or as the *commissionaires* of a boyar in trade. Nevertheless the members of this class were not all of them upon the same social level, since as an upper grade they had the association of merchants attached to the church of St. John the Baptist—the body which formed, as it were, the "first guild" of the Novgorodian mercantile community. Under the charter which Vsevolod granted to that guild about the year 1135, the right to become a *poshli kupetz* (*i.e.* a full and hereditary member of the "corporation of merchants of St. John") cost fifty silver *grivni*—a fortune in itself according to the then value of the metal. The guild possessed certain important privileges, while its council (composed of two leading merchants, under the presidency of the *Tisiatski*) supervised all commercial matters and litigation in Novgorod, independently of the *Posadnik* and Council of Magnates. Traces are to be found also of trade unions and guilds of a standing inferior to that of St. John, such as the "hundred of merchants" mentioned in a Novgorodian will of the thirteenth century. As for the fourth class of the Novgorodian community, the *tchernïe liudi*, it included all the small artisans and mechanics who received work, or wages for work, from the two upper classes, the boyars and the *zhitïe liudi*.

Such was the composition of the community of the capital. The *prigorodi*—or at all events the more important of them—show the same social divisions. Yet below the urban and rural communities in Novgorodian territory came a still lower stratum of the population—that of *kholopi* or slaves. This was a very numerous body—a fact of which the landownership of the *boyars* and *zhitïe liudi* was the principal cause, seeing that the large rural estates were settled and exploited almost wholly by *kholopi*. As for the free peasant population of Novgorodian territory, it bore the general name of *smerdi*, but was divided into two grades—namely, *smerdi* proper, who worked the state lands of Novgorod, and *polovniki*, who were settled upon the estates of private owners. The latter grade derived its name from a condition of land-tenure almost universal in ancient Rus—namely, the condition of *ispolu* or the making over of one-half of the harvest to the landlord. Nevertheless the Novgorodian *polovniki* held their land on rather less onerous terms, since they only had to surrender every third or fourth sheaf of the harvest, according to the value of the land and of agricultural labour in the given locality. Like the *zakupi* of the *Russkaia Pravda*, they appear to have been more restricted in their rights than were the free peasantry in other parts of Rus, and, indeed, to have approximated closely to absolute *kholopi*. Yet this position of dependency was not of ancient standing at all, but established during the thirteenth and fourteenth centuries—the very period of the growth of Novgorodian freedom! This is clear from Novgorod's treaties with its Princes. The earlier of those documents stipulate that the Prince's judges shall not try a *kholop* without the consent of his master, but in time this condition became altered to include also the *polovnik*, until the landowner ended by acquiring proprietorial jurisdiction even over the *krestianin* who was in his service. Again, the treaty of 1270 with Prince Yaroslav of Tver already referred to stipulated that information laid by a *kholop* against his master should not be credited, while later treaties extended this condition also to the *smerd*. Finally, a treaty of 1308 with Prince Michael of Tver arranged for the extradition from that principality, not only of *kholopi* who might flee thither, but also of *polovniki*. In Muscovite territory no such restrictions upon the movements of free peasants appear before the middle of the fifteenth century, and then only in the form of private, local measures. In the Novgorodian Charter of Law, however, we find traces of actual written agreements to that end being made between master and man, although such agreements were altogether unknown elsewhere in Rus. Likewise the Charter mentions *volostnïe liudi* as persons whom their employers were bound to produce before a court of law in case of the commission of a criminal offence by such employees. Yet these *volostnïe liudi* were not *kholopi*, but *krestiané* who had "given themselves under writing"—*i.e.* contracted themselves—to landowners under certain conditions. From this it is clear that the rural population working the great estates in the free land of Novgorod was a good deal more dependent upon the landowners than was the case anywhere else in Rus of that period.

Another distinctive feature of Novgorodian landownership was the class of peasant-proprietors. This class occurs in no other part of ancient Rus, since everywhere but in Novgorod the peasants worked either on state lands or on lands belonging to a private master. The territories of the free cities, however, furnish a rural class similar to the *krestiané* or free peasants, but holding their lands by right of pure ownership. This class was known as *zemtsi* or *svöezemtsi*. In an agrarian register of Novgorod for the year 1500 the number of *zemtsi* in the three *uezdi* of Novgorod, Ladoga, and Orieshka is computed at four hundred, working rather over seven thousand *dessiatini* [1] of land. Hence each *zemetz* must have possessed, on the average, eighteen *dessiatini*—an average showing that *zemtsi* were petty owners possessed of small establishments. Their tenure of land was marked by peculiar features. For one thing, they seldom owned land *in detachment*, but almost always formed agrarian brotherhoods or associations, based on kindred or on a written agreement. Many such associations owned and cultivated jointly, and others separately, whether in the same village or in different ones, while their method of obtaining the land was by *skladchina* (a "club" or "contribution" system)—separate ownership being usually the result of division of land thus jointly acquired. We meet with one such estate, for instance, which, though covering only eighty-four *dessiatini*, belonged to thirteen co-proprietors ! *Zemtsi* worked their lands themselves, or else leased them to *polovniki*, and, so far as husbandry and the size of their plots were concerned, were in no way to be distinguished from *krestiané*, except that they held their lands by right of absolute ownership. Of this absolute character of their tenure we have evidence in written agrarian registers of the period, in which we read that *zemtsi* exchanged and sold their estates, bought them of relatives, and gave them in dowry with their daughters. Moreover, we find instances of their wives, widows, and sisters figuring as proprietors and co-proprietors of their lands. Finally, in speaking of the events which accompanied the fall of Pskov, annals of that city roundly term the estates of such *zemtsi* their *otchini*. What, then, was the origin of this peculiar class in the territories of the free Town Commonwealths ? Traces of its origin are to be found in registers compiled by Muscovite surveyors after the fall of Novgorod—*i.e.* during the closing years of the fifteenth century. In one such register, compiled in 1500, we find the township of Orieshka set down as containing, not only *gorodchané*, or houses of burghers, but also twenty-nine establishments belonging to *zemtsi*, of whom a certain number are allotted to a sub-grade described as "*lutchi liudi*" ("best men"). The distinction between these *zemtsi* and the burghers or *gorozhané* is clearly marked, as also is that between the *zemtsi* and the *lutchi liudi*. Turning, next, to the list of rural *pogosti* or market centres in the district of Orieshka, we find that the same *zemtsi* who owned establishments in the township of Orieshka owned also lands in its *district*, as well as in sundry neighbouring ones. From this it follows that some of these *zemtsi* lived in the town and leased their rural lands to *krestiané*, while others of them, though numbered among the urban population, lived

---

[1] The *dessiatin* = 2·86 acres.

on their rural properties and let their town houses to *dvorniki* or rent-holders, who paid for them *gorodskoë tiaglo*, or town rates, along with the regular burghers.   It is a curious fact, also, that the register classes in the same grade both lands belonging to *zemtsi* and lands belonging to *kuptsi* (merchants), while among the *zemtsi* there likewise appear the names of a few *popovichi* or sons of priests attached to the churches of the town.   Thus the class of *zemtsi*, though ranking as a rural one, was formed mostly of town-dwellers.   That is to say, it consisted, not of dwellers in the country who had acquired houses in the towns, but of town-dwellers who had acquired lands in the country.   In Novgorodian and Pskovian territory the right to own land was not the exclusive privilege of the official and ruling classes alone, as in other parts of Rus, but was shared also by lower sections of the free population.   Both town and country inhabitants could acquire small estates, not only for agricultural, but also for industrial exploitation, and if they were men of no great wealth they combined, for the purpose, into agrarian associations or companies.   In Novgorod and Pskov such associations or companies bore the special juridical titles of *siabri* (comrades) and *skladniki* (contributors), and it was this *collectivity* of acquisition and ownership that distinguished the type from the boyars and *zhitie liudi*, who acquired and owned *individually*.   Thus the industrial capital of the towns—the principal lever of popular industry in Novgorodian territory—created in that region a unique class of peasant-proprietors.

Now that we have reviewed the composition of the community of Novgorod, it remains only to decide the question whether the above-mentioned social classes were mere economic grades, or whether they were classes in the true *juridical* sense of the word, with special rights and obligations, with differing legitimate (as distinguished from assumed) degrees of importance in the government and life of the commonwealth.   The answer to that question is that they were both the one and the other, since Novgorod's history furnishes few instances of coincidence of economic and political classification of the community.

In studying the basis upon which the system of social division in Novgorod rested we notice, first of all, a sharp differentiation between the political and the social organisation of the Commonwealth—between the forms of its political system and the actual relations of its social life. The forms of its political system bore a democratic stamp.   All members of the free classes were equal before the law ; all free inhabitants of the city had a place and an equal vote in the general *vietché*.   Yet the *social* life of Novgorod was not built upon any such grounds of equality, for in

Novgorodian political life the status of each class depended upon its economic position, while the political authority of each economic grade was determined by its commercial weight.   At the head of the community stood the boyars or large capitalists, with the capitalists of the secondary order—the *zhitie liudi*—in close relation to them, and these two classes formed the political directors of the local community.   Below them stood the merchants, the actual agents in trade, who worked with borrowed or entrusted capital, while at a yet lower level stood the *tchernïe liudi*, the artisans and mechanics, who likewise were placed in economic dependence upon the two upper classes.   Of least importance of all in the political life of the land ranked the rural classes, in that they stood much further than did the urban classes from the chief source of authority and wealth— namely, industrial capital (with the exception of the *zemtsi*, who, by origin, belonged rather to the urban community than to the rural).   Thus the Novgorodian socio-political scale was based upon inequality of classes proportioned to the possession of property.   This correlation between property and social standing expressed itself also in the socio-juridical enactments of Novgorod.   The order of boyars formed the ruling class— the class which, subject to election by the *vietché*, monopolised the higher posts of administration in the city.   This, however, was mere custom, since the *vietché* could have selected its *posadniki* (or any other officials) from what- soever class it liked, but in those days political custom overrode law, and the people's assembly had such a reverence for ancient precedent that it never once (so far as we know) awarded the office of *Posadnik* to a merchant or a *smerd*.   The boyars and *zhitie liudi* furnished the headmen of *Kontzi*, the sworn *dokladchiki* of the joint court of the Prince's Representative and the *Posadnik*, and the elected commissioners for such foreign relations and domestic affairs as needed to be adjusted by deputations from the capital. These important political rights were created by custom, and confirmed both by a long series of treaties with the Princes and (to a certain extent) by the Novgorodian Charter of Law.   We may take it, too, that, as regards rates and taxes, the two ruling classes enjoyed exemptions and rebates.   The same thing, again, is seen in *private* relations.   Both the treaties with the Princes and the Charter of Law established it as a fundamental rule that "all men shall be judged equally."   Yet the merchant or *tcherni* could not bring a suit in person in the "chamber of a *tiun*" (*i.e.* in a preliminary court), but was forced to procure a member of the "*dobri liudi*" or "gentle men"— *i.e.* one of the boyars or *zhitie liudi*—to represent him there.   The merchants, however, had their own class organisation, trades court, and elected administration, and were subject to trial or suit only in Novgorod itself— each man in his local *sto* or "hundred." Furthermore, they shared with the upper classes the privilege of having their lands worked by *kholopi* and *polovniki*, as well as of exercising police supervision and a certain amount of jurisdiction over those workers. Neither the *smerd* nor the *polovnik*, therefore, can be looked upon as having possessed equal rights before the law with the boyars and *zhitïe liudi*. Of the clergy we need not speak, since in Novgorod, as elsewhere, they possessed their own class organisation, their own rights and laws.

Thus, although the economic inequality of the social classes served as the basis and support of their juridical inequality, and both the one and the other inequality were protected by the people as a guarantee of self-rule, that power in no way corresponded, in its form, either to such a social adjustment or to the standing of the higher officials, who derived their authority from the *vietché*. Let us examine this contradiction in the life of Novgorod, since, though it was not the only one which worked disaster in the history of the city, it was a factor of great importance.

We have studied the relations of Novgorod to its Princes, as well as the organisation of its administration, the structure of its community, and the principal elements of its political life. Now let us glance at that life as manifested in the joint working of its forces and illustrated by the phenomena recorded in the ancient Chronicle of Novgorod.

The internal and external conditions under which the great free city lived introduced into its political *régime* two contradictions which communicated an original character to its political life, and which, later, had their share in contributing to bring about the loss of Novgorodian freedom. I have just mentioned one of those two contradictions—the contradiction between the social and the political structure of Novgorod, but it was preceded by an earlier one—a contradiction contained in the relations of Novgorod with its Princes. The city needed a Prince for external defence and the maintenance of internal order, and therefore sought him of its own accord, and occasionally supported him in his position by force. Yet it treated him with the utmost suspicion, endeavoured to restrict his rights and to allow him as little share as possible in the administrative routine, and turned him out as soon as he failed to give satisfaction, These two contradictions gave rise to an extraordinary amount of turbulence and movement in the political life of Novgorod. Indeed, no other capital city of ancient Rus can show such a record in that respect. From earliest times we see an active struggle in progress there between the various political parties, though it was one which differed widely in its character from time to time. In that regard we may divide the internal political life of the city into two periods.

Up to the fourteenth century, Princes not only followed one another in rapid succession at Novgorod, but were always mutual rivals, since they came of different lines. These constant changes of ruler gave rise to local political factions, which took sides with one or another of the Princes, and were captained by the heads of the more wealthy boyar families. Consequently the first period in the history of the political life of Novgorod was signalised by a strife of rival pro-princely parties. Yet it was not the Princes *themselves* who evoked those struggles, but rather the important local interests of which they were the protectors, and to which they served as the mere instruments and figure-heads. To Novgorod a Prince was (as already said) indispensable, not only for external defence, but also for the extension and security of the city's commercial traffic. In their treaties with their Princes the citizens invariably insisted that the latter should not " detain " Novgorodian merchants in their territories, but give them " clear road." Thus, during a difference with the city of Novgorod, the Prince of Suzdal "detained" some Novgorodian merchants whom he caught trading in his dominions ; whereupon the faction in Novgorod to which those merchants belonged at once took steps to compel the local *vietché* to make peace with the Prince. Commercial ties of this kind divided the Novgorodian boyar-capitalists and merchants into opposite parties in the struggle for rival Princes. The rich trading houses (which dealt chiefly with Suzdal and Smolensk) were generally for the descendants of Monomakh who ruled those regions, while the great capitalists (whose transactions lay more particularly with Tchernigov and Kiev) were accustomed to demand a descendant of Oleg when a Prince of the line of Tchernigov ascended the Kievan throne. Thus the strife of factions which filled the history of Novgorod with such clamour up to the opening of the fourteenth century was, above all things, a war of great trading interests.

With the opening of the fourteenth century the frequent replacement of one Prince by another on the Novgorodian throne came to an end, and a change set in in the political life of the Commonwealth. This change stands out very clearly in the pages of the local Chronicle. Between the death of Yaroslav I. and the Tartar invasion the Chronicle of Novgorod records (according to Soloviev) no less than twelve risings in the city, of which only two were altogether unconnected with a change of Prince—*i.e.* had no connection with the continual struggle of local political parties for this, that, or the other ruler.　Between the Tartar invasion, again, and the accession of Ivan III. of Moscow, the local Chronicle records a further twenty outbreaks in Novgorod.　Of these, however, only four, at the most, had any connection with a change of Prince—*i.e.* with the struggles of factions for a given ruler, while the remainder were due to an altogether different cause.　The new cause thus entering into operation with the fourteenth century was a *social* cleavage—a war between the poorer classes of the community and the richer.　Henceforth Novgorod became divided into two camps—the *liepshïe liudi* (or "*viatshïe liudi*," as the Chronicle of Novgorod calls the wealthier section of the population), and the *menshïe liudi* (lit. "lesser men"—*i.e.* the *tchernïe liudi*); so that the fourteenth century saw the struggle between the great trading houses merge into a war of social classes.　This new phase of social rivalry likewise had its root in the economic and political organisation of the city, and it was here that the second contradiction which I have mentioned comes in.　Sharp social cleavage based upon distinctions of property is a very common phenomenon in large industrial cities, especially in those in which republican forms of organisation obtain.　In Novgorod, which could boast of equality of political rights and democratic forms of government, inequality of classes on the basis of property was bound to make itself felt with peculiar keenness, until, assuming an acute character, it exercised an actively incendiary effect upon the lower classes.　That effect was increased the more by the absolute economic dependence of the proletariat upon the great boyar capitalists.　To save themselves from loss of freedom through insolvency,[1] poorer citizens who could not afford to pay their debts took to forming themselves into gangs, and, with runaway slaves for company, engaging in brigandage along the Volga [2]—a proceeding which led to embroilment of the city with Princes further down the river, and especially with the ruler of Moscow.　Though meeting in *vietché* as fellow-citizens possessed of equal rights, the "lesser men" of Novgorod were always painfully conscious of the pressure of a few rich families, yet debarred by ancient precedent from choosing any other rulers for themselves.　This gradually inspired the lower classes of the Novgorodian community with a stubborn antagonism to the upper.　Men of small means become doubly hostile to men of wealth when they are not only placed in financial dependence upon the latter, but are made to feel their authority.　Even before the fourteenth century signs of this social cleavage were not wanting in Novgorod.　For instance, in 1255, when the city entered upon a quarrel with Alexander Nevski,

---

[1] See pp. 154 and 160.　　　　　　[2] See p. 277.

the " lesser men " separated themselves from the " *viatshïe liudi*," and the latter had to concert measures for their subjugation. In this case, however, the " lesser men " did not constitute a political party, but a class at once oppressed and resentful—a mass of *tchernie liudi* whom the ruling class desired to place in subjection to itself. It was only when the order of boyars itself became divided, and there appeared at the head of the Novgorodian populace a few rich boyar families who had become separated from their fellows through political differences, that the " lesser men " acquired the character of a political party.

Thus, throughout the history of the city as a free Commonwealth the Novgorodian boyars remained arbiters of its political life. This placed the real government of the community permanently in the hands of a few leading families. From them the *vietché* selected its *Posadniki* and *Tisiatskïe*; from them were drawn the members of the Novgorodian Administrative Council, which communicated to local political life its varying tendencies. As we read the Chronicle of Novgorod we can easily discern this predominance of the boyar aristocracy—a predominance which makes that class appear practically a close-locked administrative oligarchy. Twenty-three times during the thirteenth century did the *vietché* elect a *Posadnik*, yet only fifteen persons did it select for that office, since some of those persons filled it and were re-elected again. Of them no fewer than ten belonged to two leading families only, of which one derived its origin from a Novgorodian boyar named Michalka Stepanitch, and the other from a boyar named Miroshka Nezdinitch—both of them men who were *Posadniki* of Novgorod at about the close of the twelfth century and the beginning of the thirteenth. These two families stood in permanent hostility to one another and at the head of rival political factions. The Michalkaites were leaders of the *Sophiskaia Storona*, where most of the boyars resided, and the Miroshkaites of the more democratic *Torgovaia Storona*, where the risings of the " lesser men " against the boyars usually originated. In short, the thirteenth century saw the office of *Posadnik* remain almost exclusively in the hands of two boyar families alone, while during the course of the two hundred years between the close of the twelfth century and the close of the fourteenth the Michalka family supplied no fewer than twelve *Posadniki*, not to mention holders of other less important posts. Thus the contradiction rooted in the political system of Novgorod led to the Commonwealth becoming, for all its democratic forms of organisation, an aristocratic republic, while the local community, unceasingly restless and distrustful of its superiors, remained, throughout the period of its political freedom, in the hands of a few leading families of rich capitalists.

Although dry and obscure in the manner of its exposition, the old Chronicle of Novgorod is by no means niggardly of colour in describing the faction fights of its city, and gives a vivid description of the occasions when the internal mal-adjustment of Novgorodian political life sought to right itself in the Square. The autonomy of the local communities of the *Kontzi* and *ulitzi* sometimes asserted itself by slighting the will of the general *vietché* of the capital. In 1359 the *Slavenski Konetz* conceived a dislike to the then *Posadnik*, Andreian Zacharinitch, and took upon itself to instal another one in his stead. Availing themselves of their proximity to the Square of Yaroslav, the Slavenskians armed themselves, and, falling upon the *vietché*, put the defenceless citizens of the *Sophiskaia Storona* to flight, beat and "stripped" (*i.e.* robbed) many of the boyars, and killed one of their number. Next, they swept across the Great Bridge, and for three days fought a running fight along the two banks of the river, until persuaded by the clergy to disperse. The only result of it was that, although the Slavenskians had many of their houses destroyed in the fight and numbers of innocent people were slain, the office of *Posadnik* went to a *third* boyar when peace had been established. "God did not suffer the Devil to rejoice unto the end," says the narrator in conclusion, "but did exalt Christendom from generation unto generation." The mutual enmity existing between the two sides of the city—between the aristocratic *Sophiskaia Storona* and the democratic *Sophiskaia Storona*—manifested itself very characteristically in a riot which occurred in the year 1418. One day a man named Stepanko—a man of humble means and station—seized a boyar in the street, and shouted to the passersby: "Help me, my masters, to beat this villain!": whereupon the boyar was dragged before the *vietché*, almost beaten to death, and thrown from the Bridge as a criminal of state. A fisherman, however, who chanced to be near the spot had compassion on the boyar, and helped him into his skiff; in return for which act the populace looted the fisherman's house. Anxious to avenge himself for the wrong done him, the boyar thus providentially rescued from popular execution sought out the original offender, and had him arrested. Thereupon the *vietché* was summoned to Yaroslav's Square, and the *tchernïe liudi* and boyars took opposite sides in the debate. Next the *tchernïe* proceeded in full panoply and with a flag to Kuzmodemian-skaia Street, where the boyar in question lived, and looted both the street and his house; whereupon, fearing lest worse should happen, the other boyars sent orders for Stepanko (the original offender) to be set at liberty, and requested the Archbishop to forward him, under escort of a priest and one of his (the Archbishop's) boyars, into the presence of the *vietché*. Intoxicated, however, with their political debauch, the general mass of the *vietché* refused to be appeased, and proceeded to settle old scores with the aristocracy by looting several of the boyars' streets, as well as the Monastery of St. Nicholas, where the boyars had their granaries. In fact, Prusskaia Street—a leading haunt of the upper class—was the only one to escape. That done, the mob returned to its own (the *Torgovaia*) side of the river, crying out : " The *Sophiskaia Storona* is coming to lay waste our houses ! " Immediately a clamour arose from every quarter of the city, and armed men began to converge from all sides upon the Bridge. This time a fight in earnest began, and men were falling rapidly, when all of a sudden there came a terrific clap of thunder, and the combatants stopped in terror. Seizing the opportunity, the Archbishop and his staff of clergy, robed in their sacramental vestments, pushed forwards towards the Bridge, where, standing in the middle, the Archbishop blessed with his crucifix the two contending parties. Thereafter, at the prelate's bidding, the combatants dispersed.

During outbreaks of this kind the Novgorodian *vietché* acquired an importance which it did not possess under normal circumstances. Ordinarily it only legislated, exercised partial supervision over the course of administration and justice, and removed elective officials with whom it was dissatisfied. Likewise, in an agrarian suit unduly protracted through the dilatoriness of judges the plaintiff could come and claim of the *vietché* two representatives, to compel the court to decide the said suit within a given period. No sooner, however, did the people suspect or see that the elective authorities, the ruling class in general, were devising or committing acts which seemed to it criminal or dangerous, than the *vietché* constituted itself into a supreme tribunal, and became not so much an assembly of the people as an assembly of the populace. That is to say, it became representative only of the *Torgovaia* half of the city, and, reversing the usual order of things, constituted the government in power, with the boyars as an opposition. Nevertheless, inasmuch as the movement, under such circumstances, was directed against the authority of the powers in being, it acquired the guise of popular rebellion, and its anarchistic character was further enhanced by its applying to political offences certain forms of jurisprudence which had outlived their day. Thus its throwing of offenders from the Great Bridge was a relic of an old form of the "judgment of God"—namely, the trial by water, while in the looting of boyars' residences and the expulsion of their owners from the city we see a dim reminiscence of the old penalty which the *Russkaia Pravda* termed "*potok i razgrablenïe.*" Of course, no social system which needs to be supported by methods of anarchy can be called a sound one, yet, for the Novgorodian *vietché*, rebellion was the only possible means of checking the administration when, in the popular opinion, it was menacing the public weal. Novgorod was not the only state in which recourse to such a means became necessary, as we know from the history of medieval Europe.

The real root of these faults in the political organisation and life of Novgorod lay, not in the nature of a free town commonwealth as such, but in conditions which ought not to have existed at all. Of this Pskov was a proof. Formerly a *prigorod* of Novgorod, but, from the beginning of the fourteenth century onwards, a free city like Novgorod itself, Pskov was by no means a copy of the latter. In passing, let me point out Pskov's more peculiar features, and then go on to conclude my remarks upon its "elder brother."

As the student of the history of the free cities passes from Novgorodian annals to those of Pskov he experiences a feeling of relief—a feeling as though he were escaping from a crowded market-place into a quiet alley. This is because Pskovian records treat largely of *peaceful* doings—of inspections by the Prince, of the building of churches, city walls, and baths, of signs revealed by *ikons*, of pestilence and fires, and of occasional differences with the Archbishop of Novgorod (the diocesan of Pskov)— differences usually arising out of questions of ecclesiastical legal jurisdiction or the allotment of clergy dues. Items relating to the founding of churches occur with particular frequency, and we gather that during the nineteen years 1370–88 the citizens built no less than fourteen stone edifices of this kind. No stormy scenes or faction fights are to be found recorded as occurring in the Square of the *vietché* before the Troitski Cathedral,[1] nor yet any of that heat in the relations of the city to its Princes, that social antagonism and party rancour, which so distinguished Novgorod. On one occasion we find the two *Posadniki* of the city being beaten in the presence of the *vietché* for some dereliction of duty; on another, priests being knouted for protesting against taxation of the clergy for military purposes ; and on a third, an insolent *Namiestnik*, or Prince's Representative, being dislodged from the steps of the rostrum. These, however,

[1] Cathedral of the Holy Trinity.

were mere by-happenings in the political world of Pskov. In the external affairs of the city matters pursued their course less peacefully. For three centuries after the unification of the neighbouring state of Lithuania and the rise of the Order of Swordbearing Knights, Pskov, which stood on the outermost edge of Rus, was forced to maintain a stubborn warfare with those two foes, and thus to exhaust the resources of a little province which, only some three hundred versts in length, stretched north and south in a narrow strip from the sources of the river Velikaia to the river Narova. Considering the equivocal and occasionally openly hostile attitude of Novgorod (for which Pskov, with its quadruple defences, served as an advanced bulwark towards the South and West), this struggle against aliens was a great historical service performed by Pskov, not only for Novgorod, but for the whole of the rest of the Russian land. It was this struggle, also, which, combined with the restricted area of Pskovian territory, created the distinguishing features in the political life and organisation of the city.

To begin with, the conditions just named compelled Pskov to adopt greater concentration of administration and territorial demarcation than was necessary in the case of Novgorod. Like the latter, it was divided into *Kontzi* (six in number, according to the local chronicle), and subdivided into *sotni*. For purposes of military administration each *Konetz* contained two of the twelve *prigorodi* (in this case small fortified settlements) which the province comprised, and the majority of which—Izborsk, Gdov, Ostrov, Opochka, and so on—were situated in the south-westernmost corner of Pskovian territory, where the frontier was most open to attack from Lithuania and Livonia. Each *prigorod* had attached to it also a rural *volost*, but these were only small administrative areas, and in no way to be compared to the extensive *volosti* attached to the more important of the Novgorodian *prigorodi*. Nevertheless the Pskovian *prigorodi*, like the Novgorodian, enjoyed a certain measure of autonomy— although, as strategic points rather than local territorial centres, they never attained to such independence as did some of the *prigorodi* of the superior city. On the other hand, the conditions above referred to caused the central administration of Pskov to acquire more strength and unity than distinguished the central administration of Novgorod. As a *prigorod*, Pskov never constituted a *tisiatch* (the military unit of the senior towns), nor did it form itself into one even after it had obtained its freedom. Consequently its administration did not comprise an office of *Tisiatski*, but, instead, had *two Posadniki*, who, with the *posadniki* of *Kontzi*, the *sotskie*, and (apparently) the *kontchanskïe*, constituted, under the Prince or his Representative, an administrative council similar to that of Novgorod, as well as (minus the *kontchanskïe*) a board of judges corresponding to the Novgorodian court of *dokladchiki*, and holding its sessions in what the local chronicle calls "the fore-court of the Prince." The status of Pskov as a *prigorod* of Novgorod can best be gathered from the powers of its Prince after the city had become a free commonwealth. Up to that time the Prince of Pskov, whether appointed from Novgorod or selected independently by the city itself, was the representative or "underling" of the Novgorodian Prince and *vietché*. That status he still retained, except that his share of authority passed to the *vietché* of Pskov, while he himself served that body merely as the paid commander of its warlike forces—as an official who, in return for defending the country and fulfilling all other behests of the *vietché* on the same footing as the *Posadniki*, received a stipulated amount of remuneration. The *rights* of the Prince of Novgorod—his share in legislation and administration, in the appointment and dismissal of officials—passed, not to the Prince of Pskov, but to the local *vietché*, which now added to its legislative and judicial functions in political and extraordinary matters an active share in the current work of administration. This concentration of authority in the *vietché* was rendered *imperative* by the threat of external peril and *possible* by the confined limits of the province.

The effect of these two conditions in communicating unity and compactness to the territory of Pskov can be seen even more clearly in the composition of the local community. Pskov, like Novgorod, possessed an influential order of boyars, who formed the ruling class, and in whose families the higher posts of administration passed downwards from generation to generation; while in the Pskovian *vietché*, as in the Novgorodian, high words often passed between the common people and the aristocracy. Nevertheless in Pskov the boyar aristocracy never became an oligarchy, political differences never developed into social antagonism or fired a struggle of parties, and the impulses and irregularities incidental to popular government never got out of hand or became incapable of rectification. Let me point out some of the causes which gave rise to this tendency of social relations—to these what I might call *amenities* of political life, in Pskov. The limited area of Pskovian territory afforded no field for boyar landownership on a large scale as did the unlimited expanse of Novgorodian possessions. For that reason the political strength of the Pskovian boyars found inadequate support in their economic position, and this circumstance served to check the political aspirations of the ruling

class.   Moreover, we can discern no sharp-cut inequality of classes or
chronic social antagonism of the kind which existed in Novgorod.   The
boyars were "mulcted"—*i.e.* had their lands assessed by the *vietché* for
payment of military tax—at the same rate as the other sections of the
population.   Again, Pskov, like Novgorod, lived by commerce, and therefore ranked agrarian capital above industrial equally with the parent city :
yet that this had the effect of drawing classes together which in Novgorod were sharply divided is shown by the fact that the local chronicle
represents the merchants of Pskov as equal to the boyars and superior to
the *zhitie liudi*.   The most remarkable feature of all, however, is presented
by the composition of the Pskovian *tchernie liudi*, especially in the rural
districts.   In Pskovian territory, as in Novgorodian, there became formed
a class of *zemtsi* or peasant-proprietors, though not, so far as we can see, a
class either of *kholopi* or of semi-free workers akin to the Novgorodian
polovniki.   In this respect, indeed, the province of Pskov was probably
the one exception in all Rus.   Pskovian legislation seems to have paid
great attention to the interests of the "*izornik*," as the *krestianin* or free
peasant who worked the land of a private owner was locally termed.   The
izornik was a free agricultural labourer who hired land from a private
proprietor at a rental of one shock in every three or four, and enjoyed the
right of passing at will from one landlord to another.   Everywhere in
ancient Rus the hire of land from a private owner by a *krestianin* was con-
ditioned by a loan—a transaction which seldom failed to place the former
in a position of more or less personal dependence upon the latter.   This
was the case with the Pskovian *izornik* and his loan (locally known as the
pokruta).   Yet this monetary obligation placed no restriction upon the
personal freedom of the *izornik*.   According to the *Russkaia Pravda*, a
zakup who ran away from his master without first of all indemnifying him
became the master's full slave, but under the law of Pskov an *izornik* who
absconded without first of all repaying the amount of his *pokruta* was only
liable to have such property as he left behind him distrained upon by the
landlord in presence of the local officials.   If the property did not realise
sufficient to pay the requisite sum, then the landlord could sue the *izornik*
for the balance on his return—but only on condition that no further consequences ensued for the delinquent.

These regulations as to the *izornik* are to be found set forth in the
Pskovian *Sudnaia Gramota* or *Sudnaia Pravda* [1]—a remarkable legislative
work by the local *vietché* which attained its final form during the latter

[1] Charter or Code of Law.

half of the fifteenth century and had for its fundamental source local juridical custom. Nevertheless the code is very difficult to decipher, since the only known complete copy of it is marred by clerical errors and blank spaces, as well as, here and there, by confusion of the wording. Moreover, its language contains not a few local idioms of a kind not to be found in any other work of ancient Rus, while some of the *casus* which it formulates are set forth too concisely, too much by means of references which, though, doubtless, intelligible in their day, are purely cryptic now. Nevertheless, the labour of studying it is repaid by the interests of its contents. Although, like similar ordinances or legal digests of ancient Rus, the Pskovian *Pravda* apportions a considerable place to the composition and practice of courts, it also furnishes an abundant store of norms and material law, especially of civil law. In it we find detailed regulations affecting contracts between vendor and purchaser and lender and borrower, as well as enactments concerning trading and agrarian companies and family relations with regard to property. A creditor who demanded payment of a debt before it was due forfeited the agreed interest (*gostinetz*), and the debtor could also apply for a rebate of the interest paid to date. Likewise a borrower was debarred from repaying a debt after he had forfeited the pledge upon which the debt was secured, but could recover the latter (either through process on oath or through the *sudebni pöedinok* or legal duel) if the creditor declined either to sue for the principal at once or to retain the pledge in question. Again, a person who pledged immoveable property bequeathed to him for his own personal maintenance (*kormlia*) was bound to redeem it; but, inasmuch as the pledging had been illegal, the offender was to enjoy the property no longer, seeing that he had "sold his own *kormlia*." Thus the code furnishes juridical theories calling for the exercise of a well-developed instinct for law, and provides for all legal junctures which might arise in the active and complex civil traffic of a trading city. Throughout its articles it seems, from the manner in which it defines relations with regard to property and civil obligations, to be striving to establish a mean between warring private interests, and upon that mean to construct a system governed not only by laws but also by morals. That is why, in its section on legal testimony, it gives a preferential value to the oath, and usually affords a litigant the option of having his suit decided on that basis. "If he so desire, let him kiss the Cross, and lay . . . beside the same"—meaning that, before giving evidence, the parties to a suit might swear to the truth of their testimony, and then deposit beside the crucifix either the article in dispute or its value in money. Such faith on the part of the law in the conscience of litigants can only have arisen out of the character of local life. Herberstein, who gathered his observations and impressions about Rus a few years after the fall of Pskovian independence, expressed himself with great enthusiasm on the subject of the humane and enlightened morals of the Pskovians ; saying that in all their trading transactions they were remarkable for strict honour and integrity, in that they never uttered a single word to mislead the purchaser, but set forth the matter clearly, succinctly, and without evasion.

It was in this Pskovian standard of morality that there lay the spiritual force which counteracted, in the case of Pskov, the contradictions which we have noted in the political life of Novgorod. Yet all the elements of those contradictions were present in the younger city—a Prince summoned or expelled at will, a rich and influential class of boyars in charge of the administration, a body of industrial capital able to exert pressure upon labour, and a popular assembly enabling labour to exert pressure upon capital. Nevertheless in Pskov those elements never attained any excessive growth nor lost all power of mutual agreement and harmonious action. Consequently they developed what I might call *political tact*—by which I mean that moral force, expressed in good organisation of the community, careful adjustment of the relations of the different social classes, and a humane and enlightened order of morals, which foreign observers noted in the Pskovians. In Novgorod, on the other hand, that force was centred in one class alone—namely, the clergy, and spent its energies in ceremonious sallies to the Great Bridge for pacific intervention in the brawls of the Novgorodian citizens. This difference between the political systems of the two cities showed itself most clearly in the respective relations of the boyars to their *vietcha*. According to the Pskovian *Sudnaia Gramota*, the local *vietché* could proclaim a new law only at the instance of the city's *Posadniki*, as representing the boyar Council of Magnates, by whom the law in question was first of all to be debated. In Novgorod, on the other hand, a new law was not looked upon as properly established until it had been debated by the *vietché* itself, in the presence, and with the approval, of the city authorities—*i.e.* of the ruling caste, with the Council of Magnates at its head. Without that being done, any decree by the *vietché* was looked upon as constituting an illegal and seditious act —an " arrogance of the rude *tchernïe liudi*," as the Council of Magnates expresses it in one document. In view, however, of the chronic antagonism between the masses and the ruling caste in the Novgorodian *vietché*, the lower orders seldom succeeded in attaining complete agreement with the administration, while, for their part, the boyars were able, through intrigue, to attract a certain proportion of the masses to their side, and so to give the decisions of the *vietché* the appearance of the popular will. In short, whereas in Pskov the Council of Magnates, with the boyars behind it, was an organ of legislative power, in Novgorod the boyars, with the Council of Magnates at their head, were a political party. Consequently we might term the political system of Pskov a mitigated, moderate aristocracy, and that of Novgorod a counterfeit, fictitious democracy.

The irreconcilable contradictions in the political life of Novgorod became the ultimate cause of the internal disruption of Novgorodian freedom. Yet in no other quarter of ancient Rus do we see concentrated such an assortment of conditions favourable to a wide development of political life. Early relieved of the pressure of the Princes' authority, and standing clear both of the princely feuds and of the raids of the Polovsti, Novgorod never suffered any direct persecution or intimidation even at the hands of the Tartars, nor ever saw the face of the Mongol tax-collector. Moreover, the city became the political centre of an immense industrial territory, as well as was drawn at an early period into an active commercial traffic, succeeded in establishing close cultural relations with the European West, and constituted for centuries the intermediary of trade between that European West and the Asiatic East. The spirit of freedom and enterprise, the political consciousness of being a powerful commonwealth known as "the sovereign lord, Novgorod the Great"—nowhere else in Rus were there to be found so many moral and material means for fostering in the community the qualities necessary for the organisation of a strong and upright social order. Yet Novgorod the Great so utilised the gifts bestowed by historical fortune that the internal and external conditions which, in their original combination, created the political freedom of the city gradually became transposed into a new combination which paved the way for the disruption of the city's independence. Let us, therefore, glance once more at Novgorod's fortunes, in a brief review of the faults inherent in its political life.

The nature of Novgorodian territory early evoked an active, multifarious industrial movement, and thus accorded the population access to abundant sources of enrichment. Yet this wealth, when acquired, was distributed very unevenly among the people : which fact, added to political inequality, caused the community to become broken up into sections, and *social cleavage* to set in in the shape of profound antagonism between the "haves" and the "have-nots," between the administration and labour. The troubles with which, for centuries, this cleavage filled the life of Novgorod taught the more serious and thinking section of the population to put less and less value upon the freedom of the city and more and more dependence upon the Prince, as the only ultimate hope of instilling law and order into the self-willed masses and self-seeking classes.

Political freedom helped Novgorod to expand its social forces, especially in the industrial field, since it was upon the principle of autonomy that the political life of the local communes which made up the territory of Novgorod was based. Yet the selfish or unthinking treatment of those communes by the political centre only caused this uniformity of political basis to result in *territorial cleavage.* As irregularities and abuses spread from Novgorod to the *prigorodi* and *volosti* they roused the latter to work for separation (made all the more feasible through local autonomy), while Novgorod evinced neither the will nor the wit to bind them to itself by strong administrative bonds or solid territorial interests. In his description of Novgorodian abuses the local chronicler remarks bitterly that at that period neither law nor a just judge were to be found in Novgorod, while throughout the provinces ruin and extortion, clamour and weeping, were the rule—"so that all men did curse our *starosti*[1] and our city." From the first the larger *volosti* of Novgorodian territory had sought to tear themselves away from their centre. Pskov attained full political independence in the fourteenth century, the remote Novgorodian colony of Viatka adopted an independent attitude towards the metropolis almost from the day of its birth, and the *volost* of the Dvina made more than one determined effort to wrench itself free of the capital. Even when the great city was fighting its last and decisive battle on behalf of its freedom, not only Pskov and Viatka, but also the Dvina *volost* refused Novgorod their aid, and actually sent troops to help Moscow.

We have seen how greatly the political differentiation of Novgorod from the remainder of Rus contributed to the advancement of Novgorodian freedom. Yet there still remained Novgorod's *economic dependence* upon Central or Great Rus. Novgorod could not do without imported grain from that region, and this fact compelled the Novgorodians to keep on good terms with the Great Russian Princes, since the latter, by holding up grain convoys at Torzhok, could soon make the Novgorodians aware that (to quote the local chronicler) "corn went neither unto them nor from them."

---

[1] Elders or headmen.

Prices would rise in Novgorod, and famine draw near, until finally the masses would rise against the boyars, and compel them to come to terms with the enemy.   In 1471 it was Ivan's [1] cutting off of grain supplies, together with the resultant outburst of the Novgorodian populace, which completed the Muscovite triumph first begun by the victory on the Shelona.   Yet Novgorod possessed neither the wit nor the power to make sincere and reliable friends of the Great Russian population and its Princes. Though strange—perhaps, rather, a no man's land—to those Princes, Novgorod was wealthy, and therefore offered a tempting morsel to their appetite, although, on the other hand, the organisation of the Commonwealth served as a vexatious impediment to the Princes' full enjoyment of the morsel.   Various causes also combined to breed hostility to Novgorod in the Great Russian population—those causes being the separate political *ménage* of the Commonwealth, the frequent raids by bands of Novgorodian " *molodtsi* " or " young men " upon outlying towns on the Volga and its tributaries, Novgorod's success in establishing, at an early date, close commercial and cultural ties with the German Catholic West, and lastly, and above all, Novgorod's alliance with the King of Lithuania.   This explains the delight with which Great Rus greeted the fall of Novgorod in the days of Ivan III.   The Great Russians looked upon the Novgorodians as renegades and apostates puffed up with pride.   Indeed, in the eyes of one of the Great Russian chroniclers they were worse even than unbelievers. "They are but infidels," he says, "and for long have not known God. Once were these men of Novgorod of Christendom, but of late they have begun to yield themselves unto the Latins.   The Suzerain Prince Ivan hath gone against them, not as against Christians, but as against strangers and apostates."   While Ivan's troops were battering the Novgorodian forces in the Great Russian provinces, the populace of Novgorod organised itself in large bands, and went roaming over Novgorodian territory in search of plunder: so that, as one chronicler remarks, "the whole country was laid to waste, even unto the sea."

Finally, the essential fault in Novgorodian organisation was *the weakness of the military forces*.   In its early days—to be precise, in the thirteenth century—Novgorod had to carry on a fourfold struggle with the Swedes, the Germans of Livonia, the Lithuanians, and the Princes of Rus, all of whom were rivals for the Novgorodian province.   Later on, Novgorod was foolish enough to complicate its external difficulties by quarrelling with its former *prigorod* Pskov.   In the course of these warrings the Commonwealth evolved a military organisation with, at its head, a *Tisiatski*,

[1] Ivan III.

and, as its nucleus force, a popular contingent or *polk*—the latter capable of expansion, in time of war, through a system known as "*razruba*," or equal contribution of contingents from the city, the *prigorodi*, and the *volosti*. Likewise the burden of war was lightened for Novgorod by those Princes and their retinues whom the city engaged to help it, as well as by Pskov, which, owing to its frontier position, usually had to bear the worst brunt of the fighting. With the middle of the fourteenth century, however, a calm fell upon Novgorod's external relations—a calm only occasionally broken by attacks upon the western frontier. Yet the Commonwealth made not the slightest use of that hundred years of peace to renew and strengthen its old military organisation, but left the matter in abeyance, through over-confidence that it would always be able to find an ally among the rival Princes. By the middle of the fifteenth century, however, the only Princes contending for Novgorod were those of Moscow and Lithuania, and inasmuch as the Commonwealth no longer possessed sufficient forces for its defence, it was forced to tack between the two rivals, and to buy them off in turn. At length Moscow began seriously to threaten Novgorod with loss of independence, whereupon nothing was left for the Commonwealth but to seek help from Lithuania. Yet both to the rest of Rus and a considerable section of the Novgorodian community an actual alliance with the Lithuanian king seemed tantamount to an abandonment of Novgorod's native faith and rightful territory. Truly, in its last years of independence the Commonwealth had bitter reason to repent of its neglect! In 1456 we see two hundred Muscovite foot-soldiers putting five thousand mounted Novgorodian warriors to flight, simply because the latter did not know how to fight in cavalry formation. Again, in 1471, when Novgorod had begun its last decisive struggle with Moscow, and had already lost two complete armies of infantry, it hastened to mount and dispatch into the field a heterogeneous mob of forty thousand tradesmen—artisans and mechanics who, to quote the local chronicle, "had never from birth been a-horse." The result was that, when the two armies met on the Shelona, four thousand five hundred Muscovite troops were sufficient to break the undisciplined Novgorodian mob, and to leave of it twelve thousand dead upon the field.

Such were the faults in the state organisation and life of Novgorod. Yet it must not be supposed that those faults explain Novgorod's fall. They are important to us, not so much as the cause of that catastrophe, as the results of the contradictions in the system of the Commonwealth— as, in fact, a proof that the course of historical affairs has its own logic, as well as a certain symmetry. At about the middle of the fifteenth century thinking people in Novgorod who foresaw the end were disposed to attribute the cause of the approaching disaster to factional differences in the city. Shortly before the death of Vassilii the Dark, Archbishop John of Novgorod promised that ruler that, if he would abandon an expedition against the Commonwealth which he was then planning, he (the Archbishop) would ask of God to deliver Vassilii's son Ivan from the Horde, provided that, in his turn, Ivan would undertake always to respect Novgorodian freedom. Then, suddenly bursting into tears, the Archbishop exclaimed: " Yet who could now arouse my people, or pacify the multitude of my city? Only feuds concern them, and dissension layeth them low." Yet those feuds and other faults in Novgorodian life only explain the *ease* with which Moscow overcame the Commonwealth. Even had Novgorod been free from those faults, it would still have fallen, since the destiny of the city was decided, not by local conditions, but by a *general* cause, an historical process of far-reaching scope and all-compelling power. To that process we referred when concluding the history of the Principality of Moscow during the appanage period. By the middle of the fifteenth century the formation of the Great Russian nationality was complete, and it lacked only political unity. Forced to fight for its very existence against the East, the West, and the South, it sought a political centre around which it could group its forces in the grave and perilous struggle which confronted it. How Moscow became that centre, and how the dynastic operations of the Muscovite Princes chanced to coincide with the political needs of the Great Russian population, we have already seen. That coincidence decided the fate, not only of Novgorod, but also of other self-governing political units which still survived in Rus of the middle fifteenth century. The extinction of the separate existence of territorial fragments independently of their political *régime* was a sacrifice demanded by the common welfare of the land, since Rus was now becoming a strictly centralised and uniformly organised state. The ruler of Moscow was merely the executor of that demand. Although the principles of its form of popular government caused Novgorod also to constitute an organic portion of Great Rus, it lived a life separate from the latter, and tried to persist in so doing, and to avoid sharing in Great Russian interests and burdens. For instance, in the negotiations with Ivan III. in 1477, the Novgorodians propounded a condition that they should not be sent to serve "in the lower land, towards the coast"—*i.e.* be made to defend the southernmost region of the Muscovite State from the Tartars. In short, had its political organisation been sounder, Novgorood might have put up a better fight with Moscow; but in no case could the final issue of the struggle have been different, since Novgorod must inevitably have sunk at last beneath the blows of the Muscovite Princes.

When a strong physical organism dies, its end is usually expressed in deep sighs and groans. Similarly, when a social union is dissolved after a long and vigorous existence, its disruption is usually preceded or accompanied by legends expressive of the mental ferment produced in contemporary observers by what they have seen or foreseen in connection with the event. In our history few catastrophes have gathered around them such a swarm of tales as cluster around the fall of Novgorod. Even before Ivan III. had begun his reign a feeling of approaching disaster had brought Novgorodian minds and nerves to a pitch of tension which vented itself in prophecies concerning the impending fate of the city. In the forties of the fifteenth century the Abbot of the Monastery of Klopska, near Novgorod, was a man named Michael —known among our Russian saints as St. Klopski. Him in 1440 the then Archbishop of Novgorod, Euphemius, invited to an audience, and was greeted by the Saint with the words : " To-day there is great joy in Moscow." " And wherefore, my father ? " asked the Archbishop. " For the reason," answered the Saint, " that the Suzerain Prince of Moscow hath had born to him a son, unto whom they have given the name of Ivan, and who shall one day abolish the usage of the Novgorodian land and bring desolation upon our city." Again, not long before the fall of Novgorod, there arrived in the city from a remote island in the White Sea the Abbot Zosima, founder of the Solovetski Monastery, who had come to intercede with the authorities on behalf of the needs of his institution. First of all he called upon one of the great ladies, Martha Boretskaia, widow of a *Posadnik*, who enjoyed great influence among the Novgorodian community. She, however, refused to receive him, and bid her slaves thrust him from the door. As he stepped over the threshold of the proud boyarin Zosima nodded his head gravely, and said to his followers : " The day will come when they who dwell within this house will tread in it no more, and when its gates will close never to reopen, and when its chambers will become forever desolate,"—" which of a surety did come to pass," adds the biographer of the holy man. Martha, however, repented later when she saw how the other boyars welcomed the anchorite whom she had so insulted, and begged Zosima to return and accord her his blessing. This Zosima consented to do ; whereupon Martha prepared a great feast in his honour, and invited a select circle of guests to meet him—the leading officials of the city and the chiefs of the pro-Lithuanian party, of which she was the moving spirit. While the dinner was in progress Zosima looked round the table at the guests, and then suddenly turned his eyes upward, as though smitten with speechless astonishment. This he did again, and yet again, and then, sinking his head upon his breast, burst into tears; nor, in spite of all his hostess's entreaties, would he consent to touch another morsel of food. As he left the house one of his pupils asked him the meaning of his conduct at table; whereupon Zosima replied: "I did gaze upon the boyars—and behold, some of them sat there without their heads!" These were the same Novgorodian boyars who, by Ivan's orders, were beheaded after the victory on the Shelona in 1471, as his principal adversaries. Again, when the struggle with Moscow was imminent, and the Novgorodians decided to place themselves under the protection of the Lithuanian king, they asked him to send them as his viceroy a prince named Michael Olelkovitch. Now, at about the same time Nemir, then *Posadnik* of Novgorod, who was one of the pro-Lithuanian party, went to pay a visit to the holy Michael of Klopska to whom I have just referred. "Whence comest thou?" asked the Saint. "From the house of my *pratestcha*,[1] holy father," answered the *Posadnik*. "And what hast thou in thy mind, my son, that thou dost go so often to take counsel of thy women?" next inquired the Saint. "I have heard," rejoined the *Posadnik*, "that the Prince of Moscow doth make him ready to come upon us in the summer time. Yet have we our Prince Michael to defend us." "Nay, but that Michael of thine is no Prince, but dirt!" exclaimed the holy man. "Send ye rather messengers with all speed to Moscow, and let them smite with their foreheads upon the ground before the Prince, in token of your fault. Else will he come upon Novgorod with all his forces, and ye will go forth to meet him, and the help of God will not be with you, but the Prince will slay many of you, and carry away yet more unto Moscow. As for that Prince Michael of thine, he will depart from you unto Lithuania, and be of aid to you in nought." And as the Saint foretold, so it came to pass.

[1] Mother-in-law's mother.

INDEX

A

Abraham of Rostov, 206, 215
Adam of Bremen, 96
Akindin, Archimandrite, 7
Alani, 30
Al Bekri, 64
Alexander Nevski, 241, 274, 280, 287, 309,
    315, 352
Amartol, 10, 16, 21
Amastris, 57, 72
America, 158
Andrew Bogoliubski, 182, 189, 199, 221–231,
    252, 273, 275, 279, 318
Andrew, St., 9
Andronicus, 24
Angi Patiai, 213
Angles, 58
Anti, 33
Arcadius, 326
Archangel, 171, 184, 201
Askold, 10, 20, 23, 56, 58, 59, 66, 70, 72, 81
Avars, 10, 34, 38
Avril, 214

B

Bagdad, 52, 58
Baldwin, 126
Basil, St., 212
Basil the Macedonian, 131
Bastarni, 30
Berendians, 190, 196
Beresti, 3, 244
Berezan, 85
Bertinski Script, 55, 57, 58, 67, 71
Bieliaev, 29
Bieloe Ozero, 7, 64, 71, 204, 208, 211, 227,
    257, 282, 307
Bieloi, 246
Bielozersk, 87, 96
Biezhesk, 321
Black Bolgars, 56, 82
Bogoliubov, 199
Bogorod, 281
Boleslav, 58
Bolgari (town), 44, 185
Bolgars, 16, 23, 25, 34, 38, 70, 81, 94, 129,
    131, 139, 187, 188, 200, 206, 228, 324
Boris, 7, 22, 97, 177, 197
Boris Vladimirovitch, 95
Borovsk, 282

Bosporus Cimmerius, 49
Bravlin, 57
Brinski, 198
Bruno, 86
Burgundi, 38
Byzantium, 21, 25, 35, 57, 79, 81, 134, 141,
    176, 179, 193

C

Carlovingians, 67
Casimir, 248
Charles the Great, 56
Chersonesus in Taurica, 49, 81
Chodota, 41
Chozars, 10, 17, 34, 52, 55, 58, 60, 73, 79,
    119
Chrobatians, 36, 38, 70
Cimmerians, 30
Clement, Metropolitan, 187
Clovis, 101
Constantine Copronymus, 131
Constantine of Riazan, 279
Constantine Porphyrogenitus, 3, 59, 79, 84,
    86, 92
Constantinople, 17, 20, 22, 55, 57, 64, 70, 72,
    80, 82, 96, 140
Cracow, 195
Croats, 36, 38
Crusades, 13
Cyprian, Serb, 290
Cyril of Bieloe Ozero, 298
Cyril, St., 24
Czechs, 23, 24, 36, 38

D

Dacians, 30, 32
Danes, 56, 58, 67
Daniel of Moscow, 242, 274, 279, 281, 285,
    287, 295, 316
Daniel Polomnik, 126
David of Smolensk, 127, 224
David of Tchernigov, 114, 123, 177, 192
David of Volhynia, 123
Davidoff, 108
Dazhbog, 44
Demian, 191
Dir, 10, 20, 23, 56, 58, 59, 70, 72
Dmitri Constantinovitch, 5
Dmitri Donskoi, 5, 247, 279, 282, 296, 298,
    300, 304, 309, 315

Dmitrov, 199, 256, 281
Domitian, 32
Dorogobutz, 142
Dorpat, 87
Dregovitches, 40, 62
Drevlians, 16, 30, 40, 62, 70, 74, 77, 78
Druitsk, 189
Dulebs, 10, 11, 34, 39, 70

E

Ediger of Ordin, 9
Eleutheria, St., 85
Estians, 33, 203
Euphemius of Novgorod, 367

F

Frisia, 67

G

Gaeti, 30
Galicia, 6, 37, 87, 116, 119, 183, 193, 194, 196, 234, 246
Galitch, 199, 256, 282, 303, 307, 309
Gardaric, 59, 60
Geira Burislavna, 60
George of Amastris, St., 57, 72
Georgius, Metropolitan, 153
Gleb, 7, 22, 97, 177, 197
Gleb Andreivitch, 223
Gorodetz, 199
Gothland, 33, 329
Gregory of Petcherski, 154
Grodno, 109
Guedimin, 200
Guillebert de Lannoy, 335, 344

H

Hanseatic League, 330
Heinrich II., 86
Herakles, emperor, 38
Herberstein, 334, 338, 361
Hermanric, 33, 34, 203
Herodotus, 30, 49
Huns, 34, 38

I

Ibn Dasta, 80, 129, 139
Ibn Fadlan, 44
Ibrahim, 64
Iconoclastic Emperors, 280
Igor, 11, 16, 17, 40, 59, 81, 83, 94, 139, 141
Ilarion, 88, 171, 206
Illyria, 24
Ilmen, Lake, 49, 62, 319
Ilya Murometz, 197, 232
Iskorosten, 40
Itil, 185
Ivan Kalita, 280, 282, 286, 289, 307

Ivan III., 295, 306, 352, 364, 368
Izborsk, 62, 64, 71
Iziaslav, 95, 98, 102, 107, 111, 116, 120, 129, 142, 191, 198, 200, 222

J

Jacob of Petcherski, 8, 22, 97
John of Moscow, 311, 312
John of Novgorod, 169, 174, 175, 176, 178, 180, 366
Jornandes, 33, 37, 41, 203, 204
Justinian, 135

K

Kalevala, 207
Kaluga, 198, 204, 275, 283
Karacharev, 198
Karamzin, 29, 125, 255
Kashira, 282
Kertch, 49, 57
Khan Boniak, 190
Kherson, 57, 82
Khordadbih, 52, 58
Khorse, 44
Ki, 40, 41, 42, 70
Kiev, 5 et seq.
Klin, 281
Klopski, St., 367, 368
Kolomna, 279, 281, 283
Korela, 331
Kostroma, 6, 199, 241, 256, 283
Koursk, 107, 117, 126
Kozelsk, 198
Kremlin, 184
Krivitches, 40, 46, 61, 74
Ksniatin, 199
Kuchkovitch, 227
Kudenev, 191
Kulikovo Polé, 267, 287
Kumani, 189
Kutchek, 273
Kutzkova, 273
Kvashnin, 276

L

Ladoga, 23, 62, 65, 87, 333, 346
Lechs, 24, 32, 36, 37, 87, 119, 201
Leo the Deacon, 3, 80, 82, 129
Leo the Isaurian, 131
Leontius of Rostov, 206
Lithuania, 119, 195, 200, 239, 245, 261, 266, 277, 288, 307, 315, 322, 330, 357, 364, 367
Livonia, 324, 357, 364
Lopasnia, 273, 276
Lothaire, 67
Lubeck, 330
Lubiech, 52, 71, 78, 123, 193
Ludovic the Pious, 57

M

Mal, 40
Mamai, 267, 288
Martha Boretskaia, 367
Massudi, 35
Maximus, Metropolitan, 289
Medyn, 282
Meres, 33, 65, 87, 203, 206, 209
Merovingians, 101
Meshtera, 283
Methodius, 24
Michael III. of Byzantium, 17, 19, 70
Michael Khorobriti, 274, 279
Michael of Suzdal, 229, 233
Michael of Tver, 285, 308, 346
Michalka Stepanitch, 353
Minsk, 62, 189
Miroshka Nezdinitch, 353
Moors, 192
Moravians, 24, 36
Morduines, 33, 200, 203, 207, 209, 277
Moscow, 3, 124, 230, 242, 246, 256, 264, 271-
    318, 338, 340, 344, 346, 352, 363, 365-
    368
Mozhaisk, 279, 281, 283, 303, 313
Mstislav, 3, 105, 110, 139, 170, 192, 193, 223,
    236, 327
Mtzensk, 246
Murom, 87, 96, 109, 116, 138, 197, 204, 275,
    283, 307

N

Neglina, 273
Nestor, 5, 7, 13-27
Nicephorus, 19
Nicholas the Magician, 185
Nicolaiev, 49
Niphont, Bishop, 155, 163, 175
Nishkipas, 213
Nizhni Novgorod, 199, 209, 249, 275, 283
Normans, 58
Novgorod Sieverski, 114, 117, 126, 192, 272
Novgorod the Great, 11, 21, 24, 40, 52, 57,
    60, 65, 71, 73, 94, 111, 118, 130, 137, 149,
    155, 179, 187, 189, 197, 207, 227, 233,
    235, 275, 277, 308, 313, 318-368

O

Obri, 34
Odoiev, 246
Olaf, 60
Olbia, 49
Olearius, 214
Oleg, 10, 11, 16, 17, 20, 59, 71, 72, 77, 81,
    83, 86, 139, 179, 181, 351
Olga, 16, 59
Olgerd, 278, 287
Olonetz, 184, 201
Oriekhov, 333

P

Palaei, 22
Palestine, 12
Pannonia, 24
Panticapaeum, 49
Paphnuti Borovski, 291
Patricius of Lithuania, 331
Paul, St., 24
Pavlov, A. S., 145, 280
Pechenegs, 11, 17, 23, 34, 55, 70, 73, 85, 189,
    190, 195
Periaslavl, 52, 62, 78, 83, 96, 116, 189-191,
    195, 200, 221, 256
Periaslavl Zaliesski, 199, 229, 242, 276, 282
Perun, 44, 141, 334
Petcherski Cloister, 6, 13 et seq., 124, 153,
    154, 190
Peter, Metropolitan, 289
Phanagoria, 49
Photius, 3, 58, 70, 72, 77, 81
Pinsk, 109
Plano Carpini, 195
Pochaina, 199
Pogodin, 29
Poliani, 17, 25, 30, 32, 34, 40, 46, 60, 67, 70,
    180
Poloczani, 40
Polotsk, 13, 26, 52, 62, 71, 78, 95, 109, 116,
    120, 233
Polovtsi, 14, 21, 119, 189-195, 223, 362
Polycarp (of Petcherski), 7
Pomerani, 36, 60
Prochorus of Rostov, 290
Propontis, 57
Pskov, 285, 318, 330, 333, 338-364

R

Radimizes, 37, 40, 46, 62, 74, 77
Radonetz, 281
Rhos, 87, 190
Rhoxalani, 30
Riazan, 26, 96, 109, 116, 138, 199, 204, 235,
    246, 275, 288, 302, 313, 315, 326
Rodion, 276
Rognieda, 95, 109
Romans, the, 13, 32
Roman of Volhynia, 127, 188, 194, 224, 234,
    244
Rorich, 67
Rosjdestvenski Monastery, 5
Rostislav, 95-97, 109, 111, 114, 123, 175
Rostov, 52, 78, 87, 96, 97, 116, 197, 206, 215,
    221, 226, 236, 250, 256, 275, 284, 288,
    302, 307
Rshev, 275, 322, 340
Rurik, 10, 23, 52, 59, 61, 64, 70, 73, 94, 246,
    280
Rurik of Smolensk, 99, 127, 234
Ruza, 281

S

San Mamo, 82
Saracens, 70
Sarai, 309
Sarkel, 55
Sarmatians, 30, 37
Saratov, 214
Schlözer, 29
Sclaveni, 33
Scythians, 30, 31
Serbs, 36, 38
Serpukhov, 199, 273, 281, 300, 307
Shaitan, 209
Shakmatoff, 19
Shemiaka, 310
Sieverians, 30, 40, 46, 61, 74, 77
Silvester, 8, 13, 18, 20-27
Simeon Gordii, 242, 288, 296, 315
Sineus, 10, 64
Sitomlia, 6
Slaven, 320
Smolensk, 52, 61, 62, 71, 74, 96, 97, 116,
    175, 183, 197, 233, 235, 275, 282, 322,
    327, 351
Solovetski Monastery, 211, 367
Soloviev, 24, 29, 255, 351
St. Petersburg, 124
Starodub, 199, 256, 282, 307
Stephen of Petcherski, 7
Stephen of Surozh, St., 57, 72
Stribog, 44
Sudak, 57
Suzdal, 5, 26, 96, 99, 182 et seq., 351
Svarog, 44
Svenigorod, 199, 281
Sviatopolk, 15, 17, 95, 99, 111, 115, 119, 123,
    153, 187, 190, 192, 197
Sviatoslav, 80, 81, 94, 96, 98, 114, 116, 127,
    129, 191, 208, 324

T

Tacitus, 204
Taman, 49, 96
Tanais, 49
Tartars, 28, 191, 195, 201, 239, 274, 277, 280,
    283, 285, 288, 303, 308, 328, 351, 362,
    366
Tarusa, 283, 307
Tatistchev, 7, 187, 199, 200
Taunsiai, 213
Tchampas, 209, 213
Tcheremissians, 203, 206, 214, 277
Tchernigov, 26, 52, 61, 78, 83, 96, 102, 116,
    126, 192, 198, 273, 351
Tchudes, 65, 87, 119, 205
Term, 45
Theodore of Rostov, 206
Theodosia, 49
Theodosius of Petcherski, 7, 9, 15, 22, 154,
    183, 214

Theognostes, Metropolitan, 289
Thietmar, 58, 96
Tmutorokan, 88, 96
Toropetz, 327
Torzhok, 322, 328, 340, 363
Trajan, 32, 37
Troitski Monastery, 284
Trubtchevsk, 117
Truvor, 10, 59, 64
Tur, 64
Turks, 190, 191, 195, 201
Turov, 64, 71, 109
Tver, 221, 241, 249, 283, 284, 302, 306, 312,
    315, 327, 346
Tverdislav, 327

U

Uglitch, 256, 282
Ugri, 11, 16, 24, 25, 34, 119
Uluzes, 78
Usspenski Cathedral, 289
Uzbek, Khan, 288
Uzi, 55

V

Vadim, 66
Vandals, 38
Varangians, 10, 20, 25, 29, 56, 58 et seq.
Varlaam, 321
Vassilii the Dark, 283, 284, 302, 307, 334,
    366
Vassilii III., 282
Vassilii Novi, 16
Vassilievski, Professor, 57, 72
Vassilko of Terebovl, 22, 109, 123, 188
Vatizes, 37, 40, 46, 62, 74, 88, 198, 277
Vayast, 66
Veliki Lugi, 322, 340
Venedi, 33
Verea, 281, 313
Viatcheslav, 96, 97. 105, 107, 111
Viatka, 313, 318, 363
Viebuditski Monastery, 8, 18
Visbi, 329
Vishgorod, 199, 223, 275
Vitichev, 79, 84, 123
Vladimir, St., 8, 12, 17, 60, 63, 81, 86, 88-90,
    96, 99, 109, 158, 164, 179, 187, 197, 200,
    239, 270, 337
Vladimir Monomakh, 9, 14, 41, 98, 105, 107,
    110, 114, 116, 123, 125, 129, 137, 148,
    153, 163, 173, 177, 189, 191, 193, 198,
    221, 239, 252, 268, 323, 325, 351
Vladimir of Volhynia, 243, 248
Vladimir in the West, 5, 124, 195, 243
Vladimir on the Kliazma, 199, 221, 225, 275,
    289, etc.
Vladimirko, 183
Vodi, 321
Volhynia, 26, 35, 96, 97, 110, 116, 193, 194,
    1,8, 243, 276

Volodar, 109, 123
Vologda, 284, 328
Volokolamsk, 278, 281, 322
Volos, 44, 141, 206
Voronezh, 246
Vsevolod Yaroslavitch, 96, 97, 102, 107, 116, 129, 172, 176, 179, 183, 191
Vsevolod III., 99, 127, 229, 234–238, 247, 326, 343, 345
Vsoslav, 111, 120

W

Wallachians, 21
Wesses, 65, 203, 212

Y

Yan, 7, 15, 208
Yaropolk, 23, 63, 70, 107
Yaroslav I., 11, 13, 17, 21, 36, 58, 87, 94 *et seq.*, 186, 187, 189, 193, 236, 239, 320

Yaroslav the Prudent, 194, 235
Yaroslav of Tver, 327, 346
Yaroslavl, 197, 208, 249, 256, 275, 283, 284, 302
Yazigi, 30
Yuri Dolgoruki, 27, 105, 108, 114, 183, 192, 198, 200, 221, 226, 231, 252, 272, 274
Yuri of Galitch, 309
Yuri of Moscow, 308
Yuriev, 87, 190
Yuriev v' Polé, 199
Yuriev on the Kliazma, 256

Z

Zabielin, 30, 273
Zachariah (Canonist), 143
Zaozersk, 257, 277, 284
Zemisches, John, 80, 82
Zosima, 367

END OF VOL. I